D1831894

THE ENGLISH AND INDIA

THE ENGLISH AND INDIA

NEW SKETCHES

BY

E. DE VALBEZEN

TRANSLATED FROM THE FRENCH
WITH THE AUTHOR'S PERMISSION

BY

A DIPLOMATE

Gian Publishing House

29/6 SHAKTI NAGAR • DELHI-110007 • INDIA

GIAN PUBLISHING HOUSE
PUBLISHERS OF BOOKS ON HUMAN CIVILIZATION
29/6 SHAKTI NAGAR, DELHI-110007

First Reprint in India, 1986

Printed at Goyal Offset Printers, Delhi-110035
and published by Smt. Gayatri Garg
for Gian Publishing House, Delhi-110007

PREFACE.

SINCE the second edition of this book was, about six years ago, published in Paris, the Conservative Administration, under Lord Beaconsfield, has hourly, almost continually been in power (1874–May 1880). We cannot retrace here all the events of this remarkable epoch, which are still in the recollection of every one: the Russo-Turkish conflict and the Treaty of Berlin, the wars in South Africa and in Afghanistan, and the marvellous campaign of Mr. Gladstone in Midlothian, which decided the fall of the Beaconsfield Ministry.

There are, nevertheless, certain facts that we must call to mind, for they are intimately connected with the destinies of the British Empire in the East. The Prince of Wales's trip to India (1875), the first ever made by the heir to the Crown; the proclamation of Queen Victoria as Empress of India (May 1, 1876); the purchase of the 77,000 Suez Canal shares; and lastly, the Treaty of June 4, 1878, by which the island of Cyprus was ceded to England, and a British protectorate established over Asia Minor.

It will be remarked that the military demonstration made by Lord Beaconsfield—the sending of a body of Anglo-Indian troops to Malta—caused great astonishment in England, and some of the leading papers thought, perhaps with reason, that this proceeding was somewhat unconstitutional. This warlike policy of the Earl of Beaconsfield, though by no means devoid of grandeur, was perhaps, in the then state of Europe, rather dangerous, and may have facilitated the triumph of Mr. Gladstone's policy.

Such was the situation—a very difficult one—when Mr. Gladstone was called by the Queen to form a new Cabinet. The war, which was raging in South Africa, is now ended, not without terrible disasters to the British Army. The question was much more serious in Afghanistan; but the brilliant victory of General Roberts, and the complete triumph of the Emir over his antagonist, seems to have settled the struggle for some years at least. The reader will perhaps read with interest the speech lately made on this subject by Mr. Gladstone at Leeds:—'I will now go to other regions. I go to the region inhabited by another gallant people, the people of Afghanistan. That people, if they were united to us in the bonds of affection, would form a barrier, supposing a barrier to be needed, against the power of Russia, and against her aggression equally a moral barrier. I for my part have more faith in moral barriers than I have in guns and rifles. The wisdom of successive Viceroys of India appointed by Liberal Governments—but one of them appointed by a Conservative Government—I mean Lord Mayo—these Viceroys have endeavoured, by careful attention respecting the rights of the Afghans, avoiding every occasion of interference in their affairs, and meeting their wishes in a proper spirit, to efface the unhappy recollections of our former follies, I fear I may say crimes, and by degrees there was growing up a kindly feeling between those millions of mountaineers and the administrators of the Indian Empire and the representatives of British power. About three years ago all the work of that wise policy was ruthlessly reversed. Again we invaded Afghanistan, established our troops in every stronghold of the country, shed the blood of that people freely upon its mountains and its vales, and with that blood no small portion of the blood of the gallant soldiers of the British and Indian armies. And, let me ask, for what purpose? What was the effect? Simply with the effect of converting into enemies those who ought to be our best friends, and of destroying the moral barrier between ourselves and the Russian Empire. Painful and sad is the confession which that gallant General, Sir F. Roberts, left upon record when he told the Government under which he served—"You must found all your measures upon the recollection and conviction of the unquestionable fact that you are the objects of the bitter and determined hate of every Afghan." And so we were not only invited, but compelled, with the assistance of either Parliament or the country to send seventy thousand men into Afghanistan or the North-West Frontier of India for this insane and criminal purpose. What he had to do was to see if, with due regard to the safety of all those who might have acted as our partisans, we could retrieve and draw back from the fatal position which a former Government had caused us to assume. I rejoice to say that in great part the work is achieved; that these Afghans, with the exception of one slight and outlying corner of the territory under peculiar circumstances, are again masters in their own country; and if the Afghan does not yet quite know whom to obey, that is not his fault, but ours. We brought the grey hairs of that old man who peacefully ruled in Afghanistan in sorrow to the grave. We said, through the mouths of our Ministers, that we wished Afghanistan to be one, to be independent, and to be powerful. We made it, instead of one, a collection of fragments; instead of independent, we made it enslaved; instead of powerful, we reduced it to misery and to weakness. The present Government have, at any rate, made the first stage in retracing these fatal steps, and we have every hope that by a steady perseverance in a similar policy we may, at least, efface some of the most unhappy, some of the most scandalous recollections which, I am afraid, will remain inscribed upon the page of history—happily with many good works on the other side—to sully the fair fame of England.'

It is to be hoped that England—be her Government Conservative or Liberal—will understand that her true interest is to protect the independence of Afghanistan, which will be for her a much more effective barrier against the ever-dreaded Russian invasion, than the fantastic scientific frontier invented by Lord Beaconsfield, in spite of the energetic remonstrances of the great Lord Lawrence, one of the héroes of the book which we now offer to the public.

The Indian question being of the utmost importance to England, all that has any bearing on it must be interesting; and this it is which has decided us to translate these sketches. We will add that it is always advantageous to know the opinion seriously given of a foreigner on one's own country. Moreover, very few books on this subject have been published in France. These sketches will be the more interesting to the English reader, as they are written by a Frenchman, who, whatever his affection or admiration for England, cannot be suspected of partiality to her—for he must have remembered that there was a time when France was a competitor for the supremacy in India.

Lastly, we may add that this work has been approved—'couronné'—by the French Académie.

H. L.

MIMWOOD, HERTS: *Oct.* 1881.

CONTENTS.

CHAPTER I.

ORIGIN AND BEGINNING OF THE MUTINY.

CHAPTER II.

THE PUNJAB.

CHAPTER III.

SIEGE OF DELHI.

CHAPTER IV.

CAPTURE OF DELHI—INSURRECTION AT AGRA—MASSACRE AT CAWNPORE.

CHAPTER V.

CALCUTTA—HAVELOCK'S FIRST CAMPAIGN.

CHAPTER IX.

SECOND CAMPAIGN OF SIR C. CAMPBELL IN OUDE—CAMPAIGN OF ROHILKUND.

CHAPTER X.

SIR HUGH ROSE'S CAMPAIGN IN CENTRAL INDIA—LAST DAYS OF THE MUTINY.

CHAPTER XI.

CAUSES OF THE MUTINY—END OF THE EAST INDIA COMPANY THE NEW CHARTER OF INDIA.

CHAPTER XII.

PUBLIC WORKS, EXPORTATIONS, AND IMPORTATIONS — THE ISTHMUS OF SUEZ—RUSSIAN PROPAGANDA AND INDIAN RAILWAYS.

THE ENGLISH AND INDIA.

THE SEPOY MUTINY IN BENGAL, 1857.

CHAPTER I.

ORIGIN AND BEGINNING OF THE MUTINY.

Native society and the conquerors—Origin and organisation of the native army—Its strength in 1857—Anglo-Indian officers—The soldiers of the Bengal army—Change in the relations between the European officers and the sepoys—Influence of the disasters of the Cabul expedition and the English reverses in the Crimea on the troops and the population of India—Greased cartridges and the spirit of caste—Supposed plan of the conspirators—The Chippatis—Infatuation of the civil and military authorities—Disturbance at the School of Musketry of Dum-Dum—Insubordination of the native regiments at the stations of Berampore and Barrackpore—Mutiny at Mirut—Entrance of the rebels into Delhi—Murder of Major Fraser and his officers—Defence of the arsenal—Mutiny in the cantonments—Murder of a clerk of the telegraph office—General Anson—First measures of the commander-in-chief—The Rajah of Pattgalah remains faithful to the English—Death of General Anson at Kurnaal—Sir Henry Barnard succeeds him—Fight at Ghajioudounagahr—Battle of Baddli-Serai—Results of this victory—Arrival of the Punjab guides.

THE most terrible crisis which has ever threatened the fortunes of England began on Sunday, May 10, 1857, at the station of Mirut, at the foot of the Himalaya. When Philip II.'s Armada set sail from Cadiz, when Napoleon I. was organising his legions on the coast of Boulogne, when on the evening of June 18, 1815, the remnant of the Guards was awaiting the arrival of the Prussians on the heights of La Haye Sainte, the future of England was not darker than on the day when the sepoys of Mirut raised the standard of revolt, and gave the signal for a conflagration which spread in a few days from the North-West Provinces to the furthest district of Central India. It is the fashion nowadays in England, amongst a certain political party, to speak lightly of India, and of the important part played by this magnificent dependence of the British Empire. Brilliant paradoxes cannot, however, triumph over the logic of facts. British India certainly does not furnish the mother-country with a yearly tribute of ready money such as Java furnishes to Holland or Cuba to Spain; but the resources of its budget permit England to keep up sufficient military forces to cause the weight of her sword to be felt in the balance in all the great European questions. We may count by thousands the number of English families who find an honourable means of existence in official positions, or in business in India; British capital is spread by thousands of millions over the three Presidencies in indigo and tea plantations, in railways, banks, and houses of business. For England, the preservation of the vast domains of the Honourable East India Company is a question of to be or not to be. India once lost, Great Britain, with disorder in her finances, in conflict with the political troubles caused by the ruin of her middle class, would no doubt fall in a few years to the rank of Holland or Denmark. The skill of her statesmen and the courage of her army were to preserve her from these terrible contingencies. Almost everywhere, without exception, the men in authority in India showed themselves equal to the occasion in the hour of danger. Before a single soldier sent from England had disembarked on the shores of the Hooghly, the mutiny had been put down, and there was nothing left to do for the new comers but to complete the work of the victors of Delhi and Lucknow.

In this supreme struggle, where each man did his duty, English history became richer by many new and heroic personages, forming a constellation of illustrious soldiers, in which stand out the names of Henry Lawrence, Havelock, Nicholson, Neil, and Hodson. These all fell on the field of honour, in defence of the cause of civilisation and true progress. Let us, children of modern and liberal Europe, bow with respect and without reservation before their tombs!

The great men who raised the splendid edifice of British power in India had understood, most of them, that unlimited aggrandisement would be far from adding to its solidity, and that the company's task would be all the more difficult the more extensive its dominions became. These previsions of human wisdom were completely realised in the month of May, 1857. More than half a century had passed since the day when the Marquess of Wellesley extended the modest conquests of Clive and Hastings from the kingdom of Mysore to the North-West Provinces. The formidable Sick (Sikh) army had melted away some years before on the battle-fields of Sobraon and Goujerate.[1] An extensive system of alliances with the native princes gave the country the aspect of a vast confederation under the suzerainty of England—a marvellous empire whose basis was but clay.[2] In this immense country live millions of Asiatics, unchanging in their habits and their beliefs, who are retained by apathy, timidity, and fear, much more than by loyal gratitude, under the yoke of England.[3]

For a hundred years already, under a Government ad-

[1] The British flag floated without a rival from the banks of the Indus to those of the Irawaddy.

[2] See amongst the documents the table of the population of India and of the Protected States in 1868.

[3] The whole population of India can be approximately valued at 200 millions of inhabitants, of which 50 millions belong to the Native States—properly so called, to the number of 153. Statistics give the following census of the natives subject to England according to their religion:—

Native Christians	1,100,000
Buddhists	1,000,000
Aboriginal Tribes	12,000,000
Mahometans	25,000,000
Hindoos	112,000,000
Parsees	180,000
Eurasians (Christians)	91,000
Europeans (including the army)	156,000
Jews	10,000
Armenians	5,000
Total	151,542,000

—*Parliamentary Documents.*

vancing in progress, India has seen order and the supremacy of the law succeed to disturbance and anarchy. But these benefits of the conquest have passed by without making any impression on the Hindoo race; the action of their European masters has not penetrated the rock of native society even by the smallest fissure. However extraordinary this phenomenon may be, it is not a new one in India. Before the East India Company was founded, a foreign government had for centuries ruled uncontrolled from Cape Comorin to the foot of the Himalaya. Regardless of those principles of humanity and religious toleration, which are the honour and strength of Europe of our nineteenth century, the Mussulman Emperors never recoiled from any means, however violent, in order to extirpate the Brahmin religion from the soil of India. Their power, their fanaticism, their cruelties did not succeed in shaking the Indian institutions. For 800 years, the sacred races bore the yoke of the impure conquerors; and when the throne of the Moguls fell to pieces, the only traces that remained were tombs and mosques, a few thousand Mussulman converts, lost amongst millions of Hindoos, and annals, wherein the different phases of a history (which may be comprised in two words—greatness and decay) are uniformly written in letters of blood

To explain this crystallisation of the races of India, it is necessary to go back to the distinctive features of the tribes who invaded the country in the early days of history, and who brought with them civil and religious institutions which assumed this indelible character—a religion fantastic in its dogmas, degrading in its customs; a sacred language so inimitable that it forms the basis of all human languages; society divided into four principal classes—priests, soldiers, farmers, labourers (brahmin, kchatrija, vaissa, soudra), and village communities united by the double link of blood and property in common, where a local administration supplies all the needs of a simple race.[1] In short, all those motives incomprehensible to other men, which guide the Indian in his habits and his actions, and which render his interior

[1] See Documents, No. II., 'The Extent of Native Administration.'

life inaccessible to the exterior circumstances of politics. The faithful inheritors of the traditions of the first ages met on the Indus the warriors of Alexander the Great; and, overcome in the struggle, passed under the yoke of the Macedonian chiefs. Other generations, no less faithful, supported for eight hundred years the iron yoke of the Emperor of Delhi. For the last century their children have accepted the laws of the East India Company. Everything has changed around him—the Hindoo alone has remained unchanged. In vain England has absorbed all political influence—all internal rivalries; in vain she has crushed all obstacles which opposed her victorious march; in vain do all the conquests of Rome pale before her Asiatic Empire. Seven hundred and fifty English magistrates or administrators, 25,000 soldiers of the royal army, a few thousand European soldiers in the immediate service of the Company, a native army, commanded by 4,000 English officers, it is true, sufficed to maintain under the sceptre of Great Britain a territory of 1,400,000 square miles, and a population of 150,000,000. But this power, surrounded by all the pomp of the East, protected by the living forces of civilisation, stopped short before barriers which neither brute force nor intellect can surmount. The highest representative of European might could not induce a beggar of the lowest caste, expiring on his pallet in the agony of hunger, to accept from his hand a mouthful of rice! A hundred years of Christian and liberal government have scarcely touched the surface of the constitution of Indian society;[1] and we advance nothing beyond the truth when we affirm that the uncontested power of England in India has not, and never will have any other solid basis but that of European bayonets. The very title of these sketches makes it needless to add that the East India Company was to find its most formidable enemies in the native soldiers of the Bengal army.

Before going further, it is indispensable to say a few words of the history and organisation of the Anglo-Indian army. The formation of native troops in the Company's

[1] See Documents, No. III., 'The System of Caste.'

service goes back to the middle of the last century. In 1748 a corps of sepoys was first organised in the Presidency of Madras, where the authorities, by the way, only followed the example given by the French at Pondicherry. A detachment composed of European sailors, taken from ships, by fair means or foul, was added to the native contingent. The treaty of Aix-la-Chapelle, which put an end to hostilities between the English and the French in India, did not bring about the dissolution of the little Madras army. Politics were beginning to play a great part in the affairs of the Company, which was mixing itself up more and more in the quarrels of the native rulers. Up to this time, however, the establishment of the English in Bengal had preserved its exclusively commercial character. It was the native troops of Madras and the 39th Regiment of the Royal army, a regiment whose colours have since borne the motto, '*Primus in Indis*,' that defeated, under the illustrious Clive, the Nabob of Bengal at the battle of Plassey, June 17, 1757. The remembrance of this day, so great in its results—as it opened the series of victories which gave a hundred and fifty million subjects to England—is not yet forgotten in India. We shall have occasion to class among the indirect causes of the sepoy mutiny a popular prophecy which announced that the hundredth year of England's domination should also be the last.

After this victory Clive organised at Calcutta a sepoy contingent on the system adopted at Madras.[1] The political

[1] In 1760 the Bengal army, exclusive of officers in the Artillery and Engineers, only numbered eighteen European captains, twenty-six lieutenants, sixteen ensigns. The original battalions were commonly designated by the name of the captains who had raised them; for example, Matthew or Galliez battalion (Galliez ka Pultam), from the name of their first commanders. These precursors of the Bengal army were destined to end in the same way by mutiny. In 1764, the Galliez battalion, having shown symptoms of disaffection at Chaprah, under the pretext that the Government had not kept certain promises made to them, Major Munro (since Sir Hector Munro), who was then commanding the Bengal army, felt that a terrible example was necessary. Twenty-eight of the principal mutineers were condemned to death by a council of war, and executed in one day. At the last moment, three grenadiers who were among the condemned, claimed the privilege of being bound to the cannons on the right, a position which as grenadiers they had always occupied

complications which followed the Company's quarrels with the princes it had extemporised, the efforts of the Emperor of Delhi to recover his supremacy over the provinces he had ceded to the English, led to a rapid increase of the Anglo-Indian forces. This increase enabled us to finish the war successfully in 1765 by the conquest of Bihar, and by the diminution of the power of the Emperor of Delhi and of the Nabob, the Vizier of Oude. The political conditions and interests of the Company were modified; the friend of yesterday became the foe of to-morrow. In order to defend the Emperor of Delhi against the attacks of the Mahrattas, it was necessary to occupy Allahabad, Cawnpore, Fattygarh; and the occupation of these distant points necessitated a great increase in the military forces of Bengal. In 1786, when Lord Cornwallis arrived for the first time at Calcutta as Governor-General and Commander-in-Chief of the three Presidencies, the Bengal army was composed of thirty-six sepoy and six European battalions, a little more than 40,000 men. But these forces were only formidable on paper. The Company's army, badly organised and badly paid, disgraced itself by continual mutinies, and the white troops had constantly to be employed in keeping the native ones to their duty, or reciprocally; for the European regiments, hitherto exclusively composed of sailors and deserters, only remained faithful from the hope of pay, often uncertain, and always insufficient. The new governor-general had the honour and merit of co-ordinating all these impure elements. Both soldiers and officers were paid with regularity, and discipline and military instruction were strictly insisted upon. Lord Cornwallis can be said to have prepared the victories of his successors by leaving behind him a well-organised army.

The days of the native powers were numbered. The Marquess of Wellesley had left Europe, as he proudly announced, to govern India from a throne with the sceptre of a statesman, and not from behind a counter with the yard-measure of a shopkeeper. From the very beginning he applied himself

on parade and in battle—a last favour which was not refused. The Matthew battalion was disbanded in 1784 for having refused to serve beyond seas.

to establish in the most incontestable manner the superiority of the Government which he represented over that of the native princes; the English cantonments were pushed forward in the Deccan to the north of Delhi. The policy of conquest required great military means: the Bengal army was increased to fifty-six battalions, and a corresponding increase took place in those of the Madras and Bombay presidencies. Territorial extension continued under the successors of the illustrious brother of the Duke of Wellington; and the first half of the century witnessed successively the conquest of Delhi, the dethronement of the Peischwah, the ruin of the Mahrattas, the Burmah war, the Cabul expedition, and the two Punjab wars. To meet these incessant military needs, to provide for the security of their new conquests, the Company's forces received considerable additions; and in 1857, at the moment of the mutiny, they were divided as follows[1]:—

At the beginning of the mutiny the majority of the corps[2] did not possess their full complement of 1,000 men, which was the normal strength of the battalions of the royal army; the sepoy battalions numbered 1,100 men in Bengal, and from 800 to 900 in Madras and Bombay. The effective force of the regular cavalry regiments amounted to 600 sabres, both in the royal and in the native army. The artillery, which was entirely in the Company's service, was composed chiefly of Europeans, and only a few batteries were manned by natives. In round numbers, the total of the regular forces of the three presidencies can be estimated at 220,000 men of native troops, and 45,000 men of European.

We must remark on finishing this enumeration, in order

[1]

	Bengal Army.	Madras Army.	Bombay Army.	Total.
Cavalry Regiments, R.A.	2	1	1	—
Battalions, Infantry, R.A.	15	3	—	—
The Company's European Infantry .	3	3	3	—
European and Native Artillery . .	12	7	5	24
Native Regular Infantry	74	52	29	155
Native Regular Cavalry	10	8	3	21

[2] Battalion or regiment can be used indifferently of the regiments of the royal army, as some contain two and even three battalions, and others one only.

to avoid all confusion in the mind of the reader, that in the following pages we shall principally occupy ourselves with the Bengal army, which bore alone the whole burden of the Mutiny of 1857.

The preceding table shows that the effective force of cavalry was very feeble, especially for a country so favourable to its use as the great plains in the North of India. But besides this, eighteen regiments of irregular cavalry were attached to the Bengal army. This force only differed from the regular cavalry by the number of European officers, and by certain modifications in the conditions of enlistment and pay; most of the troopers were drawn from the middle class of the people. The staff of the so-called irregular regiments only comprised five Europeans —an officer in command, a second under him, an adjutant, a doctor, and a sergeant-major. Notwithstanding the length of this nomenclature, we must still say a few words about certain other corps created according to necessity, and on a different base. The Company's representatives had not closed their eyes to the dangers which might result from the immense development given to the Bengal army. In the recently annexed countries, regiments of local irregular infantry had been organised to preserve at one and the same time the security of the frontiers and internal peace; for example, the regiments of Arracan and Assam, four of Goorkhas, and ten of Sikhs; the latter, recruited from among the Punjaubis and the tribes of Afghanistan, co-operated with the English in the most active and devoted manner during the terrible campaign of 1857. We have still to speak of the contingents furnished by the native princes in order to complete this summary of the military forces of the Bengal Government. All the Indian sovereigns who had preserved any sort of independence were bound, without exception, to the English rule by treaties under which the contracting parties guaranteed one another help and protection in case of need. But the English, fully conscious of the spirit of disorder which presided over military expenditure in the native states, had taken care to specify the forces on which they could count, and to cause the revenue of certain districts to be assigned for ever to the maintenance of these troops, and of their regimental staffs, composed of officers detached from the Company's service. The oldest of these contingents, that of the Nizam of Hyderabad, had been organised at the end of the last century; those of Gwalior and of Oude were of more recent origin. These contingents were not directly under the control of the commander-in-chief of the Company's army and, to save appearances, his orders and instructions reached the diplomatic residents accredited at the native courts, by the intermediary of the Foreign Affairs department. At the beginning of their military establishment, the Company had followed by economy the irregular system; a captain commanded each battalion and a subaltern each company. Advancement was by seniority on the general list of all the officers;[1] from whence resulted great slowness in promotion, and the choice of officers quite unfit for service through age or infirmities. There has already been occasion to remark that in the first days the greatest disorder reigned in all matters of pay, equipment, accounts, and administration; and that the regiments, both European and native, were not less wanting in military instruction than in discipline. Besides this, the social and hierarchical position of the officers was ill-defined. Each lieutenant-colonel of the royal army on his arrival in India received a local brevet, in virtue of which he assumed a superior rank to that of the officers in

[1] Officers' commissions were given directly by the Company's directors, and no other conditions were required of the candidate than having received a college education, and being between the ages of sixteen and twenty years. According to an official document, 1,976 commissions were distributed from January 1, 1836 to December 9, 1843 in the Indian army. Then commissions were divided in the following way: To sons of officers in the Indian service with the rank of captain and below, 128; to the sons of majors and lieutenant-colonels, 143; to the sons of members of the Indian Civil Service, 103; to sons of officers of the Royal army and navy, 383; to sons of clergymen, 205; to young men whose fathers belonged to the bar or were in business, &c., 938. The total of commissions distributed in less than eight years equals, if it does not surpass, the contingent of officers furnished to France during the same period by St. Cyr and the École Polytechnique, and is worthy to fix the attention of whosoever wishes to gain a clear idea of the importance of India as a portion of the British Empire.

the Company's service, whose authority was often contested even by officers of the royal army inferior to them in rank.

Lord Cornwallis put an end to this state of things in 1788, abolished local brevets for superior officers of the royal army; and as commander-in-chief granted to officers of the Anglo-Indian service brevets corresponding to the grades they held from the Court of Directors. Equality was henceforth established between the officers of both services. A few years later, in 1796, these reforms were completed by the entire transformation of the Anglo-Indian staff. Regimental promotion up to the rank of major took the place of promotion by seniority on a general list of each presidency, but for superior officers promotion still remained by seniority, in each branch of the service, on a general list. From this time forth, the highest honours of the military hierarchy were open to Anglo-Indian officers, who, under the previous *régime*, had never got beyond the rank of lieutenant-colonel, unless by exception, as in the case of Clive. At the same time, the number of general officers of the royal army who might be called to high military commands in India was fixed at two for Bengal, one for Madras, and one for Bombay. As to the regimental staff of the corps composing the regular native infantry, it was definitively settled thus: 1 colonel (a general in active service or on half pay, but always absent from the corps, as in the royal army), 2 lieutenant-colonels, 2 majors, 8 captains, 22 lieutenants, and 11 ensigns. This organisation stood the test of time without essential modification, and at the beginning of the mutiny the staff of a native regiment included 1 colonel, 1 lieutenant-colonel, 1 major, 7 captains, 11 lieutenants, and 7 ensigns.[1]

[1] Such a magnificent idea prevails in Europe of the treasures which fall to the lot of Europeans in India, that a few details of the pay of Anglo-Indian officers before the Mutiny of 1857 may not be perhaps read without interest. An ensign, on service, in the regiment received 202 rs. a month, a lieutenant 256 rs., a captain 415 rs., a major 780 rs., a colonel 1,032 rs. The command of a regiment gave an addition of 400 rs. a month, and that of a company one of 50 rs. The annual pay of a colonel actually present with the colours was therefore 17,184 rs., about 1,720*l.*; the pay of a brigadier in command was 2,900 rs. a month (250*l.*). As to retiring pensions, they varied according as the officer after 22 years' service, if he was captain, for example, passed

This 'cadre' would have been more than sufficient for the regiment's instruction and discipline, but in most of the corps it was far from being complete. At the Company's outset, in the character of a political power, it was customary to confide to Anglo-Indian officers all the functions of the military administration of the Commissariat, of the stud, and of other civil or diplomatic employments, accorded to the capacity of the individual and the necessity of the moment. These exceptional cases soon became general. The difficulty of finding men worthy of trust and familiar with the language and habits of the natives, necessitated the employment of officers in the Indian service as judges, collectors, and magistrates in the newly-acquired territory. They, however, retained their right to promotion on the regimental list. These appointments were much desired by everyone as being better paid, and giving a better position and a more comfortable existence. We have seen how, through a spirit of economy, and in order to avoid increasing immoderately the Bengal army, the Court of Directors had provided auxiliary forces under the name of irregular local, provincial, and police regiments, forming the contingents of the native princes, whose staffs were exclusively furnished by the officers of the Indian service.

This constant resort to cadre of the army pushed to an extreme extent reduced the staff of the regular army to its lowest point, and in many cases regiments were commanded for months together by captains or even by lieutenants. The regular and irregular cavalry of the Bengal army was almost exclusively composed of Mussulmen belonging to Rohilkande and to the Doab of the Ganges. The seventy-four regiments of regular infantry, with the exception of a few companies of Sikhs, belonged to the kingdom of Oude and to the North-West Provinces. The pay and the retiring pensions were relatively liberal, and were always regularly paid; volunteers vied with one another in flocking to the Company's standard.

into the invalid establishment or retired definitively. In the first case, he received full pay, but was obliged to reside in India; in the second, he might leave the country, but forfeited about a third of his pay.

The difficulty of choice amongst so many candidates was so great for a long time that only men of the highest castes, such as Brahmins and Rajpoots, were admitted into the ranks, in whom physical beauty and warlike qualities were to be found in the highest degree. Former wise rules, which prescribed the systematic mixture of religious nationalities and castes in the infantry corps, had almost fallen into disuse. On the eve of the mutiny, there was little fault to be found with the Bengal army from the point of view of instruction, discipline, and the physique of the men. The average height of the sepoys was superior to that of all European armies, with the exception, perhaps, of the Russian Guard.[1]

These fine soldiers—who were scrupulously clean, docile, smooth-tongued, and absolute strangers to the vice of drunkenness, that perfidious source of nearly all acts of insubordination in European armies—observed instinctively the strictest discipline; and in many regiments the punishment list remained blank for years. The native Bengal army had taken an active and honourable part in the dangers of the last wars. Its annals were enriched with acts of heroic valour, and certain corps were united to the most renowned regiments of the royal army by the powerful bonds of military confraternity. Services such as these did not remain unrewarded, and the officers, as well as the Court of

[1] A camp consisted in three large tents, a single man in a red coat, with a ramrod in his hand, standing as sentinel. The soldiers used to doff their uniforms and assume the Indian costume in all its simplicity, few of them having on as much as a shirt. The most wonderfully fantastic head-dresses were to be seen. One man had his head shaved close, another wore plaits of hair six feet long, another, thanks to the razor, exhibited a tremendously high forehead; a Sikh soldier had his hair turned back and knotted in a chignon like a Chinese girl. The native officers were distinguished by a necklace of beads of gilt wood; the most perfect order, the greatest quiet prevailed. Each individual cooked his own little dinner at his own little fire, or occupied himself in cleaning up. The hand of time, the civilising influence of military discipline, had passed over the unchanging character of the Hindoos like oil over marble. Three strokes of the drum—two words—and these savages, half naked a minute before, presented fine specimens of disciplined soldiers, their uniform and their muskets on their shoulders. Nothing, however, was changed in their instincts or their habits; they were the same men who, two thousand years ago, fought under the standard of Porus against the warriors of Alexander.

Directors, treated the sepoys like favoured children, and were proud of commanding men of ancient races whose well-authenticated genealogies showed a long list of ancestors, and whose military qualities and successes were patent to the whole world. The Bengal army, in a word, constituted a sort of aristocracy among the military forces of the Indian service.[1] We must remark that the marvellous progress which, thanks to steam, had taken place in the communication between Europe and Asia, soon modified considerably the original relations between the sepoy and his superiors. At the beginning of the conquest, and during the first thirty years of the century, Anglo-Indian officers—separated from their countries by a six months' voyage at least, exiled for life to India, bachelors for the most part, or united by temporary ties to native women—found a sort of adoptive family in their regiment. An officer of sepoys added a sort of paternal authority to that derived from his rank, and in consequence customs of a Homeric and patriarchal character, which are altogether out of date, were introduced in the interior life of the regiment.[2] Under the influence of rail-

[1] During the siege of Jellalabad, after the retreat from Cabul, the 35th Regiment of the Bengal army and the 13th of the Queen's became bound to one another by the strictest ties of military brotherhood. Before the separation of the brigade at Ferozepore, the sepoys gave a dinner to their European comrades, and not satisfied with plying their guests with beer and generous wines, they pushed their kind attentions to the point of providing stretchers to carry back to the barracks those amongst their guests who might be overcome by the good cheer (*inter pocula*). As a return for this politeness the Queen's soldiers gave their entertainers a native feast, diversified with yams and barley sugar, and subscribed a large sum of money, with which they bought a piece of plate for the officers' mess of the native corps.

[2] The Bengal army enjoyed the privilege, precious in the eyes of the orthodox Brahmin, of being liable to home service alone, whilst those of Bombay and Madras had to undertake general service, and might be called upon to fight or to do garrison duty beyond seas. Certain articles of the code of enlistment prove the spirit of concession to the prejudices of the Brahmin which animated those who drew them up. One is framed in these words: 'Great care shall be taken to refuse men of low caste, such as shopmen, clerks, barbers, porters, palanquin bearers, gardeners, washermen, cooks, and other low members of society.' This exclusiveness subordinated in the Bengal army the action of Government to that of a small number of Brahmins, mollahs, and fakirs, and a soldier was more afraid of offending their prejudices than committing an act of insubordination. The pressure brought

roads and steamboats, Anglo-Indian existence acquired new interests. An invasion of accomplished young ladies, of enterprising widows, peopled the solitudes of India, and gave to officers of sepoys the hitherto unknown joys and anxieties of domestic life. They now turned their eyes to Europe, and only considering India as anything but a land of exile where they had come to seek means of bringing up a family. They no longer expected their regiments to fill up a void in their lives, having interests elsewhere; the familiar intimacy of early days ceased between the men and their officers, or at least considerably diminished.[1]

It must be said, moreover, that diverse measures of military red-tapeism had done a great deal towards diminishing the authority and prestige of European officers. For many years the spirit of exaggerated centralisation, that bane of civilised Europe, had assumed exorbitant proportions, and had pushed its pernicious doctrines to the utmost extent under the influence of the superior officer—the commander-in-chief; and, following his example, those of the Bombay and Madras armies absorbed the whole power of rewarding or punishing, and even allowed the sepoys to appeal to head-quarters from the decisions of their immediate chiefs. This supervision over the regimental hierarchy bore its fruits, and very bitter ones. The officers, always afraid of being reprimanded or

to bear on the officers was such that they were often obliged to get rid of good soldiers because their companions thought them too low in caste to associate with.

[1] General Seaton, in his interesting Memoirs, tells how, on his arrival with the 36th Regiment, in 1827, he was initiated into certain customs, always faithfully observed in the older corps of the Bengal army. This was one: A Chat or poet was attached to the regiment, whose mission it was to encourage the soldiers during battle (with his voice) and to celebrate their deeds after the fight. This bard was a fine old man with a white beard falling to his waist; he had belonged to the regiment since childhood, and knew the history of all its campaigns. Every day after parade he advanced to the head of the line, struck his pike into the ground, and with his right hand raised towards heaven declaimed in a sonorous voice verses celebrating the exploits and virtues of the colonel, the officers, and soldiers of the regiment. At my first parade he introduced my name into his song, and on my thanking him by a small present for this unmerited favour, he predicted for me, with the assurance of a prophet, a future full of success and glory.—*Nine Years on the Western Frontier of India*, by Lieutenant-General Sir Sidney Cotton, K.C.B.

disapproved, only exercised timidly the right of command, and considered that they had fulfilled their task when they were able to maintain, at least in appearance, order and tranquillity in the corps confided to them. In order to do this they relied on the sepoys, whose birth or intelligence gave them a sort of supremacy amongst their comrades. The latter profited by the trust reposed in them to introduce their relations and friends into the corps. Regiments recruited in this way became large families, united by the ties of blood and interest, where all sorts of intrigues and dangerous associations could develope themselves. So that we can understand the obstinate confidence of the Anglo-Indian officers, who, to the last, rejecting all evidence, persisted in believing in the devotion and faithfulness of their soldiers, especially if we take into account the habits of dissimulation and mendacity so common among the natives. How much blood, and how many disasters this infatuation, honourable to them, no doubt—for the officers were among the first victims—was to cost England! It is credible, although the thing does not rest on unimpeachable proof, that other causes contributed to encourage bad passions and wild hopes in the ranks of the Bengal army. Those among the native princes who were either dispossessed or held in tutelage had for years cherished the dream of a mutiny in the native army; the troops, too, had without doubt always numbered in their ranks ambitious, active, and intelligent soldiers, who formerly could have risen to the first rank in the service of their natural rulers. These men of energy, finding themselves powerless to break down the prejudices of that most exclusive caste of all—the English—and having no other prospect after a life of faithful and loyal service than the position of subahdar-major,[1] must often have longed for the day when, at the head of their comrades, they should drive out their European masters; and, as in the good old days of Scindiah and Holkar, carve out for them-

[1] The rank of subahdar-major (native captain), the highest ever attained by native soldiers, never placed them on a footing of equality even with the youngest European ensign.

selves a large share in Indian dignities—a pair of epaulettes or a crown! The extraordinary good luck which for nearly a century attended the English undertakings in India, discouraged the most adventurous spirits. But in 1842 the charm was broken by the disasters of the retreat from Cabul.[1] The Hindoo and Mussulman sepoys no longer thought their masters invincible, and a spirit of discontent and disaffection crept in amongst them. The tribes of the Indian Caucasus, supported by the mutiny of the Afghan regiments in the pay of England, had forced the Europeans to evacuate their conquests beyond the Indus after immense reverses. This was a threatening example, and was calculated to impress the native army and population. Why should that which had proved successful beyond the Khyber Pass not prove equally so on the banks of the Ganges and of the Jumna? Could a handful of foreign soldiers resist the efforts of millions of Indians, backed by the native forces of the Bengal army? For fifteen years this problem agitated many minds amongst the mercenaries of the Company. Ambition, the thirst for riches, the hatred of a foreign domination, are instinctive sentiments in the heart of man, and they exist just as much under a dark as under a white skin.

The exaggerated accounts of the English misfortunes in the Crimea could not fail to increase the general uneasiness, and to inflame the passions, the hatred, and the hopes of the dispossessed dynasties.[2] The archives of the palace at Delhi

[1] See Documents, No. V., 'Cabul Disasters.'

[2] Not only the army but the population came to the conclusion that the military resources of the little far-away island (Chota, su Tapu) were exhausted by the Crimean War, when they saw the effective force of the Royal troops reduced beyond measure. After the capture of Sebastopol, insignificant measures contributed towards reviving this idea, which had been widely made use of by the native press during the war. The Patriotic Fund, for instance, which was a subscription in favour of the wounded and of the soldiers' families, helped to persuade the natives that the English power was in full decline. The great proprietors and their subordinates felt themselves called upon, and perhaps rightly so, to respond to this appeal for funds, which took the name of Russian tax (Chimdu Russ), and it was generally believed in India that its product was intended to furnish exhausted England with means to fight Russia.—Edwardes' *Reminiscence of a Bengal Civilian.*

attest that during the siege of Sebastopol, King Mohammed Shah Bahadour sent a secret mission to the Shah of Persia, asking for help against the English. Was it likely, then, that the heir presumptive would remain unmoved by the events of the battle-fields of Inkermann and Balaclava, when he knew full well that on the death of the reigning emperor sovereign honours, the right of residence in the palace of his ancestors, and the pension of twelve lakhs of rupees enjoyed by his father, would be withdrawn from him?

In the first days of 1857, Nabob Daudou Pan, better known under the name of Nana Sahib, the same who played such an important and odious part in the mutiny, left his residence of Bethour, near Cawnpore, in order to take a journey to Delhi, and soon after another to Lucknow. Most probably politics had something to do with his movements, which were totally at variance with the stay-at-home habits of the native princes. Perhaps, without conspiring in the full meaning of the word, the dispossessed masters of the soil, well aware, as they were, of the elements of discord fermenting in the native army, deemed it necessary to come to some mutual understanding, in order to be ready for any eventuality. It may be admitted, then, though subsequent investigations almost completely failed to discover any proof of it, that in the early part of 1857 the native princes and their agents were not idle, and that they neglected no means of exciting disaffection in the native army, especially amongst the troops stationed round the great centres, such as Delhi, Cawnpore, and Lucknow.

In the midst of all these elements of disintegration, the fatal innovation of greased cartridges for the Enfield rifle, with which the European and native troops had recently been armed, made its appearance. Those of the men who were dissatisfied naturally affirmed that the object of introducing new ammunition into the service was only to deprive all the sepoys of their caste, and to oblige them to embrace Christianity. Hindoos and Mussulmen were equally threatened; for the cartridges served out to the former were said to be encased with cow's fat, and those intended for the latter with pig's fat. These foolish rumours excited almost to madness minds nourished in the impure superstitions and exterior practices of the Brahmin religion. The following anecdote, borrowed from the Memoirs of Colonel Skinner, an officer whose name is gloriously connected with the campaigns of the beginning of the century, gives a very just idea of the all-powerfulness of the spirit of caste. He was wounded in an encounter with the troops of the Rajah of Oomeara, January 31, 1800, about three o'clock in the afternoon, and only came to his senses the next morning at dawn. His trowsers alone had been left him by the marauders, so that, to escape the burning rays of the sun, he crawled towards some neighbouring bushes. Two wounded men belonging to his regiment joined him there. One, a subahdar (native captain) had his leg shattered above the knee, the other, a jemidar (native lieutenant), had received a lance-thrust in the body. The three wretched beings were devoured by thirst, but not a living creature could be descried; and they spent the day longing for death. Their prayers were not heard, and night approached. The sky was clear, the moon was bright, the cold was intense. Silence was only broken by the cries of the wounded calling for water with a dying voice, and by the gnashing of the teeth of the animals devouring the dead bodies. Several times jackals advanced towards the colonel and his companions, who were obliged to make a noise and throw stones to drive them away. At last day broke; and in the dim light the wounded men saw a man and an old woman going over the battlefield, and giving each person a bit of bread and some water. Colonel Skinner received this unexpected succour with thankfulness, but the subahdar was a Rajpoot of high caste, and the charitable woman a 'chounar,' one of the lowest, so that he refused to accept either bread or water. In vain the Englishman tried to shake his companion's resolution, and entreated him to save his life. The subahdar answered stoically that in his condition, with merely a few hours' agony in prospect, the intensity of his sufferings was a matter of little importance. Could he deny his faith and die in a state of impurity in order to avoid pain? This instance shows that all the influences which act on a man, such as habit, public opinion, &c., are concentrated in the case of the Indian in the spirit of caste.[1]

Native society considers a man deprived of caste as a culprit guilty of some great crime, and the hatred and contempt of his equals pursue him everywhere. His family even cannot escape public persecution. For the pariah, for his wife and his children, there exist in this world neither relations, friends, temples, nor burial, and in the next a thousand frightful torments await them for thousands and thousands of years! A Brahmin, who loses caste, can only be compared to a great man in Europe who falls from high social rank to the lowest depths of a convict establishment. The above explanation affords grounds for affirming, however incredible it may appear to the reader, that, with regard to the sepoy mutiny, the introduction of greased cartridges was the last straw which broke the camel's back.

Here we must remark that, all-powerful as were caste prejudices where Europeans were concerned, they had ceased to exist among native soldiers through their daily contact with one another. Hindoos and Mussulmen alike, forgetting their past hatred and their religious differences, drew nearer together; and a sort of vast military freemasonry, cemented by real or imaginary interests, was formed in process of time in the Bengal army. The news of the day, or the opinions prevailing amongst the native masses, spread with extraordinary rapidity from the towns and palaces to the remotest garrisons. Must we conclude from these indications, as others have done, that organised bands kept up a secret correspondence with all the regiments, and that the conspirators intended the mutiny to break out at once in all the Indian stations on Sunday, May 10? The plan of the ringleaders is supposed to have been as follows:—To assassinate

[1] An Indian may lose caste by debauchery, by crime, by eating impure food, or by killing a cow! The worship of sacred animals is carried to such an extent in the Indian Peninsula, that the inhabitants do not use soap because cow's fat may enter into its composition.

officials and officers as they came out of church, to seize immediately on the treasure, the arsenals, and the public magazines, to open the gates of the prisons; and having done this to proclaim old Mohammed Shah, Emperor of India. The outbreaks at Barrackpore and at Mirut, which could not be suppressed by the leaders, hurried on events, and prevented, so it is said, the Indian Vespers from filling with bloodshed, on the selfsame day and at the selfsame hour, all the stations of Bengal, of the north-west provinces of the kingdom of Oude, of Central India, and of the Punjab. We must hasten to add that no trustworthy discovery, either during or after the mutiny, served to confirm the existence of plots as subtly constructed as these, worthy indeed of veteran European revolutionists, but too deep for the primitive conspirators of Asia. Still, attentive observers were aware of certain premonitory signs of the coming storm.

In the first days of March, the 'choupangis' (Anglo-Indian police agents) carried about from village to village and town to town 'chippatis' (a sort of cake), which they pretended to have received from unknown persons, and the origin of which the Administration with all its efforts could not discover. A strange thing, which proves the mystery surrounding the lower strata of Indian society, is that even nowadays, when the connection between the fact and the events of the morrow is clearly understood, the most competent judges cannot agree upon its signification.[1] Some see in it a sign borrowed from former customs, warning the native communities to put themselves on their guard against some great danger near at hand. Others affirm that the chiefs of the conspiracy forwarded these cakes throughout India, and that by the very hands of the agents of English authority, in order to alarm the population and make them believe that they would soon be forced by Government to adopt one and the same sort of food; in a word, to abjure their religious and caste prejudices.

In the midst of all these plottings, the most perfect discipline prevailed in the native army; for the sepoys, though

[1] See Documents, No. VI., 'Distribution of Chippatis.'

they imparted to their superiors their imaginary fears, aroused by no less imaginary projects of religious propaganda, rejected with apparent horror all idea of mutiny. These protestations found too easy credence among the Anglo-Indian officers, who, if they were struck by any signs of disaffection, perceived them in other regiments, but not in their own. It was admitted that bad tendencies, fomented by the native press, and a spirit of uneasiness, existed in the ranks; but the official staff reports went no further.

Even the greatest alarmists declared that no mutiny could be more than partial, and that the Hindoo element would always be ready to fight the Mussulman, and *vice versâ*. Besides this, all the men who had grown grey in the Company's service refused obstinately to believe that under the red coat of the sepoy lay dormant the wildest terror, the most ferocious passions;—the natives themselves pierced with a surer glance the gloom of the political horizon. From the early months of 1857 business became slack; and, as in the bad days of yore, bankers, merchants, and rich men buried their diamonds and treasures.

Musketry schools had been established at the stations of Dum-Dum, Mirut, and Sialkote, to which were sent detachments from the different sepoy regiments, in order to teach the men the use of the Enfield rifle. But the new ammunition was only distributed to a Goorkha regiment, which had asked for it to make a show of discipline and good-will. The agitation excited in the army by the question of greased cartridges was made known to the public by a slight fact, which exhibits so curiously the Indian customs and superstitions, that we shall mention it in some detail. A grenadier of the second native infantry regiment attached to the Dum-Dum depôt[1] was going along the road to the cantonments, when a low-caste workman of the arsenal asked to drink out of the copper cup he had in his hand. The soldier, rather astonished at such a familiarity, answered that he could not allow any one to drink out of his cup, without knowing what

[1] One of the principal arsenals of Bengal, situated in the suburbs of Calcutta.

caste he belonged to. 'You talk of caste,' the man replied, 'don't you know it will no longer exist the day that you have bitten a greased cartridge.' These words, reported by the soldier to his comrades, created such agitation in the depôt, that the commanding officer made an instantaneous report to the war secretary, who, being an old officer, accustomed to respect and give way to the sepoy's religious prejudice, at once understood the gravity of the situation. Directions were sent to explain the composition of the cartridges to the sepoys, and as a final measure the question was settled by modifying the drill, so that the soldiers had not to bite the cartridge. This extreme concession did not quiet matters, and the agitators even made use of it to assert with greater violence than ever that cow's fat most certainly and really entered into the composition of the new cartridges, notwithstanding all the Government denials. They argued, with some show of reason, that if it had not been so, why should the soldiers' drill have been suddenly changed? In the meantime, a detachment of the 34th was sent from Serampore to Barrackpore.[1] The men stationed there had followed with anxiety the different phases of the cartridge question, and had shared the fears and anger of their brothers in arms at Dum-Dum, which was near their own cantonments. The agitation created in the ranks of the sepoys of the 34th communicated itself with the rapidity of lightning to the regiments stationed at Serampore. The 24th of February—there are really ill-omened days in the history of man—the soldiers of the 19th Regiment refused, when on parade, to receive their cartridges, though they came out of the same chests as those they had used the day before. The brigadier commanding at Serampore, who had not a single European soldier with him, countermanded the distribution; and as the sepoys consented to return to barracks, no further repressive measures were taken. The Government was made acquainted with these facts, and sent steamers to Burmah to fetch the 84th Regiment of the Royal army, so as to reinforce

[1] The summer palace of the Governor-General, and a considerable cantonment of native troops, about twelve miles from Calcutta.

the feeble garrison at Fort William; but before their return blood had already flowed at the very station of Barrackpore, where, thirty years before, the insubordination of a native regiment had been repressed with such merciless energy.

Towards the middle of March, a sepoy of the 34th, called Mangal Pandy (which name was given later on to the rebels), went through the lines exciting his comrades to mutiny, and cut down his adjutant, whilst the native soldiers and officers on guard close by remained deaf to the cries and orders of the victim. Mangal Pandy and the native officers were brought before a court-martial, condemned to death, and executed. Unfortunately, repressive measures did not stop here, and with the most imprudent severity the authorities disbanded the 34th; they forgot that once in their homes, the sepoys would disseminate everywhere the mendacious report of the strange projects against native religion ascribed to Government by fanaticism or superstition. The murder at Barrackpore had scarcely opened the eyes of the military authorities to the spirit of disaffection in the native army,[1] when the haphazard of human passions gave birth to the crisis in the station, which, by reason of its very considerable European garrison, seemed the least exposed to a mutiny among the native troops. In the month of May the new ammunition was served out during morning drill on the esplanade at Mirut to ninety men of the 3rd regiment of regular cavalry selected from the different squadrons. As only five accepted it, the eighty-five others were brought before a court-martial, and condemned to five years' imprisonment. Any act of mercy would have been out of place, and would have authorised mutiny in the Bengal army. The commander-in-chief decided, justly enough, to execute the sentence in all its rigour. On May 9, the condemned men were stripped of their uniforms before all the assembled troops of the station, chains were riveted on their legs, and they were then led back to prison. A mournful silence prevailed in the native regiments present on this occasion. Not a word was said, not a gesture of insubordination was made. The dan-

[1] See Documents, No. VIII., 'Last order given to the Schools of Musketry.'

gerous moment seemed safely over, and the brigadier in command could write in his official report, with some show of truth, that he had successfully solved the greased cartridge question. The events of the following day gave the lie to this assertion. On Sunday, May 10, just as the European population of Mirut was about going to church, a great tumult broke out in the native ranks, the 3rd cavalry regiment showing itself more violent than the others. The officers who hastened to the spot to endeavour to restore discipline, were attacked furiously. Some of them fell under the blows of their soldiers, and the whole regiment moved on to the prison. By an inconceivable error of judgment of the authorities—an error which, by-the-bye, often meets us again in the scenes of the mutiny—the guard on duty, which did not even attempt resistance, was composed of sepoys. The gates were thrown open, and the military prisoners and a crowd of wretches of the worst kind poured forth. From the outset the 20th infantry raised the standard of revolt, but the 11th was still undecided, and listened, at least, to the orders of its officers, if it did not obey them. In the midst of the excitement, the mutineers of the 20th rushed into the lines of the 11th, which was still hesitating, and fired upon the staff, killing the colonel. This murder turned the scale, and for several hours the sepoys, the scum of the bazars, and the escaped convicts pillaged, burned, and murdered to their heart's content.

During this time the vacillation of an old general, weighed down with infirmities, sufficed to paralyse all action on the part of the largest number of European troops in any Anglo-Indian station. The surprise had been complete; yet we must add that the great extent of the station at Mirut, which covered a space of more than five miles, the entire separation of the European troops from the native ones, explain, to a certain point, how it was that the news of what was passing in the sepoys' lines was some time in reaching head-quarters. The day was drawing to a close before the royal troops could be assembled under General Hewett on the parade ground. Having secured the regimental chests and the barracks, they marched towards the native lines, but the rebel sepoys had already left them, and were hastening to Delhi. There only remained some small bands of stragglers, on whom the artillery fired a few harmless rounds. The station was enveloped in darkness; and the general, without troubling himself to pursue the rebels, ordered his indignant men to withdraw to their cantonments for the night. All the help given was to acquaint the Delhi authorities by telegraph with the events which had occurred since the morning. At dawn the next day, patrols were at last sent round the station to look for any families who might have escaped being massacred through the fidelity of their servants, or favoured by the darkness. The many smiling villas of Mirut were a heap of smoking ruins, from which were extracted thirty-one horribly mutilated European corpses. On May 11, at sunrise, the cavalry which composed the rebel van-guard took possession of the bridge of boats over the Jumna. No other town offered the mutineers such a safe aslyum against English vengeance as Delhi; for in its walls lived the descendant of Timour, the natural chief of the insurrection, surrounded by a crowd of ruined nobles, adventurers, and discontented persons of all kind, whose most ardent wish was for the downfall of the English dominion and the restoration of the fallen dynasties. As far back as April, a proclamation in Persian, posted clandestinely on the walls of the grand mosque, had announced that the time had come to drive the European conquerors out of India. The cantonments round Delhi, though occupied by a considerable Anglo-Indian force, did not contain a single European soldier; and this, notwithstanding that the arsenal inside the town was one of the best supplied in the Empire. It is only just to remark that the onus of this inexcusable fault must be laid on the Court of Directors, as the danger of its isolated position had been several times pointed out by the different commanders-in-chief, amongst others by Sir C. Napier.[1] The commissioner of the district, Major Fraser, was

[1] See Documents, No. IX., 'The Danger of the English Position at Delhi.'

aroused by the news of the arrival of the regiments from Mirut, and he went forward to meet the rebels, accompanied by his officers and a few police. Abandoned by his escort and fired on by the sepoys, he fled to the palace to ask help of old Mohammed Shah, but it is needless to say that he received no answer to his entreaties. The rabble soldiers, who had also entered the palace, pursued the unfortunate magistrate and his companions, and massacred them all in the apartments of the European commander of the imperial residence. These murders once accomplished, the rebels, the emperor's guard, and the dregs of the populace fell upon the European quarter, which for some hours was the scene of the most hideous excesses. All the efforts of the mutineers soon centred on the arsenal, the defence of which had been promptly and energetically organised by the staff of nine European commissioned and non-commissioned officers, as soon as they were aware of what was going on. Arms were served out to the workmen, loaded guns pointed at the entrance, and, as a last resource, a train of powder was laid to the chief magazine, to prevent its falling into the hands of the rebels. Scarcely were these preparations finished, when a messenger presented himself to demand the cession of the arsenal in the Emperor's name, and on refusal, the attack began immediately. By means of ladders applied to the walls, the besiegers entered the exterior courts, and in a few minutes a heavy fire from the neighbouring roofs, which were crowded with the enemy, disabled several of the Europeans. The workmen, to whom arms had been given, far from helping their masters, joined the attack in great numbers; and even those who remained faithful threw away their rifles and wandered about the enclosure, a prey to the wildest terror.

All hope of resisting successfully was soon lost. Lieutenant Willoughby, of the Artillery, ordered Sergeant Scully —these two names should be jealously preserved by history— to apply a match to the train. Some magazines and buildings blew up with a terrible noise, burying many of the besiegers under their ruins, but the destruction produced was only partial, and the greater part of the stores and provisions remained intact. Non-commissioned officer Scully, who was wounded in the explosion, was dispatched by the victors. Lieutenant Willoughby succeeded in leaving the town, but was massacred a few days after in a village. Three of the other European defenders of the arsenal escaped safe and sound, and managed to reach Mirut.

While the revolt was triumphing in Delhi itself, the position of the military authorities in the cantonments, two miles to the north of the Cashmere Gate, was becoming more and more critical. Successively apprised of the events of the preceding night at Mirut, of the entrance into Delhi of the rebel sepoys, of the sack of the European quarter, Brigadier Greaves hastily took some measures of defence. A circular warned English residents to meet without delay at the signalling tower on the Amballah road. Infantry and artillery reinforcements were dispatched to the town, but the troops round Delhi were infected with the spirit of revolt, and nearly all the detachments sent from the camp went over at once to the rebels.

The 54th allowed its officers to be massacred in their midst by the Mirut troopers, without offering any resistance; and even the men who preserved the most semblance of discipline and loyalty returned to their quarters only to inflame their comrades by an account of the success of the revolted regiments. The officers had lost all authority, and tumult and confusion in the camp were at their height. The 34th alone still retained some appearance of discipline; but towards the evening a few devoted soldiers came to the colonel and adjutant, and advised them to fly. They said that the troops considered themselves released from their oath of fidelity, and that notwithstanding their own goodwill, they were powerless to protect their officers against the madmen, who were little by little gaining the upper hand. All hope of resistance was gone from that time. The officers and the European families took to flight, and Brigadier Greaves, like the captain of a smoking vessel, was the last to leave. That night the victory of the sepoys was celebrated in the cantonments by fire, pillage, and assassination. The unfortunate fugitives met with the most varied fate. Some of them fell into the hands of the mutineers, and were massacred. Others were killed in Mussulman villages, where they had taken refuge. As a rule, the English were kindly treated in the Hindoo communities, and for weeks together whole families found shelter in miserable huts, to the great honour, be it said, of the ryots, and to their equally great peril; for their generous hospitality exposed them to the fiercest wrath of the rebels.

The latest and most marvellous conquest of science contributed to the safety of England in the midst of all these disasters. The telegraph clerk, who was shut up in his office at the far end of the camp, was one of the last victims on that day. As evening drew near, he was sitting before his instrument when the murderers, mad with carnage, burst into the room, and in an instant tore him to pieces. But the dispatch, which was to avenge his death, was already passing along the wires with the rapidity of lightning. The Punjab authorities knew the full extent of the disasters at Delhi before his limbs had ceased to quiver; and, meeting in council, they began preparations for future victory. The fatal news had also been conveyed by telegraph to Calcutta, and to military head-quarters. General Anson, Commander-in-Chief of the Indian Army, had for several preceding weeks taken refuge from the terrible heat of the summer at Simla. A younger brother of Lord Lichfield, a distinguished member of the Lower House, a man of fashion, renowned in the highest London society for his elegant manners, his race-horses, his first-rate talent, for which General Anson owed his position, to his family connection and to the Queen's protection; for Her Majesty still showed to the beautiful Mrs. Anson the same affection with which she had honoured the Hon. Miss Forester, the chief ornament of her court in the early days of her reign. General Anson had been scarcely two years at Calcutta, and had acquired a very slight experience of men and things in India. Besides this, his former military service was not sufficient to give him any great authority, as he had been present at no other campaigns than that of Waterloo, where, however, he did his duty bravely as an ensign in the Guards. Let us hold, to do him justice, that even if he had taken part in every battle since the beginning of the century, even if he had been gifted with the highest military genius, he could hardly have escaped the infatuation which hid from the most competent officers the hostile spirit of the native troops.

As before mentioned, nearly all those in command, in their private or official correspondence, speak of the discipline and loyalty of their soldiers with a confidence full of delusions. It is true that the mote, which none of them perceived in their own eyes, assumed the proportion of a beam in those of their neighbours; the state of the army was said to be serious, the question of greased cartridges full of danger, and certain regiments showed unequivocal symptoms of disaffection. But such contradictory reports had not led to the conclusion that the spirit of sedition had so completely permeated an army which for one hundred years had been faithful to the British flag. At any rate, no one could suppose that a mutiny would not be immediately suppressed at Mirut, where a numerically superior European force could be opposed to the native soldiery. To doubt the success of repressive measures was to refuse to see the sun at mid-day! The correctness of this estimation is settled to-day by the facts themselves. If that same evening, the brigadier in command at Mirut, recovering from his first surprise, had sent his two cavalry regiments and a rifle battalion in pursuit of the mutineers, the latter would have entered Delhi as fugitives, and in no case could have maintained themselves there. It has been seen, too, that the mutiny did not break out spontaneously in the cantonments at Delhi. The regiments hesitated before listening to appeals from the rebels, and one even remained faithful to its duty till the evening. The immediate arrival of European troops would no doubt have prevented or repressed all attempt at revolt. Both at Mirut and Cabul, of fatal memory, the incapacity of an old general ruined everything. How much blood and treasure the systematic predilection of the Court of Directors for invalid officers was to cost England! General Anson's first measures attest a judicious character full of decision, and able to look danger in the face without trembling. Three European regiments, stationed in the sanitariums of the Himalaya, received orders to descend at once to the plains, and a Goorkha regiment was dispatched to Philour to serve as escort to a siege train. The next day, the commander-in-chief left Simla for the scene of action. For European troops, the abrupt change from the healthy climate of the Himalaya to the burning plains of India, and the necessity of forced marches in May—the hottest month of the year—was a severe trial. They easily endured the fatigues of the first marches, but cholera broke out at Amballah, their first rallying point, and raged with extreme violence. This terrible plague was only an additional motive for pressing on to Delhi; but how to bring together in a few days the food and the immense apparatus, indispensable for enabling a European army to take the field at this season.

The co-operation of the Rajah of Pattgalah[1] was of immense help to the English commissariat in its difficulties. This prince, belonging to an old and illustrious Sikh family, and the chief of the most important amongst the states allied to England in the neighbourhood of Amballah, exercised a most powerful influence on the conduct of other independent native rulers. The help he afforded to the English in money, camels, elephants and carts, allowed the vanguard to leave Amballah on May 19. The head columns arrived at the second rallying point, Kumaon, on the 19th. Scarcely were all the forces united, when General Anson succumbed to an attack of cholera. But his plan of campaign survived him. If the exclusive merit of carrying the war under the walls of Delhi[2] does not belong to him, he had at least that of accepting the advice of persons who, better acquainted than he with the native character and

[1] See Documents, No. X., 'The Maharajah of Pattgalah's Accession.'

[2] See Documents, No. XI., 'General Anson's and Sir H. Lawrence's Letters.'

capabilities, represented the absolute necessity of a vigorous line of action. Did not history itself demonstrate that success had always attended the English in wars where they had gone forward with blind audacity, without calculating the number or the resources of the enemy? Major-General Sir H. Barnard succeeded Anson by right of seniority, and assumed the command in chief of the troops, which were composed of two horse batteries, of the 9th Lancers of the Royal army, of three regiments of European infantry, and of three native ones, on which little dependence could be placed. We must add to these several forces, the Mirut brigade, already on its way to Alipore, which had been chosen beforehand as a rallying point. These troops had the good luck to be the first to meet the enemy, and to avenge their military honour, which had been tarnished by involuntary inaction at Mirut. The Delhi sepoys, in order to prevent the junction of the Mirut brigade, and of the principal body of the army, occupied the approaches of a suspension bridge over the Hindum some distance from the village of Ghajioudoun gahr. The rebels made but a feeble resistance, and took to flight almost without striking a blow, and abandoned seven guns.

The result of the fight was already certain, when the English general was informed that some sepoys had taken refuge in huts in the rear of his lines. He ordered the village to be cleared, but the sepoys were so convinced of their safety that they were surrounded before they thought of flying. They defended themselves with admirable courage, repulsed the attack of a Sikh regiment, and when they finally succumbed to the bayonets of the 61st, the victory proved dearly bought. An incident had already shown that men of determination were to be found in the native ranks. Just as some skirmishers were about to take possession of a gun, a sepoy of the 11th set fire to the ammunition, and with his last glance saw an English officer and several men blown to pieces by the explosion. The attack, which the rebels began on the following day, was easily repulsed, with very little loss to the English, amongst whom fatigue, privation, and the heat of the sun made quite as many victims as the fire of the enemy. On June 7 the Mirut brigade reached head-quarters at Alipore. The arrival of this reinforcement was most opportune, as the staff reports certified that the enemy was in force in the neighbourhood. The sepoys, in fact, had determined to await an attack in the open, and occupied before Delhi a position the natural advantages of which they utilised with a skill constantly exhibited by them during the whole contest. A considerable force of native infantry was stationed to the right of the Great Trunk Road,[1] in a vast serai,[2] whose walls were pierced with loopholes, and in front of which, on a slight elevation, was a battery and a howitzer, defended by epaulements, covered by fascines and gabions. At a little distance the village of Badd-li-Serai offered excellent cover for infantry in its houses and gardens. The defence of this position was confided to seven infantry regiments, two cavalry, and an artillery battalion, all of which had belonged to the Bengal army. Besides these regular forces, the sepoys numbered in their ranks the artillerymen of the palace of Delhi and volunteers of all kinds, drawn to the scene of action by hatred of the foreigner, by religious excitement, and the thirst for blood and pillage. On June 8, at midnight, Sir H. Barnard had taken his last measure, and Brigadier Hope Grant left the camp at the head of three cavalry squadrons and two pieces of artillery, in order to turn the sepoys' left wing. Difficulties on the road impeded the march of this column, and the battle was nearly decided before it came into action. The division which had been selected for the principal attack, under the orders of the commander-in-chief left the camp at two in the morning, and arrived about sunrise at some distance from the village of Badd-li-Serai. Its defenders at once opened fire. The British artillery took up a position, and the infantry, composed of the 75th of the Royal army, and

[1] The greatest artery in India, at a time when railways existed merely on paper. It presented a continuous development of more than 1,200 miles.

[2] Serai, the caravanserai of the *Arabian Nights*, consisting of rectangular buildings with towers at the four corners, and an internal court destined to travellers.

the 1st of the Company's, deployed on the high road. It was soon evident that the British artillery was unable to silence the fire of the fortified battery to which it was opposed. Two regiments and the staff met with considerable loss. Sir H. Barnard felt that the matter could only be settled by a bayonet charge. He ordered the 75th to capture the guns, whilst the Fusiliers marched against the battlemented walls of the village. In the very moment when orders from head-quarters were about to be given, the 75th thought they were going to be charged by cavalry, and the men formed square without waiting for the word of command. The mistake was immediately recognised, but it was too late to remedy it, and they advanced on the battery over ground impassable through the depth of mud under a galling fire. In a few minutes seventy men were disabled, but the battery was taken and its defenders put to flight, or were slain at their guns. The Fusiliers were equally successful, and they occupied the village of Badd-li-Serai without severe loss. The two regiments united marched on the serai, where they battered in the gates and bayoneted all to the last man. This was the first example of those bloody reprisals which we shall have occasion more than once to make mention of. The reserves had arrived on the ground during these operations, and Brigadier Grant with his cavalry turned the sepoys' left. The Lancers immediately drove back the troops opposed to them, and took possession of two guns, on which the rout became general, and the sepoys only rallied in the suburbs of Delhi, where the pursuit ceased. Towards the afternoon the English entered their cantonments as victors. Not a month had passed since the day when they had been occupied by perjured soldiers, who had tarnished their military honours by shedding the blood of their officers. The British army numbered 54 dead, of whom 4 were officers, including Adjutant-General Colonel Chester, and 32 wounded. The sepoy losses were much more considerable. They abandoned several colours and thirteen guns. A strange detail, very characteristic of the mutiny, is that the military medals and the

Order of British India,[1] given by the Company as rewards for faithful services, were found on the red coats of dead sepoys, both soldiers and officers; and, stranger still, pouches full of greased cartridges, the final and decisive cause of the mutiny, were picked up on the ground occupied by the rebel regiments. The results of this affair were immense, for it re-established the prestige of the English in the eyes of the Asiatic population; yet it is hardly worthy of notice when compared with the enormous forces engaged and the torrents of blood shed at Solferino and Gravelotte.

The news of the sepoy defeat passed from mouth to mouth to the most remote frontiers of the Punjab, and gave decisive help to the energetic measures of Sir J. Lawrence. The European regained confidence in his superiority over the Asiatic. A handful of British soldiers, some three thousand leagues from their country, in the depths of Asia, exposed to the burning rays of a vertical sun and to the hot breath of suffocating winds, were able to look the future confidently in the face. This fortunate beginning was the precursor of still greater successes. The Punjab 'Guides,' one of the best regiments in the Indian army, came into camp on June 7. They were composed of three squadrons and three companies of infantry, and were exclusively recruited among the tribes of the Indian Caucasus. These men of iron had

[1] Two military orders were given as rewards to well-deserving soldiers in the Indian service. The first of these, the Order of Merit, was only bestowed for deeds of valour; and though the number of members was not limited by statute, it was very rarely bestowed. It was divided into three classes, each of which had to be won by some brilliant exploit. The badge of the first class was a gold star, with the motto: 'The reward of valour,' on a blue ribbon, bordered with red. For the other two classes the star was of silver. The first gave double, the second and third two-thirds and one-third extra pay; but the order was distributed so scantily, that many superior officers told the author they had never met with a gold cross in all their experience, and with very few silver ones. The Order of British India was divided into two classes of 100 crosses each; the first, destined to subahdars and rissaldars, conferred the title of Sirdar Bahadour, and carried with it two rupees a day extra pay. The second class, to which all native officers were admitted, conferred the title of Bahadour, and one rupee extra pay. In point of fact, this reward was only granted to seniority, and few of the members in possession of it were still in the service.

covered the distance from Peshawur to Delhi, some 562 miles, in less than three weeks, in the hottest time of the year; and yet from their appearance one might have imagined that they had left some neighbouring garrison the evening before to take part in a review. However important this reinforcement was from its number, it was still more so from the mere fact of its arrival; for the entrance of the 'Guides' meant that Sir J. Lawrence was undisputed master of the Punjab, which had scarcely been conquered ten years before, and was inhabited by the most warlike race in India. The help given did not stop here. Wondrous triumph of political talent and of the personal ascendency of a great statesman over a whole nation! At the call of Sir J. Lawrence the formidable Sikh population furnished the English army with men, money, and ammunition sufficient to take Delhi, not only before one of the numerous battalions sent from England on the news of the mutiny had joined the besieging forces, but even before a single one had disembarked at Calcutta.

CHAPTER II.

THE PUNJAB.

Retrospective glance over the history of the Punjab—Nanak, founder of the Sikh sect—Radical change in Nanak's institutions—Ranjit Singh—Anarchy on his death—The Punjab is annexed to the Company's dominions—English centres of action—State of the public mind—The sepoys disarmed at Lahore—Peshawur—Execution at Peshawur—Effects of the execution of June 10—Sir J. Lawrence and his staff—The flying column—Brigadier Nicholson—Insurrection at Jhelum and Sialkote—Departure of the flying column for Delhi—Flight and destruction of the 26th N.I.—Ditto of the 51st—The situation of the Punjab at the end of August.

WHILST the tempest of revolt was raging in the North-West Provinces, precursive signs of the storm were not wanting in the great plains of the Punjab. The Punjab—the country of the five rivers, as its name indicates—is watered by the Indus, the Chenab, the Ravee, the Jhelum, and the Sutlej. The first and the last mark its limits, but its political importance extends much further, and radiates over Peshawur, the lands west of the Indus, and the mountain states, such as Tskandah and Ladakh, &c. Besides these principal rivers, the Punjab is traversed by innumerable water-courses, almost all navigable, owing to the configuration of the ground, which is on an inclined plane, with a fall of 1,600 feet to the sea level. With the exception of the Indus and the Sutlej, the course of all these rivers has changed by lapse of time, and the Punjab contains a considerable number of deserted cities; some of its great towns being of comparatively recent origin. The population of the Punjab is about six million souls, distributed in the following manner:—The Lahore district, 2,000,000; in Jumna, 1,000,000; Peshawur, 600,000; Deera Ismail Khan, 450,000; Moultan, 700,000. A recent census (1868) estimates the inhabitants of the large towns as at 135,813 for Amritsur, 98,924 for Lahore, 58,555 for Peshawur, and 56,826 for Moultan. We may remark that the population of the Punjab is not exclusively composed of Sikhs, and that Sir A. Burns, the great traveller, in 1838 estimated the Sikh element at half a million only.

In the month of May 1857 scarcely ten years had passed since Ranjit Singh's kingdom had been definitively annexed to the Company's domains, and the turbulent and warlike spirit of the inhabitants gave just cause to dread that they might take advantage of the British Government's embarrassed position to revenge the bloody defeats of 1845, 1846, and 1849. These anticipations were not realised. The Punjab, far from taking up arms against its European masters, furnished them with the necessary means to bring the siege of Delhi to a successful termination. This phenomenon of fidelity to a foreign yoke deserves explanation; and it will be necessary to sketch in general terms the history of this Asiatic people, among whom, within a period of ten years, the English were to find their most formidable adversaries and their most faithful friends. At the beginning of the mutiny, subject as they had been for some time to British rule, the races of the Punjab had not submitted then for the first time to foreign domination. Since the days of Alexander, a period to which the first certain information about the Punjab goes back, to the reign of Ranjit Singh, their history presents nothing but a long series of wars and revolutions. Lying on the route of all the adventurers who have been periodically attracted from the depths of Asia to the soil of India by the thirst for pillage and conquest, it has witnessed the passage of Greeks, Parthians, Scythians, Tartars, Moguls, and English, all of whom in turn it has accepted as masters. In 1526 Baba, at the head of the Afghans, subdued the Punjab before founding the dynasty which permanently occupied the throne of Delhi, and raised the Indian Empire to the highest glory. It is probable that up to the fifteenth century the races of the Punjab remained faithful to the social and religious institutions which they possessed in the time of the Macedonian conqueror. They were Hindoos of the sect of Buddha; and, notwithstanding the persecutions of the Mohammedan princes who occupied the throne of Delhi, they were still practising their ancient ceremonial, when there appeared in their midst an extraordinary man whose influence was to extend to our days.

Nanak, a Hindoo of the Kchatriyas caste, and the founder of the Sikh sect, was born at Ralwundi, in the province of Lahore, towards 1469. After long meditations and distant journeys, he assumed the mission of reconciling the Mohammedans and the Hindoos, and travelled about the country to propagate pure deistic doctrines. The new prophet applied himself to demonstrate to his followers that good intentions and good actions are specially pleasing to the Deity, and that external ceremonies constitute the only real difference between the religion of Mahomet and that of Buddha. His preaching, which proved successful, denounced the distinctions of caste as an impious institution, taught the equality of all men before God, also absolute tolerance of all religions, and universal charity. These doctrines spread far and wide—they had their apostles and martyrs. Thousands of Hindoos, converted by fear to Islamism, regretted the belief of their fathers, but the Brahminic religion does not allow of the return of those who have once renounced it. Nanak's sect opened a way of escape to such timorous spirits, and made, moreover, many proselytes amongst low-class Hindoos, who found themselves by its means on a footing of equality with their co-religionists. The prophet's death did not arrest the development of his doctrines, and for more than a hundred years numerous neophytes continued to take the pahäl.[1] Progress such as this aroused the jealous fears of the Delhi emperors.

[1] To 'take the pahäl.' The ceremony of initiation into the religion of the Sikhs is as follows: The neophyte must declare his desire to renounce his religious faith before a meeting of five Sikhs at least, assembled in the public place, in a temple, or in any other spot. Having done this, an ordinary sort of sweetmeat, known as 'batasa,' is sent for from the nearest confectioner's shop, and is immediately dissolved in water, with which the eyes and body of the convert are sprinkled. During this time one of the Sikhs present repeats in a loud voice, and in the language he knows best, the principal articles of the religion of Nanak. The ceremony is closed by the solemn promise of the neophyte to observe them faithfully. He has now but to select a 'gourou,' or

The Sikhs became the objects of bloody persecution; and Raj Bahadour, Nanak's ninth successor, was beheaded in the imperial palace at Delhi, in the presence of Aureng-Zeb and his Court. The tradition goes that Raj Bahadour, who passed, if not for a prophet, at least for a mighty magician, with Aureng-Zeb's courtiers, was begged by them to give proof of his occult powers before his death. He traced some words on a paper, which he folded up, bowed his neck to the executioner, and his head rolled on the pavement to the great astonishment of those present, who expected some feat of jugglery. The paper contained a Persian play on words, which can be translated thus:—'I have given my head and not my secret.'

Persecution led to resistance; and Gourou Govind, Nanak's tenth successor, completely modifying the spirit of the first institution, changed the sect into a sort of military confraternity. The Sikhs, who till his time had been devoted to peace and charity, became soldiers; they were obliged to carry arms, to let their beards grow, and to wear blue garments. Adepts received the name of Singhs (lions), and the Khalsa (community) chose for its war cry the proud motto 'Victory to the state of the prophet' (Wa garujee ka Khalsa). The proselytism which Nanak had tried to carry out by preaching and teaching, Gourou Govind attempted by force. Fortune did not crown his efforts, and he succumbed in the struggle against the Delhi emperors, after seeing the Khalsa decimated by war and persecution. The line of inspired prophets, conformably to the terms of the sacred books, which fixed their number at ten, ended with Gourou Govind. His successor possessed political and military powers. The influence of the chief of the Khalsa, stripped of all religious prestige, disappeared little by little; and towards the middle of the last century the constitution of the Sikh race offered a striking resemblance to that of European nations in the Middle Ages. The sect was divided into twelve misals (clans), each commanded by a special chief or sirdar. The

spiritual master, to teach him the language of the sacred books, and to explain their doctrines.—*Asiatic Researches*, vol. i.

strength of certain of these misals amounted to ten and twelve thousand horsemen, and the united strength of the community to 70,000. At the beginning the chiefs were generally of low birth, and simply owed their position in the first rank to their talent or their audacity. Later on, hereditary succession was introduced into the 'misals,' and family alliances acquired great influence. Matrimonial diplomacy played a considerable part in the confraternity, and contributed greatly, for example, to the high fortune of Ranjit Singh's family. In case of war a chief, named by election, exercised supreme power, but his authority ended with the hostilities. A sirdar was by no means absolute; his companions had a fixed share in the booty; and, in a word, performed for him the same services that he rendered to the confraternity. Such confraternity was wanting in any solid bond of union; a common danger or the hope of a rich plunder might maintain temporary union amongst its members, but once the special occasion over, it inevitably fell a prey to intestine quarrels. Moreover, in this new state of things, the Sikhs forgot the pure doctrines of their first prophets. Professional thieves, they became celebrated for their debaucheries and cruelties. These impure elements, with little coherence, were to become in clever hands the basis of one of the greatest empires whose rise Asia has ever witnessed. Ranjit Singh, son of Sirdar Maha-Singh,[1] was born towards 1776. An orphan at twelve years old, he received no education, and was revelling in the debaucheries of the harem, with all the ardour of youth, when the invasion of the Punjab by the Afghans, under Shah Mohammed of Cabul, stripped him of his paternal dominions. Misfortune developed the energy of an ambitious and enterprising nature. Too feeble to oppose force by force, the young sirdar insinuated himself into the good graces of the conqueror, and managed to reconstruct his inheritance piece by piece. Shah Mohammed's conquests were only transitory; and during the perturbations which followed his precipitate retreat to Cabul, Ranjit Singh took possession of Lahore and of a vast extent

[1] See Documents, No. XII., 'Genealogy of Ranjit Singh.'

of territory. Such was the basis of the vast edifice at which he worked without cessation until his death. This man, who deserved amongst all the surname of the 'Lion of the Punjab,' had the mind and the resources of a great statesman, and his achievements almost allow of associating his name with those of the two political meteors, whose prodigious fortune has astonished modern times—Napoleon I. and Mahomet Ali. The interest which in Asia centres in Ranjit Singh's name, authorises us perhaps to reproduce the portrait traced of the royal adventurer by one of the prominent members of the Indian service, Major Henry Lawrence, since Sir Henry Lawrence.

At the age of fifty Ranjit Singh, marked by the smallpox, deprived of one eye, with a miserable constitution, ruined by debauchery of every sort, did not prepossess in any way by his exterior. Ignorant, but gifted with great intelligence and powerful memory, he was thoroughly master of the art of governing. Economical to parsimony, always meditating ideas of reform, all the affairs of the kingdom passed under his eyes; and the vigour of his memory enabled him to follow the most complicated accounts. Active, enterprising, naturally a friend to justice, he possessed to a certain point the fine qualities which make good and great kings. Kindly, generous towards those around him, who adored him, but forgetful and frivolous, the Oriental proverb, 'A dog near the master is of more consequence than a brother at a distance,' was applicable to him. This changeableness led him rarely to give a refusal, without however remaining absolutely faithful to his word. He was accused several times, and justly, of rapacity and bad faith; but it must be said that the actions which stained his life must rather be attributed to the necessities of Oriental despotism than to the vicious propensities of the man. Ranjit Singh was brave, and killed several enemies with his own hand in battle; he rarely shed blood deliberately, and invariably granted liberal pensions to the families of the princes he dispossessed. He annually visited the different provinces of his empire, and preserved an exact recollection of all he saw. Easy of access to every one, he habitually excited quarrels amongst his servants, and carefully remembered the indiscretions which escaped them in the heat of the disputes. Given up to the excesses of drunkenness and of the harem, his primitive immorality became apparent in his dealings with the English. It is said that in an interview [1] with the Governor-General, Ranjit Singh having learnt that Lady Bentinck had not accompanied her husband, he graciously assembled some of his most beautiful bayadères in a tent close to the English camp. It is useless to say that as soon as the puritanic Lord Bentinck knew of his gallant attention, both tent and dark beauties were immediately restored to their owner. The Maharajah's gift did not, however, pass unperceived or unappreciated by all. Without any apparent motives several aides-de-camp received the order to leave the staff and reform their regiments. From being a fugitive, dispossessed of his small state towards the end of the last century, Ranjit Singh, in 1809, had become, by the help of his own good sword and diplomacy, the supreme chief of the formidable Sikh community. Gifted as he was with political views of a high order, he forebore to extend his personal power or to reform primitive institutions more than was necessary. The sirdars kept their fortresses, their titles, and their honours,[2] but the skilful hand of their new master so divided their power as to establish equilibrium amongst the great feudatories, and to prevent or repress all attempt at rebellion. Ranjit Singh's sagacity was not less conspicuous in his dealings with his formidable European neighbours.[3] A treaty,

[1] See Documents, No. XIII., 'Interview of Ranjit Singh and of Lord Bentinck, October, 1831.'

[2] They say that in 1815 when Ranjit Singh refused to join the League of the Indian Princes against the English, the principal sirdars, exasperated by his inaction, offered him in the durbar women's clothes, hoping by these ironical presents to stimulate his warlike ardour; but the blind passions of his *entourage* did not triumph over the great political sense of the Maharajah.

[3] The first foundation of the *entente cordiale*, to which Ranjit Singh faithfully adhered all his life, was laid in 1808 by Mr. Metcalfe, then attached to the Anglo-Indian Foreign Office, and who since, under the titles of Sir Charles and Lord Metcalfe, played a considerable part in the colonial history of Great Britain. Mr. Metcalfe, then on a mission to Lahore, was ordered by his Govern-

signed at Amritsur with General Ochterlony in 1809 established the basis of an *entente cordiale* with the Company, to which the Lion of the Punjab remained constantly faithful, even when the disasters of the Afghan War seemed to offer unexpected and sure chances of giving to his empire limits worthy of that of the Moguls in its best days.[1] Free to aggrandise himself towards the north, conformably to the terms of the treaty with General Ochterlony, on condition of abstaining from any attempt at conquest on the left bank of the Sutlej, Ranjit Singh successively seduced Peshawur and Cashmere, and was governing a population of more than twenty million souls at his death. The military forces which sustained this grand edifice were proportioned to its power—50,000 regular troops, 50,000 militia, and 200 pieces of artillery, all remarkably well organised; but that mainstay of any well-disciplined army—certain pay—was always wanting to his soldiers, and was generally a year at least in arrear. The officers could only obtain an instalment by declaring in open durbar

ment to demand that Ranjit Singh should withdraw his troops from the right bank of the Sutlej, and hand over the Sikh states on the left bank to the suzerainty of Great Britain. Mr. Metcalfe began negotiations one evening that he was having an intimate conversation with the Maharajah on the terrace of his palace. The Prince rose without speaking, went down into the courtyard, mounted one of the horses which always stood ready saddled and bridled, and rode furiously several times round the maïdan (lawn). After this violent exercise he rejoined the astonished negotiator, and showed great surprise at the impudent demands he had made in the name of his Government. 'What!' said the Maharajah, 'you English, who refused to protect the independent Sikh states on the left bank of the Sutlej, now coolly ask me, who had no scruples on that score, and have just succeeded at the cost of much blood and treasure in subduing them to my rule, you coolly ask me to withdraw my troops and give them up to you. What a proceeding on the part of friends!' Mr. Metcalfe did not attempt to dispute the justice of the Prince's argument, but he judiciously pointed out that a timely adhesion to the demand of the English Government would secure their sincere and durable friendship for him, and that were he once certain of his frontiers to the south, the Maharajah might extend his conquests in a more profitable direction. Ranjit Singh seized upon the idea at once, granted all that was asked, and to the last day of his life never lost an opportunity of testifying his gratitude for the good advice given by Mr. Metcalfe.—*Adventures of an Officer*, by Major H. Lawrence.

[1] See Documents, No. XIV., 'Text of the first treaty of Ranjit Singh with the English.'

that their men, dying of hunger, were ready to mutiny. The army of the Khalsa sufficiently proved its courage and its excellent organisation during the hard-fought campaigns of 1845, 1846, and 1849. From the very beginning Ranjit Singh appreciated at their true value the advantages of European tactics and discipline, and engaged in his service deserters and others who had been employed in the Company. Later on, French and Italian adventurers attained high military rank in the Punjab. Such was General Allard, a brave officer of the armies of the First Empire, who left behind him in the country a reputation for honourableness and disinterestedness which time has not yet effaced.[1]

The years which followed Ranjit Singh's death proved an orgie of bloodshed almost unparalleled even in the history of Asia. The Lion of the Punjab had reduced the anarchical passions and ambitious tendencies of his vassals to impotency, but had not annihilated them; and when he died the land was divided into two rival factions ready to sustain their projects by arms.[2] We shall not enter into long details about the terrible struggles which stained Lahore with blood after the great chief's death, and which set upon the throne Duleep Singh, a supposititious son of Ranjit Singh, under the regency of his mother the Ranee—a favourite dancer whom an old man's caprice had drawn from the ballet corps to place her upon the steps of the throne. The debaucheries of the principal personages of the kingdom assumed towards this time proportions worthy of Bacchus's Court in the palmiest days of the Indian Conquest of the God of Wine. The English envoy, in certain important circumstances, could not obtain audience of a single Minister, all the Cabinet members being for some days under the influence of strong drink—'dead drunk,' the despatches said. On another occasion, the same diplomate, going unexpectedly into the durbar, found the Grand Vizier disguised as a bayadère, and indulging in voluptuous dancing under the eyes and to the great delight of his colleagues. As soon as the Lion of the Punjab's

[1] See Documents, No. XV., 'Staff of Ranjit Singh.

[2] See Documents, No. XVI., 'The two grand factions in the Punjab.'

inheritance was open to the world, a strong military party formed itself in the army, who, disregarding the wisdom of his foreign policy, coveted the spoils of British India. Either weakness, infatuation, or the hope of finding in foreign warfare a vent for intestine struggles, prompted the Ranee and her advisers to give full scope to the passions of the soldiers; and after consultation with astrologers, the Sikh army crossed the Sutlej at the end of November 1845, without any previous declaration of war.[1] In the midst of its disorders, the army of the Khalsa had retained many noble military virtues, and the battles of Moudki, Ferozshahar, and Sobraon are numbered amongst the bloodiest ever won by the English in India. That of Sobraon, where the waters of the Sutlej carried away more than 20,000 Sikh corpses, placed the Punjab at the feet of England; and in the treaty of peace, signed immediately after at Lahore, the conquerors showed wise moderation. The Governor-General, Lord Hardinge, according to instructions brought out from London, respected the independence of the Punjab, and contented himself with such rectification of the frontiers as was necessary for the defence of the Company's dominions. This treaty did not, however, terminate the work of pacification. It was evident that on the departure of the British troops the country would fall back into the state of anarchy which had preceded the war. The Ranee and her favourites, and even the most influential sirdars, were incapable of maintaining order amongst a population of soldiers whose violent tendencies had been developed by seven years of revolution and a recent bloody campaign. The durbar besought the conquerors to continue to occupy the Punjab, hoping to shelter its weakness and folly behind British bayonets. This proposal, though seductive in appearance, was unacceptable. A civilised Government could not consent to afford a blind protection to the caprices and iniquities of a Lahore durbar. But it was agreed that during Duleep Singh's minority affairs should be managed by a council of the principal chiefs under the control of a Company's agent. An English force was

[1] See Documents, No. XVII., 'First War against the Sikhs.'

to garrison the country, and a sum of twenty lakhs of rupees was assigned on the public revenues for its maintenance. This convention was ratified by an assembly of the principal sirdars, the composition of which will give an idea of the gaps made in the ranks of the great families of the country during the last seven years. Of the seventy sirdars who made up the Punjab States-General, only eleven remained in 1846. Of those who had passed away, seven alone died a natural death. The experiment attempted by the English at Lahore, in accordance with the traditions of Asiatic history, where at every page one sees the authority of a great name perpetuated under that of a crowned puppet, could not resist the test of time. However, the revolt was not against the young Maharajah, but against the Feringees, the strangers who were trying to prop up the throne of Ranjit Singh's successor. The murder of two officers in the Company's service at Moultan in November 1848 gave the signal which foretold the storm. The British staff scattered over the Punjab, and surrounded by disloyal or wavering troops, braved the storm with rare heroism, and gave time for an army to appear on the scene.[1] The beginning of military operations was not fortunate. The battle of Chillianwallah, undecided at the best, where the English lost some colours and four guns, brought back matters to the state they were in the darker days of 1846. Still the Company's fortunes were to issue victorious from this crisis. Lord Gough's rapid march on Lahore, the victory of Goujerate, the capitulation of the Sikh forces intact, put an end to hostilities and to the independence of the Punjab. After the events of the last few years there could no longer be any thought of restoring Ranjit Singh's throne, and the annexation of the Punjab was almost fatally imposed on England's policy. The young Maharajah was deposed. On March 29, 1849, a proclamation announced that the land of the Five Rivers was definitively added to the Company's possessions, which now extended beyond the Indus to the foot of the mountains of Afghanistan.

[1] See Documents, No. XVIII., 'Second War of the Punjab.'

Three principal centres of action—Lahore, Moultan, Peshawar—were naturally the subjects of much uneasiness to the English. First in importance came Lahore, with a population of 100,000 souls, a turbulent and warlike town. Next to Lahore, Ferozeporé, the chief arsenal of the Company. This second-class fort, situated on the left bank of the Sutlej, commanded the road between the Punjab and Delhi, and played an important part in military events by the very fact of its position. The Lahore district comprised besides the holy and populous city of Amritsur, and the fort of Govindargh, which derived its importance neither from its strategical position nor its arsenal. Named after the celebrated Gourou Govind Singh, rich in traditions and relics, this citadel was a sort of holy ark for the Sikhs. Its possession conferred a certain legitimacy on the European conquest, and its loss would have seriously compromised the fortunes of the English in the eyes of the superstitious population. The cantonments of Mian-Mir, six miles from Lahore, contained three native regiments of the Bengal army, the 81st of the Royal army, two European horse batteries, and four artillery companies of the European reserve. Moultan, on the left bank of the Chenab, served as principal emporium for the trade between Corberel and Cashmere on the north, and Scinde, Arabia, and the Persian Gulf on the south. Since the insurrection of the North-West Provinces, Moultan assured the communications of the Punjab with Bombay, and through Bombay with Europe. Its garrison was composed of sixty Europeans and one battalion of the Bengal army. Yet its population and that of the neighbouring country abounded with elements of tumult and brigandage. Finally, Peshawur was the keystone of the edifice of European power in the Punjab. The valley of Peshawur, at one extremity of which is situated the town of the same name, terminates at the other at the Khyber Pass, connected with the most terrible defeat ever suffered by the English in India. The surrounding country is inhabited by numerous nomadic and warlike tribes, accustomed to a life of intestine struggles. A few vigorous lessons taught the nearer ones the weight of their new neighbour's arm, and the regularity and justice of an European administration soon completed the work of pacification. The border tribes, constantly driven to revolt by the summary and capricious proceedings of Ranjit Singh's proconsuls, easily became accustomed to live on peaceful terms with masters who were satisfied with moderate taxes, and who in return provided efficacious protection to all their interests. But beyond the circle of the outposts, the state of public mind was singularly bad. Outside a certain territory, the whole native population had shown its hostility to the European authorities by the commission of more or less serious crimes—the murder of an officer or of a police agent, asylum given to malefactors, thefts and attacks in arms on allied tribes or on the cantonments. All communication with Peshawur and the outposts was strictly forbidden to the refractory population, and those who dared to cross the English lines were kept prisoners until the submission of their respective tribes. To give some idea of the difficulty of the English position, we must add that the forces of some of these clans, the Mohmunds, the Afridis, the Euzossaics, were superior in number to the English troops scattered along the right bank of the Indus, viz., in the cantonments close to Peshawur the 70th 87th regiments Royal army, four batteries of artillery, eight companies of the reserve at the station of Nowshera, at the extreme end of the valley[1] the 27th—in all, 3,000 Europeans. As to the native troops, they amounted to 10,000 men, of whom 9,000 were poorbeahs, or soldiers in the Bengal army. This force, which amply sufficed in ordinary times, allowed of detaching columns in pursuit of hostile tribes, without materially weakening that which defended Peshawur and its suburbs. But the actual state of affairs had never been anticipated even by the most experienced officers of the Indian service; for the danger was not in the hostile dispositions of more or less distant tribes, but existed in the camp in the very heart of the army.

[1] In the Punjab all men born to the east of the line of the Sutlej go by the name of poorbeahs.

The native soldiers, thrice as numerous as the Europeans, might, according to the example of their brethren of Mirut and Delhi, raise the standard of revolt, and inaugurate a work of destruction which would promptly receive the co-operation of the wild tribes beyond the frontier, and of the population of the Punjab. To complete this sketch, we must say a few words of the state of feeling on the other boundaries of the Punjab. Some miles from the Sutlej was the Rajah of Bawalpore, who, although he owed his throne to the friendship of the English, showed himself inimical to their cause from the early days of the mutiny; on the south was Scinde, newly conquered, with its Beloochee population, well known for their religious fanaticism; finally, to the north, Goulab Singh,[1] Maharajah of Cashmere, a crafty and perfidious prince, and the tribes of Thibet, who might at any moment attack the sanitariums of Simla and Missouri, where, as usual, the Europeans had sought a refuge against the heat of summer.

The dangers which threatened the large centres were not less formidable in the important towns and small stations, where two or three European magistrates and a small police force represented the Company's authority. The aspect of the whole country seemed to portend one of those great cataclysms which shake nations to their foundations. Could it be otherwise in that distant land where time had not yet consummated the work of conquest? Scarcely ten years had passed since an energetic race, without love or respect for aught but martial glory, had accepted the yoke of masters from whom they were separated by religious belief, customs, language, and even the colour of their skin. A great number of the vanquished of Ferozshahar and Sobraon were still in the prime of life. What wrath, what desire for vengeance must have been burning in the hearts of these lions of the Khalsa! Was not fate fulfilling all their wishes, and could

[1] Goulab Singh, the then Maharajah of Cashmere, whom we have already had occasion to mention amongst Ranjit Singh's intimates, owed to him his fortune. Poor, but of good family, he was serving as a sowar (trooper) in a Sikh regiment, when he killed a comrade in some dispute. He was pursued by the victim's friends, and took refuge in Ranjit Singh's tent, who, charmed by his appearance, forgave him and admitted him into his *entourage*. This was the first step of the ladder which led the astute Goulab Singh to the throne of Cashmere.

any better opportunity for revenge ever offer itself to their swords? Discord was in the conqueror's camp, the mutinous sepoys were masters of Delhi and of the North-West Provinces, and sedition was smouldering in all the military stations of the Punjab. This obvious view of the case only touched the problem of the situation on the surface; other elements of considerable importance had to be taken into account; for instance, the nullity of all the military or religious chiefs of the Khalsa, the hatred felt for centuries by the Sikhs against the Mogul Emperors and their subjects, and the profound impression produced on the population by the foreign government that had given them order, peace, and, above all, perfect religious liberty. The Sikhs could not retain confidence in chiefs whose dissensions, not to say treacheries, had been the principal cause of their disasters. The most prominent sirdars had disappeared from the political scene. Duleep Singh, a convert to Christianity, was living on his Scotch property; Shere Singh, the most courageous and the most honest man in the Khalsa, was a prisoner at Calcutta; Bikram Singh, the high-priest of the sect, and one of the last descendants in direct line from the founder of the Sikh religion, Baba (father) Nanak, was without influence, and bowed down by age and infirmities. He was, moreover, under police surveillance at Amritsur, the Holy City. But even had he possessed as much power over the minds of the faithful as his great predecessors, how could he forget the persecutions of the Mogul emperors? To preach a holy war in favour of the restoration of the throne of Delhi, would have been an outrage on the memory of their martyrs, a disavowal of the prophecies of Tej Bahadour. Besides the colour of the skin, there was no real link between the Sikhs and the mutinous sepoys. The soldiers of the Bengal army had done even more than their European comrades to wound the pride of the vanquished of Sobraon and Goujerate by their caste prejudices and their aggressive manners, in *cafés* and bazars. These feelings were noticeable also in civil matters. If popular hatred pursued the Hindoos employed in the police and finance departments,

E 2

all of them grasping and corrupt in the Punjab, as in the Company's other possessions, general respect, if not affection, was felt for the civil and military officials—courageous, upright, and enlightened men, who for ten years had given to the land that great benefit of modern civilisation, absolute religious toleration—the most complete liberty for all religions!

The system of government inaugurated in the Punjab may be considered as a successful application of the enlightenment of Europe to the government of an Asiatic nation. At its head was a chief well known for his skill, daring, and profound acquaintance with the language, the customs, and the instincts of those he had to govern. Under his orders were picked officers and civilians, whose extensive powers were, within wise limits, left free from the tyranny of rules and instructions. We must name amongst the eminent men about to appear in the first rank in this political conjuncture, Sir John Lawrence, Chief Commissioner, who had succeeded his brother Sir Henry as Governor of the Punjab; Mr. Montgomery, Judge at Lahore; Colonels Chamberlain, Herbert Edwardes, and Nicholson, all employed in some capacity, civil or military; and under them a staff of which, it has been said with justice, that it was composed of the right men in the right place. It is necessary to remind the reader that the population of the Punjab does not only consist of Sikhs—the Hindoo and Mussulman elements are largely represented. The sympathies of the Hindoos, almost exclusively engaged in commercial and banking pursuits, were given, in accordance with their interests, to the Government which enforced order and security. The Mussulmen of the country, the towns and the frontiers who were better disposed towards their co-religionists of Delhi, were separated, on the other hand, from the Sikhs by the bloody barriers of the past. Ranjit Singh's reign witnessed the pitiless revenge taken on the Mahometans by the proselytes of the Khalsa: mosques converted into stables, and holy tombs profaned by coarse sirdars. These recent injuries were still festering in the minds of the sons of the prophet, so that hereditary hatred divided the children of the soil, whilst their foreign masters, though only a handful of men, were united in a common work and in a common peril. Without illusion as to the dangers of the situation, thoroughly persuaded that it was a question of conquering together or dying together, the English had besides for them the superiority of intelligence, discipline, and military science. The position, though bristling with difficulties, was not hopeless. With the help of a good pilot and a devoted crew the storm-tossed vessel might yet reach the port in triumph.

'The mutineers of Mirut are masters of Delhi. Mr. Todd and several Europeans have been massacred; the office must be closed.' This was the last telegram which the unfortunate clerk had time to send from the Delhi cantonments to the central station at Amballah, before falling under the blows of his assassins. In a few minutes the news reached Lahore, Peshawur, and Moultan. Other messages sent from Amballah on May 12 left the Punjab authorities no doubt as to the extent of the Delhi disasters—disasters well calculated to fill with affright the stout hearts of the representatives of British authority at Lahore, where the scum of a large town might at any moment come to the help of the rebellious regiments quartered at Mian Mir. The head of the Government, Sir John Lawrence, who had left some days before to pass the hot season on the breezy heights of Murri, was at this moment at the station of Rawal-Pindi; and in his absence supreme authority had been delegated to Mr. Montgomery, chief justice of the Punjab. The political clear-sightedness and the energy of this magistrate were equal to the occasion. He immediately assembled in council the chiefs of the garrison; and after a long discussion, in which the commanders of the native regiments, completely deluded as to their men's disposition, resisted a general disarming, it was decided to remove the caps from the sepoys' muskets, and to reinforce the garrison of the Lahore citadel. The fort, situated in the town which it commanded, contained the finance offices and the public treasure. Under ordinary circumstances, it was held by a sepoy battalion, relieved the first and fifteenth of every month, a European company changed monthly, and some artillerymen, about a hundred in all. On the following day certain discoveries made by the police necessitated more energetic measures. A Brahmin, employed in the department for the repression of Thuggee, came, proof in hand, to denounce to the authorities a plot, the execution of which was fixed for the next day. On May 15, at the moment of changing guard, when both guards would be together in the fort, the two native battalions were to fall on the Europeans and massacre them. On one side would have been 1,100 sepoys, on the other about a hundred men taken unawares. The result could not be doubtful. On being informed of the success of the enterprise by a preconcerted signal, the native regiments stationed at Mian Mir were to murder their officers, and to attack without delay the quarters of the English troops. The plan was well concerted, and seemed to promise every chance of success. Later information proved that the plot had ramifications in all the stations near Lahore, and was intended to break out almost simultaneously at Ferozepore, Philour, and Jellandar. Incomplete though they were, these revelations left no doubt as to the imminence of the danger. The fate of the entire Punjab was bound up with that of Lahore, and there were only a few hours remaining before the moment fixed for the outbreak. Mr. Montgomery and Brigadier Corbett, the military commander, assuming discretionary powers in face of such perils, disregarded the protest of the sepoy officers, and resolved on immediately disarming the native regiments. Secrecy was indispensable to carry out this measure. The native troops were called out on morning parade to hear an order of the day relative to the disbandment of the 19th Native Infantry at Barrackpore.[1] The precautions taken did not stop here. By a singular chance, a ball was being given that night by civilians to the officers of the 81st of the Royal Army, whose hospitality had so often enlivened the dark

[1] See Documents, No. XIX., 'Order of the day for the disbanding of the 19th Regiment, B.A.'

winter evenings. Nothing was changed in the programme of the *fête*. The ball took place. Never, to borrow a celebrated phrase, had dancers trod a more fragile crust on the edge of a volcano. The last sounds of the music were still lingering in the ball-room, the remains of the supper were still on the table, when all the troops of the station were marched towards the parade ground. The fate of all India—one may say—was hanging on the result of that morning's work. Twilight had followed a fine night. Notwithstanding the early hour, the ball guests and the whole European population of Amarkati (the civil cantonments of Lahore) had betaken themselves to the ground. What anxiety was perceptible on those pallid countenances, which certainly no trivial curiosity had attracted to the scene! All present knew of the disasters at Delhi, all felt that their own life and the lives of those dear to them were at stake in the game about to be played out under the first rays of the sun. The troops were disposed by columns of battalions on the same front. To the right were the two European batteries of artillery, and four companies (about 300 men) of the 81st R.A.; in the centre the three infantry regiments, and to the extreme left the 8th regular cavalry, B.A. On the general's arrival a change from front to rear of the left wing was executed. The columns began to move, but the European companies only appeared to do so, and the artillery, imitating them, were able to load their guns without the sepoys perceiving it. This manœuvre accomplished, the sepoys having faced about found before them, in their new position, the English line deployed on the left in order of battle. Behind this line, the artillery had placed its twelve guns in position. A mounted adjutant rode to the front of the sepoys, and read an order of the day, announcing to the native regiments that, to prevent them from taking part in a mutiny which would be followed by the most disastrous consequences, the general had decided to disarm them. Before the sepoys could recover from the surprise caused by this unexpected order, a loud voice commanded them to lay down their arms. Some signs of hesitation were shown, but meanwhile the British half battalion, moving by platoons, had passed between the guns and had reformed in line of battle under cover of artillery. Instead of a feeble line of infantry the native soldiers had before them twelve pieces of cannon, with lighted matches. A single shout, a mutinous gesture, and their ranks would have been mowed down by grape-shot. Behind the silent and threatening guns, the Queen's soldiers were loading their muskets. The sharp click of the locks alone broke the silence of this solemn moment. The native ranks bent down. The ground was covered with muskets and cavalry sabres; the victory was won. Without striking a blow, more than 3,000 privates and troopers had laid down their arms before less than 600 Europeans.[1] Operations had not been less fortunate nor

[1] For the sake of greater clearness, we think it well to give a sketch of the formation of the European and native troops on this day, which may be said to have decided the fate of India:—

FIRST FORMATION.

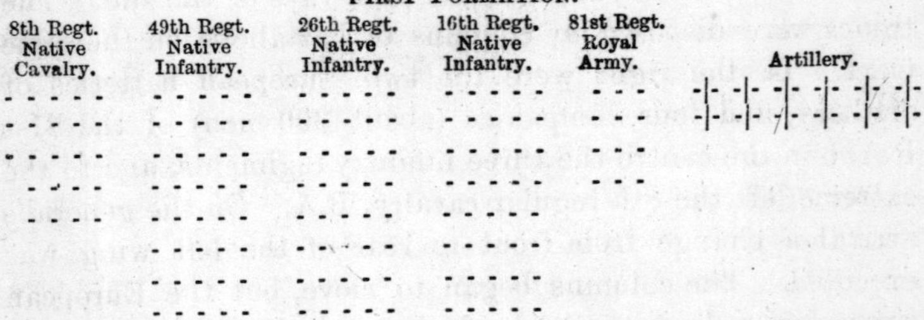

SECOND FORMATION.

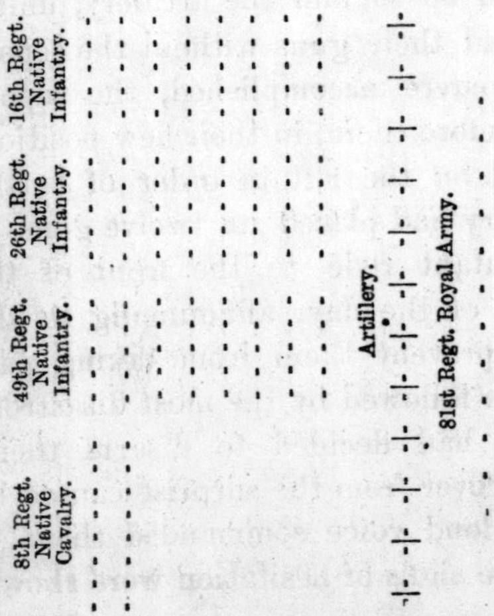

less well managed in the citadel, where the European detachment, reinforced at the critical moment, had disarmed the two native battalions.

At Moultan, the same thing was done with equal success. Major Crawford Chamberlain, brother of the General Chamberlain whose name will recur often and gloriously in the following pages, himself a distinguished officer, disarmed the 62nd and 69th of the Bengal army without resistance. This operation was all the more noticeable and the more noticed, in that Major Chamberlain had only sixty Europeans, a battalion of native horse artillery B.A., of doubtful loyalty, and two regiments, one of cavalry and one of infantry, belonging to the special Punjab force, to oppose to the sepoys. It showed, in the most convincing manner, moreover, that the English could count on the fidelity of the Sikh soldiers.

The telegram announcing the outbreak at Mirut reached Sir J. Lawrence at Rawal-Pindi, a station some hundred miles from Peshawur. Though little prepared for the cataclysm which was opening the soil beneath his feet, the chief commissioner of the Punjab measured the abyss with the eye of a statesman, and descried chances of success in its very depth. His consummate experience of the character of the people of India gave him every reason to hope that the principal sirdars and, in their wake, the mass of the population, would be likely to wait till matters before Delhi had taken a decisive turn. His first care was to put himself in communication with such officers, influential through their rank or services, as were in the neighbourhood of Peshawur; for instance, Major-General Reid, commanding the division; Brigadier S. Cotton; Lieutenant-Colonels N. Chamberlain, Herbert Edwardes, J. Nicholson—all highly gifted men, who added to well-proved valour intimate knowledge of the country and its inhabitants. England's interests could not have been placed in better hands. Sir J. Lawrence, from Rawal-Pindi, took part, as it were, in their sittings; and by means of the telegraph wires assisted at their deliberations. The situation which events had created for the Punjab authorities was one of those which no instructions, however complete, had so much as contemplated. The chief commissioner and his advisers did not hesitate to break through the bonds of routine, and to assume an immense responsibility in face of an immense disaster. In the first instance, it was necessary that the depositaries of civil and military power should consult with one another without having recourse to the post or to the telegraph, which might be interrupted at any moment. It was decided that Major-General Reid, the senior officer in rank beyond the Sutlej, should take the command in chief, and fix his head-quarters at Rawal-Pindi. This measure had the advantage of placing under Sir John's energetic hand the general whose advanced age might give reason to fear some weakness on his part. The Council resolved also on organising a flying column, destined to act against threatened points, and to inspire terror as much by its rapidity in marching as by the vigour of its action. The command of the corps was given to Brigadier N. Chamberlain, one of the most eminent officers in the Anglo-Indian service. Measures were also taken to remove the suspected regiments from seditious influence, and to send them immediately into parts where religious prejudices most strongly divided the inhabitants from the sepoys. This done, the members of the Council separated to return to their several posts, and in twenty-four hours all the troops beyond the Jhelum were in motion. In addition to general measures, special ones, necessary to ensure the safety of Peshawur, were not neglected. Though the intensity of the passions raging amongst the natives was not yet known, a state of siege was declared in the cantonments. The two European regiments, backed by artillery, took up strong positions at either end of the camp where they were. A large house, easy of defence, which had belonged to General Avitabile, was chosen for head-quarters, and the European families in Peshawur were secretly warned to seek refuge there in case of danger. Only Brigadier Cotton and Brigadier-General Nicholson, who were entrusted with the command of the frontier, remained in the town. The first shock caused by the events of Mirut and Delhi had passed away, but the atmosphere was still threatening, and the apparent calm was not able to hide the approaching storm from far-seeing men. Yet a few days more and the danger was to be revealed in all its gravity. About May 12 letters of the sepoys opened at the post-office had given precious information as to the fermentation in the native camp. This first intelligence was soon completed by a letter seized at Sukkaddar, and by some documents found on a fakir arrested in the vicinity of the camp by the police. Absolute proofs such as these did not yet shake the confidence of the officers of native regiments in the fidelity of their soldiers, and they pleaded their cause in the Council with an energy which betrayed itself by actual insubordination. Colonel Nicholson vehemently opposed the illusions of his comrades; and Brigadier Cotton, having yielded to his opinion, it was resolved that the sepoys should be deprived of their arms. Marked success attended this energetic decision. The 24th, 27th, and 51st Regiments, B.A., laid down their arms at the first summons in presence of the European brigade. A certain small number of native troops not comprised in this order preserved a passive attitude on parade, and returned to their quarters in perfect order. This apathy was not imitated by a few Anglo-Indian officers who, having protested to the last against a general disarming, threw their sabres indignantly amongst the muskets of their men, making a display of temper which was wisely overlooked. Notwithstanding the secrecy maintained, the chiefs of the Hill tribes in the neighbourhood of Peshawur were not ignorant of the issue of this struggle. The victory once decided, they came into the English camp, bringing congratulations and offering services which they were not slow to perform. In the following night, twenty men of the 51st deserted in the hope of finding an asylum amongst the neighbouring tribes. But disarmed sepoys were no longer for the mountaineers the respected soldiers of the Honourable East India Company. Colonel Everard set a price on the heads of the fugitives, and nearly all of them were brought in by the mercenary natives. By submitting passively to disarmament, the sepoys had not only averted from themselves the severities of martial law, but had besides, by this species of pacific compromise, succeeded in veiling the extent of their defeat from the eyes of the population. The mutiny of one regiment in the cantonments of Peshawur was about to afford the English an occasion to make that display of proscriptions and executions which in the eyes of the Orientals is the exclusive and inseparable attribute of victory. Towards the end of May, the 55th, recently arrived in the cantonments of Nowshera, mutinied, and took the route to Delhi, with baggage and ammunition. A tragic episode followed their departure, and attested once again the depth of the illusions of most sepoy officers. Lieutenant-Colonel Spottiswoode, of the 55th, had never left the corps since he joined it four years before. On the eve of the mutiny he was still guaranteeing on his head, both in his private and official correspondence, his men's discipline and devotion. Till the last moment this unfortunate officer remained in the ranks, trying to re-animate an expiring loyalty. When, at last, he understood the futility of his efforts, he withdrew broken-hearted, and put an end to his existence by a pistol shot. A just punishment fell upon the rebels. A column, commanded by Colonel Nicholson, overtook them on their march to Delhi, and the sepoys, after a vigorous resistance, were dispersed, leaving 120 prisoners in the victor's hands. They were brought back to Peshawur, and were all condemned to death, but the English recoiled from such wholesale slaughter,[1] and decided to execute one man only in three.

At sunrise, on June 10, the European and native troops were drawn up on one of the parade grounds, forming a square of which the two Royal regiments and the three disarmed ones formed three sides. Ten guns occupied the fourth, and in one corner were grouped, either standing or crouching, the forty condemned, heavily ironed. Martial pomp was displayed in its utmost severity. The men's muskets, the officers' revolvers were loaded, and lighted matches were smoking near the guns. Brigadier Cotton and his staff were saluted on their arrival by ten rounds of cannon,

[1] See Documents, No. XX., 'Extract from a Letter of Sir F. Lawrence.'

as on a gala day, and went at a foot's pace round the four sides of the square. The sentence of death was read, and the execution began. A man was tied to the mouth of each of the ten guns. The officer in command of the battery lowered his sabre; and heads, legs, arms, and frightful fragments of human forms, exhaling a horrible smell of burnt flesh, were blown in every direction. There were four discharges, and four times the European regiments trembled with horror at the cruel sight. The native ones remained silent, motionless, impassible at the terrible spectacle. Nearly all the condemned died with the heroic indifference which the Hindoos knew so well how to preserve in face of death. 'Captain Sahib,' said a fine sepoy of herculean form, some twenty years old, to one of the officers who superintended the execution, carelessly running his hand over the instrument of death, 'Captain Sahib, there is no need to tie me up, I don't wish to escape.'

The events at Peshawur exercised a magical influence over the northern populations of India. With the first success of the mutiny before their eyes, the Sikhs and Afghans might have thought that, according to predictions which had been long in circulation, the Company's reign begun in 1757 would not outlast its centenary. But ever faithful to their habits of prudence, grandees, old soldiers, and warrior tribes, before declaring themselves waited to see which side fortune would favour. After the native regiments were disarmed at Peshawur, and particularly after the execution of the forty sepoys, all indecision ceased. Not even Aureng-Zeb, Nadir Shah, nor the most terrible despot in history had ever traced a bulletin of victory in such terrible characters. The discharges of June 10 re-echoed to the furthest extremities of the Punjab, and by their lurid light the populations discerned the finger of the God of battles. The victory was won, as public common sense could not fail to see, not by cowardly mercenaries, incapable of fighting even to save their brothers in arms, but by a handful of Europeans strong in union, patriotism, and wild audacity—that audacity which causes the loss of empires when they fall into the hands of demagogues intoxicated with success, and which leads to salvation when it animates real statesmen. Then followed a strange fact, unique, one may say, in history. All the furious passions which ferment in the heart of man—religious fanaticism, secular vendettas, a warlike spirit, the thirst for blood and pillage, changed into a feeling of absolute devotion to masters, strangers by race and belief. The ill-will entertained by the Sikhs towards the Company's government disappeared before the ancient hatred and bloody reminiscences of the Mogul emperor's oppression. The hour had struck for the accomplishment of the ancient prophecies; the road to Delhi was open. The Sikhs were about to revenge their martyrs and the murder of their saint, Gourou Tej Bahadour. The principles of religious tolerance scrupulously practised by the European Government had borne their fruits. Adhesion to the English cause was not less energetic nor less popular amongst the frontier tribes. The recollection of the great invasions of India was still alive in the mountain population, and Delhi's reputation for fabulous riches excited the most ardent cupidity. What did it matter to these men athirst for war and pillage under what flag they fought! We must add that certain chivalrous instincts inherent in the hearts of strong men were not unconnected with the zeal shown for the English by the Afghan tribes. The rough mountaineers of the Indian Caucasus had heard with horror of the atrocities committed on women and children by the Delhi mutineers; and pointed out, not without pride, that in the fatal retreat from Cabul they had protected all prisoners whose age or sex entitled them to respect. The most hostile tribes sued for peace, paid a fine, and offered volunteers, which were thankfully accepted. Was it not already a first success, whilst waiting for better things, to have rallied to the European cause a set of marauders always ready to swoop down on the plains, and to transform discontented neighbours into paid soldiers if not devoted friends?[1]

Towards the latter half of June, patrols of horsemen, in

[1] See Documents, No. XXI., 'Recruiting at Peshawur.'

strange and glittering costumes, armed with lances and matchlocks, appeared in the streets of Peshawur; a month earlier entrance into the city would have been forbidden to these wild auxiliaries, or at least each one would have been obliged to lay down his arms before entering its walls, and could not have remained beyond sunset. But the English authorities knew these savage inhabitants of the mountains thoroughly, and did not suspect their fidelity as long as there was a chance for them of being led to Delhi, and taking part in the pillage of the imperial city. Fortune was again about to bestow her favours on the most audacious. It is only right to recall here that Sir J. Lawrence himself discussed and almost accepted the necessity of the evacuation of Peshawur.[1] But the urgent solicitations of Colonel Edwards and Sir S. Cotton, who being on the spot were able to form a correct judgment as to the effect a retreat would produce on the population of the frontier, succeeded in turning the governor from his disastrous purpose. 'He who wishes to rule the Punjab must be strong, daring, and pitiless; his horse's tread must cause all to tremble within two miles of him,' is an old Asiatic saying. Neither strength, daring, nor cold indifference to the culprits' fate were wanting to Sir J. Lawrence. The part forced on him by the mutiny and its success was one which no human wisdom could foresee. In a few days, by the mere force of circumstances, the Governor of the Punjab became the supreme head of all that remained to England beyond Allahabad. The telegraph, after having put the authorities on their guard, was included in the general ruin, and its destruction was of distinct service to the mother country. What would have happened if the Punjab officials had been obliged to submit all their actions to the control of the Calcutta Government, and allow measures to be discussed in the Indian Council, which, in order to succeed, had to be put into execution as soon as conceived? Would the Governor-General, Lord Canning, and his advisers have placed sufficient confidence in their skilful

[1] See Documents, No. XXII., 'Correspondence relative to the evacuation of Peshawur.'

colleague in the Punjab as to give him *carte-blanche*; and in the contrary case, would not the discussions, the delays in answering have seriously compromised the best concerted plans? The question was solved by the wires being cut, and Sir J. Lawrence immediately concentrated the supreme authority into his own hands.

Communications between Lahore and the capital were not, however, completely interrupted.[1] Postal communication with Calcutta was continued through Moultan by way of the Indus, or of Central India and Bombay; but thanks to the difficulties and length of the journey, a reply from Calcutta could not be expected under two months at Lahore. The entire edifice of the Anglo-Indian hierarchy had disappeared beneath the first shock of the mutiny. England's vital interests did not suffer thereby. The postal and telegraphic service was not interrupted in the Punjab itself, and thus the English had for them all the forces of governmental civilisation without its heavy burden of useless rules and hierarchical routine. The hand that controlled the mainspring could judge of the evolutions and the slightest motion of the wheels. Sir J. Lawrence, however, full of confidence in his officers, abstained from restricting their authority, and left to each the care of watching over the general safety in the measure of his intellect and his powers. The chief's example and noble patriotic sentiments, the certainty that in case of defeat no European would escape, gave rise to acts of the most unheard of audacity. No measure of precaution was neglected—guards were placed at all the fords, bridges, and gates of towns. The country had been inundated with fakirs, more or less connected with the mutiny; they were sent away or thrown into prison. Most of the subaltern agents employed in the departments of finance, justice, and police, belonged to the North-West Provinces and Bengal, and the very fact caused their loyalty to be doubted. They were dismissed, and ordered to leave the country. The publications of the native press were con-

[1] See Documents, No. XXIII., 'Difficulties of the English agents for the communication between the Punjab and Calcutta during the mutiny.'

trolled by a strict censorship. From the beginning every sepoy's correspondence had been opened, and henceforward all letters passed under the eyes of the officials. Constant perquisitions brought to light numerous stores of arms, and in a month more than 60,000 sabres and muskets fell into the hands of the English. The sale of sulphur, saltpetre, and arms was absolutely prohibited. Religious preaching was under the strictest supervision, and more than one Moulvi was arrested in the midst of his congregation. The police had emissaries everywhere—in the markets, temples, mosques, hospitals, prisons, regimental or town bazars, about wells, or in the midst of the villages. An iron hand held the Punjab, and a thousand-eyed Argus spied out the slightest movement of the population. An imprudent word or a false step was followed by immediate and terrible chastisement. An ocular witness says, energetically, that one hair of a European weighed more in the scales of justice than the head of a native. The sword of Damocles, though suspended over every head, only fell on that of the evil-disposed, chiefly Hindoos or foreign Mussulmen, and rarely touched the natives, who remained neutral spectators of the struggle. Sir John Lawrence,[1] as we have already had occasion to remark, felt that the Indian question would be decided under the walls of Delhi, and from the first had neglected no opportunities of despatching reinforcements of men, arms, and ammunition to the English army. The disarming of the native troops had scarcely been effected at Lahore and Peshawur, when Sir John, after making a last appeal to the sepoys' loyalty[2] in a public proclamation, sent a corps of Guides, the picked regiment of the irregular Punjab force, to Delhi. A certain number of Sikhs were among the dis-

[1] Sir John gave advice as well as help to the military authorities. It is said that on receiving, during the early part of the mutiny, a telegram showing perceptibly a wish to fortify Amballah, Sir John, who was at a whist table, replied by the laconic words: 'Trumps are clubs and not spades.' This was all the more piquant, that General Anson, then Commander-in-Chief, had published a few years before, under the initials 'Major A.,' a treaty of whist, well known to all lovers of that noble game.

[2] See Documents, No. XXIV., 'Proclamation of Sir J. Lawrence.'

armed soldiers—these men, who had no sympathy with the mutiny, were again entrusted with arms. Some infantry of the R.A., who had previously served in the cavalry, were formed into a squadron of dragoons, and the men necessary to man two batteries of artillery were furnished by the Queen's army as well. Finally, when the native population showed itself favourable to the English cause, after the execution at Peshawur, their goodwill was made use of on a vast scale, and Sikh regiments appeared literally as if evoked by magic. Their number, originally six only, was carried to twenty-two, and then to twenty-five. The military resources improvised by the Governor's energy did not stop here, and the Philour arsenal furnished the Delhi army with a formidable siege train, large guns and ammunition, which contributed considerably to the success of the operations.

We have seen that a flying column was ordered to be formed to patrol the country and lend assistance to the authorities everywhere at the first signs of rebellion. Lieut.-Colonel Chamberlain, one of the glories of the Anglo-Indian army, was placed in command, and received besides a local brevet of brigadier, which gave him superior rank to that of any officer he might come in contact with during his campaign. The new general lost no time in taking the field; and leaving Wazirabad at the end of May, he proceeded successively to Lahore and Amritsur, where he repressed some attempts at mutiny with inflexible rigour.[1] In the latter town, the news of the revolt of three native regiments at Jallandar on June 7 had just been heard of. The indecision of the brigadier in command at Jallan-

[1] Brigadier Chamberlain's speech to the native troops, after the execution of two mutineers belonging to the 35th Regiment, Lahore, June 9:—'Officers, non-commissioned officers, and native privates of the 35th,—You have just seen two of your comrades tied to the mouth of a gun and blown to pieces. This punishment will fall to the lot of all traitors. Your conscience will tell you what they must suffer in the next world. These two soldiers have been blown from a gun and not hanged, because I wished to spare them the degradation of the hangman's touch, and thus show that the Government, even in this crisis, does not intend offending in any way your prejudices of caste or religion.'

dar, his concessions to the infatuation of the sepoy officers against the repeated orders of his immediate superiors, had led to the most deplorable occurrences. On June 7, the troopers of the 6th cavalry, B.A., deserting their lines in the night, poured tumultuously into the encampment of the 36th infantry, which rose immediately, massacring its European officers or forcing them to fly. The rebels then advanced on the cantonments of the 61st, where some show of discipline was still maintained, and induced them to follow their example. An havildar (non-commissioned officer) and some faithful soldiers devoted themselves to defend their officers, and found means, at the peril of their lives, to conduct them to a place of safety. The brigadier, who had neither known how to foresee events nor obey orders, did not make amends for his fault at the decisive moment. The 8th, R.A., remained without orders during the struggle, and the mutineers had already been several hours on the way to Delhi, when he resolved on sending a few European companies and a battery of artillery in pursuit. At Philour, the ranks of the Jallandar regiment were swelled by the defection of the 3rd of the Bengal army, thus bringing their number up to about 2,000 men, and they pursued their march rapidly on Loudianah, a station on the left bank of the Sutlej, which commands the road from the Punjab to the North-West Provinces. The energetic magistrate of this district at the head of a few native troops attempted to bar their passage, but was deserted by a portion of his men, and obliged to give up the defence of the river. The sepoys entered Loudianah as conquerors, opened the doors of the prisons, pillaged and burnt the establishments of the Protestant missions, and finding themselves pursued again, took the road to Delhi. They succeeded in entering the town without having been overtaken by the English troops, who had followed them from Jallandar, and who now joined the besieging forces. The passage of the mutineers through the Sutlej districts excited much commotion amongst the population, and the native regiments that were not yet disarmed, together with the flying column, were ordered to scour the country. Their former commander, General Chamberlain, had just been appointed to the Delhi army, and replaced by Colonel Nicholson with the provisional rank of brigadier.

We will here give a sketch of the career of this officer, who in a few months' campaigning won for himself a foremost place in the military annals of Great Britain. He arrived in India in 1839, at the age of twenty, as an ensign in the Company's service, took an active and brilliant part in the Punjab and Afghan wars, and though only a captain in his regiment, held the brevet of lieutenant-colonel. In this capacity he long exercised important commands on the most exposed frontiers, and everywhere acquired unlimited influence over the native population. When he gave up the command of the province of Hazara, a religious confraternity was formed which devoted itself to the worship of Nicholson, just as the Sikhs had done to that of Nanak.[1] The initiated took the name of Nikkal Scynes, wore salmon-coloured garments, and assumed black felt hats as a distinctive sign. Their worship consisted in singing hymns, with the chorus: 'Gourou Nikkal Scynes.' The new believers, in the full meaning of the word, were living peacefully in their community when Nicholson, on his way to Cashmere in 1854, stopped at some distance from the convent. A deputation was instantly sent to their patron saint, which, on admission to his presence, threw themselves without preamble at his feet, chanting his praises. Nicholson at first modestly declined these homages, but his remonstrances proving of no avail, and the wandering sheep persisting in rendering him divine honours, he ordered his servants to administer a few vigorous blows in the hope of thus bringing them to their senses. This remedy produced no effect; on the contrary, the devotees, rejoicing in their stripes, unanimously declared that the impurity of their life fully justified the rigour of the master, who, as a last resource, took to flight to escape their importunities. On the receipt of the news of Nicholson's glorious death at the assault of Delhi, one of the brethren declared he could no longer live in a world deprived of such a bright and shining

[1] *Friend of India*, October 18, 1860.

light, and at once cut his throat. Another followed his example, and a third became a convert to Christianity out of fidelity to the memory of his patron.

The reader must excuse this characteristic anecdote of the individual. We shall now return to the military operations of the officer, which entirely justified the trust showed by Sir J. Lawrence. On his way to the Sutlej, Nicholson disarmed some native regiments without firing a shot, re-established the Company's prestige by severe examples; and on his arrival at Philour, matters presented a sufficiently peaceful aspect to justify the hope in both officers and men of speedily reforming the forces which were besieging Delhi. An unexpected order recalled them to the northern extremities of the Punjab.

The duration and difficulty of the siege of Delhi, and the necessity of reinforcing the army before that town becoming more and more apparent each day, Sir J. Lawrence, before weakening his European forces, wished to stamp out any chance of military insurrection by disarming those Bengal regiments whose attitude hitherto had not given sufficient cause for so doing. The help of the flying column was indispensable in order to strike this blow. At Rawal-Pindi and Amritsur the measure met with no resistance. But at Jhelum, the 14th infantry withstood, with the greatest energy, 270 men of the 52nd, three guns, and some platoons of irregular cavalry sent to disarm them. This proved one of the bloodiest fights of the whole war. Lieutenant-Colonel Ellice, who commanded the expedition, fell grievously wounded. The sepoys, driven from their cantonments, retired to the bank of the Jhelum, where they maintained themseves till night, and then, under cover of darkness, crossed the river and entered Cashmere. Goulab Singh's kingdom did not afford them a safe asylum. Arrested in great numbers, by order of the prudent Maharajah they were given up to the English authorities, and executed. The fight of Jhelum was followed on the next day, July 9, by the mutiny of the forces stationed at Sialkote—that is to say, of the 46th B.A., and a wing of the regular cavalry. Brigadier

Brind, an old and much respected soldier, the chief surgeon, and many officers, were massacred by the sepoys; but the women, children, and a portion of the Anglo-Indian staff found shelter in the neighbouring fort. Brigadier Nicholson, on his way to the North, at the head of the flying column, had just disarmed the 59th N.A. at Amritsur, when he received information of the occurrences at Sialkote, and the order to cut off the rebels from Delhi. A strong detachment of the 9th cavalry, which had mutined at Sialkote, formed part of the flying column. Nicholson disarmed it, and having successfully accomplished this preliminary measure, bent his energies towards finding means of transport for his infantry. It was necessary at any cost to overtake the mutineers, and to march without halting under the terrible sun of the Punjab, more terrible even in that season of the year than in Bengal during the greatest heat.[1] In a few hours, two hundred ekkas (small carts of the country) were assembled, soldiers able to ride mounted the horses of the disarmed native squadrons, and at nine o'clock on the evening of July 10 the flying column began its march. It was composed of the 52nd Royals, of a battery of artillery, and of some recently formed companies of Sikhs. The moveable column arrived at Godanpore on July 11 towards six o'clock, having accomplished a distance of forty-four miles in less than twenty hours. The halt could not be long. The next day at nine, General Nicholson was warned by spies that the

[1] The Mahomedan tradition gives the following picturesque explanation of the torrid heat of the Punjab:—'Formerly there lived at Moultan a holy man named Pir Schamsch, who was entirely given up to his devotions, and begged his meal from charitable souls, when the necessities of the body made themselves felt. One day, seized with hunger, he obtained an excellent cutlet through the philanthropy of a butcher, a good Mussulman. Pir Schamsch, his breakfast in his hand, at once went to a cook and begged him to grill it on the gridiron for the love of the prophet. This cook, a man of little faith, took the cutlet and threw it in Pir Schamsch's face. The latter humbly picked up the piece of meat without any thought of revenge, and raising his eyes to the sun, he entreated that the slight service he had asked of the miscreant might be done for him. The reply from on high was not long in arriving. The sun at once descended three degrees, a position which it has since retained, and grilled Pir Schamsch's cutlet to the right point.'—*Twelve Years on the Frontiers of the Punjab*, by Colonel H. Edwardes.

mutineers were leisurely crossing the Ravee at Trimmon Ghat, a fort ten miles from Godanpore; and the column, resuming its march, soon overtook them. The troopers of the 9th charged the English artillery resolutely, but being received by rounds of grape-shot turned bridle, and their infantry, also losing courage, soon followed their example. At the end of half an hour, the mass of the rebels, leaving two hundred dead or wounded on the field, was in full retreat upon the Ravee. The want of cavalry did not allow Nicholson to complete this first success. The sepoys managed to reach a neighbouring island, and the English proceeded to Godanpore.

A sudden rise of the river prevented operations from being carried on for several days, but on the other hand, the sepoys were unable in consequence to leave the island where they had taken refuge. On the 16th, the necessary boats having been procured, the 52nd R.A. crossed the Ravee, whilst a sustained fire from the English artillery drew off the attention of the insurgents. The slight fortifications raised by the rebels, and the only gun they possessed, were carried at the point of the bayonet; and the sepoys, pursued with vigour, perished in arms or found a watery grave. A few fugitives who crossed the river were pursued by the natives, eager to gain the price set on their heads, and were given up, with few exceptions, to the English authorities. The brigade that mutinied at Sialkote may be said to have been completely annihilated; the fight at Trimmon Ghat terminated the military operations of the flying column in the Punjab. Fortune had hitherto favoured Sir J. Lawrence's plans, but England's skilful representative was not a man to flinch at the decisive moment from any danger or sacrifice necessary to ensure the success of the work of repression. Rightly persuaded that the tranquillity of the Punjab was secured for the moment, and that the Gordian knot would be cut under the walls of Delhi, he did not hesitate to reduce his European forces to their lowest figure, and ordered the flying column to join the besieging army by forced marches. Four European regiments, a few batteries of artillery, the

81st at Lahore, the 27th at Rawal-Pindi, the 70th and 87th—about 4,000 men—alone remained to guard the entire Punjab and more than 10,000 disarmed sepoys. Never had a statesman risked his reputation and his life with such absolute disregard of himself. The Punjab was still to be the scene of strange and terrible events before the siege of Delhi came to a decisive conclusion. On July 30, the 26th N.I., which had been disarmed in May, deserted in a mass the cantonments of Mian Mir, near Lahore, after massacring the major in command and the European sergeant-major. Favoured by a storm, the fugitives eluded a detachment sent in pursuit, and arrived the following day at a ford on the Ravee, where a native police guard had been placed. The latter resolutely defended the position till the arrival of the district magistrate, Mr. Cooper, accompanied by an escort of irregular cavalry. This feeble reinforcement decided the day's fate; and the sepoys, completely routed, sought safety in the river, and succeeded in reaching a little island near at hand. Exhausted and faint for want of food, the fugitives did not attempt to continue the struggle, and surrendered to the soldiers who, by the help of boats, had reached their last asylum. They numbered, all told, some 282 men, and were taken to the police station at Myala, where they were confined for the night in the casemates. Next morning they were assembled in a body in the open air, and a list of their names was hastily drawn up. This simple formality over, without further form of trial, the prisoners were chained together in gangs, and the head of the column moved to the place of execution, where the firing platoon was awaiting them. The magistrate, sitting under a tree and surrounded by his staff, watched each detachment of the lugubrious procession defile before him. Repeated discharges, sure messengers of death, reached the ears of the sepoys, and called forth the most diverse emotions on their countenances—astonishment, despair, and stoic calm. As they passed some prophesied, with cries of rage and furious gestures, a speedy death to the foreign judge who presided over the bloody execution; others, notwithstanding their chains, flung themselves wildly about in a mad sort of dance, blasphemed the religion of the Sikh soldiers surrounding them, and invoked the help of the goddess Ganga. The firing had gone on for several hours, 170 human beings had ceased to live, when one of the men of the firing platoon—one of Ranjit Singh's veterans—having fainted, a respite of a few minutes was granted. The work of death was resumed without delay, and number 237 had just been called, when the English magistrate was informed that the rest of the prisoners, about fifty, refused to leave the casemate where they had been confined the preceding evening. When the door was broken down, the last scene in this frightful tragedy appeared in its full horror. The narrow space only contained corpses; the fifty had died of exhaustion, suffocation, hunger, and thirst. The Christian judge who appears in history as the perpetrator of this awful massacre can doubtless invoke peremptory arguments in his favour. Alone, in the midst of a wavering population, having no other means of sustaining his prestige but pitiless severity, perhaps he could not do otherwise than punish deserters, whom all military codes would certainly have condemned to death. What nothing can justify, is the light and easy tone of the book in which he recounts the event, and which we have not ventured to reproduce even when giving the above horrible details.[1]

These terrible examples were not sufficient to impress upon the disarmed regiments the fact of their weakness. Towards the end of August, the Peshawur police called attention to the purchase of arms by men belonging to the disarmed regiments. In order the better to verify the fact, the military authorities made the sepoys vacate their usual huts, and placed them under canvas. On August 28, at a given signal, whilst the 51st B.A. was effecting its temporary change of quarters, all the soldiers of the corps deserted. Punishment was immediate and terrible; the guns and the infantry opened fire on the fugitives, who besides were pitilessly pursued by the Sikh cavalry. The official documents attest

[1] See Documents, No. XXV., 'Extracts from the Reports of Mr. R. Montgomery to Parliament.'

that out of 870 sepoys who left Lahore on the morning of August 28, 659 were dead on the following day.

This episode closes the lugubrious necrology of the mutinous regiments of the Bengal army in the Punjab. Repression was carried out pitilessly and ceaselessly, and the public documents furnished to Parliament give the following numbers:—

Sepoys shot or blown from the mouth of guns by order of the military authorities . . .	628
Sepoys, ditto, by order of the civil authorities .	1,370
Sepoys hung by order of the military authorities .	86
Ditto, by order of the civil authorities . . .	300
Total	2,384

However, notwithstanding this frightful total of executions, which does not comprise sepoys slain in arms, the interior situation of the Punjab was most serious towards the end of August, and we cannot better explain the difficulties of the position than by borrowing the very words of Sir J. Lawrence: 'As the months went by, the inhabitants of the Punjab felt that our power was growing weaker, for all our valuable forces were despatched to Hindostan, and no reinforcements arrived from Europe. The native correspondence depicted our isolated position in the metaphorical style of the country. It began to be believed, which no one had dared to do at the beginning of the mutiny, that the end of British rule was at hand, and the fire of disaffection, hitherto stifled, burst here and there into flames. Prudent men, who admitted the possibility of a speedy revolution, tried to guess who might be masters in the future, and to conciliate them. Our friends and our most loyal adherents took precautions to ensure the safety of their families in the troublous time about to occur. Enterprising spirits, though they did not delude themselves with the thought of restoring Ranjit Singh's kingdom, cherished at least the hope that the original Sikh community would rise from its ashes, whilst many turbulent minds longed for disturbances and the possibility of pillage. Peaceful chieftains made preparations for active life in their country homes; the inhabitant of the southern deserts rejoiced at the notion of resuming his habits of brigandage, and the mountaineer of the North was full of aspirations to recover his independence.'

In a few weeks future events were to throw a clearer light on the gloom of the situation, and to justify the confidence and plans of Sir J. Lawrence. Before the end of September the capture of Delhi rewarded the patriotic efforts of the Governor of the Punjab and his comrades. From the highest to the lowest all had done their duty, and Sir John, after his victory, could with pride and justice say of his staff, both civil and military: 'Never has a chief been better served than I have been, nor owed more to his officers.'

CHAPTER III.

SIEGE OF DELHI.

A few words on the history of Delhi—The disruption of the Mogul empire—Discontent of the population in the North-West Provinces—Its cause—The police—General wish for the restoration of the dynasty of the Great Mogul—Mohammed Shah Bahadour is proclaimed Emperor of Hindostan—Massacre of the English prisoners—State of feeling in the British army—Sir H. Barnard and his staff—Major Hodson—Delhi and Sebastopol—Beginning of the siege—Affair of June 19—Ditto of June 23—Arrival of reinforcements in the British camp—Change of the monsoon—Death of Sir H. Barnard—Major-General A. Wilson succeeds him—The sepoys maintain intelligences in the British camp—Fight of July 14—General Wilson takes measures in favour of the natives—Aspect of the camp—Dissensions amongst the mutineers—Insolence of the military chiefs to the old king—Fight at Hasaffsarh—Difficulties of the besiegers' position—Sanitary condition of the British army.

The history of the chief city of Hindostan is but one long series of foreign invasions, intestine wars, murder and rapine. As far back as the 361st year of the Hegira (1001) the rude tribes of the Indian Caucasus poured into India under the guidance of Mohammed Guzni. The object of these invasions, which followed at short intervals, was less religious propaganda than thirst for pillage. In 1391 Timour Khan took Delhi and massacred the inhabitants, but his descendants did not long retain the throne of India, which passed to another family known in history as the Imperial House of Lodi. Delhi was once again conquered in 1526 by Sultan Baber, of Timour's lineage, at the head of an Afghan army. Sultan Baber's victories, misfortunes, romantic adventures, generosity and devotion to his subjects, his friends and children, impart to the legendary hero of the East the charm with which the annals of Europe surround the character of Henry IV. and Gustave Adolph. Royal virtues were perpetuated for some generations in the posterity of Baber. Sultan Akbar, for instance, was both a perfect horseman, an intrepid warrior, and a patron of science and of the fine arts. Gahan the Magnificent built the new town of Agra, where he erected in honour of his faith the mosque known as the Mother-of-Pearl Mosque (Moh Musjid); and to the memory of the beautiful Sultaness Nourmahal that admirable tomb, the 'Taj,' which still ranks amongst the marvels of art.[1]

Finally, we have Alamghir, better known as Aureng-Zeb, who shone in the foremost rank in this constellation of sovereigns, and died at eighty-nine in the fiftieth year of a glorious reign. After him we note in the descendants of Baber a degeneracy which had begun long before in those of his companions of glory and adventure. Under the gilded roofs of palaces, and amidst the cool shades of delightful gardens, the great-grandsons of the conqueror forgot the warlike exercises which formed the joy and the glory of their ancestors. The luxuries of a second Capua also enervated the daughters of the robust peasant women, who used to carry the fruits of their gardens to the market of Cabul, or who cut grass among the rocks for the one horse of the family. The harem became a sacred enclosure, beyond the walls of

[1] This building, which is entirely of white marble—floor, walls, and roof—contains no ornament but bas-reliefs representing flowers of exquisite workmanship; and the chaste and majestic simplicity of its *ensemble* only pales before that wonder of Indian art, the Taj. The death of the Sultaness Nourmahal, which the latter was intended to commemorate, was accompanied, if we are to believe tradition, by supernatural and romantic circumstances, which explain the reverence, approaching to worship, shown by her husband for her memory. Amongst other things, she demanded of him not to re-marry, and to execute his promise of raising a mausoleum in her honour which should transmit her name to posterity. The emperor accordingly erected a temple where the pomp and art of the East have done their utmost. What pen can do justice to the harmony of form of this fairy mosque, built on the banks of a river, on a terrace flanked by four towers, in the midst of ever-verdant groves. Both interior and exterior are of white marble; the slabs of the pavement, the coating of the walls, even the openings through which filters a dim light are of marble, and some idea may be formed of the amazing amount of work lavished on the windows when we say that each contains eight hundred lights. In the centre of the mosque a marble balustrade, fretted like lace, protects two cenotaphs, exactly corresponding with the tombs of the Sultan and his wife, who rest in a vault below.

which the great ladies of the Mogul empire never stirred. The conquering race lost its strength and vigour, the structure raised by brute force was on the decline, and new invaders were about to aid the children of the soil in throwing off the yoke of degenerate masters.

The years which followed the death of Aureng-Zeb (1707) and preceded the establishment of the Company's power in India, witnessed the disruption of the Mogul empire and the revolt of its twenty-two tributary provinces. The successors of the prince, who emulated in Asiatic annals the glory with which modern history has crowned Louis XIV., were unable to maintain his inheritance intact, and in a few years their throne fell to pieces. Scarcely forty years had passed since the death of Aureng-Zeb, when Nadir-Shah, at the head of a Persian army, took possession of Delhi, and only relinquished his prey after having given up the city to the sanguinary excesses of his troops. The Rohillas formed for themselves an independent power to the east of the Ganges. The 'subahdar' of Bengal made himself absolute master in his province. The 'subahdar' of the Deccan proclaimed his independence, and became Nizam of Hyderabad. The Mahratta confederacy rose to be a first-class power. The great functionaries preserved a merely nominal link with the central power. Anarchy overspread the country. Great feudal lords and chiefs of armed bands occupied fortresses and kept up an incessant warfare, stained with frightful excesses. In the midst of this crisis the agents of the Honourable East India Company appeared upon the scene: the ambitious followers of those humble English merchants whom the love of gain had first attracted to the three Presidencies. Other Europeans had taken part before this in the intestine struggles of Asia, and in the first rank we find those brilliant French adventurers who opened the way for future conquests. Clive and Hastings, profiting by the traditions of French policy, favoured by fortune and well backed up by the mother country, realised the glorious future which the genius of Dupleix and La Bourdonnaye had aimed at. It must be well understood, however, that the Company's representatives during the second half of the last century did not make these conquests in the name of England. After subduing by arms and negotiation the great vassals who had rebelled against their suzerain, they substituted, it is true, the vigorous authority of the Company for a decrepit rule, but all change stopped there; and the semblance of supreme power was scrupulously preserved to the feeble heir of the great Mogul. Fate had finally decided against the empire of Hindostan. Scindia, with his Mahratta army, had occupied Delhi for some time (1803), when he was driven from his new conquest by the British forces under Lord Lake. The aged emperor, Shah Allum, in the hope of recovering his family patrimony, received the Europeans at first as liberators. His illusions were soon dissipated, and he merely obtained, as we have mentioned above, a nominal power, surrounded by the externals of royalty—such as a guard, the right of residence and of jurisdiction within the walls of the imperial palace, and a civil list of 12 lakhs of rupees. But the Mogul emperor, dethroned *de facto*, never formally renounced his rights, and his cause always found sympathisers, especially amongst the Mussulman population of the empire.

England's rule gave to the North-West Provinces[1] years of peace and prosperity the like of which they had never enjoyed before, and yet in the hour of trial their inhabitants showed themselves favourable in general to the restoration of the fallen dynasty. The numerous auxiliaries found by the rebellious sepoys in this important part of the Anglo-Indian empire can only be explained by a few details on the subject of the land-tax and the corruption of the native police, which were a double source of secret and deep discontent to all parties. Though we humbly avow that we have neither the intention nor the ability to guide the reader through the labyrinth of Indian finance,[2] yet it is indis-

[1] The territorial division known as the North-West Provinces comprises the two great cities of the Mogul empire—Agra and Delhi.

[2] Jacquemont once asked an Anglo-Saxon official to explain in a few words the different systems of land tax in vogue in India. The gentleman answered that for twenty years he had been at work on them without being any the wiser

pensable, in order to explain the state of feeling in the North-West Provinces, to say something of the land-tax, which had been introduced there thirty years before against the energetic and repeated protests[1] of all who remained faithful to the earlier policy of the Company. An honest, liberal, and well-intentioned government had aroused more hatred by a too complicated and too severely applied system of land taxation than had been produced by the exactions and tyranny of the fiscal agents of the great Moguls. The statesmen and financiers who, towards 1830, under the governorship and somewhat under the influence of Lord W. Bentinck, arranged the different parts of the new system, were thoroughly convinced, and rightly so, of the corruption and rapacity characterising the middle and higher classes of native society. They therefore attempted to bring the village communities and the revenue officers into immediate contact by suppressing, as far as possible, the intermediary talukdars and zemindars,[2] which was the exact contrary of what had been done at Madras and Bombay, where the conquering government had taken special pains to follow the traditions of its predecessors in matters of taxation and property. Those who made the new law meant doubtless to protect equally both great proprietors and humble peasants, but their good intentions were completely frustrated. The new machinery, directed by a hand of iron, crushed down the whole population of the North-West Provinces to one same level of degradation and poverty. The judges, called upon to decide the vexed questions to which the land-tax gave rise—questions so numerous in a country like India, where property rests upon a vague and ill-defined basis—showed the blindest and most deplorable party spirit in their decisions. Their judgments laid it down as an axiom that the right of the village communities in the soil was inalienable,

[1] See Documents, No. XXVI., 'The Land-tax in the North-West Provinces.'

[2] The 'taloukdar' enjoys no right of property, and is merely a sort of hereditary collector who contracts to pay the land-tax on certain properties into the coffers of the state against a certain commission. The 'zemindars,' on the contrary, combine extensive seigniorial rights with those of landed proprietors.

and that all 'taloukdars' were to be considered as forgers and impostors. In a word, a high official could write that 'the one aim of justice was to reduce large properties to lesser proportions, and to substitute village communities for individual proprietorship.' The ardour of innovation blinded the Anglo-Indian authorities, and systematic persecution estranged from the Company the very classes of society which ought to have proved its most faithful supporters.

The system of land taxation put into practice in the North-West Provinces on their annexation—a system which differed essentially from the one in use in Bengal and in the rest of India—was based on a survey of the soil and of the rights attached to it. A foreign government thus subjected the interests of several million subjects to a supervision so minute that a large proprietor could scarcely exercise it over his own tenants. To work without injustice, such a system m[illegible] be strictly accurate in its smallest details; and how was it possible to obtain the requisite accuracy in a country where the inhabitants, plunged in ignorance, were incapable of taking part in the drawing up of public acts affecting their most vital concerns? Besides this, constant changes in the title deeds of property in a few years completely altered the whole register, and placed the people at the mercy of the native revenue officers, a corrupt and rapacious set. Recent changes had still more intensified the evil. In the first years of the conquest, the 'patwari,' the most important of the revenue agents, continued to fill the position he occupied under the great Moguls. From time immemorial this official had exercised the functions of village notary and accountant, and the English courts had recognised the patwari's register and testimony as without appeal in all questions of ownership. The patwaris succeeded one another from father to son; and, united by a common interest with the persons whose rights they administered, they usually deserved and justified the confidence and respect shown them. Soon, however, the English authorities felt the necessity of more regularity and uniformity in the keeping of official documents and accounts than these simple men were capable of. Accordingly, all patwaris actually occupying a post were ordered to pass an examination, in order to ascertain their fitness for their position. Most of them, alarmed at this prospect, resigned their employment; and the Company, in an evil hour, completely reformed an institution both useful and dear to the hearts of the natives. Each collectorship was divided into circles (halquahs), subdivided again into several patwaris. At first the management of these circles was to have been given to any of the former native officials who had satisfactorily passed the examination, and had been elected by the vote of the population; but the elective system failed almost everywhere. The new patwaris, who were arbitrarily named by the Government, and were mere ordinary fiscal agents, proved generally corrupt, and inclined to use the power placed in their hands for their own ends, to the detriment of justice and truth.

We must add that the land tax was very high, and could never have been collected in its entirety, if the natives, in their profound attachment to the soil, had not preferred sacrificing their last penny to losing their hereditary possession. British officers who, in order to escape from the rebels, were obliged to seek refuge in the villages, and lived for months together in daily contact with the ryots, have unanimously testified to the deep distress of the lower classes, and to the kind treatment they met with from the Hindoos.[1] The small proprietors, unable to pay the excessive land-tax, fell of necessity into the hands of usurers, often the agents or accomplices of the subaltern *employés* of the Administration, and were most of them legally deprived of their land. These changes in property brought about little by little the dissolution of native society. The ruined proprietors remained as farmers on the properties once their own, but irritated and humiliated by a degradation which they justly ascribed to the iniquities of the inferior Government agents, and consequently to the Government itself. The 'zemindars,' or great proprietors, had their own subjects of complaint and suspicion. Though long shorn of their feudal rights by foreign rule, they still retained

[1] See Documents, No. XXVII., 'Relation of Dr. Beatson, 74th N.I.'

great influence over their former vassals. The European conquest had not entirely destroyed the links of a *régime* which did not exclusively recall an age of tyranny, but rather one where feelings of mutual confidence and affection often bound together the weak and the strong, the lowly and the powerful, the vassal and his lord. The zemindars learnt that a project of law was under consideration, having for its object the recognition of the right of permanent possession in those farmers who could show proof of having occupied their holdings for a certain term of years. This measure assumed in their eyes the character of an absolute confiscation, so that both small and great proprietors and ryots, ruined and discontented all of them, only waited for an opportunity to protest by arms against the Company's rule.

The corruption of the police was again a fruitful source of ill-feeling by its tyrannical and mischievous action. The 'burkundazes' (the subaltern agents of the native police), grasping and badly paid, and easily evading the supervision of their European superiors, who were few in number and too widely scattered, refrained from no exaction that could bring an increase to their salary. Any infraction of the law, any offence against social order, murder, theft, or outrage, was a source of ignominious gain to the unfaithful agent. On the first news of a crime, the burkundaze used to wait upon the two or three great proprietors in his district, in order to receive from them the remuneration to which he seriously considered himself entitled, if he did not implicate them in the affair, even as witnesses. Infanticide, the murder of girls at their birth,[1] that special crime of Asia, which is practised there on so large a scale, presented the richest harvest to the police agent. A proud Rajpoot would make any sacrifice rather than allow the officers of the law to violate the sacred precincts of his harem. We will not dwell on this subject, for the corruption and exactions of the Indian police in the period preceding the mutiny are exposed in all official documents. We scarcely dare hope that this state of things has been modified by the changes

[1] See Documents, No. XXVIII., 'Infanticide in Rajpootana.'

which have taken place in the last twenty years, and that the police of the present day has ceased to be the curse of the country. Doubtless, as heretofore, the Administration makes honest efforts to bring the chaos of Indian police into something like order; but the vices inherent in a government of conquest, in the impure elements from which the inferior agents are recruited, in the ignorance, the timidity, the dissimulation and untruthfulness of the native population, constitute an incurable evil not to be triumphed over by all the skill and vigilance of European magistrates.

The causes of discontent and disaffection which we have just enumerated greatly influenced public feeling in favour of a restoration of the throne of the Moguls. The rightful heir of Aureng-Zeb, who in European eyes scarcely preserved a shadow of fallen greatness, exercised a marvellous prestige over the Mohammedans, and even over the Hindoos. The politic moderation with which the English had used their victory encouraged popular delusions. As we have seen, old Mohammed Bahadour continued to occupy the hereditary palace of his ancestors, where he saw himself surrounded by all the pomp of sovereign power. He could confer honorary titles, and still retained the semblance of supreme authority, and the least favours shown by him were more highly prized by the natives than the greatest rewards granted by the Government *de facto*. Up to a few years previously indeed, the Company's representative, in all interviews with the dispossessed emperor, had done him homage by presenting an offering (nazzar) of gold pieces.[1]

All the native princes who still enjoyed a show of independence openly recognised the suzerainty of the prisoner of Delhi, and the very inscriptions on the coins of their several states gave proof of the faithful allegiance they still felt towards him. Besides this, the long years of internal peace which India owed to the vigorous rule of the Company, had done a great deal towards calming if not destroying the religious prejudices and secular antipathies

[1] See Documents, No. XXIX., 'The last nazzar given to the King of Delhi by English officers.'

which before the conquest had divided Mussulmen from Hindoos. A sentiment of nationality—the nationality of colour—had to some extent developed itself amongst the native population, and was stimulated by the natural hatred between master and subject, between the conquerors and the conquered. The progress made by the country in the path of civilisation—a postal system excellently organised, electric telegraphs, the security of transit, and the extension of commerce—had drawn the population nearer together, and contributed to pacify the divisions of past times. In many cases, the benefits conferred by fifty years of orderly and peaceful government proved active agents in the service of the mutiny. The success of the rebellion at Delhi had the double result of giving it a capital and a chief. The mutineers were not yet masters of the cantonments, when Mohammed Shah Bahadour was proclaimed Sultan of Hindostan, to the sound of drums and with discharges of artillery. Notwithstanding this precipitate action, it can be safely affirmed—and the proceedings of the court-martial before which the ex-Emperor appeared after the capture of Delhi prove it—that he was never more than a passive and resigned instrument in the hands of the rebels. This restoration of the throne of the Moguls met with great popular favour. The Emperor invested more than forty princes with robes of honour in a durbar held in the great hall of the palace, and the mutineers took an oath of fidelity at the foot of the throne.[1]

A scene worthy of the barbarous days of Tamerlane inaugurated the new reign. Forty-nine European prisoners, mostly women and children, had been brought to the palace the day following the revolt. They were confined in a low room without windows, where air and light were alike wanting, and received only the coarsest food. Mrs. Aldwell, a convert to Christianity, married to an Englishman, who escaped from death by a timely return to her former religion, related the events of those terrible days in something like the following terms, when called upon to give her testimony

[1] See Documents, No. XXX., 'Proclamation of the sepoys of Delhi.'

before the military court, sitting in judgment on Mohammed Shah: 'We were shut up in a dark room with a single door and no window. One prisoner alone could not have lived in this hole, and we were fifty. We were huddled together, but we kept the door closed as much as possible, though this deprived us of air and light, in order to prevent the sepoys from frightening the little children. The soldiers constantly entered the room with fixed bayonets, whenever the fancy seized them, and asked us with horrid threats if we would consent to embrace Islamism, and become the king's slaves, if our lives were spared. The men appointed by the court to guard us incited the sepoys to massacre us, and cut us into pieces to serve as food for crows and magpies. On the Tuesday, the sepoys openly announced that our last hour had come, and that we were to be blown up. Our food was of the coarsest kind, but the King twice sent us some a little better.' The miseries of captivity were not to last long. On May 16, a band of sepoys, in a state of wild excitement, presented themselves in the private apartment of the King, and demanded that the prisoners should be given up to them. An affirmative answer was instantly given. 'Some officials of the palace, accompanied by sepoys,' says Mrs. Aldwell, 'appeared at the door, and ordered us to come out without delay. The women and children burst into tears, exclaiming that they were being led to death. The Moslems swore by the Koran, the Hindoos by the waters of Jumna, that they only intended to lead the prisoners to a better residence. These repeated assurances induced the poor creatures to come out. They were counted and carefully bound together in a compact mass, as is usually done to prisoners on the march. The group was dragged towards the large courtyard, and got as far as a fig-tree, which overshadowed a small reservoir. Then the murderers began the massacre, striking right and left with their sabres. Some of the princes, the sons or grandsons of the King, looked on at the bloody scene from behind lattices or comfortably seated on terraces.'

To be impartial, we must add—what trustworthy witnesses affirm—that Prince Feroz-Shah, a near relation of the King, unable to check the murderers' rage, reproached them so vehemently with violating the law of Mohammed by killing women and children, that he was obliged to fly from their vengeance. The palace record found after the assault, describes the horrible crime in these words: 'Forty-nine English were prisoners. The army demanded that they should be given up to them. The King answered, "The army can do as it pleases with the prisoners." Consequently, they were slain by the sword.'[1]

Whilst the crowd of sepoys and officials, actors in, or spectators of, the horrible tragedy were grossly insulting the victims in their dying agonies, the town population, more especially the Hindoos, reprobated these cruelties, and openly proclaimed that the gods would not look favourably on a cause stained by such crimes. Round about Delhi anarchy broke out from the first; and the wild tribes, such as the 'Gojars' and 'Ramghars,' would not recognise the authority of the new King. A hundred years of peace and order had not appeased their intestine dissensions. The villagers attacked one another, and settled by main force quarrels dating far back but never entirely forgotten. Other portions of the population, who had apparently hailed with satisfaction the restoration of the ancient dynasty, soon began to regret the peace they had formerly enjoyed, and employed force to protect themselves against the exactions of the new finance agents. Every vestige of order and law disappeared, and the right of the strongest became the only one paramount in the provinces round Delhi.

The military forces which, under Sir Henry Barnard, re-occupied their former cantonments after the battle of Gazioudoudnaggarh on June 8, were composed as follows:—The 9th Royal Lancers, two squadrons of Royal Carabineers, the 60th and 75th R.A., the 1st and 2nd European Fusiliers in the Company's service, the Timour battalion (Goorkhas), a detachment of engineers, eight pieces of 18, four

[1] The first accounts stated that the princes of the Imperial house had taken part in the massacre with unheard of refinements of cruelty. The English officers firmly believed these reports, which were not afterwards fully borne out by official investigations, and this explains the terrible reprisals they inflicted on their prisoners.

mortars, four howitzers, besides the guns captured from the enemy; in all, 800 cavalry, 3,600 infantry, and sixteen siege-pieces. The day following the battle, the British army had been reinforced, as we have seen, by the Punjab Guides, numbering about 1,200 men. The ardour of the soldiers made up for their small number. The officers joyfully exchanged their tranquil garrison life and all the luxury of the mess for the hardships of war, poor fare, and muddy water. For the first time during the Indian wars, European soldiers found themselves called upon to undertake duty outside the camp; and their provisions were both insufficient and bad in quality. But what mattered privations such as these, and exposure to climate and sickness, when it was a question of life and death. The spot where the camp was fixed was eminently calculated to excite the martial spirit of the men. The tents were pitched among the ruins of the former cantonments, and at every step broken furniture, shreds of clothing, or half-destroyed houses recalled the fatal 12th of May. The men left the hospital without asking the doctor's permission, or even concealed their wounds, in order to lose no occasion of fighting against their treacherous comrades. This was, indeed, the true image of civil war with all its sanguinary excesses—civil war, where individual passions and ferocious instincts exercise a more powerful influence than the sentiment of duty or fidelity to the colours. Military organisation, if not discipline, was still preserved in the ranks of the mutineers. They marched to battle in their scarlet uniforms, and the British flag floated side by side with the green standard, which was the symbol of the insurrection. The word of command was given in English, and during the fight the sepoy bands played the favourite airs of the Royal troops or, stranger still, 'God save the Queen.' These insulting proceedings, and the accounts of the massacres, which one after another kept reaching the army under the walls of Delhi, fired all hearts with the wildest desire for revenge. A dark skin became an object of hatred and disgust to European eyes. Native servants, so useful, so indispensable, and some of them so devoted to their masters, were grossly abused and ill-treated on the slightest pretext. The soldiers, who gave no quarter in battle, did their best to torment the prisoners under their charge. A usual and favourite amusement was to strike the captive sepoys with the butt-end of their guns or the flat of their sabres, and worse still, to force them, by threats and brutality, to eat pork or cow's flesh. The officers, who presided over the courts-martial, were blinded by passion. It was a matter of certainty that every accused person would be condemned, and the sentence was invariably death. 'Make short work of Delhi,' was the last laconic message telegraphed by the Governor-General to the Commander-in-Chief before the wires were cut. There were many strong reasons for bringing the siege to an early and successful termination. To deprive the insurrection of its temporary leader, of its capital, and of the immense resources contained in the Delhi arsenal, was to break its neck. This would also ensure order in the Punjab, which province had inspired keen and legitimate anxiety. Could any one have foreseen that Sir J. Lawrence would not only maintain order in his government, but also furnish the reinforcements necessary to reduce Delhi? The orders of the Government were thoroughly conformable, as we have seen, to the wishes of the whole army. Both officers and men fully comprehended that in the actual circumstances success was possible only by making up in audacity what was wanting in numbers. The new Commander-in-Chief, Sir H. Barnard, who had scarcely landed in India when General Anson's death conferred on him, by right of seniority, the command of the British troops, knew nothing of the habits and languages of the country. But recently engaged in the tremendous struggle at Sebastopol, his impressions and the strategy with which he was familiar inclined him naturally and very strongly to credit the sepoys with skilful combinations, and a power of resistance worthy of his former adversaries in the Crimea. Besides this, his inexperience of Indian affairs obliged him constantly to have recourse to the advice of his staff, which was divided into two very distinct schools. The one consisted of the old generals, who had risen by seniority—brave and experienced officers—but incapable of displaying energy or of taking part in daring enterprises; the other, of officers still young in years, who had had the good fortune to gain brevet-rank by exceptional services, or by exposing their lives, with true Oriental fatalism, in desperate enterprises—impetuous partisans, prompt, vigorous, and clever, little disposed to spare their own blood and that of their men. Foremost among the latter we must mention Major Hodson, who became one of the principal heroes of the siege of Delhi, and whose career, for this reason, we shall describe in some detail.

His adventurous life gives a good idea of the trials and labours of an officer in the Anglo-Indian service. Hodson, the third son of the Archdeacon of Stafford, was born in 1820, in Gloucestershire. After passing through Cambridge, he entered the Guernsey militia as ensign, and thence entered the Company's service. He arrived in India in 1844, and immediately on landing, took part in the bloody campaign on the Sutlej. His courage, intelligence, and excellent education obtained for him the friendship and patronage of influential personages; and at the end of the war he received as a staff appointment the management of the Lawrence asylum—a military orphanage. The second Sikh campaign, 1849, found him in the exercise of these peaceful functions, and he distinguished himself in it no less than in the first. Fortune still favouring him, he was called, on the conclusion of peace, although only with the rank of lieutenant in his regiment, to the command of the dreaded Punjab Guides. His brilliant career was suddenly cut short by the discovery of certain irregularities in the regimental accounts, which fact was used against him by his enemies, and he was once more a lieutenant in the 2nd European Fusiliers of Bengal, to which he had originally been attached, when the mutiny broke out. The very interesting volume, dedicated by the Rev. A. Hodson to his brother's memory, shows us this brilliant officer as director, architect, and accountant of an educational establishment which had then no existence, except on paper. With an ingenuity worthy of Robinson Crusoe, Hodson improvised plans of construction, scaffoldings, and even manufactured nails on an isolated table-land of the Himalaya. As commander of the Punjab Guides, he became the supreme head of a vast extent of frontier, and found himself called upon to maintain order in his district, to exercise justice, and to collect taxes. All civil and military power was concentrated in his hands. He wielded the most marvellous power over the natives: whether as an impetuous guerilla chief he pursued predatory tribes at the head of his men, whether as arbitrator in quarrels between neighbours, he pronounced capital sentences in a court of justice, or whether at evening, before a roaring fire and surrounded by the native chiefs, he listened, whilst the pipe passed round, to the story of the day's hunting—his influence was supreme, his word was law. Hodson was gifted with all those physical qualities which are so much admired by primitive races. Slight and tall, a capital horseman, prodigiously active and inured to all privations, he enjoyed the rare privilege of being able to sleep on horseback. Skilled in the use of the sabre, he was always to be found in the van, exciting the courage of his men by voice and gesture, in the style of Homer's heroes. When events took a serious turn in the mutiny, Hodson's rare talents pointed him out naturally to the authorities as the person to fill an important post, and he was entrusted with the Intelligence Department of the staff. He discharged his new functions so successfully, that it was familiarly said in the English camp that he knew in the morning the *menu* of the dinner prepared in the evening for the successor of the great Mogul.

The position of the British forces before Delhi has been compared, and not unreasonably, to that of the 'allies' before Sebastopol. The besiegers, as in the Crimea, drew their resources from the rear, and were too few in number to surround the town, whilst the besieged possessed enormous numbers of men and stores in abundance. Considering the numeric weakness of the British forces, there could be no question of laying regular siege to a town of the importance of Delhi, which had a population of more than 150,000 souls, a circumference of seven miles and a half, and was enclosed by walls, defended by a glacis to a third of their height, with a ditch in front of twenty-four feet, and flanked at intervals by twelve gun bastions. A part of the town was likewise protected by the channel of the Jumna, on the right bank of which is built the modern Delhi. The siege operations, wisely adapted to circumstances, were limited to the portion of the works comprised between the 'water bastion,' which defends the Cashmere, and the 'Mouri bastion,' which defends the Cabul Gate. All other issues remained as free as if the town were not besieged. The front of the attack offered a development of two miles and a half, from 'the Hindoo Rao House'[1] to the Villa Metcalfe, at which was stationed the last picket on the extreme left. The British camp was three miles and a half in depth, and was cut in two by the high road, the possession of which was absolutely necessary to ensure communications with the Punjab, and therefore with Europe, as every other issue was blocked by the besieged town and the insurrection in Central Asia. The front of this species of untrenched camp was composed of a series of batteries planted on a plateau, the approaches of which were defended by broken ground. To the left, excellent lines of natural defence were formed by the Jumna, and in the rear by a canal which takes its rise in a neighbouring pond (the Nasafgarh Taël), and joins the Jumna to the north of Delhi. The right was partly defended by an aqueduct which crosses the canal, and then running parallel to the Great Trunk Road, enters the city by the Cashmere Gate. But on this side of the aqueduct, from the Cabul Gate to the British advanced posts, were the suburbs of Telawari and Kissenganje, the mosques, palaces, and gardens of which served to cover the attacks and protect the retreat of the enemy. These positions formed the extreme point of the besiegers' line of defence. The Hindoo Rao House, the nearest point in the

[1] Hindoo Rao House, a country residence built by a Mahratta prince of the house of Scindia, who lived at Delhi in a sort of exile. It formed the extreme point of the right of the British forces.

British lines to this dangerous neighbourhood, had been entrusted to the Goorkhas [1] of the Timour battalion, who proved as brave as they were faithful.

The doomed city could be seen in all its Oriental magnificence from the Hindoo Rao House, and formed, indeed, a splendid panorama. The eye ranged over the almost perfect oval of its vast enclosure, with its picturesque gates and bastions. On the left, in the midst of shady groves, and bathed by the waters of the Jumna, rose the curious pile of the palace of the great Mogul, and the lofty tower of Telun Garh, the guns of which commanded the bridge of boats over the river. In the interior of the town appeared the long thoroughfare of Chundney Chowke, with its smiling gardens, and the domes and minarets of the beautiful mosque of Jamma.[2]

[1] The Goorkhas come from Nepaul, and descend originally from the Hindoos of the plains. Without contemning the Brahmin religion, they despise caste prejudices, eat meat, drink fermented liquor, and assimilate European customs better than any other Indian races. Small in stature, broad-shouldered, square-faced, singularly ugly, but strong and intrepid, they retained in the highest degree the feeling of honour peculiar to the old Rajpoots. Numerous attempts were made to shake their loyalty during the siege, but always in vain. The position they defended for four months was exposed to a galling fire. In one day two cannon shots killed or wounded, one ten and the other seven men out of the garrison. The wounded and sick Goorkhas refused to leave the post of honour to go to the hospital. Major Reid, who commanded the battalion, was worthy of his brave soldiers; he only left the walls of the Hindoo Rao House to take part in the assault, in which he was severely wounded.

[2] Islamism has retained all its power and prestige at Delhi, and the Jamma mosque is in every respect a splendid edifice. The temple portico is entered by a grand staircase, on the steps of which are shops full of woven stuffs, eatables, and bird sellers with thousands of pigeons—the Prophet's favourite birds. Galleries, supported by sculptured columns, surround the court, the details of which can be taken in at a single glance. In front lies a courtyard paved with white marble and adorned with a large basin full of the clearest water. The background is filled in by the mosque itself, with its red brickwork, its minarets, its domes and its large halls, which are approached by three Gothic arcades. The daylight was waning as I arrived at the mosque, and in the semi-darkness my eyes only imperfectly distinguished a misty assemblage of shapeless outlines, floating above the surface of the ground. The varied attitudes, characteristic of Mussulman devotion, soon gave me the key to this mystery. The faithful, prostrate a minute before on their faces, rose at the voice of the man, and the building was filled, as by magic, with a crowd dressed in white, looking like so many dim shadows.

The immense ruins of ancient Delhi, silent and unimpeachable witnesses of the grandeur and disasters of past days, stretched for miles into the neighbouring country, whilst at one's feet lay the formidable machines which science and intellect have applied to modern warfare. The sight was both picturesque and terrible, and foreshadowed the length and difficulty of the struggle which was to decide the fate of India.

The siege of Delhi offers this further resemblance to that of Sebastopol, that after the affair of Gazioudoudnaggarh, as after the battle of the Alma, an audacious *coup de main* might probably have carried the place. The court, the sepoys, and the population were all in equal consternation, and no serious preparation for defence had yet been made. The skirmish was over in the morning, and the English soldiers might have been called out in the evening without too great a strain on their powers. An assault given on June 8 at sunset would have offered the best chances of success—at least so said the inhabitants of Delhi after the town was taken; but the opportunity was not made use of, though Sir H. Barnard, acting on the advice of the more energetic members of his staff, decided on a desperate course a few days after his arrival before the place. On the night of June 13 two regiments were marched against the city, and ordered to blow up the gates with petards. Through some unforeseen delays day broke before the beginning of the attack, and the General-in-Chief, no longer hoping to surprise the enemy, countermanded the assault. This prudent resolution was not matter for regret; had they succeeded in entering the town, the British forces would have been too few to defend at the same time the camp, and to carry on the fighting in the streets.

The day after the affair at Gazioudoudnaggarh the sepoys took courage again. The incessant and well-directed fire from their batteries showed that they were acquainted with the range of the positions occupied by the English. Their chiefs utilised the advantages of the climate and of the ground with rare skill. The sorties began at midday, at the very moment when the terrible June sun at its zenith exercises a most deleterious effect on European constitutions. The besiegers were harassed by repeated attacks. The alarm was sounded two or three times a day in the camp; for the sepoys, without undertaking extensive strategical movements, constantly engaged in skirmishes, to which the ground in the environs of the city was specially adapted, being covered with jungle and with ruins of all sorts. The Hindoo—patient, silent, and subtle—is better fitted for a warfare of ambush than the European, who is always ready to rush into danger, and offer his unprotected body to a concealed enemy.

Skirmishing was of a desperate character from the first, for religious fanaticism had reached its height both among Hindoos and Mussulmen. The thirst for Christian blood excited by the massacres of Mirut and Delhi was not yet assuaged. Besides, not a single man in the ranks of the mutineers could have any doubt as to the fate reserved to him in case of defeat. The sepoys had no choice but to perish in arms or to meet with an ignominious death at the cannon's mouth, or on the gallows. Daily examples gave evidence of the implacable rigour of the English towards the prisoners who fell into their hands. However, the insurrection had fair chances of success, notwithstanding recent reverses. The Delhi arsenal contained inexhaustible resources in arms and ammunition, and the mutinous regiments flocked to the capital from every part of the empire. The immense numerical superiority of the besieged allowed them to bring up fresh troops to each attack, whilst the English were under fire several times in the course of the day. Though the sepoys were always repulsed, the constant struggle exhausted the victor's forces. Were we to enumerate all the skirmishes that took place before Delhi, they would offer little historical interest, so we shall content ourselves with noticing the more important ones only.

On June 19, in the night, the Intelligence Department was informed that a serious attack would be made by the brigade which had mutinied at Nacirabad. This brigade, composed of the 15th and 30th N.I., and of one foot and one horse battery, had entered Delhi the evening before, and the military authorities of the insurgents had decided that the new contingent should not receive any pay before it had engaged the English. At sunrise, a considerable force was seen to leave the town to the right and disappear into the suburbs. Only towards the middle of the day the whole scope of the enterprise was revealed. A great tumult broke out suddenly in the rear of the camp on the other side of the canal, in the middle of the plain, where the mules and cattle and the huts of many camp followers were situated. In a moment the whole space was covered by a motley crowd of terrified men, women, and children, camels, oxen, and elephants—all pressing towards the bridges over the canal. The surprise was complete, for the sepoys had penetrated to the rear of the camp. The horse artillery under Major Tombs first appeared on the scene of danger. The guns, exposed to a galling fire, were only disengaged by a brilliant charge of the Punjab Guides, inspired by the example of their commanding officer, Captain Daly, who, however, was soon disabled by a severe wound.

Brigadier Hope Grant's Lancers, who next came to the assistance of the artillery, met with serious losses when charging in a narrow street. Sir H. Barnard, who was the last to hear of the attack, at once sent off the infantry necessary to reinforce the troops; but they were slow in arriving, and the British forces were too weak in any case to defend all the points attacked. The horrible confusion was still further increased by the approach of evening, for fighting went on till nightfall, and the flashes of the guns and of the musketry shed a sinister light over the scene. At last darkness put an end to the combat, and the British troops returned to their quarters dejected by the fatigues and uncertain issue of the day. For the first time since the opening of the campaign the sepoys had resolutely maintained their ground against English bayonets.

These impressions were slightly modified on the following

day, when a column sent to the rear, in order to definitely repulse the enemy, found only the dead and wounded abandoned by the sepoys on the battle-field. The column had not yet re-entered the camp when the tumultuous scenes of the preceding evening were repeated, in consequence of a demonstration in the rear by a few of the enemy's cavalry, and the British troops marched in hot haste against aggressors who had already withdrawn behind walls of Delhi. The Nacirabad brigade[1] earned for the first time in the fight of June 19 the renown it retained through the war. No native corps preserved so long nor so completely a regular organisation and strict discipline. The sepoys' loss was estimated at 300 or 400 men, that of the English at 100 killed and wounded. A picket was stationed in the rear, and if this precaution had been taken at the right moment the losses and alarm of the last skirmish would have been avoided; but the soldiers were so few in number and so overwhelmed with work that it was difficult to guard all the weak points of the camp.

The struggle which was to recommence on June 23 had been predicted long before. Brahmins, astrologers, dervishes, and magicians had all prophesied, whilst the mutiny was yet unthought of, that the British rule would not last beyond hundredth anniversary of the battle of Plassey, when England's star had first shone victorious over India.[2] The centenary of this event fell on the first day of the new moon, at the beginning of the Feast of the Might of the Gods, one of the great solemnities of the religion of Vishnu and Juggernaut, and was believed to be propitious both by the Mohammedans and by the Hindoos—a double consideration—not

[1] This horse battery was well known in the Company's army for its brilliant services, and in recompense of their valiant conduct at the siege of Jellalabad (1842) the guns were decorated with a mural crown.

[2] The actors in the battle of Plassey had not all disappeared from our world a few years ago. In 1856 we enjoyed the honour of offering our respectful homage in the shape of biscuits and rice to the oldest veteran of our army at Barrackpore—an elephant captured by the English at the battle of Plassey, in 1757, as was attested by the regimental register of the commissariat, and who bore with severe dignity the weight of years and military services.

without importance to those who directed the strategy of the insurrection. At three o'clock in the morning the town batteries opened fire, and the sepoys occupied the suburbs of Sabzi-Mandi and Kissenganje with a considerable force, composed of the three regiments that had mutinied at Jallandar, and had only joined head-quarters a few hours previously. This movement was crowned with success, and in this new position the sepoys' fire enfiladed the British camp and batteries. Two English columns were immediately despatched against Sabzi-Mandi, whilst another detachment went to meet the expedition sent from Jallandar in pursuit of the mutinous regiments, and which had notified the preceding evening its speedy arrival in camp. The suburbs were thrice carried by the English, and re-occupied as many times by the sepoys. Sir H. Barnard directed operations from a neighbouring height; but he was unable to follow the various phases of the fighting going on in the streets or in the gardens, and many officers complained afterwards of having received orders to retire when they ought to have advanced, and *vice versâ*. The struggle continued all day long, under a tropical sun, without any decisive advantage on either side. However, towards evening the sepoys evacuated Sabzi-Mandi, which the English immediately occupied.

The dearly-bought experience of the day—more than 150 men having been killed and wounded—had demonstrated the weakness of the British lines before Sabzi-Mandi. A strong guard was henceforth stationed in that place, in an easily defended seraï, which was connected with Hindoo Rao House by a battery known as 'Sunny House,' and noted in the siege for the havoc caused by its fire..

The gaps made during these two days in the British ranks were filled up at once. On the very evening of June 22, the expedition sent by the Punjab authorities in pursuit of the regiments that had mutinied at Jallandar, and had just evacuated the enclosure of Sabzi-Mandi, an expedition composed of some companies of the 75th R.A., and of a Sikh regiment, in all 850 men, arrived in camp. Other troops were near at hand. On June 25, the 8th R.A., 400 men strong, to which number the effective force of most of the Queen's regiments was reduced, and a few days afterwards the 61st R.A., the 1st Punjab infantry, and a squadron of the 5th Punjab cavalry appeared as reinforcements. Eventually the British troops under the walls of Delhi numbered 6,600 men, of whom 3,000 were Europeans.

Whether by chance or calculation the sepoys, by beginning the mutiny in the month of May, had selected the period of the year in which the fatigues of war are most trying to Europeans. In time of peace every European regiment is rigorously confined to barracks from sunrise to sunset, and if a white sentinel shows his pallid face in the full glare of day, it is always under the shade of a gate or of a rampart. The sentiment of military duty and the thirst for vengeance inspired the English army with strength to support the frightful heat of the climate, though the burning rays of the sun and the scorching breath of the hot winds had from the first proved most potent auxiliaries of the sepoys. In every battle sunstrokes, and their terrible consequences, apoplexy, delirium tremens, and fevers of all sorts, made many victims amongst the English. Luckily, the rains, which set in on June 27, allowed of the siege operations being carried on in the daytime without exposing the men to the fierce ardour of the sun. The rains, moreover, facilitated the defence of the English lines; for the inundations of the Jumna protected the left flank of the camp by an impassable sheet of water, whilst the overflow of the canal in the rear rendered any enterprise on the enemy's part difficult, if not impossible in that direction.

A few days after the change of the monsoon, on July 5, Sir H. Barnard was carried off by a violent attack of cholera. The old general had not been able to resist the cares and fatigues attendant on his command, and died before bringing to a successful end the difficult task entrusted to him.[1] If he can be reproached with having let pass the opportunity of striking a great blow on June 8, after the victory won before Delhi, it must be said that, as a new comer in India,

[1] See Documents, No. XXXI., 'Last Letter of Sir H. Barnard.'

he could not fully appreciate the prestige exercised by white soldiers over the natives. The ruses, stratagems, and extraordinary feats of audacity (constantly neutralised by a lack of perseverance), which form the distinctive characteristics of Asiatic tactics, astonished and bewildered the veteran officer. His death cast a noticeable gloom over the army, where his genial manners, his generosity of character, and his high courage had won for him as an individual the affection and respect even of those who blamed him most severely in his capacity of general-in-chief. The command of the army passed, by right of seniority, to Major-General Reid, who, however, tendered his resignation almost immediately, for reasons of health. He was succeeded by Major-General Archdale Wilson, who had long been in the Company's service as an artillery officer, and who, from having spent most of his life in India, was well acquainted with the inhabitants and habits of the country. He had besides already distinguished himself in several affairs since the first rising at Mirut. Other changes took place about this time in the higher grades of the staff. Brigadier Chamberlain, whose brilliant exploits in the Punjab the reader has doubtless not forgotten, replaced as adjutant-general Brigadier Chester, who fell in the battle of Gazioudoudnaggarh, and Lieutenant-Colonel Baird Smith, of the Engineers, succeeded Colonel Laughton in the direction of the siege operations.

The first proceedings of the new General-in-Chief were not fortunate. On July 9, whilst the sepoys were attacking Sabzi-Mandi in mass, 150 sowars (troopers) surprised the advanced post in the rear of the Mussulman cemetery. Major Tombs, of the Artillery, always one of the foremost in battle, withstood the enemy's onset almost single-handed, and won the Victoria Cross by saving the life of a wounded comrade. This daring attempt, which merely resulted in creating a short-lived panic in the camp, showed that the enemy kept up close communications with the native troops. There could be no doubt as to the treachery of the sentinels of the picket of the 9th irregular cavalry regiment. Some native artillerymen profited by the confusion to desert. The cavalry regiment was sent back to the Punjab, and the native battery to which the deserters belonged was disarmed. The corps was almost exclusively composed of veterans of the Afghan and Punjab wars, who a few weeks before had not hesitated to fire upon the mutinous regiments at Jallandar. Profoundly humiliated in their military honour, these old soldiers gave up their guns with ready obedience, but with tears in their eyes. Their resignation and the entreaties of their officers obtained for them some mitigation of punishment, and they were allowed to retain their sabres and continue to man the siege batteries, where they showed the most exemplary fidelity. Strange contrast! The 9th irregular cavalry, which had been treated with relative indulgence, deserted almost to a man before reaching the Punjab frontier..

On July 14, at dawn, the sepoys attacked the advanced posts of Hindoo Rao House and the seraï. They were repulsed, and General Chamberlain, with two regiments, pursued the enemy into the suburbs, and having overcome all obstacles arrived within 200 feet of the ramparts, from whence a heavy fire was immediately opened. The English fell back in disorder, pursued by the sepoys, but the arrival of the 1st European Fusiliers compelled the rebels to retire behind the fortifications. This unimportant affair cost the English 200 killed and wounded, including sixteen officers. General Chamberlain was wounded in the shoulder, and though he gave fresh proof of his heroic courage during the day, he added in this affair nothing to his military reputation. It was a mistake undoubtedly on his part to have led his men, without any settled purpose in view, within range of the enemy's batteries. These constant and useless skirmishes began to excite great discontent in the camp. Even in the very presence of their officers, the men complained of the thoughtless manner in which they were exposed to danger. To carry the self-same positions every day, and abandon them afterwards, was to play a game which was calculated to try the courage of the most valiant. General Wilson possessed the rare merit of exactly appreciating the difficulties and resources of the situation. It was impossible to carry the place by surprise. A few secret agents in the midst of the many thousand natives scattered about in the British camp, sufficed to betray the secret of the most skilfully laid plans to the inhabitants of Delhi. The British army was so weak numerically, that, to get together any considerable storming force, it was necessary to leave the camp, the artillery, and the hospitals, without sufficient protection. What would become of these precious objects if, whilst street fighting was going on, the sepoys were to attack the English lines in considerable numbers? Besides these reasons, there were others no less decisive—no attack of the enemy on the right wing had yet succeeded even for a few hours, and the left, covered by the overflow of the Jumna, was henceforth unapproachable. Considerable reinforcements were expected shortly, and an abortive assault, a serious check before Delhi, would at once be followed by the insurrection of the Punjab, the fall of Holkar-Scindia, and the ruin of all the allies still faithful to England, and, even worse, might cause the temporary ruin of British rule in India. Under these circumstances, General Wilson resolved to let the siege drag on until the time when an increase of his forces should enable him to strike a decisive blow. The batteries were ordered to slacken their fire, and the officers commanding pickets were strictly forbidden to risk the safety of their men by sending them uselessly in pursuit of the enemy. Other measures showed General Wilson's profound knowledge of the nature of the struggle, and did honour to his sentiments of humanity. We have already had occasion to remark upon the implacable severity of the English towards their prisoners, and the ill-treatment which fell to the lot of the natives in the camp-followers. At the beginning of the siege, the few wise and experienced officers who had tried to make their infuriated brethren in arms understand the vast importance of the native element in the coming struggle, had been met by accusations of weakness, and almost of treachery. In the British camp, the natives were four times as numerous as the Europeans.

All supplies of the camp depended upon them, and their services were even more precious and indispensable in the hospitals. The most incomprehensible devotion was evinced by numbers of individuals akin by blood to the murderers of Mirut and Delhi. For a small salary the khansammahs (major-domo) used to cross in silence the Valley of Death, so called on account of the incessant fire it was exposed to, a basket on their arm, in which to carry to their masters, at the appointed time, the customary morning cutlet or evening roast beef. At the foreposts, the palanquin bearers (caste of the Kaharvaris) fell under the enemy's fire, close to the wounded they were carrying to the ambulance in the faithful discharge of their duty. And yet many of these brave and unfortunate adherents remained for weeks ill and dying on the bare ground, exposed to the inclemency of the weather, whilst the doctors were unable to obtain huts for them. General Wilson felt that victory, and even the prolongation of the struggle, was impossible without the assistance of the natives; and one of his first acts of authority was to forbid that they should be maltreated in any way. An order of the day to this effect, backed by severe examples, restored confidence to the threatened followers of the army, and brought back to the camp abundance of supplies. Sellers of goods, knowing that they would be protected, re-opened their shops, and the English lines suddenly assumed the appearance of a town, created as by magic, of which an ocular witness has traced the following picturesque description:—

'What a sight our camp would be, even to those who visited Sebastopol! The long lines of tents, the thatched hovels of the native servants, the rows of horses tied by the heels, the parks of artillery, the English soldier in his grey cotton coat and trowsers (he has fought as well as ever without pipe-clay); the tall, wiry Sikhs, with their long hair tied up behind their blue turbans, the olive-complexioned Afghans, with their wild air, their gay head-dresses and coloured saddle-cloths; and the little Goorkhas, their natural ugliness set off by black worsted hats and woollen coats, the truest, bravest soldiers in our pay, dreadful and hideous as death. There are scarcely any poorbeahs left in our ranks, but of native servants many a score. In the rear are the booths of the native bazars; and farther out, on the plain beyond, the thousands of bullocks, camels, and horses that carry our baggage. The officers are talking by their tents, the men are loitering through the lines of the bazars. Suddenly the alarm is sounded; every one rushes to his tent, the infantry soldier seizes his musket and slings on his pouch; the artilleryman gets his gun harnessed; the Afghan rides out to explore. In a few minutes every one is in his place; troops are moved towards the points that are attacked; they return towards evening faint and weary, leaving some of their number in the hospital-tents. The slain are sewn up in sacks to be carried to the churchyard in the morning. The chaplain of the force is always ready, or the priest, if the dead be of the Romish Church. A few words, a few shovelfuls of earth, mayhap a few tears, and all is done.'[1]

Whilst the re-establishment of order and discipline in the English camp gave promise of speedy victory, internal divisions were multiplying more and more among the mutineers. Towards the beginning of July the Delhi army was reinforced by the arrival of revolted regiments from Bareilly, Mouradabad, Schahjahanpore,—about 3,000 men in all. These regiments had recognised as their chief a certain Bakht Khan, formerly an artillery subahdar well known in the Company's service, and who rose to be one of the most important personages among the mutineers. Corpulent, obsequious, intelligent, possessing great importance in the Wahabit sect, Bakht Khan soon obtained so much of the King's confidence that he gave him, though a man close upon sixty, the chief command of the troops, much to the displeasure of Prince Mirza Mogul, who had hitherto held that post. Mirza accordingly instigated certain regiments to protest against the Royal decision, which they did so violently that Mohammed Shah, in order to calm them, was obliged to give the prince an independent command over the

[1] *History of the Siege of Delhi*, by an officer who served there.

brigades that mutinied at Mirut and Delhi. The dissensions amongst the generals spread to the ranks. The colonels, who were almost exclusively old subahdars, worn out by age and service, incapable of enduring fatigue and hardship, could not exercise much authority over their men. Only by dint of skilful concessions did they manage to maintain some show of discipline. Any project, any military operation was submitted not only to the approbation of the officers, but also to that of the men. As to the old King, his power was merely nominal, and the generals unscrupulously covered their defeats by the most bare-faced lies. For instance, guns just taken out of the arsenal were on two or three occasions paraded before the eyes of the Padishah as trophies of victory. The emptiness of the Royal treasury still further aggravated the state of affairs. In the beginning of July the soldiers were reduced to half-pay, and this necessary measure gave the finishing stroke to the little discipline that remained. To hang or shoot without further form of trial any person suspected of favouring the enemy's interest, to take merchandise by force out of the shops, to carry off the wives and daughters of peaceful citizens and pillage their dwellings, became the daily occupation of a lawless soldiery.

The scenes that were enacted in the streets were reproduced in the palace. The sepoy chiefs appeared before the King in undress uniform, whilst in their manners they displayed an entire want of respect. Such insults stirred up the blood of his illustrious ancestors in the Sultan's veins; and after having been treated with greater disrespect than usual at some durbar, he denounced in an official proclamation the affronts against his dignity and the excesses committed on his subjects, and declared his intention of retiring to Mecca.[1]

[1] Two or three regiments that are encamped in the town pillage the bazars, force the locks of houses, openly steal merchandise, and take by force the horses of the cavalry. Those who are guilty of such excesses in a town that has not been taken by assault, forget that even the odious tyrants Gengir Khan and Nadir Shah always respected the places where they met with no resistance. The soldiers overwhelmed the King's faithful servants with threats

This abdication manifesto once made public, Mohammed Shah Bahadour proposed to deliver up to the besiegers the gates of the city, if they would agree to spare his life and to continue to allow him the pension he had enjoyed up to that time—a proposal which was scornfully rejected. The ringleaders of the insurrection, who knew but too well what would befall them in case of defeat, were doing their utmost to reanimate the zeal of their partizans, who were now almost without hope. Secret agents were despatched to the Madras and Bombay armies, in order to excite the spirit of revolt in their ranks. The Delhi mosques resounded with calls to arms. Fakirs preached the holy war in every street, and emissaries, disguised under some religious garb, even went to implore assistance from the Emir of Cabul, from the Maharajah of Cashmere, and the Shah of Persia. This state of things was known down to the slightest detail to the intelligence department of the English army, which was managed with skill by Major Hodson,[1] and under him by an extremely intelligent native of Delhi, named Rajah Ali. Certain friends and relations of the latter, who occupied high positions at court, informed him daily by word of mouth or by letter of the rebels' plans of operation and of the fluctuations of public opinion. Their correspondence, a real masterpiece of Oriental calligraphy, was so perfectly managed that a thin roll of paper hid in a pen handle or in a pellet of bread contained several pages of ordinary writing. It is useless to add that these agents were richly paid, for they would have met with no mercy from the sepoys had they been discovered. As to the go-betweens, their danger

and insults. Notwithstanding the most formal orders, the Royal Tarash-Khana is full of infantry, and cavalry horses are feeding on the grass of the gardens. Hitherto these spots have been respected. Neither Nadir Shah nor Mohammed Shah, nor any other Governor-General, ever dared to cross the precincts of the palace on horseback. We vow to consecrate the rest of our life to God, to repudiate the title of sovereign, so full of cares and misery, and to prostrate ourselves in the dress of a pilgrim before the tomb of the most holy Khwaja Sahib, and to proceed from thence to Mecca.—*Proclamation of the King of Delhi.*

[1] Lieutenant Hodson, lately captain by seniority, was immediately afterwards made brevet-major.

was quite as great. If they succeeded in eluding the guard at the gates and the detached parties of mutineers scattered all round the camp, they had still to dread the brutality and dulness of comprehension of the English sentinels, who frequently mistook them for enemies. Information was constantly conveyed by word of mouth, and Rajah Ali, or oftener the head of the department, Major Hodson himself, had to disentangle the truth from the mass of exaggerations and lies with which the emissary invariably surrounded it. Fortunately, the major never failed to detect the shifts and evasions of the natives, and to comprehend the various shades of meaning they gave to words.[1] His services did not stop there. At the first alarm, he was seen in the saddle at the head of the savage-looking Afghans, who, attracted by his renown, had joined him, and whom he had been authorised to form into a free corps. At other times, he disappeared with his men for days together in search of adventures, from which he always emerged with fresh honours, thanks to his knowledge of the country and to the blind devotion of his formidable companions.

Notwithstanding all internal dissensions, the sepoys did not slacken their resistance, and few days went by without some attack being made on the besiegers. Towards the middle of August, a serious sortie had just been repulsed, when an important reinforcement, consisting of troops of the Punjab, entered the camp.[2] This column was commanded by General Nicholson, one of Sir J. Lawrence's most able and active coadjutors, who had replaced Brigadier Chamberlain as adjutant-general a few weeks previously, in consequence of the latter having received a severe wound. His military talents were soon put to the test. On August 24, information was received that a considerable force had left Delhi with eighteen guns to intercept a siege train just

[1] Major Hodson once had in his hands some verses in which Mohammed Shah bewailed the cares of royalty. Here is one extract: 'The army came and surrounded me. The happy days are over, and there is an end to all pleasure.'

[2] One European horse battery, the 52nd, and a detachment of the 61st R.A., the 2nd Punjab infantry, and a regiment of Moultan cavalry.

sent off from Ferozepore to the English camp. The sepoys were immediately pursued by 2,000 men, with sixteen guns, under General Nicholson's order. The British began to march at four o'clock in the morning, the next day crossed with great difficulty the inundated ground at the back of the canal, and found themselves, after a short halt at noon, in presence of a strong rebel corps—the brigade that mutinied at Nimach—which had taken up a position on the further side of the water at some distance from the village of Nasafgarh. The struggle was short and decisive. Before sunset, the sepoys were dislodged from all their positions, leaving thirteen guns, their tents, and ammunition in the hands of the English. The divisions amongst the mutineers were felt most disastrously for them in this combat. Whilst the Nimach brigade was resisting the British onset, that of Bareilly, commanded by Bakht Khan, remained in a prudent inactivity. The King was incensed at this conduct, and sent orders to his favourite not to re-enter the town without engaging the enemy. Apparently ashamed of what they had done, both general and soldiers promised to obey, if supplied with food and artillery. As their demand was not complied with, the whole brigade re-entered the gates with flying colours and drums beating.

Whilst General Nicholson was fighting at Nasafgarh, the besieged attempted a sortie which was vigorously repulsed, and only afforded additional proof of the intelligence maintained by the sepoys in the English camp. The length of the siege of Delhi began to make men doubt what might be the final result. The promised succour did not arrive from Europe, and letters, official or otherwise, sent to the besiegers, most of them of little weight, and, as they had to pass by way of the Punjab, old in date, were far from inspiring confidence in the future. Information was received at short intervals of the massacre at Cawnpore, the revolt in Oude, and the death of Sir J. Lawrence. The rumour of Havelock's first victories had caused men to hope for a time that the heroic veteran would be able to co-operate in the siege. But impeded by difficulties, resulting from the season of the year and by the weakness of his forces, Havelock had not even been able to march to the assistance of his countrymen who were shut up in Lucknow. The European colony at Agra, the most important town in the North-West Provinces, had been obliged to take refuge in the fort, where they were sustaining a species of siege. In a recent sortie, the little garrison had met with severe losses, and at any moment the insurgents might be reinforced by the regiments that had mutinied at Mhow, Indore, and Gwalior.

Besides political considerations, sanitary reasons of the highest importance made it desirable to push on operations vigorously. Till quite lately the establishments for receiving the sick and wounded had almost sufficed to meet the exigencies of the case, and as soon as the former cantonments were re-occupied, some three or four houses that had escaped destruction were converted into hospitals. But the sick and wounded generally preferred remaining under canvas; the medical staff was at its full complement, and was amply supplied with everything but quinine—in a word, there was little fault to be found with the sanitary department, and its efforts were crowned with success. During the first month, moreover, endemic sickness had been of a relatively mild character. But the situation soon assumed a gloomier aspect. Delhi has always been considered, and with justice, one of the unhealthiest stations in India during the autumn months, and the extent of the inundations clearly showed that the end of the rainy season would be exceptionally fatal to Europeans. Towards September, all the special diseases of India—fever, dysentery, and cholera—appeared in their most virulent form in the English camp. The hospitals were full of sick and wounded, to the number of 3,074; and the time in which the British troops would be without one able-bodied man could almost be computed with mathematical certainty. No one knew better than the Governor of the Punjab the difficulties with which the besieging force had to contend, and the importance of speedy success. The struggle before Delhi was a matter of life and death, in which one or the other of the contending parties must infallibly succumb. Sir J. Lawrence, thoroughly cognizant of the necessity of the situation, had stripped the Punjab of troops for four months past, in order to fill up the gaps in the besieging army, but his resources were drawing to an end, and the last reinforcement that could be expected from him reached General Wilson's encampment on September 6.[1] The army now numbered 11,000 men, of whom 3,307 were Europeans. The decisive moment had arrived—a final blow had to be struck. To avoid destruction Delhi must be taken, and England's brave soldiers were worthy of the task that fate had assigned to them.

[1] This column was composed of detachments from the 8th and 60th R.A., the 4th Punjab infantry, a half battalion of Beloochees, and a corps of 2,000 auxiliaries, furnished by the Maharajah of Cashmere. Sir J. Lawrence had secured the assistance of Ranjit Singh, Goulab Singh's successor, by recognising his hitherto doubtful right to the throne.

CHAPTER IV.

CAPTURE OF DELHI—INSURRECTION AT AGRA—MASSACRE AT CAWNPORE.

Preparations for an assault—Breaching batteries—The sepoys resist—First day of the assault—Anxiety felt in the evening by the British staff—Capture of Delhi—Mohammed Shah gives himself up—Death of the three princes Abou-beker, Mirza Mogul, and Mirza Kischer Sultanet—Implacable severity shown by the English—Result of these extreme repressive measures—Rewards distributed to the victorious army—Insurrection at Agra—Massacre at Cawnpore.

FROM the middle of August the greatest activity had prevailed among the artillery and engineers. Gabions, fascines, scaling ladders, platforms for guns lay on the ground ready for use. Sikhs and labourers from the neighbourhood, attracted by the high pay, formed a body of workers intended for employment in trenches. The inadequate number of artillerymen was supplemented by volunteers who, drawn from the European cavalry, went through a very summary process of drill. Colonel Baird Smith, who directed the engineering operations, chose for the point of attack that part of the town which abutted on the river, and which was comprised between the Mouri bastion and the bastion by the water-side. As the simple parapet which connected these works was not defended by artillery—an oversight which the sepoys vainly tried to remedy when too late—it was certain that as soon as the fire from the bastion was silenced, a breach could easily be made in the wall. On the night of September 7, a first battery was traced out seven hundred paces from the Mouri bastion; this operation having attracted attention in the place, two successive rounds of grape-shot were discharged on the workmen. The sepoys, however, thinking that it was merely a foraging party, ceased firing, and work went on during the night with increased activity. By daybreak, notwithstanding the zeal of the men, one gun only was mounted on its platform. The severe fire from the place could not prevent the armament of this battery, the projectiles from which soon dismantled the old wall of the Mouri bastion, and rendered it untenable. A second breaching battery was erected on the night of the 10th, under shelter of the vast buildings of the Custom-house—magazines which, by the most astounding negligence, the besieged had forgotten to destroy. When they recognised their mistake, the sepoys fired upon the workmen, killing many of them; but the work was none the less successfully carried out. The besiegers' system of attack was completed by a third battery, destined to make a breach in the wall which separates the Cashmere bastion from that on the water-side; and finally, by a battery of ten guns, thrown up in the gardens of Rodsia Bagh. The native workmen, most of them Masbi Sikhs,[1] gave proof once more, whilst serving in the trenches, of that passive courage so signally characteristic of Asiatic races. 'If a man fell in the ranks of the workers,' says an eye-witness,

[1] The Masbi Sikhs were originally Hindoos of the Sweeper caste. When Govind Singh, the warrior Gooroo of the Sikhs, resolved on destroying all caste distinctions among his followers, this hitherto despised class saw the door opened for themselves to the 'baptism of the sword;' and though perhaps never admitted to the higher ranks of the Sikh community, they held a recognised position among their co-religionists; perhaps the more so, that the body of the murdered Teg Bahadour had been brought away from Delhi by men of their caste. Of this class hundreds were to be found in all parts of the Punjab at the annexation; and although unwilling to enter into the ranks of the Bengal army, where the demon caste still held fatal rule, they were ready to avail themselves of the field for labour opened before them in the extensive public works which soon covered the Punjab, more especially on the different canals in the course of formation in the Doab. Here they were employed by hundreds when the mutiny broke out, and put a stop to all such works. Thus thrown out of employment, these men were living idle, congregated at the heads of the several Doabs, till the chance of labour should return. When the call was made upon them, they eagerly seized the opportunity, came forward for service, and were drafted off in large numbers to Delhi, where they might be seen during the weary weeks of the siege nobly braving danger and enduring privations. They dug trenches, raised batteries, and even sometimes worked the guns, and throughout did good and faithful service.—*Punjab and Delhi*, by the Rev. Cave Brown.

'his neighbours dropped their pickaxes, and silently raised the dead or wounded individual, whom they placed side by side with those already disabled. A few eyes showed signs of emotion, and the entire gang continued working without a word.' During the six days employed in constructing the batteries, the besiegers lost 327 dead and wounded. Three months' experience had taught the English soldiers how to utilise the inequalities of the soil, and they skilfully profited by the ravines, ditches, and garden walls abounding in the environs of the town, to bring reinforcements in men and ammunition to the siege batteries, and to carry off the wounded.

By September 12, all the breaching batteries were ready, and fifty guns poured shot and shell upon the doomed city. The spirit of resistance was not yet quelled in the sepoys; though the artillery of the bastions could not be used, sharpshooters, hidden in pits in front of the trenches, kept up a heavy fire upon the artillerymen. At nightfall some siege pieces were brought to the ramparts, and their fire distressed the English considerably. Sorties were attempted on different points, and the enemy's cavalry attacked the rear of the camp in order to create a diversion. As might have been foreseen, the imminence of the peril only excited further divisions amongst the chief mutineers; and during a council of war held in the palace, the old King, tearing his beard, invoked the malediction of Heaven on the generals whose ambition and discord had brought ruin upon him. All was confusion and disorder in the interior of the city. The distracted inhabitants offered high prices for means of transport of any kind—horses, camels, or ox-carts—though no one, under any pretext, was allowed to pass out of the city gates. On September 13, the whole population was summoned by beat of drum to repair, without delay, with their tools to the Cashmere Gate, in order to throw up a battery there, which would enfilade the British positions. The decisive moment had arrived, and Colonel B. Smith advised the Commander-in-Chief not to delay the assault. That same day, in the evening, four Engineer officers having ascertained, under cover of darkness, that the breaches were practicable, all necessary preparations were made for storming the town. Four columns [1] were told off for the assault. The two first were to enter by the breaches in the Cashmere and water bastions, the third by the Cashmere Gate, and the fourth, after traversing the Kissengange suburb, the scene of so many desperate combats, was to pass through the Lahore Gate. On entering the town, the troops had to follow the route which had previously been determined on. A fifth corps, forming a sort of reserve, intended to guard the camp, was almost exclusively composed of native infantry. General Nicholson, who commanded the first column, had the chief direction of the operations.

At dawn, on September 14, the fire of the siege batteries, which had been very violent during the night, suddenly ceased, and the smoke from the guns, condensed by a heavy dew, covered the ground with a thick mist, through which appeared only the summits of the bastions and of the walls. The early morning was beginning to break. The storming columns were awaiting the signal of attack, for it was expected that under cover of darkness the sepoys would have made the breaches impracticable. At length the expected signal was given in the direction of the Cashmere Gate, in the shape of a cloud of smoke followed by a loud report. This was succeeded by a sharp fire of musketry, and the English rushed towards the place at double quick time. Lieutenant Fitz-Gerald, of the 75th R.A., was the first to mount the breach in the Cashmere bastion, where he met with a glorious death. He was at once followed by his comrades, and the whole of this work, after a sharp but short struggle, fell into the power of the assailants. The success of the second column was quite as rapid and complete at the

[1] The first column comprised the 75th Royals, the 1st European Fusiliers, B.A., the 2nd Punjab infantry, and was commanded by Brigadier Nicholson. The second, the 8th Royals, the 2nd European Fusiliers, B.A., the 4th Punjab infantry, commanded by Brigadier Jones. The third column, the 52nd R.A., the Kumaon battalion, the 1st Punjab infantry, commanded by Colonel Campbell. The fourth column, the Punjab Guides, the Cashmere auxiliaries, a Goorkha regiment, and som European companies, commanded by Major Reid.

water bastion. The heroic conduct of the officers and men of the Engineer corps, who had been ordered to blow up the Cashmere Gate, so as to facilitate the entrance of the third column into the town, deserves to be related in some detail.

This detachment was composed of Lieutenants Home and Salkeld, of Sergeants Carmichael, Burgess, and Smith, of Trumpeter Hawthorne, of Havildar Madhon, and of eight native sappers. In consequence of some delay at the last moment, the full light of the sun betrayed the audacious undertaking. Lieutenant Home and four sappers, carrying sacks of powder, were the first to cross the exterior palisade and the half-destroyed drawbridge. The enemy in their surprise withdrew behind the gate. The sappers placed the sacks against it, and, jumping into the ditch, rejoined the storming party safe and sound with Lieutenant Home. The second detachment, which followed with petards and a lighted match, was less fortunate. The sepoys, recovering from their first alarm, fired almost point-blank at the valiant party through the loop-holes, and the last preparations were made under a shower of balls. Lieutenant Salkeld fell mortally wounded, just as he was about to apply the match to the powder. Sergeant Carmichael and, after him, Sergeant Burgess, met with the same fate. But the latter succeeded in his attempt, and the crackling of the flames gave warning of an approaching explosion. Hawthorne caught up the dying officer in his arms, threw himself into the trench, and, having placed his precious burden in safety, dashed across the ruins of the gate at the head of the victorious column, sounding the charge.[1]

The besiegers had entered the town, but the most dangerous part of the enterprise lay before them yet. Fighting in the streets, a thousand times more to be dreaded than on the ramparts, was about to begin, and the sepoys were well prepared for it. Not a building but was converted

[1] The author relates with all the more emotion the different phases of this episode of the siege of Delhi, in that he retains a charming recollection of the pleasant days he spent under canvas at the foot of the Himalaya, in 1855, with Lieutenants Home and Salkeld, then cadets in the military school at Kourki.

into a citadel, whether mosque, palace, or private dwelling. After the capture of the two bastions, the first and second column effected their junction conformably to the plan of attack, in order to march along the wall and meet the fourth column, which was to carry the Lahore Gate. Formidable obstacles presented themselves at once. It was necessary to pass through a street so narrow that four men could scarcely march abreast. A barricade bristling with guns defended the issue, and the flat roofs of the houses were crowded with sharp-shooters. Twice the English entered this terrible defile, and twice they were obliged to fall back before a volcano that belched forth grape-shot and bullets. Nicholson, in the hottest of the fire, encouraged his men, by voice and gesture. Almost all the officers were killed or hit, and at length, an irreparable loss to England, the heroic general himself fell mortally wounded.[1]

The English troops, decimated in this struggle, retired to the Cabul Gate, carrying off their wounded, and entrenched themselves strongly there. Meanwhile, the third column, after forcing the Cashmere Gate, marched along the Chandney Chowke, the principal thoroughfare of the city, and arrived in the neighbourhood of the grand mosque, where the sepoys were entrenched in great numbers. By the most inconceivable forgetfulness neither artillery nor powder had been provided, and the troops were obliged to renounce battering down the gates, and to retire with great loss. The fourth column, composed almost exclusively of native troops, was still more severely handled. In the neighbourhood of the

[1] Let us here sum up the services of this valiant soldier, who, wounded on September 14, survived his victory a few days only. Nicholson was born on December 22, 1822, went to India in 1839, and was attached as cadet to the 27th native infantry of the B.A. In its ranks he went through the disastrous campaign in Afghanistan, and was made a prisoner at the capture of Ghuzni; he was not set at liberty till after the Khyber Pass had been forced by General Pollock. Nicholson then took part in the two wars in the Punjab, was present at the battle of Chillianwallah and Goojerat, and distinguished himself by carrying the fort of Attock, on the Indus. In recompense for these services, he successively obtained the brevet rank of major and that of Lieutenant-Colonel. At his death he was Lieutenant-Colonel of the 27th infantry, General by local brevet, and a C.B.

suburb of Kissengange they found themselves confronted by a considerable corps of sepoys, who easily put to flight the Cashmere contingent. The Goorkhas made a more serious resistance, but, overwhelmed by numbers, and deprived of their beloved chief Major Reid, who had been disabled by a severe wound, they retired in disorder.

The danger was pressing. Intent on pursuing the English, the sepoys were on the point of penetrating into the camp and cutting off the storming parties. In vain did General Chamberlain, rising from a sick bed, his arm in a sling, attempt to rally the fugitives. The evil seemed irreparable, when Major Tombs's Horse Artillery, Brigadier Grant and the Queen's Lancers, Hodson, at the head of his Afghans, arrived simultaneously on the spot in hot haste, notwithstanding all the difficulties of the intervening broken ground. Thanks to this opportune assistance, the rear of the storming columns was out of danger; and the forward movement of the sepoys was arrested though not repulsed. The assailants scattered themselves over the ground as skirmishers, and showered bullets on the defenders of the camp. There were so many obstacles and difficulties to be contended against in the shape of ravines, rocks, ruins, and walls, that the cavalry could not act; and for several hours the troopers, with drawn sabres, stood under a shower of balls, in a position they dared not abandon without endangering the issue of the day. Towards evening, there arrived some companies of foot soldiers, who dislodged the sepoys from their hiding-places, and drove them back into the town. The serious nature of the losses met with was attested by the long procession of red ambulance palanquins from the walls of Delhi to the camp:[1]—

[1] The assault of Delhi was one of the bloodiest encounters relatively to the number of the combatants that the English were ever engaged in in India. This is proved by the following table:—

Battles	Generals in command	Forces engaged	Dead and wounded
Assaye, 1803	Sir A. Wellesley	4,500	1,540
Laswari, 1803	Lord Lake	6,500	900
Mehidpore, 1817	Sir F. Hislop	4,000	800
Ferozshahar, 1843	Lord Gough	8,500	3,287

Sixty-seven officers and 1,104 men, about a quarter of the forces engaged, were killed or wounded. Out of the seventeen Engineer officers only seven escaped unhurt. In certain regiments, the whole staff was disabled, and yet the besiegers had only attacked one quarter of the town. The sepoys were still masters of the palace, of the Selimgarh fort, and of three-quarters of Delhi as well. Their forces, vastly superior to those of the English, would allow them to make a fresh attack on the European camp through the Kissengange suburb, and not only that, but other and more formidable enemies—the thirst for pillage, the fatal love of strong liquors—had ranged themselves on the side of the mutineers. Once in possession of the European quarter, the soldiers no longer listened to the orders of their officers. Some left the ranks, enticed by the hope of booty; others, and these were the greater number, broke into the wine and liquor shops. Whole regiments dispersed, all discipline was gone. Pillagers broke in the doors of houses, forced the locks and, overcome with drink, fell asleep in the cellars among broken bottles. Others, in a state of furious excitement, ran about the streets, and the sentinels, stupefied by liquor, let themselves be massacred without resistance. An immense disaster was threatening the fortunes of Great Britain. It is said that, in view of the pressing danger, General Wilson thought for a moment of evacuating the town, but, fortunately for his honour and the salvation of his country, his hesitation only lasted an instant, and he adopted the opinion of those of his advisers who insisted on continuing the struggle at any price. The storming columns were ordered to encamp on the positions they had conquered. What remained to be accomplished was less difficult than the resistance offered on the first day might have led one to imagine. The 15th was spent in restoring order and discipline in the ranks. Such wine and spirits as still remained in the shops were emptied into the gutter; an order of the day again promised the division of the spoils of the place to the troops; and to put an end to excesses, pickets, stationed at the gates, stopped the exit of any booty. This measure did not prevent the Sikhs, who were thorough masters of the art of looting, from safely concealing all they had robbed at the first moment. By means of cords and ladders they passed their plunder to comrades posted outside the walls, and by these means jewels, shawls, silken stuffs, and even women gave evidence of the English victory to the very furthest extremities of the Punjab. On the 16th, the offensive was resumed, but the bloody experience of the first day had not been in vain, and artillery, together with sapping and mining operations, was employed as need arose. The arsenal was occupied without great loss, and the magazines were found to contain an immense quantity of ammunition and 200 pieces of cannon. On the same day, the sepoys completely evacuated the suburbs of Kissengange, whilst on the following one the English re-took the bank whose vast gardens overlooked the Chandney Chowke. The numbers of the enemy diminished visibly, and resistance was evidently drawing to an end. On the morning of the 18th, an eclipse of the sun increased the consternation already existing in the sepoys' ranks. The population passed in crowds through the gates that still remained free, and many sepoys, distinguishable by their scarlet uniform, were seen amongst the multitude hurrying over the bridge of boats across the Jumna. An honourable feeling of fidelity still kept a few thousand devoted men in the works round the palace, in order to cover the retreat of the old King and his family. On the 19th Hodson, making a reconnaissance round the walls with a handful of native troopers, reached without obstacle a camp occupied by the mutineers outside the town near the Delhi Gate. The tents were deserted; arms, ammunition and fires still burning, showed that the retreat had been recent and sudden. As a just reward of his exploits, the bold adventurer was the first to ascertain the victory to which he had so much contributed. A few hours later the palace doors were burst in. The few remaining defenders, the sick and the wounded who had sought refuge there, were pitilessly massacred. The eventful drama of the siege of Delhi was at length at an end. The British flag floated over the Selimgarh tower; the

Giaour sullied with his presence the sacred enclosure of the harem and the beautiful hall of the Divan Khas, with its white marble walls, covered with poetical inscriptions and flowers of precious stones. The pale-faced soldiers defaced with their bayonets the verses celebrating the glories of the place, 'If there be a paradise on earth, it is here, it is here.' The victory of the English was complete; the throne of the great Moguls had for ever disappeared into the abyss.

The insurrection had lost its capital, but its nominal leader had escaped the conquerors. Protected by the devotion of his faithful subjects, Mohammed Shah, with his wives and other members of his family, had succeeded in leaving the palace, and offered therefore a rallying point to the insurgent army, which had reached the plain, severely weakened by its losses, but still formidable by its numbers. Had the existing forces of the insurrection grouped themselves round a single chief, a terrible struggle might have ensued, from which the already much tried army might not have issued victorious. Fortunately, this possibility was not realised. Be it despair, want of physical strength, or love for his house, Mohammed Shah refused to fly to any distance, and took refuge in the neighbouring ruins of the Koutab column,[1] a relic of the splendour of Mahommedan palaces, which exists some seven miles from Delhi. The prince's retreat was soon known to the English intelligence depart-

[1] The Koutab is situated about seven miles from Delhi. It is a gigantic erection of red stone, that rises in the shape of a truncated cone, 300 feet high, on a base of 42 feet in diameter. It is divided into four stories of unequal height, marked out by balconies, whose entablature is sculptured with rare delicacy. Everything in this curious monument bears the stamp of grandiose art. Round about the Koutab stretch galleries, supported by columns of primitive architecture, covered with eccentric sculptures, sometimes of a very indecent character; but all carefully mutilated. These mutilations and other indications seem to point out that the Koutab was built in the 13th century by the Emperor Koutab, the first sovereign of the Afghan dynasty, to serve as minaret to a mosque built on the ruins and out of the ruins of twenty-five Hindoo temples. A winding staircase leads to the top of this singular edifice, and the panorama which from thence unrolls itself before the visitor's eyes amply rewards him for an ascent whose least drawback is fatigue. Tigers, panthers, and hyænas often take refuge in the staircase, or, at any rate, the account of their visits and exploits is never wanting in the tales of the native cicerone.

ment, and Rajah Ali caused overtures to be made to the Sultana Zinat Mahal, in order to induce the unfortunate couple to constitute themselves prisoners. After some hesitation, the fugitives consented to do so, on condition that their lives should be spared. Major Hodson, who had managed the negotiation, was commissioned by the Commander-in-Chief to be present at the fulfilment of the treaty. Accompanied by Rajah Ali and 290 troopers, this bold officer, leaving camp on the morning of September 22, passed through the ruins where the population of Delhi had sought refuge, and arrived at the tomb of the Emperor Houmayoun, in the recesses of which were concealed the Royal fugitive and his suite. It was a vast building, which might easily have been defended. A numerous escort of armed adherents still surrounded the fallen sovereign. Rajah Ali got off his horse and entered the mosque, to try and induce the prince to fulfil his engagements. He was obliged to have recourse to both entreaty and threats before he could convince his listeners, but at last he carried the day, and two palanquins appeared borne down the steps of the ruined staircase. In the first were old Mohammed Shah Bahadour and Jamna Baksch, one of his sons; in the other, the Begum Zinat Mahal. Timour's descendants placed their sabres in the hands of the English officer, and the march began. A strange and sad procession it was, worthy of the chronicles of former days. Two palanquins, surrounded by dark-visaged horsemen with bright-coloured turbans and drawn sabres—behind them a pale-faced man, with a perfectly impassible countenance, and a few steps further, an immense crowd convulsed with passion, and expressing its grief by the wild cries and frenzied gestures peculiar to Orientals. The palanquin which advanced first along the dusty road, borne by its bearers in measured tread, contained within its gilded frame the legitimate heir of the highest earthly dignities. His glorious ancestors had enjoyed and deserved the titles of 'King of kings' and 'Sun of the Universe.' The most renowned poets had sung their glory, and the most precious jewels had shone in their diadem; their palaces, the tombs where now they rest are to-day the wonders of the earth, and travellers stop before these marvels of art, filled with admiration and respect. For Mohammed Shah, a wretched captive, overwhelmed by age and misfortunes, the present, frightful as it was, paled before the anticipation of the future. What could await him but the anguish and agony of a shameful death; or, worse still, a process of slow dissolution within the damp walls of some remote citadel! Then only would fortune cease to persecute the dethroned descendant of the great Akbar! A man of foreign race, a simple cavalry major, was presiding over this species of entombment; but he represented all the living forces of modern civilisation, Christian faith, military discipline, political intelligence, science and industry. Hodson, as the instrument of destiny, was merely executing the decrees of that irresistible law of progress which condemned the decrepit monarchies of Asia to pass under the sway of free and happy England.

No attempt was made on the road to rescue the prisoners, and they were brought safely to the general-in-chief's presence. As some sort of reward, Hodson was allowed to retain the two sabres that had been given up to him; one bore the seal of Nadir Shah, the name of Jahanghir was engraved on the other.[1]

A still bolder enterprise was reserved to this daring officer, and we shall here give a verbatim extract from a letter addressed to his family by Lieutenant MacDowell, Hodson's friend and faithful companion, and a chief actor in the tragedy that ensued. One hundred sowars, Rajah Ali, an ignoble member of the Royal family in the pay of the English police, and the two friends, composed the whole of the force sent on this expedition, worthy of the Cid Campeador.

On September 23, the little column set off at eight o'clock

[1] The story goes that on the entrance of the party into the town, the officer in command of the Cashmere Gate, astounded at the success of the expedition, paid his victorious comrade the following short and flattering compliment, 'By God! Hodson, you ought to be made commander-in-chief.'

in the morning, and took the direction of the tomb of Houmayoun, where there were still three important members of the Imperial family, Abou Bekr, son and presumptive heir of the King, and his two cousins, Mirza Mogul and Mirza Kischer Sultanet, at the head of a number of armed men. At the distance of a mile Hodson stopped his troops and sent an emissary to the princes, demanding their immediate surrender. After a long parley the messenger returned to ask, in the princes' name, that their lives should be spared. 'No conditions' was the answer given, and the emissary went back. A strange noise, a tempest of human voices apparently issuing from the depths of the earth, followed his return. It was known afterwards that the soldiers and court officials, who numbered 3,000 or 4,000, had demanded with cries of rage and despair that their masters should give them the signal of resistance. The negotiation succeeded, however. Dejected by their recent reverses, and having learnt that the King's life had been spared, the princes decided to give themselves up without conditions. The emissary came to Hodson to announce their speedy arrival. Ten men were sent to meet them, and the rest of his troop was placed across the road. The three cousins soon appeared, huddled together in a 'rath' (a small country cart) drawn by oxen. The ten horsemen closed round the vehicle, whilst a few steps behind them a furious crowd followed, brandishing arms of all sorts with frenzied gestures and cries. The two English officers advanced towards the captives, whose humble greeting they received with haughtiness; and the squadron, at the command of its chief, quickly formed behind the cart and moved towards Delhi. It was an all-important moment: the crowd undulated like a wave before breaking on the prow of a ship. Hodson advanced alone on horseback towards the serried ranks, and waved them backwards with a gesture of command. Incredible as the fact may appear, this mass of human beings wavered before his determined glance, and in a few seconds the last man had disappeared into the dark recesses of the tomb of Houmayoun. We shall now allow

Lieutenant MacDowell, one of the actors in this affair, to relate the story in his own words:—'Leaving the men outside, Hodson and myself (I stuck to him throughout), with four men, rode up the steps into the arch, when he called out to them to lay down their arms. There was a murmur. He reiterated the command, and (God knows why, I never can understand it) they commenced doing so. Now you see we did not want their arms, and, under ordinary circumstances, would not have risked our lives in so rash a way; but what we wanted was to gain time to get the princes away, for we could have done nothing, had they attacked us, but cut our way back, and very little chance of doing even this successfully. Well, there we stayed for two hours collecting their arms, and, I assure you, I thought every moment they would rush upon us. I said nothing, but smoked all the time, to show I was unconcerned; but at last, when it was all done and all the arms collected, put in a cart, and started, Hodson turned to me and said, "We'll go now." Very slowly we mounted, formed up the troop, and cautiously departed, followed by the crowd. We rode along quietly. You will say, why did we not charge them? I merely say, we were one hundred men and they were fully six thousand. I am not exaggerating; the official reports will show you it is all true. As we got about a mile off, Hodson turned to me and said, "Well, man, we've got them at last," and we both gave a sigh of relief. Never in my life, under the heaviest fire, have I been in such imminent danger. Everybody says it is the most dashing and daring thing that has been done for years (not on my part, for I merely obeyed orders, but on Hodson's, who planned and carried it out). Well, I must finish my story. We came up to the princes, now about five miles from where we had taken them, and close to Delhi. The increasing crowd pressed close on the horses of the sowars, and assumed every moment a more hostile appearance. "What shall we do with them?" said Hodson to me. "I think we had better shoot them here; we shall never get them in." We had identified them by means of a nephew of the King, whom we had with us, and who turned Queen's evidence. Besides, they acknowledged themselves to be the men. Their names were Mirza Mogul, the King's nephew, and head of the whole business; Mirza Kischer Sultanet, who was also one of the principal rebels, and had made himself notorious by murdering women and children; and Abou Bekr, the nominal commander-in-chief, and heir-apparent to the throne. This was the young fiend who had stripped our women in the open street, and, cutting off little children's arms and legs, poured the blood into their mothers' mouths. This is literally the case.[1] There was no time to be lost; we halted the troop, put five troopers across the road behind and in front. Hodson ordered the princes to strip and get again into the cart; he then shot them with his own hand. So ended the career of the chiefs of the revolt, and of the greatest villains that ever shamed humanity. Before they were shot, Hodson addressed our men, explaining who they were, and why they were to suffer death. The effect was marvellous. The Mussulmans seemed struck with a wholesome idea of retribution, and the Sikhs shouted with delight, while the mass moved off slowly and silently.'

What one has just read explains the furious wrath which filled the hearts of the two young men, but it does not justify the murder in cold blood of defenceless prisoners by an officer, an English gentleman. The crimes of the princes do not excuse the impetuous soldier for having imbued his hands in blood. This should have been reserved for the executioner. The work of death was done in the open day. At a few yards from the extempore scaffold were thousands of co-religionists, friends, and followers of the culprits weeping like women or trembling like cowards. A word, a gesture, the presence among that base multitude of a single manly heart would have caused the two Europeans to disappear like a tempest-tossed ship into the depths of ocean. Those who slay with the sword shall perish by the sword.

[1] These lines show the entire conviction with which the young officer accepted the first accounts of the massacre, which accounts later investigation, on the trial of the Emperor, did not confirm.

Hodson and his friend a few months subsequently met with a glorious death on the battle-field. Taking these facts into account, impartial history will doubtless give the benefit of extenuating circumstances to the author of this triple but heroic assassination. It is indispensable to add, as a characteristic trait of Asiatic races, that the bloody execution excited the highest admiration in the Punjab. Naturally inclined to regard might as right, the Sikhs, moreover, considered the death of the three princes as a punishment decreed by Heaven for the persecution their saints had suffered from the house of Timour. A sort of religious halo seemed to crown the military career of Hodson, and young men from the noblest families in the Punjab solicited in crowds the honour of forming part of the irregular regiment to the command of which he had been appointed in recompense of his services. The success of the expedition, and the catastrophe with which it closed, aroused the admiration of his companions and chiefs. The spirit of the times was not in favour of clemency. The Anglo-Indian press made itself remarkable by the ferocity and wildness of its appeals for vengeance. It demanded the entire destruction of Delhi, or, at least, of the beautiful Jamma mosque, the suppression of caste, and the wholesale transportation of the Mohammedan population to Australia! The inhabitants of Delhi dearly expiated their adhesion to the mutiny. They had taken refuge in the neighbouring ruins, where for months they were subject to the most terrible distress, and it was not till the month of December that the Hindoos were allowed to return to their desolate homes. The Mohammedans only obtained this favour by giving proof that they had held aloof from the insurrection. As to the military prisoners, who were very numerous, they were treated with the utmost severity. Besides, sepoys taken in arms, sick and wounded, whose wounds had not once been dressed, were found almost in all the houses in Delhi. The medical service, in point of fact, had been very badly attended to from the first among the insurgents, as nearly all the native doctors attached to mutinous regiments had remained faithful to the British cause. Ill or well, the prisoners were brought before the court-martial, whose judgments, given without discussions and in the fewest words, varied merely by the nature of the death awarded to the condemned. For months together the gallows stood always ready, and the match remained lighted alongside of the cannons. More than 3,000 men were condemned and executed, amongst whom were 29 members of the Royal family.

These immense hecatombs cannot be compared to the horrors committed by the Spaniards in America nor to the atrocities of the proconsuls during the wars of the 'Vendée,' nor to any of those frightful historical crimes the thought of which still causes humanity to grow pale after the lapse of centuries. Traitors to their colours, and assassins of their officers, the mutineers deserved the severest punishment. But once the fate of arms had been decided, and the victory won by England, was it necessary that implacable justice should cause the Bengal army to disappear to the last soldier in a sea of blood? The wholesale executions, revolting from a humanitarian point of view, and opposed to the dictates of a wise policy—by reducing the Hindoos and the Mohammedans to despair—produced no other effect than that of rendering the struggle longer and more sanguinary. The capture of Delhi had irreparably ruined the chances in favour of the insurrection. Once deprived of its capital, its leader, and its military resources, an entire defeat was inevitable. Yet the hostilities might have been prolonged. The rebels had evacuated Delhi about 30,000 strong. These armed bands, unpaid, without artillery and demoralized by loss and privations, no longer presented, it is true, the cohesion of the formidable regiments that had fought in the first days of the insurrection. Still such a number of desperate soldiers constituted elements of resistance that, in the hands of a clever leader, both could and ought to have been made use of. One of the princes of the house of Timour who escaped from the massacre—Feroz-Shah—at the head of his sepoys resolved to sell his life dearly, and proved to the English, by many hazardous expeditions, sometimes crowned with success, that the interests of policy and humanity often go together, and that the smouldering ashes of revolution are not to be extinguished by blood alone.

It was several months after the fall of Delhi before the English authorities busied themselves with the fate of the ex-Emperor. Victory had not appeased his enemies, and neither his age, his birth, nor his misfortunes could protect him from the unworthy treatment we regret to have to record. A letter dated from Delhi, January 4, 1858, and inserted in the Anglo-Indian paper the 'Mofussilite,' describes in these words the captivity of the aged prisoner: 'It is not true that Mohammed Shah is treated as a king. He lives in a little room with no other furniture but a charpoy (folding bed), and is daily exposed to the insults of the soldiers and officers, though the Commissioner of the district, Mr. Saunders, makes a point of treating the dethroned monarch with the politeness of a gentleman. Rude visitors take a mean pride in forcing the old man to rise and salute them on their entrance. It is even said that recently one of them laid hold of him by the beard. And not only this, the Begum and the Royal princesses have come to share the prisoner's captivity, and find themselves exposed to the eyes of strangers, who enter the rooms of the captive whenever it suits them; such familiarity would be considered a gross insult even by a woman of the lowest caste. The soldier who furnished me with these details tells me that he has often entered the room of the ex-Emperor, even when the embroidered slippers placed at the door announced the presence of the women. At the sight of him the unfortunate Sultanas, in a state of bewilderment, turned their faces to the wall, and remained stiff and motionless as stone statues.' This useless rigour was followed by a trial. Notwithstanding the capitulation which guaranteed his life, Mohammed Shah was brought before a court-martial composed of five officers. We shall dwell in some detail on this trial, which is without precedent in history. The discussions, interesting from the rank of the accused, will show the reader the inextricable difficulties which met the English when they attempted to raise the veil still surrounding the origin and causes of the insurrection.

The heads of the accusation against the ex-Emperor can be summed up as follows: That he had taken part in the intrigues of his son Prince Mirza Mogul, and of Bakh Khan, an Anglo-Indian artillery subahdar, and other unknown ers, with the object of inducing the Bengal army to revolt and make war upon the legitimate sovereign; that he had allowed himself to be proclaimed Emperor of Hindostan, and had in that capacity taken possession of Delhi, and had within its walls resisted and sanctioned an armed resistance to the Company's troops; and finally, that he had been a consenting party to the murder of the Europeans massacred in the palace of Delhi on May 11 and 16, 1857. The discussion on the intrigues prior to the insurrection affords curious details of customs, which, while they show once again the absolute unchangeableness of Orientals, seem to be borrowed from some tale of the 'Arabian Nights.' Hassan Akari, an astrologer and magician by profession, had acquired immense influence over old Mohammed Shah, and had managed to persuade the credulous monarch that he had prolonged the King's life by the sacrifice of twenty years of his own existence. Thanks to the impostor, black magic and dreams played an important part in the councils of the court of Delhi. One night, Hassan Akari saw in a dream a terrible tempest coming from the west, followed by a still more terrible inundation; on the surface of the waters the King seemed to float in peaceful slumbers. This was enough for him to predict that the King of Persia and his army would overthrow European might in India, and restore the fallen monarchy. A few days afterwards, a eunuch was despatched to Teheran, furnished with credentials and confidential papers signed with the Emperor's seal. In one of those documents, Mohammed Shah complained of the proceedings of the English, and asked for assistance, in return for which, remembering doubtless that a similar concession had won over the Persians to the side of his ancestor Haluym, he bound himself to become a convert to the Schïyas sect. Certain witnesses affirmed that after visiting Teheran, the diplomate was to have proceeded to Constantinople and St. Petersburg, but all reliable information stopped here, and no trace of any results from the mission could be discovered.

The mystery connected with the distribution of the cakes (chippatis) was not cleared up satisfactorily. One officer deposed that his men believed the delivery of these parcels to have been encouraged by Government in order to signify to the people that, before long, there would be only one sort of food, and consequently one religious belief. 'The same food, the same faith,' is an Indian axiom, and the similarity of food is the fundamental basis of the Brahmin religion. A distinguished member of the Civil Service, Sir. C. Metcalfe, said, on the contrary, that the sending the cakes was merely an alarm signal, and had no object but to put the native community on its guard against some near and serious danger. The participation of the ex-Emperor in the intrigues formed amongst the soldiers before the mutiny was but vaguely proved. A former Court secretary, Mankand Lal, stated that Mohammed Shah was in the habit of giving his genealogy to the sepoys who came to do him homage, and of offering them a red handkerchief in token of a blessing. An order of the commissioner had soon put an end to these presents. What, however, proves the little connection between the Emperor and the army is that not a single red handkerchief was found during the siege among the effects of any one sepoy, dead or alive. The depositions incriminated more seriously the Royal family and its immediate adherents. The Court officials had been wont, at the very door of the private apartments, to expatiate on the approaching mutiny of the army, on the entry of the rebels into the palace, on the restoration of the Emperor, and on the promotions and rewards which would fall to the lot of the devoted servants of the Crown after the fortunate event. The young princes had openly announced the speedy arrival of assistance from Persia and Nepaul; finally, the King's son, Tamna Baksch, well known for his hatred of the English, who had refused to recognise him as heir-apparent, had spoken shortly before the insurrection of the approaching massacre of the European colony at Delhi, in presence of several witnesses. The accused's passive complicity in the murders committed after the entrance of the Mirut mutineers into the Imperial palace was fully established. On their arrival at Delhi, on the morning of May 12, Mohammed Shah had with him a body of 1,200 men, besides artillery, entirely at his orders and paid from his own purse. This force was not employed to protect the Europeans, as the terms of the existing treaties required. These soldiers and the Court officials took part in the murder of Mr. Fraser, the commissioner, and of Captain Douglas—two murders which followed immediately on the irruption of the hordes from Mirut into the palace. The work of death over, the sepoys presented themselves before the King to report what they had done, and to ask of him help and protection. 'I have not summoned you,' answered the old man, 'and you have acted wrongly.' The sepoys, surprised by this cold reception, replied that if the King would not give them his support, they were undone, and must agree among themselves as to their future conduct. These words overcame Mohammed Shah's resistance. He seated himself in an armchair, the sepoys defiled before him one by one, bending low as they passed, and he extended his hand over each head in sign of protection. That very day, at three o'clock, a volley of twenty-one guns announced that Mohammed Shah had re-ascended the throne of his ancestors. Almost simultaneously the principal officials and their soldiers were taking part in the siege of the arsenal. Again the King did nothing for the defence of the Europeans brought captive to the palace, though he might easily have saved them, more especially the women, by assigning them a refuge in the harem. In order to avoid the reproach of exaggeration, which was rightly made against the first accounts on the English side, we have borrowed the principal details of the massacre, given in the preceding chapter, from the formal deposition of Mrs. Aldwell, a Mahommedan married to an Englishman, whom her religion had protected from the fury of the murderers. There is no need to dwell upon this lugubrious episode of the mutiny; we will only add that a gravedigger, called upon to give his witness, stated that out of the forty-nine victims he buried, only four or five were men.

The attitude assumed by Mohammed Shah during his trial was that of an old man bowed down by age and infirmities. His only defence, which he repeated on every occasion, was that he had been a mere instrument in the hands of his family and the mutineers. His wretched health obliged the sittings to be constantly interrupted, and the trial, begun on January 27, occupied twenty-one sittings, and lasted two months. On March 29, a solemn day in the history of Asia, the very tribunal that would have been barely competent to degrade an English officer, guilty of negligence or indiscipline, pronounced a sentence of dethronement on the last descendant of the great Mogul emperors. Found guilty of the different charges made against him, Mohammed Shah was sentenced to imprisonment for life. The justice of this decree cannot be denied when we consider his passive complicity in the massacre of the Europeans and in the military events of the siege of Delhi. Misfortunes so great must, however, appease the bitterest animosity. Mohammed Shah did not evince before the court that judged him the Royal virtues so eminently exhibited by the kingly martyrs of European history; but like Charles I. and Louis XVI. he drained the cup of bitterness to the dregs, and fell from the throne to the profoundest depths of human misery. For this reason he deserves a last word, if not of praise at least of pity. Despatched from Delhi to Calcutta as soon as the roads were open, he was afterwards sent to Rangoon in Burmah, where he died in captivity, November 7, 1862.

The capture of Delhi aroused patriotic joy of the most legitimate kind in all British hearts. Promotions and the Victoria Cross rewarded the valiant remnant of the besieging army. The losses had been considerable.[1] Neither disease nor the enemy's fire had spared the Europeans and their auxiliaries, and there were few among the survivors of the siege who had not passed through the hospital. General Wilson received a baronetcy, which perpetuates the remembrance of his successful enterprise. The division of the spoils led to long and disagreeable discussions, and did not take place till some years later, in February, 1861.[2]

The labours of the victors were by no means terminated by the capture of Delhi, and as early as September 24, a body of troops was despatched to pacify the neighbouring districts, relieve Agra, and march down to Cawnpore, where the forces destined to repress the insurrection in Oude were being organised. This column, commanded by

[1] Losses of the Anglo-Indian forces during the siege of Delhi:—

	European officers	Native officers	Non-commissioned officers	Drummers	Soldiers	Total
Killed	46	14	80	7	865	
Wounded	140	49	207	10	2,389	3,837
Missing	—	—	1	—	29	

In this table, the officers who died in consequence of their wounds are included among the dead. For the rank and file only those killed on the battle-field have been counted. The actual total is therefore much higher than the one given above. Out of the general total there were 2,151 Europeans and 1,686 natives.

[2] The distribution of the booty dragged on for several years, and perhaps a few details on the subject may not prove uninteresting. The Commander-in-Chief had promised his troops that the plunder should be divided among them, and no one doubted the fulfilment of this promise, when after three months' delay, an official notification was made that no one could dispose of what belonged to the Government. This document, without settling anything as to the destination of the objects found in private houses, which formed the best part of the booty, granted six months' batta to the troops. 'Batta' is the indemnity given to troops during a campaign. The measure excited such recriminations that the Government, on second thoughts, declared the stores of the arsenal should alone be reserved, and recognised the army's right to the plunder which had not been State property before the assault. The donation of the batta was again confirmed. It was, however, only on February 9, 1861, after more than three years and a half, that the official decree appeared, authorising the shares to be given to those who were entitled to them. The whole amounted to 34 lacs—61-213 rupees. The shares were calculated according to the pay of European soldiers, that is to say, one share per diem. The native soldiers had half shares. For the first time the camp followers were allowed to take their part in the spoils.

Colonel Greathead, who had specially distinguished himself during the operations of the siege, was composed of one battery of artillery, of the 9th Lancers, of the remains of the 8th and 75th Royals, and of a squadron of Sikh cavalry, forming in all an effective force of 450 men, besides the 2nd Punjab infantry, now reduced to 120 men. After taking the fort of Malagarh, the residence of a rebel chieftain, and re-occupying the town of Aligarh, the expedition arrived, on October 12, under the walls of Agra, where it was anxiously expected by the Europeans who had sought refuge in the fort. Thanks to the presence of some hundred white soldiers, the station of Agra, the chief town of the North-West Provinces, and the residence of the Lieutenant-Governor and of the high court of justice, had escaped the dangers of the first days of the mutiny. But on July 4, at morning parade, the Kohat contingent, that formed part of the Agra garrison, fired upon its officers and quitted the station, leaving behind it two guns and a small number of artillerymen, still loyal to England, in order to join the insurgents of Nimach and Mahidpore, who were scattered over the neighbouring country.

On the following day, July 5, Brigadier Polwelhi, who was in command at Agra, marched against the enemy with about 500 men of the 3rd Bengal European Fusiliers, a battery of European artillery, and some volunteers, infantry and cavalry. The enemy occupied in force the village of Schahgange, four miles from Agra. The English battery opened fire at the distance of 600 yards on the village, which formed the key to the position, and was vigorously responded to by the battery on the other side. The combat continued till the sepoys, encouraged by the explosion of an ammunition waggon, which did much damage in the English ranks, charged their adversaries with the bayonet, and were repulsed with loss by a heavy fire from the European battalion. The British infantry advanced in its turn on the village, and success seemed assured, when a shell caused the explosion of a second ammunition waggon, and rendered another gun useless. The cartridges of the European soldiers were exhausted, and the handful of volunteers on horseback could not, with the best possible will, make any impression on forces fifty times as numerous as themselves. The signal was given to retreat on Agra. Worn out by the heat, attacked on every side, the little column withdrew to the fort through the cantonments which the enemy's cavalry had just set on fire. Astride on a gun, brave Captain D'Oiley, though mortally wounded, continued to watch over the safety of his cannon till the last moment, and died just as he reached the fort.

The handsome dwellings of the civil officials and the public establishments of the Catholic missions [1] were pillaged and burnt by the victorious sepoys, who, moreover, opened the doors of the prisons, containing 4,000 wretches of the worst description.[2] The insurgents did not, however, venture

[1] The Agra mission, a splendid Roman Catholic church, possesses several educational houses for the two sexes. The establishment for girls is directed by French sisters belonging to the order of Jesus and Maria, and is in no way inferior to the best managed convents of Europe, in point of order and general appearance. The inmates are divided into three distinct categories: first come the children of rich parents, then the orphans of soldiers of the Indian army, thirdly, children of Indian Catholics. Before coming into possession of these splendid establishments, the missionaries passed through long and painful trials, as is attested by the following account given me at the Agra episcopal palace by an amiable Capuchin father: 'One of the first founders of the mission was returning one evening to his hut, when he suddenly found himself in presence of a most formidable looking tiger. Entirely without means of defence, the valiant father at once made up his mind what to do, and brought his cowl well down over his head, and ran towards the tiger, which turned and fled as if the devil, and not a Capuchin, had been in pursuit. Another time, the same father was obliged to take refuge in a tree, in order to escape from a second tiger that refused to be frightened by the cowl. But the beast, either from hunger or the wish to taste what the flesh of a Capuchin was like, stationed itself below the tree. The poor father kept a long and anxious vigil midst the branches, till at length, inspired by his patron saint, he determined to set fire to his sack-cloth gown, and to throw it, metamorphosed into another tunic of Nessus, on the tiger. The animal instantly took to flight. The monk got home to the convent in light attire, having nothing on but his wooden shoes, but safe at last and unhurt.'

[2] See Documents, No. XXXII., 'A Visit to the Prison of Agra.'

The citadel of Agra, begun by the Emperor Akbar in 1563, and finished, it is said, in four years, is quite equal to those remains of the past which the astonished traveller encounters in the deserts of Syria and Upper Egypt. A paved passage leads through massive walls to that part of the fort which commands the town and the river. A few listless sepoys and some artillery

to attack the ramparts of the fort, and took the road to Delhi, laden with spoils. During the two succeeding months, the old-fashioned fortifications sufficed to protect the garrison and the refugees who had withdrawn into the fortress, in order to be safe from a sudden attack of the roving bands of troops on their way to the head-quarters of the insurrection. The position of the Europeans at Agra offered some appearance of danger only after the capture of Delhi, when the remnants of the rebel army overran the neighbouring country in considerable numbers. The alarm had become very great amongst the garrison, where the civil element was in the majority, so that the arrival of Colonel Greathead's column

are not sufficient to give an appearance of life to this fortress, originally built to contain an army; and it is through a wilderness of ruins that visitors arrive at the palace erected by Shah Jehan inside the ramparts. A miserable wooden door, closed by a padlock, is the only barrier which protects the entrance of this Indian Louvre, which is approached by the bath-room reserved to the monarch. Though the rooms are in a state of dilapidation, through damp and the absence of care, they reveal something of the splendour which in its palmy days surrounded the throne of the great Moguls. The floor is paved with white marble, and the walls are alternately adorned with slabs of dark enamel, covered with flowers in relief, and with porcelain of exquisite workmanship interspersed with mirrors. Blue and gold painting ornaments the ceiling, and hundreds of white marble niches open in the walls to receive lamps.

Water flows in abundance in a marble reservoir richly carved. The other apartments are equally magnificent. Everywhere is to be seen marble and the most delicate ornaments, columns encrusted with jewels, an unheard of luxury in a deserted and fairy-like palace. The terrace, reserved for audiences, is partially covered by a gilt dome, sustained by elegant columns, enamelled with mosaics of cornelians, turquoises, and emeralds, and realises the marvels of the 'Arabian Nights.' Before one lies a garden worthy of Semiramis, with fountains flowing into white marble basins, groves of rose trees, and jessamine, and in another direction a bird's-eye view of one of the finest panoramas it is possible to see. An immense and verdant valley, in the midst of which rise those majestic edifices the tomb of Akbar and the Taj, and through which wind capriciously the waters of the Jumna. Within the ramparts, close to this palace, worthy of the 'Arabian Nights,' is another royal abode of earlier date. Red stone alone has been used in this building, which possesses several gracefully proportioned halls and some fine sculpture. Finally, the citadel contains a mosque known as the Moti Musjid (Mother of Pearl Mosque), built in 1656 by Shah Jehan, entirely of white marble, and whose only ornamentation consists in marvellously carved flowers. The majestic simplicity of this temple is only surpassed by that of the Taj. At the gate of the mosque a number of gigantic tamtams and prodigious drums give a frightful idea of what court concerts must have been in those days.

was the occasion of great rejoicing. The Europeans left their asylum to meet the victors of Delhi, and the officers obtained or took permission to return these visits. In the midst of the general delight, the necessary vigilance was not observed; and suddenly a heavy artillery fire opened on the British position, and the enemy's infantry poured into the camp. The negligence of the sentinels was soon repaired. The infantry fell in, the troopers sprang to the saddle, and the artillery opened fire upon the sepoys, who, amazed at this unexpected reception, took to flight, leaving behind them twelve guns and several hundred dead and wounded. They were commanded on this occasion by Bakht Khan, a favourite general of the Emperor of Delhi during the siege. Their forces were composed of the regiments that revolted at Mhow and Indore, and of the remains of the Mirut brigade, about 6,000 men in all. After this success, General Greathead's column continued its march, and arrived in the first days of November at Cawnpore, where the British had already met with their greatest reverse. We cannot pass under silence the frightful episode of the Cawnpore massacre, and our readers must kindly return with us to the beginning of the mutiny.

Cawnpore, a most important strategical position, is situated on the extreme frontier that separates the Presidency of Bengal from the North-West Provinces and the kingdom of Oude. It forms the head-quarters of one division of the Indian army, and contains numerous military establishments which extend for five miles along the Ganges. In the early days of the conquest, the European troops had always occupied the Cawnpore cantonments in considerable numbers, but their effective force had been gradually diminished, and in the spring of 1857 there were in them only fifty-nine European artillerymen and 205 soldiers belonging to different regiments. On the other hand, the Bengal army was represented by the 1st, 53rd, and 56th infantry, by two regiments of regular cavalry, and one battery of native infantry. Cawnpore owed its importance not only to its excellent military position, but also to the large European population that had taken refuge there. Civilians, merchants, engineers, agents of the Ganges canal, and railway *employés*, proprietors of the neighbouring indigo factories, and the women and children of the 32nd R.A., which was stationed at Lucknow, numbering about 850 individuals, were all crowded into the town. General Sir H. Wheeler was in command of the division. Though he had passed most of his life in India he was not sufficiently on his guard against Asiatic deceit and treachery in his dealings with Nana Sahib, the leader of the insurrection at Cawnpore. This Mahratta prince, who at a single stroke, dealt, it is true, with a master's hand, won for himself a fatal distinction in the list of diabolical and brutish beings, in which the Roman Cæsars and the Jacobins of 1793 shine pre-eminent, was the adoptive son of Bagi Rao, the ex-Peischwah of Poumah, and lived some ten miles from Cawnpore, in a stronghold situated in the midst of his domains. At the death of the ex-Peischwah in 1851, the pension of eight lacs of rupees which he enjoyed was, with a hitherto unexampled parsimony, refused to his heir.

The right of adoption forms the fundamental basis of the Brahmin religion, and confers on an adopted child the full rights of a legitimate son. British policy had already sanctioned in many cases this characteristic trait of Indian customs, by admitting the claims of an adoptive son in cases of Royal inheritances, as, for instance, in those of Scindia at Gwalior (1844) and those of Duleep Singh in the Punjab (1845). The measure of which Nana Sahib was the victim was all the more severe that it had nothing to do with politics.[1] Dissimulating, however, his anger with true Asiatic perfidy, Nana Sahib lived on the most friendly terms with the Europeans of Cawnpore, who were frequent guests at his nautch-shows and hunting parties. Azim-ullah-Khan, one of his confidential servants, a Mahommedan of most insinuating manners and crafty mind, visited Europe during the Crimean war, and returned to his master,

[1] See Documents, No. XXXIII., 'Adoption of Nana Sahib.'

bringing back the most exaggerated notions of the difficulties in which England was involved.[1]

[1] I spent a few days at Constantinople after the check the Allies met with before Sebastopol, on the 18th of June, a check which was followed by the death of Lord Raglan and a pause in offensive operations. There I met several times an elegant-looking young man with an olive complexion, richly dressed in Oriental costume, and his hands covered with rings. He spoke English and French, and dined at *table d'hôte*. I took him for an Indian Prince returning home after an unsuccessful suit against the East India Company. He had made acquaintance with Mr. Boyne, superintendent of the gang of military workmen formed by Sir John Paxton, and the former introduced him to me one evening that we were smoking on the terrace of the hotel. I remember that the Hindoo evinced a great wish to obtain a passage to the Crimea in order to get a nearer view of the famous city, and of the great Roustams (Russians), who had beaten the united forces of the French and English. He added that he was at Malta on his way to Calcutta, when he learned the results of the assault of the 18th of June, and that the news had determined him to go at once to Constantinople, from whence he hoped to reach Balaclava. In the course of conversation the stranger spoke with evident pride of his successes in London society, and affected great familiarity with people of the highest rank; in a word, his manners inspired me with anything but sympathy. He not only bragged of his 'bonnes fortunes,' but bluntly declared that women in Europe not being imprisoned in harems, as in the East, rush like moths to a candle and perish in the flame. Some weeks later, a gentleman on horseback presented himself at my hut in the Crimea and gave me a letter from Mr. Boyne, begging me to obtain permission for the bearer, his friend Azim-ullah-Khan, to visit the trenches. The new comer was none other but my Indian prince of Constantinople. I ordered the horse to be put up in the stable, and went to the general in command in order to ask for the requisite permission. The sun was setting, and the Russian batteries had just opened fire, according to their usual custom; bullets were falling on the heights where the stranger was standing, and a shell burst close to him. I was not able to procure the pass at once, and I found on my return that Azim-ullah-Khan had retired into the cemetery, where he was attentively watching the fire of the Russians. I explained what it was necessary for him to do, regretting at the same time that an invitation to dine at the mess of the Light Infantry prevented me from being his companion. 'Oh,' he replied, 'this is an admirable post for seeing what is going on, and as it is late, I shall ask you to accompany me another day, and I shall remain here till night-fall.' He added laughingly: 'In my opinion you will never take this fortress.' I proposed that he should dine with me at the mess, and assured him he would be very welcome, but Azim answered, with a mocking smile: 'Thanks; remember I am a good Mussulman.' I observed that I had met him at the *table d'hôte* of the Missirie Hotel. 'I was only joking,' he answered, 'I am not mad enough to believe such nonsense —I have no religion.'

That evening when I came home the stranger was asleep in my bed, and my servant declared that he had drawn largely on my provisions and my liquors. Next morning he departed without taking leave. A piece of paper was left on my table with the following lines in pencil: 'Azim-ullah-Khan

The Nana was acquainted with the feeling of disaffection current in the native army, and was prepared for a speedy outbreak in that quarter. In the early months of 1857 he successively visited Delhi and Lucknow, and this fact authorises us to believe that he was unwilling to forego the chances offered to his ambition and vindictiveness by the discontent rife in the Bengal army.[1] Beyond this no proof exists of any plotting on his part, and it was only at the last moment that the understanding between him and the mutineers came to light. According to the usual custom of Indian princes, Nana kept up a species of military state, having about 500 men and a battery of artillery in his service.

The news of the mutiny at Delhi and Mirut arrived at Cawnpore on May 14, and during the following days the ill-feeling existing among the native regiments assumed a yet more serious character. A fire, evidently the work of an incendiary, broke out in the lines of the 1st regiment. The sepoys complained in private that they would shortly be called upon to use new-fangled cartridges, and openly announced their intention of resisting by force any act that might outrage the prejudices of their caste or religion. The hostile spirit of the native troops was so apparent, that in order to avoid even the shadow of provocation, the usual Royal salute was not fired on May 24, Queen Victoria's birthday. At this serious conjuncture, Sir H. Wheeler took the fatal course of accepting Nana Sahib's good offices. Hitherto, the prince had testified the warmest sympathy for England in every word and act. He offered to take charge of the public money, and on May 26 his soldiers replaced the detachment stationed at the Treasury. On the same day the passage of an irregular regiment of the Oude army through Cawnpore increased the already existing excitement among the native troops, and the authorities ordered their dangerous guests to continue their march at once. Subsequent events justified the opportuneness of this measure.

presents his compliments to Russell, Esq., and thanks him for all his kindness, for which he is very grateful.'—W. H. Russell, *My Diary in India*, 1858-59.

[1] See Documents, No. XXXIV., 'Visit of Nana Sahib to Lucknow.'

At a short distance from the town these troops mutinied, and massacred their European officers. No misconception could exist any longer. Every day, every hour increased the danger; Sir H. Wheeler ordered all Europeans to meet in the buildings hitherto occupied by the women and children of the 32nd. The citadel in which the British were seeking an asylum was but a miserable refuge. It was composed of two one-storied buildings, covered with thatch and tiles, surrounded by verandahs and brick walls of no great strength, intended to lodge a company of a hundred men each. At some distance there was a well and the necessary offices for cooking and washing. Trees, and magazines, in course of construction, commanded the defences, which had never been more than traced out. The scarcity of labour, the hardness of the soil calcined by the heat did not even allow of completing a trench of insufficient depth round the buildings. The position was defective in every respect, but as Sir H. Wheeler could expect no help either from Oude or the North-West Provinces, he was obliged to concentrate his forces at the extreme point of the station, the nearest to the road to Calcutta, through Allahabad, and the only one by which a relieving force could arrive. The work of provisioning the camp was not more advanced than that of raising the hastily extemporised fortifications. Only a few cartloads of provisions and ammunition had been brought in, and, as a final error, the arsenal, with its well filled stores, was confided to Nana's care. The infatuation of the English authorities was promptly dispelled. As soon as he got possession of the arsenal, Nana threw off the mask, and his emissaries openly preached sedition in the sepoy lines. On June 6, at two o'clock in the morning, the two cavalry regiments and the 1st infantry deserted their cantonments with arms and baggage, though without attacking their officers. The mutineers, after pillaging and burning the European bungalows, and throwing open the doors of the prison, encamped at Kuliempore, on the Delhi road, where they were joined in the evening by the remaining native troops in garrison at Cawnpore. Their departure was fatal to Nana's plan; for, if reduced to his own forces, he would not have dared to undertake anything against the English. He went himself in the night to the sepoy camp, and by entreaties, promises, and large gifts of money, induced the insurgents to alter their plans and return to Cawnpore. The sepoys retraced their steps, and under Nana's influence took part in one of the most atrocious crimes that has ever dishonoured humanity. On June 7, at ten o'clock in the morning, a battery opened fire on the entrenchments where the unfortunate British colony had sought refuge. The defences were most imperfect, as we have said; the number of men in condition to bear arms was scarcely equal to that of Leonidas and his Spartans at Thermopylæ; and yet these soldiers, besides their own lives, had to defend more than 300 women and children. The little garrison did wonders to defend their precious charge. Incessant sorties were made, in which the guns of the besiegers were captured and spiked; but what availed successes such as these, in presence of the overwhelming numbers of the rebel regiments, augmented by all the bandits of the neighbourhood and the scum of Cawnpore, whose assistance had been purchased by the Nana's gold!

As soon as the besieged re-entered their lines, the batteries were re-established and re-opened fire. The enemy's sharpshooters poured a heavy fire from the neighbouring houses and from the tops of trees into the very heart of the place. Could any position be more terrible than that of these doomed victims, exposed to a storm of grape-shot and shells? Round about them were the Nana's batteries, and over their heads was the merciless sun of India, whose rays strike only to kill. The two small barracks, shattered and riddled by shot, no longer offered even the slight protection of a roof to the numerous refugees, and it was necessary to extemporise defences behind barrels, sacks filled with earth, stones, and such walls as still remained standing. It was impossible to procure a single drop of water during the day without risking certain death; for the well, which was placed in the midst of the entrenchments, was the special mark for the enemy's bullets. From the beginning of the siege, it was necessary to serve out the ammunition with a sparing hand, and yet it was rapidly exhausted. There were neither hospitals nor ambulances for the sick and wounded, and soon fever, cholera, and all the plagues of India claimed their part in the grand banquet of death. Hope, immortal hope, had deserted all hearts! for three weeks they had received no news from the outer world. 'This is worse than the siege of Jerusalem,' says an inscription found afterwards on a ruined wall.

In these awful circumstances, General Wheeler, hard pressed by necessity and yielding, it is said, against his will to the advice of his staff, committed the irreparable error of placing faith once more in the Nana's word, and consented to sign a capitulation which in very ambiguous terms guaranteed the lives of the Europeans.[1] On the morning of June 27 the little garrison, to the number of 500 men, women, and children, was placed on board the boats which were to convey them to Allahabad. Scarcely had they embarked, than at a signal given by Tantia Topee, one of the Nana's confidants, the boatmen set fire to the barges, whilst guns concealed beyond some rising ground opened fire upon the wretched fugitives. Only two boats managed to gain the middle of the river—one of them was speedily damaged by the balls. A few of its passengers were fortunate enough to reach the other frail vessel, which proceeded down the river under a shower of bullets and grape-shot. Their agony was uselessly prolonged, for fate reserved yet more implacable enemies to the thirty miserable beings on board. The boat stranded six miles from the starting point. She got off at nightfall; eight miles further on, near the village of Muzapgarph, she again grounded, and the sepoys, who were following along the banks, as tigers might follow their prey, attempted to board her. Their attack was repulsed, and a violent storm which happened in the night disengaged

[1] The principal clause of the capitulation was: 'All soldiers and others unconnected with the administration of Lord Dalhousie, who will lay down their arms and give themselves up, shall be spared and sent to Allahabad.'

the boat from the sand-bank, and she again proceeded on her way. At daybreak the fugitives ran aground for the third time. They were now at Souraypore, thirty miles from Cawnpore; a large body of men, sent in pursuit, were awaiting their opportunity on the river side. Fourteen English disembarked and drove back the enemy; but, carried away by success, they went too far inland, and on their return the boat had disappeared. The waters, more clement than the sepoys, had swallowed up her human freight.

The Nana's soldiers had, however, not abandoned their prey, and the fourteen Europeans, to escape them, took refuge in a little temple close at hand.[1] One was killed before crossing the enclosure. The enemy, some hundred in number, not daring to assault the building, which was quite unfitted for defence, brought up artillery, and the shells producing no effect on the massive walls, piles of wood were placed against them and set on fire. The supreme moment had come. To avoid suffocation, the English rushed headlong upon their assailants; six were killed in the sortie, and the seven others threw themselves into the Ganges. Of these seven survivors three were shot in the water. The four others, of whom three were wounded, to wit Lieutenants Thompson, Mowbray,[2] and Delafosse, and Privates Murphy and Sullivan, of the 32nd Royals, managed to swim to a station occupied by the troops of Maharajah Dey Bezah Singh, Rajah of Raischwarah, in Oude, who received them with humanity. The Maharajah approved the conduct of his soldiers, kept the Europeans for a month under his protection, and at the end of July gave them the means of rejoining Havelock's corps. The second boat that got out into the stream was soon stopped, as we have said. The Nana's agents brought back the unfortunate passengers to their former cantonments after three days of suffering, and all the men were at once massacred. The women and children

[1] The Indian temples are without windows or lateral openings, and there is no means of firing on the assailants.

[2] Now Lieutenant-Colonel, found himself, by a singular chance, at Gwalior when the pretended Nana was taken prisoner.

were added to the number of prisoners already in the Nana's hands. This number comprised the women and children of the Cawnpore garrison, who had escaped being murdered on June 27, and some women and children from the station of Fatteyzarh on the Ganges, who, having embarked in order to fly from the mutineers, had run aground at Cawnpore. All the men with them had been killed on the spot. The miserable creatures, confined in a country house known as Bibi-Garh, were about two hundred in all. We must now retrace the most horrible scene of this most horrible drama.

CHAPTER V.

CALCUTTA—HAVELOCK'S FIRST CAMPAIGN.

Illusions of the supreme authorities of India—Misunderstandings at Calcutta between the Government and the European population—First military measures—March and operations of the first reinforcements sent from Calcutta—Benares—Mutiny of the 6th B.A. at Allahabad—Allahabad is re-occupied by the English—Excessive severity shown in repressing the revolt—Difficulties encountered by the Commissariat department—The Nana is proclaimed Peischwah—Havelock marches on Cawnpore—Massacre of the women and children at Cawnpore—Punishment of their murderers—Havelock's first campaign in the kingdom of Oude—The situation on the arrival of Sir Colin Campbell—Koër Singh—Lord Canning—The Madras and Bombay armies—Major-General Sir James Outram—Warlike spirit shown by the English.

THE telegraphic despatches announcing the mutiny at Mirut and the taking of Delhi by the sepoys fell like a thunderbolt on the population of Calcutta,[1] the City of Palaces.[2]

[1] The first despatch received at Calcutta announcing the outbreak at Mirut was from the Governor of the North-West Provinces, in these words:—'Agra, May 11, 1857,—Last night a lady received from her niece, a sister of the postmaster at Mirut, the following telegram:—"The cavalry have mutinied. Have burnt their tents and some of the officers' houses. Have killed or wounded all the officers and Europeans in the lines. If my aunt intends to leave to-morrow, she will have to put off her departure, as the mail will not leave." No further message has been sent, and communication is interrupted, why I know not. Whatever news reaches me shall be forwarded at once.'—*Parliamentary Documents.*

[2] The City of Palaces. This ambitious name is fully justified by the appearance of certain quarters of Calcutta, and there are few towns that possess so fine an approach as the capital of Bengal can boast of when entered by the Bridge of Alipore. Before one lies a vast expanse of verdure, four or five times the size of the Champ de Mars, in the midst of which rise the ramparts of Fort William; to the right stretches the line of palaces bordering the Chowringhi Road; to the left winds the Ganges, covered with vessels; and as background, one has the Governor-General's palace, of which the architecture is incorrect, but the general effect grand, by reason of its enormous mass. Some statues raised by public gratitude to the great men of

On the previous evening, Calcutta offered the strange and marvellous spectacle of the civilisation of the nineteenth century, side by side with the barbarism of the primitive ages. The usual procession of well-mounted horsemen, elegant women, and fine equipages had appeared at the evening promenade. The regimental band had played as usual in the Auckland Gardens, and the breeze had carried the melodies of Meyerbeer and Rossini to the copper-coloured crowd, performing their ablutions on the banks of the Hooghly. On their return home at night, the merchant princes of the city had sought their rest as usual under the cooling influence of the punkah after an excellent dinner and a pleasant rubber of whist. The following day was a terrible one. Scarcely had the fatal writing on the wall been deciphered than dismay became universal. The Europeans, who had retired to rest the preceding evening in the most complete security, awoke to find themselves exposed to the most formidable dangers, complicated by a military insurrection and a war of races. Though relatively better informed, the Government did not fully appreciate the violence of the storm which was breaking.[1] At the beginning they affected to doubt the gravity of the crisis, and to consider the events at Mirut and Delhi as local disturbances, which the European regiments would easily put down. The illusions of the Governor-General and his council are amply shown by the nature of the last telegram despatched to the Commander-in-Chief: 'Make short work of Delhi.' Could it have been otherwise? We have already had occasion to notice the blind

India give proof, it is true, of no very high standard of taste, but notwithstanding this, the first aspect of Calcutta is really splendid. But no one, however, should venture even a few steps beyond the well-to-do quarters if he does not wish to come across as wretched hovels as any to be found amongst the miserable dwellings of Timbuctoo. On the one hand is civilisation, on the other barbarism. Here the nineteenth century is represented by a handsome equipage, in which sits a young Englishwoman dressed in the latest Paris fashion. There a half-naked Hindoo drives a primitive cart, belonging rather to the time of King Porus of the conquests of Bacchus, or to those far-distant ages when the god Brahma dwelt upon earth.

[1] See Documents, No. XXXV., 'Letters of Sir Henry Lawrence and Lord Canning.'

confidence felt, with few exceptions, by the sepoy officers in the loyalty of their men. The Secretary for War, who could only obtain his information through the official reports of those in command, necessarily shared the error into which even the most experienced officers had fallen. Besides this, most of the high Anglo-Indian functionaries had risen to the posts they occupied by serving only in the great centres of administration, and, therefore, were not intimately acquainted with the country they were called upon to govern. Their sojourn in a large capital had caused them to forget the instincts, prejudices, and wants of the Asiatic, so diametrically opposed to those of the European. They were surrounded by all the resources and luxuries of modern civilisation, such as scientific institutions, rapid and easy communication between every part of the globe, and journals of the highest class. The Hooghly, covered with the newest specimens of naval architecture, flowed at their doors; and on its banks an amount of traffic, worthy of one of the greatest marts of the commercial world, followed its ceaseless course day and night. In presence of these wonders, the governing body forgot the sand on which the foundations rested.

For years the policy of the India Council had been guided by a spirit of innovation, and a desire for experimentalising. Whether yielding to the incitations of the press, or to the imperious necessity of supplying material wants—whether from a noble desire to propagate civilisation, or to shake off the selfish lethargy which had marked the first sixty years of the Company's rule, the Anglo-Indian officials had launched out perhaps too blindly on the stream of progress. Railroads were constructed even in the most remote parts of the empire, whose soil was speedily covered with a network of telegraph wires. Fertility was restored to the North-West Provinces by means of a vast system of canalisation continuing that of the great Moguls. Model penitentiary establishments were set on foot in order to improve the moral condition of the prisoners. The unlimited liberty of the press gave the native papers the opportunity of exciting hatred and suspicion against their foreign rulers. The education of the indigenous population was the object of incessant experiments and generous sacrifices. Moreover, the religious and caste prejudices of the Hindoos had received a serious blow by the prohibition of infanticide and suttee, and by innovations in the internal discipline of prisons.[1] Quite recently the promulgation of the law authorising the remarriage of native widows had provoked protestations of the most seditious and violent character.[2]

In a word, the attempt had been made to introduce the magnificent conquests of mind over matter, which constitute modern civilisation, in the midst of a race stationary for centuries, and congealed, so to speak, in its antique prejudices and habits. Noble though the undertaking was, before attempting it the Government ought to have foreseen that by outrunning the instincts and needs of the population, a catastrophe might one day result from so many discordant elements, and ought, in short, to have anticipated the possibility of disastrous consequences. Not only had no extra precautions been taken, but the number of the European forces, the only ones to be relied on, was less than before the vast increase of territory, acquired in the east and west, during the preceding ten years.

In addition, all the European regiments had been massed in the Punjab under the false impression that any danger from a military point of view could only come from the north, and in the shape of Russian aggression. Scarcely a few hundred European soldiers were to be found in Bengal and in the greater part of the North-West Provinces. It has already been said that the Anglo-Indian authorities were not alone responsible for this state of things, and that the Court of Directors, influenced by the meanest considerations of economy, had refused to increase the European forces, even after the annexation of the Punjab and of Oude. The same short-sighted policy had defeated all projects of adding to

[1] See Documents, No. XXXVI., 'Difficulty in reforming the Discipline of Prisons.'

[2] See Documents, No. XXXVII., 'Extracts of petitions against the Marriage of the Widows.'

the internal defences of the country by the construction of fortresses. Between Calcutta and Agra—a distance of more than 900 miles—the only fortified point that could afford protection in case of a successful insurrection was the citadel of Allahabad. The native army was entrusted with the care of the treasuries, the arsenals, and the prisons, so that the sepoy mutiny shook the British power in India to its very foundation.

In the midst of this crisis of life and death, internal dissensions divided the European colony in Calcutta. These unseasonable disputes can be explained in a few words. Until the renewal of the East India Company's charter in 1832, Europeans had possessed no recognised legal existence outside the capitals of the three presidencies. As aliens they could neither hold nor acquire landed property, and few men of any standing cared to establish themselves in a country where they were not protected by law. The few adventurers who sought their fortune in India mostly deserved the suspicions and distrust they inspired. The European element was considerably increased and modified by the changes made by Parliament in the constitution of India, and by the establishment of steam communication with Europe. A stream of emigration set in towards the British possessions in Asia, and the European colonies of Calcutta and Bombay acquired immense importance by the progressive development of their riches and the honourable character of their members. Unfortunately, the mutual dislike between civilians and other Europeans continued to exist. Official arrogance and haughtiness on one side, excessive sensitiveness and petty jealousies on the other, perpetuated the work of disunion, and divided the representatives of the Anglo-Saxon race in the peninsula of the Ganges into two hostile camps, even in time of peace. The Government committed the mistake of allowing itself to be influenced by tradition and prejudice, when all Europeans ought to have been united in presence of a common danger. Restrictive measures applied to the press and to all who were in possession of arms—measures which made no distinction between

Europeans and natives—excited great discontent in the Anglo-Saxon population, and were violently denounced by the London papers. Soon other causes of discord appeared. The revolts and massacres which were constantly occurring in the various stations placed half the inhabitants of Calcutta in mourning, and filled them with intense alarm for themselves and their families. The military authorities, influenced by the blind confidence of most of the sepoy officers, hesitated whether or not to disarm the native forces at Calcutta and Barrackpore. Their indecision greatly increased the general discouragement, and several regular panics ensued. On June 18, for instance, a vague report having been spread that the native regiments had mutinied at Barrackpore, and were marching on Calcutta, a great number of European inhabitants took refuge on board the ships anchored in the river. Notwithstanding its apparent inaction, the Government had taken measures as early as the middle of May to bring together in Calcutta troops on which it could rely. On the first news of the insurrection at Mirut,[1] the Governor-General addressed a proclamation to the native army, and in order to increase its effect steamers were despatched to Madras, Burmah, Ceylon, and the Mauritius, with orders to take on board the European regiments in garrison in those several places. A providential chance supplied England with assistance as unexpected as opportune. Within the few preceding months the English and French Governments had combined a more or less justifiable expedition against China. The troops sent out from England round the Cape of Good Hope, in the propitious season of the year, arrived at Singapore just at the outbreak of the mutiny; and Lord Elgin,[2] who had the direction of the expedition, appreciating at its full importance the danger threatening India, took upon himself the responsibility of altering the destination of his forces. The

[1] See Documents, No. XXXVIII., 'Proclamation of the Governor-General to the Bengal Army.'

[2] See Documents, No. XXXIX., 'Letter of Lord Canning to Lord Elgin, Commissioner-General of the China Expedition.'

ships carrying the 90th and 78th Highlanders appeared off Singapore in the month of May, and were at once despatched to Calcutta, where they arrived in time to turn the scale in favour of the English. Thanks to these reinforcements, the sepoy regiments were disarmed, and any chance of serious troubles in Calcutta or in the neighbouring districts was averted.

Help from England took longer to arrive. A portion of the strong garrisons of Corfu, Malta, and Gibraltar might easily have been embarked on board the Mediterranean fleet and landed in a few days on Egyptian soil. In less than two months, as the news of the mutiny at Mirut arrived in England towards the middle of June, steamers sent from Calcutta or Bombay—where they abounded—to Suez might have landed the Queen's regiments on any point whatsoever of the Indian coast in the early part of September. Nowadays the opening of the Canal would allow England, with the help of her merchant fleet alone, to send all the forces of the United Kingdom to the Indus or the Hooghly. In the days of the mutiny, M. de Lesseps's great work was scarcely begun. The British Government hesitated to create a precedent which would infringe the neutrality of Egypt, and all reinforcements were sent to India *viâ* the Cape of Good Hope, so that whether from want of initiative or from the necessity of making concessions to European policy, the first regiments despatched from England disembarked in India in December, only in time to take part in the winter campaign. The first reinforcements that arrived from any Asiatic colony were composed of some companies of the 2nd European Madras Fusiliers under the order of Colonel Neil, an energetic officer who had taken part in the Crimean War, and had commanded the Anglo-Turkish Contingent under Sir R. Vivian. Before leaving Calcutta, Colonel Neil had occasion to give proof of the iron will he was to display later on in the field. At the proper hour for the train to leave, the detachment was not complete, owing to some delay or other, and as the station-master persisted in giving the signal to start, Neil ordered four soldiers to take possession of the engine. This argument was irresistible, and the train only moved out of the station when all the soldiers had taken their places in the carriages. The progress of the small column was so rapid, by means of transport improvised on the spot, that it arrived at Benares in the early days of June. The state of the Holy City inspired the greatest anxiety. This Jerusalem of the Brahmins, built on the point of Sivàs Trident, in contradistinction to all other parts of the globe that rest on one of the ten thousand heads of the Serpent Anarita, is, owing to this fact, safe, as everyone knows, from earthquakes.[1] Moreover, a pilgrimage within its walls ensures plenary indulgence to the faithful, and whoever is fortunate enough to expire there escapes the numerous transmigrations which abound in the Hindoo creeds, and is at once absorbed into the bosom of the deity. This belief explains the immense number of pilgrims who yearly come to seek salvation in the Holy City. Besides the fermentation of spirit natural to a population over-excited by devotion, the station of Benares contained other elements of

[1] The panorama of the Holy City offers a most animated and fantastic sight, more especially at sunrise, to the eyes of a stranger. The grand staircases are covered with bathers, who ascend and descend like the tide on the sea-shore. Sacred bulls, marked with their special sign, move slowly and majestically through the serried ranks. Stern-visaged officials, in red turbans and girt with sabres, sit on the benches below the ghaut, and demand from the poorest the tribute of a few annas. A multitude of men, women, and children bathe in the river, whilst thousands of small brass pots, deposited by them on the lower steps of the ghaut, reflect the first rays of the sun. Though very few venture into the middle of the river, accidents, not however to be ascribed to chance or imprudence, occur frequently. Wretches, skilful in the art of diving, are said to seize and drag down women and children in order to steal their ear-rings and bracelets; and one of them is believed to have exercised with impunity his abominable trade for several years, using as a disguise the head of a crocodile. Often, too, fanatics seek voluntary death in the sacred waters, and commit suicide by tying large earthen jars to their necks. Equipped in this fashion they throw themselves into the current, and soon find the death they seek. The scene we have attempted to describe, worthy to be reproduced by the brush of a painter, who might wish to represent India from its most picturesque side, is to be witnessed as far as the walls of Aureng-Zeb's mosque. From the minarets of the temple the Holy City presents quite a different aspect. The houses of the town, with their flat roofs, occupy a vast space, but the courtyards and streets are so narrow, that this immense mass of masonry, inhabited by more than a million of men, looks like a vast solitude, enlivened only by flocks of pigeons and parrots.

disturbance. The garrison was composed of the 37th infantry of the Bengal army, of a half regiment of Sikhs, of a corps of irregular cavalry, and a half battery of European artillery.

The sepoys had for some time been giving proof of bad feeling when Colonel Neil appeared before the Holy City with 250 men of the 10th Royals. The presence of this little force, and the representations of its energetic leader, determined the authorities to disarm the native contingent. Unfortunately, this measure was carried out without any settled plan and with the greatest precipitation. A parade was ordered on the exercise ground near the huts of the 37th. This regiment arrived on the ground simultaneously with the detachment of the 10th Royals and the European semi-battery. On being ordered to lay down their arms, the sepoys offered resistance, and were driven back into their lines hotly pursued by the infantry. At this moment the irregular cavalry and the Sikhs made their appearance, whilst the guns were still smoking. The irregulars passed over to the enemy. The Sikhs hesitated for a second or two, then seized with panic, and imagining they were being led to certain death, broke out into unearthly shouts, and began firing in the direction of the European artillerymen. The guns answered this attack immediately. Three times did the Sikhs charge the half battery, and three times were they repulsed by the storm of grape-shot that decimated their ranks. The struggle ended almost as soon as it began. Sepoys, irregulars, and Sikhs dispersed in hot haste over the neighbouring country.

This lamentable occurrence, which might easily have been prevented by the exercise of a little tact, had no serious consequences beyond the parade ground, though a Sikh company was on guard at the public treasury. Great anger was, however, excited amongst the men stationed there on hearing of the events of the day, but they were calmed down by the explanations and exhortations of Sirdar Sourat Singh. This Sikh chief, who had been actively concerned in the second Punjab war, had been put into confinement on the conclusion of peace, and was living at Benares under the surveillance of the English authorities. In gratitude for the way in which he had been treated, Sourat Singh sided resolutely with the English, and managed to extricate the public money from the hands of his compatriots. A strange fact, no less strange in its way than the action of Sourat Singh, was that the diamonds of the Ranee of Lahore, the mother of Duleep Singh, were, together with much silver money, in the treasury.

This attempt at mutiny produced no commotion even in the town itself, and a Mahommedan demonstration, in which the green flag was hoisted, passed away without serious consequences. Matters were far otherwise in the country round about, where the fugitive sepoys stirred up the population and occasioned disturbances, which were repressed by the English with the utmost severity. Perhaps nowhere in the whole course of the insurrection was so much blood shed so recklessly.

As there was no further fear of a rising in Benares or the environs, Colonel Neil continued his route towards Allahabad, where his orders, as well as the serious nature of events, urgently required his presence. Allahabad is situated some eighty miles from Benares, and occupies one of the most important strategical positions in India. Placed at the confluence of the Jumna and the Ganges, it commands all the great lines of communication by land or by water between Bengal and Northern India. Its importance had been recently increased by the annexation of Oude. The citadel, built some centuries back, was nevertheless provided with all modern appliances for defence, and contained an arsenal well stored with war materials. The garrison comprised sixty Europeans, invalids drawn in haste from the establishment at Chounar, the 6th B.I., some companies of the Sikh Loudianah regiment, and a squadron of irregular cavalry from Oude. The native troops occupied cantonments about three miles from the fort, which was held by a mixed detachment of two infantry companies. The 6th B.I. gave proof of more duplicity, and had recourse to more shifts and evasions than any other native corps, and one can well understand how it happened that its officers, without being specially infatuated, retained confidence in their men to the very last moment.

In the early days of June, the whole regiment petitioned the authorities to be sent against the Delhi rebels. Their request was transmitted by telegraph to the Governor-General, who lost no time in showing his appreciation of their fidelity. At evening parade on June 6, Colonel Simpson read an order of the day of thanks and congratulations, amidst the cheers of his soldiers, and the troops returned peacefully to barracks. On meeting at mess that night, the officers might be excused for thinking that the storm had passed off completely, or at least would not burst for a long time. Vain delusion! Scarcely had they left the table when the alarm was sounded in the cantonments. The whole of the 6th had taken up arms, on hearing of the events at Benares. The officers strove to restore order in vain; five were killed, and eight young ensigns, mere lads, who had only just landed in India, were pitilessly massacred by a party of mutineers, who met them as they were leaving the mess room.[1] Colonel Simpson escaped by a miracle; and his horse, though mortally wounded, had sufficient strength to carry him to the postern gate of the fort. The position was most critical, and it was an open question whether the Sikhs in the citadel would not make common cause with the 6th, in which case all was lost. Fortunately for England, Lieutenant Brazier, who was in command, and who, by a very rare exception, had risen from the ranks during the last Punjab war, had acquired over his men that wonderful, nay almost inexplicable influence, which Europeans sometimes exercise over Asiatics, and the Sikhs remained faithful to their salt. Their attitude, and the presence of a few guns, served by the sixty invalids, overawed the mutineers, who laid down their arms without resistance. England was thus spared an immense disaster, though the results of the disturbances in the cantonments were serious. That very night the natives rose simultaneously in

[1] The only one of these unfortunate youths who escaped (by hiding in a ravine) died some days after in consequence of his wounds.

the town and the neighbourhood, in such a way as to arouse suspicion that the plot had been carefully planned beforehand. The prison doors were broken open. The criminals confined in them, with irons still on their legs, joined the bands of pillagers. Under cover of darkness the European dwellings, the magazines, and the docks of the steamboat companies were completely sacked and burnt. For a short space the public money escaped, for the sepoys on guard resolved, in a moment of generosity, to offer it untouched to the King of Delhi. Other counsels prevailed, however, next morning, and when it was put to the vote, the 6th decided to divide the 300,000*l.* amongst themselves. Each soldier received three or four bags of 100*l.* in silver, and the regiment at once dispersed. By common consent the men returned home to place their share of the booty in safety, but few of them reached their destination. The spirit of rapine was abroad, and many sepoys who had bragged of their good fortune were murdered by peasants and robbers. Next day there was an attempt to restore order, and a Mussulman, celebrated for his fanaticism, strove to organise a sort of provisional government in the name of the Emperor of Delhi, which, however, only lasted a few days.

As we have said, Colonel Neil had been sent to Allahabad with a European detachment. This first reinforcement, conveyed in ox-carts by forced marches, arrived on June 7. The bridge of boats was in possession of the rebels. There was some delay in procuring a steamboat, and the troops entered the fort on June 9 only. Colonel Neil followed the next day. Before departing he had received a telegram from the Governor-General, conferring on him the chief command at Allahabad, in token of satisfaction at the energy he had displayed in disarming the rebels at Benares. This new mission offered many difficulties, for though the good ship had escaped the abyss she was floating helplessly amongst the rocks. The absence of will and decision amongst those in authority paralysed all attempt at action, and threatened to be the cause of disaster. Colonel Neil's arrival inspired[1]

[1] The sentinel on guard at the gate of the fort, on recognising Colonel

courage in all hearts, and matters at once assumed a new aspect. The mutineers were driven from a village near at hand at the point of the bayonet, and the English re-occupied the bridge of boats, by which 100 Fusiliers of the 2nd Madras regiment arrived that evening. This accession of strength enabled Neil to restore discipline among the Sikhs, whose excesses he had been obliged to overlook, as he had no means of repression at command. These sons of the Punjab had been unable to resist the temptation to plunder that presented itself at every instant, and they had especially turned their attention to the liquor shops and the docks of the river companies, where the best European wine was stored in abundance, claret and champagne, Cognac brandy, port, &c. The Sikhs, on their return from such expeditions, used to sell at a nominal price the larger share of their booty to their European comrades, and drunkenness, with indiscipline as its consequence, was prevalent in the fort. Neil bought up all the wine still in the Sikhs' possession for the commissariat, and to make things more sure, he marched his turbulent auxiliaries outside the fortifications, and made them encamp within range of the guns. Having taken these precautions, he stormed the suburbs on June 17, and re-occupied the town on the 18th without encountering resistance. The provisional government took to flight, and the inhabitants, fearing a possible bombardment, deserted their homes to a man.

Success was complete. The punishment inflicted on the vanquished was terrible. Up to this period all the victories of the English had been marked by much bloodshed; but at Delhi and in the Punjab, those who perished on the gallows, or were shot, were mutineers taken in arms, who would have been condemned to death by any military code, by any judge. At Allahabad the sepoys disappeared laden with the plunder of the treasury, and repressive measures were exercised on the simple, ignorant populace, guilty at most of having followed the exhortations

Neil, summed up the position with soldierly frankness in these few words: 'Thank God, sir, you will save us yet!'

of fanatical priests, and succumbed to an irresistible temptation to pillage. It suffices to examine the Anglo-Indian papers of the day, in order to discover letters in which both actors and spectators speak with an animation, almost humorous, of horrible butcheries. Nowhere during the mutiny was blood spilt so abundantly and with such levity as at Allahabad and in its environs. Alas! in every latitude, amongst every nation, the red-hot lava that burns in the furnace of great political crises is only the impure mixture of heroic virtues and savage passions. We recoil before the painful task of casting a slur on the conduct of the English in their struggle with the sepoys, by reproducing in detail cruelties worthy of the worst days of Tamerlane or Hayder Shah. These excesses were followed by immediate chastisement. In no former wars had events been more pressing, nor time more precious. It was not only necessary to re-establish the Company's authority in the northern provinces, but also to relieve Cawnpore, which was seriously threatened by the Nana's forces. Feeble entrenchments, thrown up in haste, protected some hundreds of women and children, besides the small garrison. A few hours' delay might occasion the most frightful catastrophe. The difficulty of getting together the numerous servants, workmen, porters, bearers, &c., without whose help no European troops can move in India, caused considerable delay in taking the field. The natives fled on all sides from the pale faces, who brought terror and death with them. The English had, by their excessive severity, slain the goose with the golden eggs. In addition to this, cholera, resulting from the heat and the fatigues of the latter marches, broke out with extraordinary violence amongst the European soldiers. In thirteen days, the little English troop lost seventy-three men. Colonel Neil and his staff triumphed, however, over these obstacles, by dint of activity, and on June 30 the vanguard of the expedition left Allahabad. It was composed of 400 Europeans, of a Sikh regiment, and of two squadrons of native cavalry. They advanced by short stages until, on July 2, a communication from Sir Henry Lawrence, Commissioner of Oude, announced that the mutiny had assumed the most formidable proportions, that Cawnpore was in the hands of Nana Sahib, and that under no pretext was a forward movement to be made by less than two European regiments at their full complement. The effective of the vanguard being far below this limit, it halted to await the principal body of the army.

The news received was but too true. We have already shown how shamefully the Nana, by the massacre of June 27, had violated the capitulation which had made him master of the Cawnpore cantonments. The murderers were still pursuing the wretched fugitives along the river's bank, when Nana Sahib betook himself to his stronghold of Bithour, where he caused himself to be proclaimed Peischwah.[1] His coronation was accompanied by all the ceremonial sanctioned by tradition. The new monarch placed himself on a throne, whilst Brahmins of the highest caste traced on his forehead the special marks emblematic of royalty. The largesses to the people, the discharges of artillery, the illuminations and fireworks that concluded the evening, recalled the pomp and grandeur of the Mahratta princes. Was this event the last act in the long prepared intrigues concealed under the mask of abject submission to the rule of the conquerors; or was it merely inspired by the intoxication consequent on an easy and ignominious victory? Without attempting to solve this problem, we shall merely point out that days of peace and quiet did not long fall to the lot of the upstart Peischwah. The Cawnpore Mussulmen did not accept the rule of a Mahratta prince without a struggle; and the claims of one of them, a man of ancient lineage, conspicuous by his persistent animosity during the siege of the cantonments, were put forward by local intrigue. The first hours of the new reign were, moreover, troubled by the information that the English were massing troops at Allahabad, with the intention of taking the offensive. The

[1] The Peischwah (leader), a kind of president of the powerful Mahratta Confederation, often proved the successful rival of the Mogul Emperors in the latter half of the eighteenth century. The power of Bagi Rao, the last of the Peischwahs, and the adoptive father of the Nana, outlasted that of the throne of Delhi; and he only surrendered to the English in 1818, after the Pindari War.

Nana left Bithour for Cawnpore, where, in accordance with the custom of Oriental despots, he drowned his terror and anxiety in every sort of dissipation. We may observe, incredible though it sounds, that the proclamations issued from the harem by the Nana incontestably prove the superiority of Asiatic conspiracies over European ones in the art of official mendacity.[1]

The British forces gradually came up. In the early days of July 1,200 men were assembled, and offensive operations began. The expedition, intended more especially for the relief of Cawnpore, was commanded by Brigadier Havelock, recently arrived from Calcutta, whose name will be for ever associated with the heroic defence of Lucknow. The English were soon to find themselves in the presence of the Nana Sahib and his allies. On the 13th they encamped five miles from Fattypore. The men, exhausted by the heat of the day, were waiting for the baggage, when the insurgents' cavalry, thinking doubtless that it was confronted by a weak vanguard only, advanced in an imposing line of several thousand horsemen. A well-directed fire from the European infantry caused great confusion in their ranks, and the English, marching rapidly in pursuit, occupied without resistance Fattypore, which had been deserted by the inhabitants. This victory did not cost Havelock a single soldier, but gave convincing proof how little reliance could be placed on the native cavalry attached to the expedition—some ten troopers alone having obeyed their officers and followed them in the charge against the enemy. The following day, at dawn, the insurgents threatened the baggage, and the European troops were obliged to begin the struggle anew. In the morning, intelligence had been received that the sepoys had occupied with artillery a bridge of masonry on the high road near Pandore Haddi. The bridge and guns were carried by the Madras Fusiliers, but the want of cavalry (18 sabres in all) made it impossible to follow up the victory. The feeble European force cut its way through thousands of the enemy, arrived

[1] See Documents, No. XL., 'Proclamation of Nana Sahib.'

within 25 miles of Cawnpore, and captured 16 guns, without having more than 28 men disabled. This beginning promised well. On July 16, at the junction of two roads, leading one to the Cawnpore cantonments and the other to the native town, the English came upon redoubts defended by strong artillery and imposing masses of sepoys, numbering more than 20,000 men. Notwithstanding great difficulties presented by the state of the ground, which had been soaked by torrential rains, the works were carried at the point of the bayonet. The sepoys, however, fought with more energy than they had done hitherto, and the struggle lasted far into the night. This victory made Havelock master of Cawnpore, which he entered on the following day, July 17.

During this short campaign the English, surrounded by innumerable enemies, had captured 23 guns and re-occupied Cawnpore with a total loss only of 105 men killed and wounded. They had, however, passed through severe trials. For seventeen days they had experienced the vicissitudes of the most uncertain season of the year—at one moment scorched by the burning rays of the sun, at another drenched to the skin by deluges of rain. But suffering and privations developed all the manly qualities of the British soldier. Neither hunger, sun, rain, nor incessant marches over heavy roads drew forth complaints or murmurs, for there were hundreds of women and children to be rescued from the hands of the Nana. Havelock set the example of courageous resignation. For seventeen days he never took off his uniform. He seemed gifted with ubiquity, and was present everywhere—in the ambulances, in the magazines, in the thickest of the fight. Charging the enemy, sword in hand, at the head of the attacking column, he had two horses killed under him. Victory crowned his efforts at last. Cawnpore was retaken and the Nana put to flight. Alas! it was too late.

We have already spoken of the misery endured by the little garrison at Cawnpore after their surrender, and of the massacre of the men and officers when they were about to embark on the Ganges, according to the capitulation signed by the Nana. Several hundred women and children had survived the butchery of June 27, and had remained in the Nana's hands. These poor creatures, imprisoned in a tiny bungalow known as Bibi-Gahr, without air, almost without food, attacked at the same moment by fever, cholera, and dysentery, all hope denied to them, experienced every possible species of suffering. The more favoured among them were employed in grinding the corn of the Mahratta chief, and accepted this task, emblematic in the East of slavery, without complaint, because it enabled them to bring back a little extra food to their famishing children.

Their captivity, with its attendant horrors, was drawing to a close. On the afternoon of July 15, hearing that Havelock's army had passed the Pandore Haddi, the cowardly Rajah, who with several thousand men had not been able to make head against a handful of European bayonets, resolved to perpetrate the foulest of massacres as an act of defiance to the victorious foe. Three or four men, forgotten amongst the women, were sent for and cut to pieces under the eyes of the Nana. A platoon of the 6th Regiment received orders to put an end to the remaining prisoners by firing at them through the doors and windows of their prison. Some feelings of humanity, however, still existed in the breasts of these soldiers, and they fired their muskets into the ceiling. This only prolonged the agony of the victims. The Nana, in a state of exasperation, called in the assistance of some Mussulman butchers in addition to his own guard, and these demons entered the Bibi-Garh, brandishing their weapons. Never were Christians in the circus given over to more ferocious wild beasts. The dead and dying remained the whole night long in this charnel-house. The next morning the corpses were cast into the neighbouring well, and then ensued a horrible scene. Children who had escaped, thanks to their small size, were seen to creep from under the dead bodies and run wild with terror and covered with blood round the mouth of the well. The Nana's executioners, worthy servants of such a master, without taking the trouble to despatch the little creatures, threw them alive among the heaps of human remains. Not a single European was left to relate the horrible tale. On their entrance into Cawnpore on July 17, Havelock's soldiers found the still reeking corpses of the victims in the well. The Nana, after blowing up the ammunition in the place, had taken refuge at Bithour, a stronghold belonging to him some miles from the town. The proximity of his home did not inspire the monster with the courage in which he was wanting, and on the approach of some companies of Madras Fusiliers, he evacuated the place with 5,000 men and 43 guns, abandoning his treasures and 15 battering-pieces. Since then no certain trace has ever been found of this Asiatic Nero, though several times the report of his capture has caused great excitement in the public.[1]

[1] At the time that this work was printing, an individual, supposed to be Nana Sahib, was taken captive, and the fact caused the greatest excitement in England. We borrow the details of this strange story from the columns of the *Times*:—On the evening of October 21, a letter written by Nana Sahib's secretary was brought to Maharajah Scindia. In it Nana Sahib stated that he was applying to Scindia as to a brother, that after wandering several years in the desert he had returned to Hindostan, and now placed his life in his hands. On receiving this intelligence, Scindia placed himself at the head of two hundred horsemen, and proceeded with them to the neighbourhood of Lackhur, where Nana was said to be. Scindia seized his correspondent and brought him prisoner to his palace. Round the building he placed a guard of 3,000 men, and sent for the political agent of the province, who arrived towards evening, and received the captive's deposition, which was something to this effect:

Though Scindia was younger than the Nana, he had known him in his childhood, and is said to have recognised him immediately. Moreover, the Nana took care to establish his identity by relating certain incidents of his life, which he alone could know.

As son of Baji Rao, Peischwah and Nana of Bithour, he had been constrained, under pain of death, to place himself at the head of the mutineers. He had taken no part in the murders on the river, and still less in the massacre of Bibi-Gahr. After the capture of Cawnpore, he had sought a refuge in the forests of Nepaul, where he lived several years. He had then passed into Assam, and had remained a year at Gowhatty disguised as a fakir. Finally, worn out by this wandering existence, he had come to Bareilly, and from thence to Gwalior, where he had been for twenty-four hours only. The secretary, who wrote the letter to the Maharajah, declared that he had met the Nana at Bareilly, and that having no employment he had entered his service, but that he had only known that the fakir was the Nana when the letter to Scindia had been dictated to him. It appeared afterwards that the Maharajah, not wishing to consign to certain death a man who had voluntarily sought his protection,

The name and standard of the Peischwah, however, afforded a centre round which the insurrection continued to rally up to the very last. The Nana's accomplices and executioners did not escape condign punishment. On July 25, Colonel Neil, who commanded at Cawnpore under Havelock, published the following order:—'The well which contains the mortal remains of the women and children massacred by command of the miscreant Nana Sahib shall be filled up and banked over carefully in the shape of a tomb. A detachment of European soldiers will perform this pious duty to-night, under command of an officer. The house and the rooms in which the massacre took place shall not be cleansed nor white-washed by the fellow-countrymen of the victims. The brigadier intends that every drop of innocent blood shall be removed or licked up by the condemned before their execution, in proportion to their caste and to the share they have had in the massacre. Consequently, after the sentence of death has been read, each criminal shall be brought to the scene of the massacre, and forced to cleanse a stated portion of the floor. Care shall be taken to render the task as revolting as possible to the religious feelings of the condemned, and the provost marshal shall not spare the

and who was a Mahratta as well as himself, demanded that the life of his prisoner should be spared; but on the persistent refusal of the British agent, he finally gave him up without conditions. The Nana, escorted by Scindia's men, was despatched to the cantonments of Morar, where he was carefully handcuffed and confined in the camp prison under the guard of an officer and a company of the 26th Royals. The secretary was shut up in a separate cell.

The pretended Nana now says that he is a mere fakir, and that he can prove it. He asserts that the letter written to Scindia contains not a word of truth, that his deposition made to the political agent is completely false, and that when he thus wrote and spoke he was under the influence of haschisch. The prisoner is about forty years old; he has a bushy beard and long black hair, which at first were supposed to be dyed, though no proof of that is forthcoming. His height is five feet nine, his face is marked by small-pox. According to official information, Nana Sahib would be now about fifty years old; but as the prisoner seems not more than forty, it is thought that possibly he may not be the Nana, notwithstanding the accumulated proofs against him. In presence of these facts, anyone who is familiar with the habits of deceit ingrained in the Asiatic character, will reserve his opinion, and incline to believe that there has arisen a new claimant in India whose identification will be profitable to none but lawyers and solicitors.

lash if needful. When the appointed task has been accomplished, the sentence shall be carried out on a gallows, raised in front of the house.' Colonel Neil, merely by outraging their prejudices of caste and religion, had succeeded in making death a thousand times more horrible to the natives than if they had undergone the most barbarous tortures. He says, in a private letter: 'The first to be executed was an infantry subahdar, a huge brute of the highest caste. A broom was given him by a sweeper. At first he refused to use it, but the provost-marshal's lash descended so energetically on his shoulders, that he screamed like a madman, and accomplished his task in hot haste. He was hanged afterwards, and buried under the road. A few days after came the turn of others among the condemned. Amongst them was a Mahommedan, who before the mutiny had been employed in one of our courts. He was a vile wretch, and one of the leaders of the revolt. He attempted some resistance, but the lash soon brought him to his senses, and he cleansed with his tongue the stain of blood assigned to him. This is not a measure to be judged by ordinary rules, but it is well adapted for the present emergency, and I trust no one will interfere with me before the place is entirely cleansed.'

Havelock's work was only partially done. His orders and his own feelings equally urged him to hurry on, without delay or hesitation, to Lucknow, where the Residency was besieged by immense multitudes, reinforced by all the regular troops stationed in the kingdom of Oude. After the recent massacre at Cawnpore, could any Englishman, any man, contemplate without terror the fate that threatened the feeble garrison, encumbered with women and children, and cooped up behind incomplete entrenchments, where provisions and ammunition were alike wanting? How, nevertheless, was the perilous enterprise to be undertaken with no forces but the skeleton of an army? In the first place, it was necessary to traverse the Ganges, with its tremendously swift current, swollen by the rains, by means of a small steamer and native boats. The essentially warlike population of Oude was in arms, and had hitherto not been subdued—only conquered by a stroke of the pen. Havelock had neither cavalry nor field artillery, and there were scarcely 200 European soldiers between Calcutta and Cawnpore.

At his earnest request the Government of the metropolis parted with every soldier fit to take the field. These reinforcements arrived successively at Cawnpore, and towards the end of July the European troops numbered about 2,000 men. This feeble effective force had to be still further reduced, in order to provide a garrison for Cawnpore, where the baggage of the army was left. Rapidity being the first condition of success, ammunition and provision for a few days only were taken. This involved the exposure of the men to all the vicissitudes of the weather, and also to the necessity of bivouacking on the bare earth. On July 28, the expedition, comprising 1,700 men and ten guns, crossed the Ganges, and by the following day came face to face with some of the difficulties of the undertaking.

All the villages had been put into a state of defence, and furnished with artillery. At Omaou, six miles from the river, the enemy offered a vigorous resistance, and set fire to the town before leaving it. The sepoys formed again, as soon as the place was taken, and another combat was necessary, in order to retain the ground occupied. Towards evening the Nana's troops appeared on the left flank of the English, but with their usual cowardice did not venture to take part in the action. On August 3, at Basseratgange, a town surrounded with walls and ditches, with a tower armed with five guns, the fighting was still more serious. The Madras Fusiliers and the Highlanders only carried the entrenchments and entered the town at nightfall at the cost of many lives. The English were decimated by the enemy's fire, and the diseases of the country, with cholera at their head, were already raging with intensity. Every stretcher in the ambulance was occupied, and the expedition was reduced to 1,200 men. It was impossible to advance.

That evening orders were given to retreat, and though circumstances but too sadly justified this retrograde movement, it excited much murmuring in the ranks. Havelock persisted nevertheless, though never did wounded lioness, obliged to leave her whelps in the hunter's hands, deplore more bitterly the rigour of fate. But prudence is also a military virtue, and had the march forward on Lucknow been continued after the losses experienced, a frightful disaster would have infallibly ensued. On the other hand, speedy assistance was expected, and recent intelligence from the Lucknow authorities was reassuring up to a certain point. A loyal sepoy, who had passed the enemy's lines, had just brought to head-quarters despatches from the military commander of the besieged Residency. The garrison, though hard pressed, still held out manfully, and was provided with provisions and ammunition for several weeks. This information was soon made known to the whole army, and somewhat mitigated the bitterness of retreat. By the first days of August, General Havelock had taken up his position in the cantonments of Mangalwar, on the left bank of the Ganges, and was occupied in reorganising his small force whilst waiting for the arrival of reinforcements promised by Sir J. Outram, who had recently been appointed to the supreme command of the Oude expedition.

As soon as the Court of Directors was informed of General Anson's death, they replaced him by Sir Colin Campbell, a veteran of the Peninsular War. Sir Colin Campbell had just taken a glorious part in the siege of Sebastopol at the head of the Highland brigade, whom a community of danger and almost of costume had united to our Zouave regiments then, alas, at the height of their fame.[1] No general ever assumed a command in more critical circumstances than those in

[1] Sir Colin Campbell counted among his best friends the brave General Vinoy. I was able to give the Commander-in-Chief news of General Vinoy, with whom I had travelled from Calais to Paris, and who had spoken to me in the warmest terms of his friend Sir Colin, without forgetting the revolver he had received from him as a mark of friendship, and which he had made a good use of at the assault of the tower of Malakoff. The amicable relations between the two officers have not ceased, and his Excellency told me that he had just received a letter in which General Vinoy expressed his heartfelt wishes for the triumph of our cause, at the same time begging his friend not to show himself merciless towards the rebels. 'Believe in my experience of war, reprisals are always useless,' said the French general.

which India found itself when the new General-in-Chief arrived at Calcutta towards the end of August. India was slipping from the grasp of her conquerors, according to the energetic expression of one high in authority. Even the most far-sighted did not anticipate the success soon to be achieved by the troops before Delhi.

The situation can be summed up as follows: Direct communications between Calcutta, Delhi, and the Punjab were completely interrupted, and the Delhi army, little more than 4,000 strong, was scarcely able to maintain its position. Its base of operations was the Punjab, by the line of Loudianah. Sir J. Lawrence, with heroic devotion, despatched his European regiments to Delhi, but it was doubtful whether the besieging force would be able to remain before the city till their arrival. The last news from the North-West Provinces, now a month old, received at Calcutta *viâ* Bombay, announced without comment that the Agra garrison had been obliged to take refuge in the fort after an unsuccessful combat. It was also known that the Lucknow garrison was hemmed in, in a weak position without casemates, and defended by a few field-works at most. Could it be hoped that a handful of Europeans, encumbered with women and children, would hold out long against a multitude of enemies? Havelock had retaken Cawnpore, and had attempted to march on Lucknow at the head of the first reinforcements sent from Calcutta, but his small army, powerless against the rebellious regiments with whom the whole population of Oude made common cause, had been obliged to retreat to Cawnpore.

The first duty of the new General-in-Chief was to make the communications between the capital and the advanced post of Cawnpore. As the strategical points on the road—Allahabad, Ghazipore, Benares, Dinapore—were still in the hands of the English, such reinforcements as could be spared to Havelock arrived without much difficulty at their destination, chiefly by means of river steamers.

Unfortunately, shortly before the arrival of Sir Colin Campbell, Lower Bengal, till then quiet enough, at least on the surface, began to feel the effects of the events at Delhi and Mirut. Towards the middle of July, the Dinapore brigade, then stationed at Bangalpore, and composed of one cavalry and of two native infantry regiments, deserted its quarters with arms and baggage. Armed bands were formed, and one of the most influential men of the district placed himself at the head of the movement. Koër Singh, though more than eighty, was one of the foremost leaders in the mutiny, owing to his intelligence and indomitable energy. Belonging to one of the highest families in India, and possessor of an immense fortune, his influence not only extended to those who were in immediate contact with him, but also to the Bengal army, in whose ranks many of his vassals were serving. For a time the rebels occupied the high road between the Soane and the Ganges, cut the telegraph wires, stopped the posts, and isolated Calcutta from the rest of India. A tremendous panic seized on every one; all along the river banks the European population fled in haste from their houses, and the authorities, in order to meet the peril, detained the reinforcements intended for Havelock.

However, before their arrival, certain resolute men had boldly confronted the danger. A magistrate of the Arrah district, Mr. Walker, and Mr. Boyle, a railway engineer, who had taken refuge with some sixty men, of whom eighteen were Europeans and fifty Sikhs, in an imperfectly fortified house at Arrah, resisted for more than a week all the attacks of Koër Singh's forces, numbering 4,000 men. The perilous position in which the valiant garrison found itself was soon known to the neighbouring authorities, who despatched a first reinforcement, consisting of two companies of the 10th Royals. Captain Lebas, too desirous of fulfilling his mission as soon as possible, lost his way in the jungle during the night, and was cut to pieces with more than half his men, his guns falling into the enemy's hands. This was one of the greatest reverses the English met with in the course of the mutiny. The relief of the place was, however, only delayed thereby. On August 2, Major Vincent Eyre, with 200 men of the 5th Royals and two pieces of cannon, completely routed the Dinapore brigade and Koër Singh's bands at Bibi-Garh, and effected a junction with the heroic defenders of Arrah. Some days later he was reinforced by the arrival of 200 men of the 10th Royals, and immediately took the field again. On August 12, the enemy was encountered, and the soldiers of the 10th, burning with rage at the sight of the adversaries who had made such havoc in their ranks, when they were defeated under Captain Lebas, rushed forward with fixed bayonets, and dislodged the sepoys from the jungle and stronghold of Indespore, the principal fortress of Koër Singh. Discouraged but not despairing, the old chief retired towards the frontiers of Nepaul, and, from an inaccessible retreat, watched for a favourable opportunity of resuming the struggle. The mutiny was nearly over in Lower Bengal, and the sepoys crossing the Ganges, soon took the road to Delhi.

The difficulties were not less at Calcutta, where, notwithstanding the efforts of the Government, the means of transport and the supplies of horses, ammunition, and arms did not correspond to the necessities of the army. Horses fetched as much as 100*l.* a piece. A cavalry regiment from Madras having refused to serve beyond the limits of the presidency, all its horses were embarked for Bengal. The military establishments at Cossipore were at work day and night, casting cannon and manufacturing Enfield cartridges. A large quantity of tents were prepared at Allahabad. In the hands of Sir Colin Campbell the military preparations were pushed forward with the utmost despatch. The waters of the Ganges were now falling, and in order to obviate the delays and inconveniences of the river route, a service of bullock-carts was organised, and stationed in relays along the high road. Then was witnessed a strange sight! On leaving a train or a steamer, the Queen's soldiers were seen to step into and travel in the curious vehicles which the Ninevite and Babylonian bas-reliefs show to have been used to convey the warriors of the kings of Assyria. During the great heat of the day, the trains stopped at stations where provisions that needed to be cooked were prepared beforehand. The service was so well organised that finally 200 men could be despatched daily from Ranigange, the last halting-place on the railway, to Allahabad, a distance of 809 miles, in less than fifteen days, without subjecting them to either privation or fatigue.

The conduct and policy of the Governor-General could at length be judged impartially. A new-comer in these distant lands, Lord Canning committed the mistake of adopting without reserve all the opinions of his *entourage*. Deceived by delusions entertained by the best qualified authorities as to the fidelity of the sepoys, he refused in the beginning of the mutiny to take such rigorous measures as might have delayed, if not altogether prevented, the outbreak. A still more grave error was signing decrees, breathing a spirit of distrust, which made no distinction between Europeans and natives. To throw doubts on the loyalty and devotion of the European press and of the Queen's subjects at such a crisis was to encourage the revolt by sowing discord gratuitously amongst the English population, and to create difficulties in the way of the local government of which the effects would be felt in Europe itself. Had an appeal been publicly made to the English journalists, showing that the gravity of the circumstances necessitated a restriction of their liberty, it is more than probable that the Anglo-Indian press would not have supported Lord Canning's Government less warmly than it did that of Lord Auckland at the time of the Cabul disaster. Subsequent events showed, moreover, that wherever Europeans, whether they were planters, merchants, lawyers, or writers, were called upon to assist in the work of repression, they proved valiant auxiliaries, and rendered services which amply testified the loyalty and courage of the Anglo-Saxon race. Once alive to the dangers of the situation, Lord Canning's Government showed no want of initiative or energy, whilst he himself firmly resisted all the appeals for vengeance that issued from every mouth and from every pen.[1] The surname of

[1] The *Friend of India*, one of the most important journals of Calcutta, recommended the following political programme :—'First, that in the districts under martial law, the lives and properties of the inhabitants should be dependent on no law but that of military necessity for the whole duration of the insurrection. Secondly, that every rebel sepoy, whether in arms or a

'Clemency Canning,' conferred on him in derision by his compatriots, whose wild desire for revenge he had not gratified, remains as his highest title of glory in the eyes of posterity. By refusing to authorise monstrous reprisals, such as were clamoured for by the thousand voices of the Anglo-Indian community, Lord Canning avoided separating India from her European masters by an impassable river of blood. He understood the real interests of his mission, and if the work of pacification has now been finished these fifteen years, the honour of it belongs in the first place to the generous sentiments and the horror of bloodshed that so especially characterised Lord Canning. Personally he made himself conspicuous by his impassive courage, and retained in the interior of his palace his native body-guard, whose much suspected loyalty never wavered. In giving this slight sketch of the modest and amiable statesman, it would be unjust to pass by in silence the noble and graceful figure of Lady Canning, the devoted companion and partner of all her husband's perils. In the hour of trial, the great court-lady gave proof of the almost virile firmness, peculiar to Anglo-Indian women, but soon paid her tribute to the deadly climate and the anxieties of high position by ending her life on the heights of Simla.

In order to complete this *résumé* of affairs in August 1857, we must say a few words about military matters in other parts of India. The Madras and Bombay Presidencies possessed, each of them, a considerable army quite distinct from that of Bengal:—

REGIMENTS.

		Regular Infantry	Irregular Infantry	Regular Cavalry	Irregular Cavalry
Effective force of the army of	Madras	52	8	8	—
„ „ „	Bombay	29	6	3	6

Each regiment of regular infantry comprised 1,000 men, each regiment of irregular infantry 800 ditto, and each

deserter, should be put to death. Thirdly, that every Indian taken in arms should be executed. Fourthly, that in any village where a European had been killed, telegraph wires cut, or the post stopped, a court-martial should exercise summary justice; that any village where a European had been insulted or had been refused aid and assistance should be heavily fined.'

regiment of cavalry, whether regular or irregular, 500 sabres.

The adhesion of these forces, formidable alike by their numbers and organisation to the cause of the mutiny, would have occasioned the most disastrous complications for England. The past history of the Madras army was full of most disquieting events, and no one could remember without apprehension that one of the most serious military revolts that ever broke out in India took place at Vellore in 1806.[1] Since then good treatment on the

[1] In the spring of 1806, in consequence of orders given to the sepoys to trim their moustaches in a uniform fashion, to do away with earrings and special signs of caste when in full uniform, and to adopt a new style of head-dress, symptoms of disaffection and indiscipline became apparent in the Bengal army. Certain summary measures seemed to have repressed the agitation, when a mutiny broke out at Vellore. The garrison of the fortress was composed of two battalions of the 23rd, of one battalion of the 1st Madras, and of four companies of the 69th Royals. In the night the sepoys shot down the European sentinels and attacked the main guard of the 69th, all the men of which they killed, and then set fire to the barracks. The officers and their families were murdered in their houses; the sick in the hospital met with the same fate. Colonel Fancourt, the commander of the garrison, was one of the first victims, and fell pierced with bullets at his own door. Colonel MacKerras, the second in command, was shot a few minutes later. By morning the mutineers were masters of the fort, with the exception of the European barracks, which two officers had succeeded in reaching. Attacked here by superior forces, the English took up their position at a postern gate, and would have all succumbed, notwithstanding their bravery, but for providential assistance. At the beginning of the outbreak, an officer had swum across the moat of Vellore, and escaping from the alligators with which it abounds, had brought information of the event next morning to Arcot, some sixteen miles off, where a considerable body of troops was stationed. Colonel Rollo Gillespie started immediately at the head of the 19th Royal Cavalry, and being better mounted than his companions, arrived the first under the walls of Vellore. Dismounting under a storm of balls, he was drawn up by a sort of ladder made of hides to the last stronghold, where the handful of European soldiers were still defending themselves. The arrival of his forces turned the scale, and the sepoys who escaped death left the fort, and took refuge in the neighbouring country. The English losses in this nocturnal massacre were considerable—twenty officers and their families and 164 soldiers were murdered. The mutiny was ascribed to the intrigues of the princes of Mysore, Tippoo Sahib's sons, who were prisoners in the fortress of Vellore. They cannot, however, have been seriously implicated, as they were not included in any of the subsequent trials. They were, however, expelled from the Madras Presidency, and ordered to reside in Calcutta, where their descendants still exist.

part of their officers and the long-continued influence of discipline had created a strong feeling of loyalty in the ranks. The Mohammedan sepoys no doubt entertained a secret sympathy for the cause of the mutineers; but living at a greater distance than their Bengal comrades from the centre of the traditions of the Mogul empire, they did not share their impatient longing to throw off the yoke of the European conquerors. Moreover, a good half of the Madras army was recruited from the Tamil population—a race without traditions of caste, and who, satisfied with regular pay and a paternal discipline, remained faithful to their salt, according to an Oriental expression. A cavalry regiment that showed signs of insubordination was disbanded, and no other act of severity was needed to maintain order. The state of the Bombay army, on the other hand, though recruited on precisely the same system, caused great anxiety on several occasions. Placed nearer the scene of events and worked upon by the emissaries of the mutiny, a mere spark would have sufficed to spread disaffection in certain regiments. Severe examples made short work of all criminal aspirations, and the turn of affairs, now more favourable to the English, soon repressed any idea of revolt.

Major-General Sir James Outram had been appointed to the command of the Oude expedition, as we have seen, and we shall not be going beyond the limits of these sketches if we give a few details of the life and deeds of one of the greatest European heroes in Asia. Sir J. Outram, on whom Sir Charles Napier has conferred the title of the 'Bayard of the Indian army,'[1] had for thirty-nine years been pursuing a brilliant and laborious career in the Company's service. As soldier, administrator, diplomate, or sportsman, on the battle-field, in the cabinet, or in the depths of the jungle, everywhere

[1] Towards 1843, Sir Charles Napier, who afterwards found a most resolute adversary in Sir J. Outram, had drunk his health at a public banquet in the following characteristic terms: 'In the sixteenth century there lived in France a knight as famous for his bravery in warfare as for his wisdom in council. It was Bayard. Gentlemen, I propose the health of the "Bayard of India," my friend Colonel Outram, of the Bombay army.'

he had given proof of rare courage and eminent faculties. Having joined the Bombay army as ensign in 1819, Outram had to await six years in obscure regimental duties the opportunity of exhibiting his brilliant qualities. In 1825, a native chief of Kauteisch, after attacking the town of Bartpore, retired to the fortress of Kittour, situated on the summit of a mountain, from whence he fomented outbreaks all around him. Outram, with 200 sepoys, scaled the rear of the fort, killed the chief with his own hand, and in recompense for this feat was entrusted with the formation of a corps of Bhils. The Bhils, a sect of professional thieves, given up to debauchery and brigandage, lived in a perpetual state of warfare with their neighbours. The young lieutenant soon showed what the influence of a single man might effect among the wild inhabitants of the jungle, and the new regiment became renowned for its discipline and courage. Gifted with that art of managing the natives with which all the great men of British India have been endowed, Outram exercised the most wonderful fascination over the rebellious population of the district by his justice, his vigour, his conciliatory character, his skill and daring in manly sports, so that, as a mark of approbation for his services, he was called to an important post in the province of Myhi-Kanta. In 1838 Captain Outram, then attached to Lord Keane's staff, took part in the siege of Ghuznee and in the Afghan war. Having been appointed to be the bearer of the news of the taking of Khelat, he traversed the whole seat of war, some 360 miles in extent, alone, disguised as an Afghan, and mounted on a Cabul pony. For seven days he was exposed to fatigue of all sorts, and escaped pursuit as by miracle. During the disasters at Cabul, Major Outram, who had been placed in command of Lower Scinde and Beloochistan, succeeded in maintaining order in these dangerous border-lands. Thanks to the excellent terms on which he stood with the Emirs of Scinde, they not only abstained from hostilities, but also furnished the British army with provisions and means of transport. When he resigned his command, public gratitude testified in a strange way to his immense popularity. He was presented with a sabre enriched with jewels by the Bombay community; with a prayer-book by the Anglican bishop of the Presidency; with a gold medal by the Pope, for services rendered to the Roman Catholic population, and with a richly damascened lance by his pig-sticking comrades.[1] Outram remained faithful to his friends in Scinde, and when, against all justice, the Emirs were stripped of their territory and their property, he refused, though a poor man, to accept the share assigned to him by law (some 10,000*l.*), and renounced his career, rather than lend his name to an iniquitous policy.

He retired to England, and was living there in semi-disgrace when the revolutions that succeeded one another at Lahore after the death of Ranjit Singh made serious complications probable. At the instance of, and with the warmest recommendations from the Duke of Wellington, his ever-zealous patron, Outram returned to India, where he successively fulfilled the important functions of Resident at Aden and Baroda, and of Resident and afterwards Commissioner at Lucknow on the annexation of Oude. Having attained the highest distinctions, and already a member of the Indian Council, Major-General Sir J. Outram had sought rest in Egypt, when he was entrusted with the supreme command of an expedition against Persia. A glorious peace had scarcely crowned his campaign in that country, when circumstances recalled him to the battle-field. His popularity and his services assured him a place in the first rank, and to the general satisfaction he was appointed to the command of the British forces at Cawnpore, intended to act against Oude. General Outram lost no time in joining the troops committed to his charge. The perils of the besieged residents at Lucknow occupied his every thought, and at one time he conceived the idea of marching directly from Benares,[2] and so turning

[1] Pig-sticking is, as everybody knows, one of the favourite sports of the Anglo-Indian community.

[2] See Documents, No. XLI., 'Letter of Sir James Outram to the Governor-General of India.'

the rivers and canals, whose passage had offered insurmountable obstacles to Havelock's first expedition. This plan failed to meet with the approval of his superiors.[1] The means of defence of the besieged in the Residency inspired at this time greater confidence than previously.[2] Outram organising means of defence all along his route, and pressing the arrival of reinforcements with indefatigable energy, arrived at headquarters on September 12.

His first acts were worthy of his noble character. The double right of seniority of rank and the choice of the Government called him to the command of the expedition destined to relieve Lucknow. Yet with the delicacy peculiar to certain choice souls, he would not deprive the brave officer who had risked so much in order to succour the besieged garrison, of the glory of bringing the heroic enterprise to a successful close, and he placed himself as volunteer under Havelock's orders.[3]

Disinterestedness and patriotic feeling vibrated in unison in every member of this little army. Never had officers and men alike been inflamed with more sincere and generous ardour. All hearts swelled, all eyes filled with tears in presence of the fatal well at Cawnpore, than which a more ghastly spectacle has never been witnessed.[4]

[1] See Documents, No. XLI., 'Letters of the Commander-in-Chief and of the Governor-General to Sir J. Outram.'

[2] *Ibid.*, 'Letter of Sir J. Outram to Mr. Mangles.'

[3] See Documents, No. XLII., 'Orders of the day of Sir J. Outram and of Brigadier Havelock.'

[4] It was at first intended to build a memorial church over the well at Cawnpore, but after long deliberation this project was given up. The monument raised over the remains of the Nana's victims, and in their honour, is from the design of Colonel Yule, of the Engineers, and is composed of an octagonal colonnade in the Gothic style, in the midst of which is the fatal well. The orifice, closed with a stone facing, serves as pedestal to a white marble statue representing the Angel of Mercy, one of the last works of the celebrated Marochetti. The statue was ordered by Lord Canning, who was Governor-General of India during the mutiny, and was paid for out of his own private means. Around the monument are gardens full of trees, which offer a pleasant promenade to the inhabitants of Cawnpore.

The memorial church rises on the site of the old hospital, which sheltered many death-bed agonies during the siege, and is placed in the centre of a large plain, on the south-west portion of which stand the European barracks.

They beheld its yawning mouth stained with blood, and choked with human remains; limbs scattered in every direction; the mother and the child at the breast united in death as in life. They beheld the sun's rays, the loathsome worm, and the voracious bird of prey doing their worst on these sad victims of human ferocity. A soldier summed up his emotions by tracing the words 'Remember Cawnpore!' with the point of his bayonet on the stone border. Who could ever forget that day, fatal above all others! Not a knapsack but contained some relic of the martyrs—letters,

A macadamised road, planted with trees, leads from the station to the plain, the scene of so much combined suffering and heroism. Traces of General Wheeler's entrenchments are still visible here and there in the shape of piles of discoloured bricks or of inequalities in the ground, almost concealed by grass. The church, which is not yet finished, is full of interest from the associations it recalls of the glories and triumphs of the Anglo-Saxons during the fatal year 1857. For instance, one meets with inscriptions such as follow:—

In memory of the Engineers of the East India Railway,
Who died from illness or from wounds
During the great Mutiny of 1857.
In affectionate remembrance,
Their comrades of the North-West Provinces.

In memory of 3 officers, 2 sergeants, 1 corporal, 1 drummer,
And 20 men of the 34th Royals,
Killed in the fight before Cawnpore,
On the 27th of November, 1857.

In memory of Captain Stuart Beatson,
Havelock's Adjutant-General,
Who, in the agony of cholera and carried in a palanquin,
Did his duty in the fight of Pandore Haddi,
And at the re-capture of Cawnpore.

In memory of 14 officers and 448 men and women
Of the 32nd R.A.,
Who died during the sieges of Lucknow and Cawnpore,
Or in the course of the Mutiny.

The lines consecrating the memory of the martyrs of Bibi-Garh are more poignant still:—

In memory of Mrs. Moore, Mrs. Wainwright,
Miss Wainwright, Mrs. Hall,
And 48 soldiers' wives, and 55 children,
Massacred at Cawnpore in July 1857.

fragments of playthings, pages torn from prayer-books, or locks of hair stained with blood. To men burning with the desire for vengeance, to hearts inflamed with the noble desire of rescuing the besieged of Lucknow from a frightful death, what mattered the fury of the elements, the fire and the steel of the enemy, or any of the plagues of earth! Forward, ye avengers. The Indian shall never fill another well of Cawnpore with dead!

In a reserved enclosure surrounding the church, which is protected by a walled embankment, crowned by an evergreen hedge, are still to be found many recollections of the disaster. On a tombstone carefully railed off the following lines are to be read:—

In the three graves inside this railing
Rest the mortal remains of Major E. Vibart,
Of the 2nd Bengal Cavalry,
And of about 70 officers and men,
Who, after escaping from the massacre of June 27th,
Were taken prisoners by the mutineers of Shoreapore,
And put to death on July 1st.

The victims who fell during the siege rest neither in the enclosure round the church nor in the church itself, and their last home must be sought for in a spot shaded by trees near barracks No. 4. There, at the time of the struggle, existed a dry well, which received the bodies of about 250 of the besieged. This well, surrounded by a railing, has been closed by a stone covered with mosaic, in the midst of which is a cross with this epitaph:—

In this well were placed, by their companions in misfortune,
The bodies of the men, women, and children,
Who died
During the heroic defence of Wheeler's entrenchments,
Besieged by the Nana.

A portion of Psalm cxli. is inscribed below.

THE INSURRECTION OF THE BENGAL SEPOYS, 1857.

CHAPTER VI.

SIEGE OF LUCKNOW—HAVELOCK'S EXPEDITION.

Condition of the kingdom of Oude before the annexation—Excess of feudal power—Powerlessness of Anglo-Indian diplomacy—Annexation of the kingdom of Oude—Errors of the new administration—Hostility to the new *régime* shown by the veterans of the Bengal army living in Oude—Blind confidence of British authorities—Conciliatory dispositions of the new commissioner, Sir H. Lawrence—The English residence at Lucknow—Position of the troops—Mutiny of the 7th irregular Oude Infantry—Preparations for defence—Mutiny of three regiments of the Bengal army on May 30—News of the disaster at Cawnpore—Insurrection in the provinces—Massacre at Aurangabad—The English are defeated at Chinhat on June 30—Death of Sir H. Lawrence—Intestine dissensions amongst the mutineers—The garrison during the first weeks of the siege—Attack of the 21st and 22nd of July—Arrival of the sepoy Angad with despatches from Havelock—Correspondence with the authorities at Cawnpore—March on Lucknow—The assault—The garrison during the assault—Military operations of September 25th and 26th—Massacre of the wounded—Losses of the British army.

The siege of Lucknow ranks, with the campaigns of Havelock and Sir C. Campbell, among the most important events in the struggle between England and the rebellious sepoys. However, before giving any account of it, it is indispensable to say a few words of the condition of Oude before its annexation.

We have already had occasion to point out that a considerable extent of territory in the Indian peninsula had remained under the rule of the native princes. Amongst these allies, or, to speak more correctly, amongst these vassals of England, the King of Oude occupied the foremost rank, on account of the extent, the wealth, and the population of his kingdom.[1] Friendly intercourse between the two powerful neighbours goes back to the year 1801, when Lord Wellesley concluded an offensive and defensive alliance with Saadat Ali Khan, Nabob of Oude. The reign of Saadat Ali Khan was both long and prosperous. A clever monarch, he weakened feudal power, recovered from his nobles the possessions they had obtained through the weakness of his predecessors, and on his death left 14,000,000*l.* in specie, an enormous sum for the period. His immediate successor received the title of king from the Company in 1819, but supreme rank developed royal virtues neither in him nor in his descendants; and all of them, vying with each other in incapacity and prodigality, opened the way to anarchy and disorders of all sorts. In the reign of the last king, Wajad Ali, the Court of Oude, during the years that preceded the mutiny, offered, even more than the palace at Delhi, a faithful picture of men and manners as they appeared in the decline of the Mogul empire. To complete the resemblance, King Wajad Ali,[2] his courtiers, and about a tenth of the population followed the law of Mahomet in this good, old-fashioned kingdom, whilst the rest of the inhabitants remained faithful to that of Brahma. The Rajpoots of Oude, the direct descendants of those warrior-priests who were masters of India before the Mohammedan conquest, had preserved intact the proud and exclusive traditions of their ancestors. The sombre mysteries of the religion of Khali and Bohwani were still celebrated in the temples of the kingdom, and on the high roads the sect of the Thugs destroyed numbers of travellers.

[1] The provinces forming the kingdom of Oude contained at the last census in 1870, 11,220,232 inhabitants, or 474 inhabitants to the square mile; 89·3 of this population belonged to the Brahmin religion, and 10·7 to the Mahommedan.

[2] The King of Oude had four wives by marriage, according to the Mahommedan law, twenty-nine acknowledged wives by 'Motah,' and four hundred female attendants called 'Motah' wives, but not permanently united as the others.—Captain Hutchinson's *Events in Oude.*

The agricultural population of Oude, from which two-thirds of the Bengal army were drawn, had preserved all the ancient Hindoo institutions untouched, and society among them rested exclusively on the system of village communities. The village, as a community, was the only legitimate proprietor of the soil, and its members alone had a right to alienate their share of the common property by sale, deed of gift, or mortgage. The village itself was a complete organisation—a kind of small republic, with all necessary functionaries, such as a head man, a notary, a priest, a smith, a carpenter, a washerman, a rural policeman, whose salaries were paid in dues by the inhabitants. The land-tax, one of the oldest established institutions of the country, was paid to the Government by the head man in proportion to the fields, the ploughs, and the numbers of the community. No people carry so far the love of the paternal acres as the Hindoos of Oude. But as the excess of population made it difficult to gain a livelihood in the country districts, most of the enterprising young men were accustomed to try their fortunes in foreign parts, and especially in the military service of the East India Company. All these soldiers, without exception, returned to visit their families when on leave, and retired on their pension to die in the village where they had been born. These details show what an intimate connection existed between the agricultural population of Oude and the Bengal army, and explain the interest felt by the sepoys, whether retired or with the colours, in the soil of that kingdom. Notwithstanding the ardour of this restricted patriotism and the fertility of the soil, it is unfortunately certain that Oude was one of the most wretched provinces of India, as was amply proved by the sight of lean, famishing cattle, ruined wells, and miserable and deserted villages in all its districts. This state of things was partially due to the exactions of the taloukdars, or collectors of the land-tax. These functionaries, originally chosen from among the chiefs of great families and connected with the village population, used to show a laxity in the collection of the tax, which was no longer the case when they were replaced by fiscal agents appointed by the Crown or the local authorities to be the intermediaries between the Government and the tax-payers. Moreover, in many cases the taloukdars disputed the hereditary rights of the village communities, and succeeded in getting hold of them themselves.

The imbecile weakness of the last king, Wajad Ali Shah, greatly tended to encourage this state of things. Invisible in the recesses of his harem, surrounded by 500 legitimate wives or concubines, his life had no object but pleasure, and the whole weight of public affairs rested on the Grand Vizier, Ali Naeki Khan. The latter, a man of limited intelligence, had made it a rule to satisfy all the wants and caprices of the begums, the eunuchs, and the buffoons, who were assiduous and welcome guests at the palace, in order to retain the favour of his master. Hence a shameless squandering of public money at the Court, and anarchy and a general disorganisation of the public services outside its limits.

Under this feeble and corrupt government, the power of the great nobles and of the taloukdars naturally would and did assume immense proportions. From out of the general ruin, a sort of feudal authority had arisen which ruled the provinces, and left but a nominal power to the King of Lucknow. Before the annexation, 250 forts, each held on an average by a garrison of 400 men, with two guns, were to be found in Oude. This formidable force of 500 guns and 100,000 men only served to sustain the royal power, settle intestine quarrels, and in the last resort to pillage peaceful citizens. The King's army,[1] 60,000 men strong but badly

[1] The raggedest costumes of the Paris carnival can give no idea of the tattered condition of the uniforms of the King of Oude's soldiers. Shakos with damaged crowns, extraordinary feathers, waistcoats without sleeves, and by way of compensation sleeves without waistcoats, trousers covered with patches of every colour, and often full of rents; this is only an imperfect sketch of soldiers so fantastically dressed that, by their side, the poorest Spanish tatterdemalions might have passed for well-dressed men. The population of Oude furnished, however, the great majority of sepoys belonging to the Bengal army, specimens of which in the correctest of uniforms were to be seen on guard at the British Residency. If, however, the regular government and well-filled treasury of the East India Company could transform the wild

paid, badly organised, and badly officered, was of little use to the cause of order, and inspired as much terror to the population as the band of robbers and brigands whom it was its duty to disperse. Independent *de facto*, the great lords living in their strongholds gave way without restraint to their cupidity and sanguinary passions. Both in family quarrels or in disputes between neighbours, fire and steel were the irresistible arguments that finally decided all litigation. Atrocious crimes, scandalous usurpations, if they found at court the interested assistance of some courtesan or some base courtier bought with gold, were easily forgotten or justified. The same influences made themselves strongly felt in the matter of taxation, and rarely did more than a third of the legal income reach the public treasury. The greater the personal power of a criminal, the surer he was of impunity; for the means of corruption he possessed were irresistible.

Informed of this condition of things by the Resident, one of the highest of Anglo-Indian officials, the Company's representatives had for many years addressed sage and severe remonstrances to the Court of Lucknow. But as the right of direct intervention was not recognised by treaty, British diplomacy met with at most apparent adhesion to advice and protests. If, at the request of the Resident, resolute action was taken, with the help of the Company's troops, against some band of robbers whose exactions and cruelties knew no limit, all trace of such salutary rigour soon disappeared. Once the fortress taken, and the band dispersed, the dispossessed chieftain obtained permission from the Court, by means of back-stairs influence, to rebuild his fortifications. A few months after their summary expulsion, the brigands returned triumphant to their stronghold, which was repaired and restored. For forty years the remonstrances of the Company's Government had met with nothing but evasive

men composing its troops into well-dressed soldiers, this prodigy was far beyond the capability of the ignorant ministers who managed affairs in Oude, and their poor soldiers, whose pay was often several years in arrear, before thinking of clothing their body, had to exercise all their ingenuity in order to fill their stomachs.

answers from the Court of Lucknow, which could have been annihilated with the utmost ease by its powerful neighbours. Had not the time arrived for destroying the last vestige of the India of former days, and adding to the Company's dominions the fertile provinces of the kingdom of Oude?

The final annexation, a measure which was warmly controverted at the time, has since brought reproaches on its author, Lord Dalhousie, as one of the decisive causes of the mutiny of the Bengal army. It is only fair to point out, in justification of the eminent statesman, whom a premature death has taken away that at the period when annexation was determined on (December 1855) weighty political considerations militated in its favour. The conspiracy which was slowly undermining the Bengal army was then a sealed book, the mystery of which no European eye had sounded. All the adventurers, all the ruffians of the Indian peninsula were assembled in the kingdom of Oude, which at any moment might become the seat of civil war and drag the British Government into an intervention costly if not dangerous. The example of the anarchy in Oude was not without danger for the neighbouring population; so that the three last British Residents at that Court—Colonel Sleeman, General Low, and Sir J. Outram—all of them eminent men in the Indian service, gave their full assent to the measure of annexation. Sir J. Outram, who had not hesitated to sacrifice his career and a share of booty almost amounting to a fortune in the cause of the Emirs of Scinde, thus sums up his opinion on the point in question:—'I have always been the upholder of native states as long as they retained a spark of vitality, and we could recognise them without infringing our treaties or our suzerain power. It is, therefore, most painful for me to have to acknowledge that if we persist in maintaining this feeble and corrupt dynasty, we shall be sacrificing the interests of ten millions of individuals whom we are bound by treaty to protect by ensuring them a good government, capable of defending the life and property of its subjects.' This testimony on the part of the Bayard of India suffices to protect Lord Dalhousie from the unjust reproaches with which his memory has been pursued.

The Governor-General, in deposing a king unworthy of the sceptre, aimed at something higher than shedding lustre on the close of a tenure of office so brilliantly inaugurated by the conquest of the Punjab. In order, however, to root out the evil, it was not only necessary to dethrone a crowned puppet but to re-establish order as well, in a country that for many years had been in a state of revolution, and to bring the great nobles under the power of the law by dismantling their fortresses and disarming their soldiers. This task, it is evident, was beyond the strength and intellect of any native rulers, so that an inexorable necessity imposed upon Lord Dalhousie a direct intervention in the affairs of Oude. The traditional policy of the Company enjoined treating the King of Oude like the Emperor of Delhi, and assuming the government of the kingdom, whilst leaving the appearance of supreme power to Wajad Ali Shah. The seductive example of the Punjab, which had submitted to European rule for eight years without resistance and almost without a murmur, caused the prudent lessons of the past to be forgotten.

On February 6, 1857, the Governor-General, in conformity with the instructions of the Court of Directors, announced in a proclamation the annexation of Oude. This document, couched in the short authoritative style characteristic of Lord Dalhousie's writings, stated that, since 1801, the Company had faithfully observed all treaties, the disregard of which by the Court of Oude had not exhausted its patience. For fifty years the advice, remonstrances, and threats of the British residents had remained without effect. What had been the result of so much forbearance? At Court ruled a king regardless of state concerns, and surrounded by buffoons and idle courtiers; in the provinces were fiscal agents who exhausted the population by their exactions; royal troops without fixed pay, who paid themselves by pillaging the inhabitants, law and justice unknown, life and property at the mercy of bands of brigands! The Governor-General added that after many vain efforts to recall Wajad Ali and his *entourage* to their duty, the Government, faithful to the treaties, now assumed the right of protecting an unfortunate people against careless tyranny.

A few days before the proclamation was published, Sir J. Outram appeared at the palace and informed the King that the Court of Directors had resolved on taking in hand the government of the kingdom. If the prince would accede to this measure, he should retain the title of king for himself and his descendants, together with a liberal revenue. In case of resistance, proceedings would not be stayed, and he would be entirely dependent on the Company's tender mercies. Wajad Ali received this announcement with a dignity which even the most degraded Orientals often manifest in the great trials of life. Unfolding his turban, he placed it, in sign of mourning, in the hands of the diplomatist, and replied that the English, who had bestowed the throne on his family, might resume the gift at their pleasure. The Company was all-powerful, and he, therefore, accepted without a murmur its decrees for himself and his family, asking nothing and desiring nothing. His rank, his honour, and his crown he was prepared to lose, but at least he would never formally ratify his degradation by accepting a pension from British charity. The resignation, the sobs, and despairing gestures which accompained these words, for once worthy of Wajad Ali's birth, went straight to the generous heart of Outram. But his instructions were peremptory, and he could not even grant to the dispossessed monarch the favour of going to London to appeal to the Queen's compassion. As Wajad Ali refused to reconsider his resolution, General Outram, on the third day following this interview, published the proclamation relative to the annexation of Oude, and the fallen sovereign was sent off to Calcutta, under escort, where he was henceforth confined.

A government accurately modelled on the one which had proved so satisfactory beyond the Sutlej, was formed at Lucknow. Sir J. Outram, the last Resident at the native court, was appointed to govern the new dependency of the

Anglo-Indian empire under the title of chief commissioner. At the very outset, unfortunately, Sir J. Outram, whose experience and chivalrous character might perhaps have triumphed over the difficulties of the situation, was obliged to return to Europe on account of his health. The unskilful and violent measures that followed soon stirred up everyone against a *régime* which, at first, had been accepted with the greatest equanimity.

Sir J. Outram's temporary successor, a painstaking administrator, gave his whole attention to small matters of finance and law, without noticing the germs of anarchy and revolution which were smouldering around him. As it has been already said, the kingdom of Oude contained, either in the King's service or in the pay of the great vassals, 150,000 men, who, from their childhood upwards, had had no other career open to them but that of arms. The Company paid up the arrears due to the royal army, and recruits from its ranks went to form the army of Oude,[1] properly so-called. The disbanded soldiers returned to their homes, where they remained quietly as long as their savings sufficed for their daily wants. The great landowners, on their side, with the political tact possessed by Asiatics to such a remarkable degree, waited to see what the future would bring forth, and abstained from all hostile demonstrations. As they felt no attachment to the fallen government, the nobles were quite disposed to judge the new system on its merits, and more especially from the standpoint of their own interests. The higher classes became uneasy only when they perceived that the authorities insisted inexorably on the payment of taxes and arrears.

As the Company had taken on itself the debts of its predecessor, it had an undeniable right to all that was owing to the ex-sovereign. The payment of these sums, rigorously exacted, led to some few cases of resistance, which, when they did occur, were easily put down. But questions of revenue involved questions of property; and prosecutions, due to the too great zeal of functionaries, led the English judges to

[1] Artillery, 30 guns; cavalry, 3,400 sabres; infantry, 16,400 men.

contest the rights of the most powerful personages in the kingdom. Private lawsuits followed in immense numbers, and were all the more difficult to settle, that for years the law of the strongest had always prevailed, and many even of the most respectable families were unable to produce the title-deeds of their hereditary domains. The good faith of the European judges led them to be deceived by the false testimonies and false documents which are invariably forthcoming in India in all judicial debates, and in many instances their decisions dispossessed legitimate owners for the benefit of impostors. These deplorable mistakes shook the tenure of landed property to its foundations. The influential families of the country, hitherto uncertain as to their line of conduct, became hostile to the English administration and the whole agricultural population, threatened in its interests, waited with impatience for an opportunity of appealing by force of arms against such inopportune severity.

When evil days come, fortune often overwhelms men and nations with blows as rapid as unexpected. One of the elements of the population of Oude, which, judging by appearances, ought to have shown fidelity amounting to devotion in the cause of annexation, sided against it. The kingdom of Oude was the birthplace, as we have seen, of more than-two thirds of the Bengal army,[1] and under the native government, the veterans belonging to the Anglo-Indian service formed with their families a sort of privileged class specially under the protection of the English Resident, who was the intermediary and the mouth-piece of all their

[1] Under the old regulations of the native army, the sepoy invalided, after fifteen years' service, retired to his home on a monthly pension of four rupees. It was a matter of surprise to see young and strong men, in the full enjoyment of health and vigour, relinquishing a service which offered to them certain promotion and increased pay, in order to retire upon this scanty pittance. And yet it was so. Men starved themselves for months, and became weak and emaciated, solely to pass for invalids. By the new rule it was directed that a sepoy who was declared unfit for foreign service should no longer be permitted to retire to his home on invalid pension, but should be retained with the colours and employed in ordinary cantonment duty.—Mr. Gubbins, *The Mutinies in Oude.*

complaints. This privilege, which at first only extended to the soldiers' wives and children, soon extended further. The pensioners traded on their position, and sold their name and influence to distant relatives, and even to strangers. A sepoy was so important a personage that false sepoys constantly appeared who, by means of cast-off uniforms and forged papers, obtained the protection of the Resident for themselves and their friends. All this was put an end to by the annexation, and the whole population was replaced under the common law, to the great benefit of justice in many cases. But the sepoys and their families, stripped of the privileges they had enjoyed so long, thought themselves victims of the ingratitude of their former masters, and swelled the ranks of the disaffected. In the course of the year 1856, it was remarked that the European officers, who, when on journies for the service of the Government or their own pleasure, had been hitherto received as respected friends in the villages inhabited by retired sepoys, no longer met with anything but incivility and rudeness from their former hosts.

The levity with which the English Administration had entered upon the most thorny internal questions was but a venial sin compared with the blind confidence which caused the simplest measures of precaution to be neglected. The taloukdars, it is true, were invited by proclamation to dismantle their fortresses, and give up their artillery, in return for a liberal indemnity. The proclamation remained a dead letter as regarded fortifications, but many chiefs, attracted by a sum which made the operation a profitable one, handed over numbers of useless old guns. Events close at hand were to cause excellent arms of all sorts to appear as by magic, and to show that the measure of disarmament had not even been imperfectly executed. Another fault, of which the onus must not fall exclusively on the Indian Administration, properly so-called, was the following one. In anticipation of difficulties which might arise from the annexation of Oude, Lord Dalhousie had asked the authorities at home that the Royal army, which under his rule had reached a minimum it had never before attained, should be reinforced by a few thousand soldiers. His request was refused by the Court of Directors, governed as usual by a spirit of petty economy. And not only this, but after Lord Dalhousie's departure, the new Governor-General, Lord Canning, deluded by the favourable reports he received of the state of Oude, conceived the fatal idea of despatching to the manœuvres at the camp near Amballah, in the early part of 1857, all the European troops which had been stationed at Lucknow to facilitate by their presence the annexation. The 32nd R.A., about 700 men strong, was the only regiment retained in Oude, and yet, the Anglo-Indian forces which formed the majority of the Lucknow garrison being connected by numerous ties with the native population, their entire devotion could not be depended upon. Neither in the capital, nor in the whole extent of the country, was there a single citadel or entrenchment worthy of the name, where, in case of necessity, the European authorities and their defenders might find shelter for a few days.

When, in the beginning of March 1857, Sir Henry Lawrence succeeded the functionary who had temporarily replaced Sir J. Outram, the absence of political system, and the exclusive attention to the interests of the public treasury, had already borne their fruits. The country was bristling with fortresses and infested with disbanded soldiers, who were utterly without resource, and only fit to gain their living by thieving and brigandage. The whole population, unsettled by intrigues and secret manœuvres, blindly accepted the thousand and one rumours held up to its indignation of the projects of the English Government against the native religion and the spirit of caste. Waggons full of powder made of old bones had arrived, it was said, at Lucknow, and this substance, mixed with flour and sweetmeats, was intended to defile the whole population. It is useless to add that no one, for love or money, was able to procure even an ounce of the impure matter. The report did not the less pass from mouth to mouth, from bazaar to bazaar, and became a certain and indisputable fact in the eyes of the credulous multitude.[1]

Intelligent and large-hearted man as he was, Sir H. Lawrence understood at a glance the faults that had been committed in subordinating political to financial interests. The fiscal agents received orders to be very moderate in their demands on private individuals; and the great landowners were officially informed that the vexatious and administrative persecutions to which they had been exposed since the annexation would not occur again. Sir H. Lawrence, moreover, neglected no means of destroying the germs of indiscipline and revolt which were all around him. His measures met with temporary success, and during the months of March and April, the intrigues of conspirators and the appeals to insurrection made by fakirs and pandits led to no very serious case of insubordination. They even afforded an opportunity of ascertaining that a feeling of loyalty to their colours still existed in the hearts of the sepoys. Several times, secret emissaries and seditious priests were denounced by soldiers. Such acts of devotion were systematically and liberally rewarded; and yet, so difficult is it to appreciate and explain the motives that guide Hindoos in their actions, a few weeks from that time, the same men, officers and privates, whose loyalty had been recompensed by promotion or pecuniary gratifications, rallied almost without exception to the cause of the mutiny.

Sir H. Lawrence soon became conscious of the error com-

[1] A very curious example of similar credulity, which I witnessed some years ago at the hill station of Simla, may be quoted here. A report got abroad among the hill men of that sanitarium, that the Governor-General had sent orders to have a certain quantity of human fat prepared and sent down to Calcutta; and that for this purpose the authorities were engaged in entrapping hill men, who were then killed, and boiled down for their fat. It might be thought that it would not have been difficult to disabuse them of so absurd a notion. A number of hill men are employed about every household at Simla in carrying letters, and in a variety of domestic duties, which bring them into daily contact with Europeans. But, for a long time, the attempt to undeceive them was of no avail. The panic increased and spread, until a large number of hill men fled from the station; nor were they, I believe, ever thoroughly convinced of the falsehood of the report.—Mr. Gubbins, *The Mutinies in Oude.*

mitted in neglecting to provide a fortified place where, in case of danger, the European authorities might take refuge until the arrival of the reinforcements necessary to carry on the struggle in the open field. By his order, provisions, grain, and cattle were collected as early as the month of May, and entrenchments were thrown up round the Residency, before which all the efforts of the insurgents were destined to fail. The Residency, a sort of European quarter, was situated on the banks of the River Gounti, outside the town, and in close proximity, on its north side, to the Char-Bagh, the Chattar-Manzil, and other royal palaces.[1]

A post of native troops at the Gate of Honour (Bailie Guard) was originally its only defence. A macadamised road, that crossed the River Gounti on an iron bridge, led from the Residency to the different camps. At some distance from the bridge were the ruins of the Machi Bhowan. This ancient stronghold had played an important part in the days when a constant struggle was going on between the native chiefs and the viceroys representing the Mogul Emperors, who then resided at Faizabad, and by its strong position and historical associations exercised an immense prestige over the population of Lucknow. Sir H. Lawrence bought

[1] The Marquis de Carabas himself, that celebrated landowner, according to the tale of the 'Chat Botté,' might have lamented, and not unreasonably, the inequality of the favours of fortune, if chance had led him to the city of Lucknow and its environs. Everywhere, at every step, one found oneself in presence of public monuments, palaces, pleasure-houses, and mausoleums bearing the insignia of native royalty: two fishes by way of coat-of-arms on the façade, and gilt parasols on the top of the building. What explains this number of royal properties is the custom of each new sovereign on his accession to build a new palace; so that most of these edifices, abandoned the day after their erection, were falling into ruins, and the condition even of those inhabited by the King left much to be desired. As to the furniture of the royal abodes, nothing more mean could be imagined.

All this is very far from that India of the 'Arabian Nights' which the traveller carries naïvely in his imagination. One could, however, form an idea of some details of the private life of Indian royalty, which were not altogether devoid of interest. The apartments reserved for the harem occupied more than half the building in all royal habitations, for the King of Lucknow was one of the greatest polygamists on earth; his seraglio contained 500 women, and on one occasion he conceived the curious idea of having himself married four times in the same day, married, be it understood, with all the rites of Mohammedan law.

this building, which he designed to use as a basis of defence. Works were begun, intended to assure the communications between the Residency and the Machi Bhowan, and to restore the dismantled ramparts of the latter. But the events which followed one another with startling rapidity, and the imperious necessities of the moment, did not allow the full completion of the system of defence, as we shall see further on; and the lines never extended beyond the enclosure traced round the Residency.

The military forces assembled at Lucknow (about 8,000 men) were not all massed on one point. The 32nd R.A. were a mile and a half away in barracks, known under the name of Chowpeyrah Issabal. The greatest agglomeration of troops was in the camp of Muriaon, three miles and a half from the town, and consisted of one battery of European artillery, of the 13th, 48th, 71st B.A., and of three batteries of native artillery. The 7th regular cavalry, B.A., was at the camp of Moudkipore, which was a mile and a half distant from that of Muriaon.

The first acts of insubordination did not take place in the ranks of the Bengal army, but in those of the regiments that had been recently organised, in order to take the place of the Royal army. In the first days of May, the 7th irregular Oude infantry refused to receive cartridges when exercising. The explanations, entreaties, and threats of the officers only produced an apparent submission, and after long hesitation, the regiment deserted its lines with arms and baggage. Pursued by a superior force, the mutineers were overtaken, disarmed, and brought back to the town.

As an additional proof of the curious vacillations of even the most mutinous corps, we will mention that this regiment remained quietly in its quarters for several weeks. It was only after the mutiny of the troops belonging to the Bengal army, which were stationed at Lucknow, that the native officers of the Oude regiment announced to the superior authorities that they and their men intended to abandon the Company's service. The entire corps dispersed without violence and without other formalities.

The inquiry which followed on these beginnings of mutiny proved that there existed a previous understanding between the local forces and the 48th B.A. A mutiny was imminent, but, notwithstanding the disastrous news received at that time from Mirut and Delhi, there was a few days' respite, of which the Chief Commissioner took advantage with great activity and foresight.[1] Martial law was proclaimed, and everything was put on a war-footing. Under different pretexts, strong detachments were sent into distant provinces, and the effective force of the native troops was thereby diminished. A volunteer corps was formed of officers without regiments, of civil functionaries, of merchants, and planters. The business of collecting provisions and the work of the fortifications were not neglected. Indefatigable and always at work, the energetic Sir Henry scarcely allowed himself a few hours' rest, and wandered at night in disguise about the populous quarters of Lucknow, in order to judge for himself of the state of the public mind. The utility of all these measures soon became apparent.

On the morning of May 30, the 71st and 48th infantry, and a part of the 7th regular cavalry B.A., raised the standard of revolt in the lines of Muriaon and Moudkipore. We shall not dwell on the scenes of murder and pillage that marked the day with bloodshed. The brigadier in command, his aide-de-camp who hurried to the spot on the first news of the disturbance, were killed, as well as several other officers. A strong detachment, sent the next day against the cantonments of Moudkipore, where the mutineers had concentrated their forces, was attacked, on the skirts of the plain in which the camp was situated, by about 1,500 men deployed as skirmishers. As the artillery was in the rear, the action could not be begun at once, and the native horsemen forming the vanguard made use of the delay to desert in great numbers to the enemy. Notwithstanding their defection, when once the struggle commenced the issue was

[1] See Documents, No. II., 'Letter from Sir H. Lawrence to Colonel Inglis.'

not doubtful for an instant. As soon as the European guns opened fire, the sepoys dispersed in the direction of Sitapore, where they remained inactive for several weeks. This first nucleus of the mutiny was composed of a little more than a half of the 48th and 71st N.I., of the 7th regular cavalry, and of some companies of the 13th B.A.—about 2,000 men in all. The want of unity and initiative amongst the mutineers was of great advantage to the English. It gave Sir H. Lawrence a few days' delay, which he utilised in providing for the defence of the place.

Other, and equally severe trials were reserved for the representatives of English authority in the kingdom of Oude. In the early part of June, there arrived successively intelligence of the Nana's treachery, and of the dangerous position of the garrison at Cawnpore, and also a letter from Sir Hugh Wheeler imploring help and protection for the women and children.[1] Secret instructions authorised the evacuation of the kingdom in case of urgency, and it may be believed that, had the Commissioner-General listened to the entreaties of General Wheeler, and united the garrison of Lucknow to that of Cawnpore, this concentration of forces would have sufficed to save many victims. But on the other hand, it could not be denied that the evacuation of Oude would strike a terrible blow at the prestige of the English in India. The victorious flag of the mutiny already floated on the walls of Delhi, and were the second town of the Peninsula abandoned to the rebels their hopes would be raised to the highest pitch. The evacuation of the recently annexed kingdom would not merely be a strategical movement; it would be, *de facto*, a proclamation of its independence. Whatever might be the danger for him and his, Sir H. Lawrence resolved, perhaps wrongly—if an heroic resolution can be wrong in the eyes of history—to remain faithful at his post.

Round him all was disaster and ruin. The mutiny had devastated the European stations of Faizabad, Sitapore, and Setone in the beginning of June. At Schahjahanpore, on

[1] See Documents, No. III., 'Letters of the Besieged at Cawnpore.'

Sunday, May 31, the sepoys of the 28th B.A. rushed into church during divine service, killing the collector and several officers; but the greater part of the European colony, that is to say, fourteen civilians or officers, nine women, four children, and a little half-caste drummer-boy, succeeded in escaping from the mutineers, and in reaching the neighbouring station of Mohamdi.

The arrival of the fugitives caused great commotion amongst the garrison of Mohamdi, which consisted of a detachment of the 9th irregular Oude corps, and a rising became imminent. Under these circumstances, the commander of the station, Captain Orr, assembled his native officers, and made an appeal to their humanity, which moved them so greatly, that, crossing their arms on the head of one of their comrades, they swore to conduct the Europeans to the station of Sitapore.

'The convoy left Mohamdi,' says Captain Orr, 'at five o'clock in the evening, and arrived towards the middle of the night at Barwar. Before departing the sepoys divided amongst themselves 110,000 rupees, which were in the public chest, and let loose the prisoners from the jail. Next morning we started for Aurangabad, the men on foot or on horseback, the women in a carriage and on the baggage waggon at the head of the column. After two hours' march, a first halt had just been ordered, when a horseman galloped past us and told us to go wherever we wished. We did not need to have the words repeated, and hope was beginning to rise again in all hearts when we perceived that we were pursued. Notwithstanding all efforts to hasten the pace of the carriage and waggon, our miserable convoy was soon overtaken and surrounded by soldiers. We were proceeding quietly, when suddenly, at a mile from Aurangabad, a furious sepoy seized a gun which Captain Key carried in his hand, and shot down old Lieutenant Shields, who was riding along with the others. This was the signal for a general massacre. By a sort of instinct we took refuge behind a large tree, and the women hastily got down. Bullets were whistling in all directions, and the air resounded with the most hideous clamour. The poor women fell on their knees in prayer, and awaited death with admirable firmness. Resigned to my fate, I was standing amid the wretched victims, when the thought of my wife and child stirred up all my desire to live, and I ran forward towards the murderers. I was recognised by the sepoy Gourdhan, of the 6th company, who called out to me to drop my pistol and have confidence in him. I obeyed mechanically, and Gourdhan and several of his companions, pressing round me, made a rampart of their bodies. The work of death went on for another ten minutes. I was scarcely three hundred paces from the fatal tree. I saw poor Captain Lysaght on his knees in the middle of the plain, his arms crossed, and his gun unloaded by his side. His commanding attitude so overawed the murderers, that they only dared approach him when he fell pierced with bullets. Women, children, every one was massacred with infernal cruelty. The life of the little half-caste drummer-boy alone was spared. The dead bodies were then stripped of their clothes.'

A few fugitives, more fortunate than the authorities of Schahjahanpore, met, it is true, with generous protection in the houses of great chiefs and even under humble village roofs; and, after enduring every species of anguish and suffering which the heart and body of men can support, succeeded at last in reaching Lucknow. Alas! for such sorely-tried ones many dangers were still reserved for them in the haven where they sought refuge, but at least they were to have the consolation of dying with arms in their hands, under the shadow of the flag of their country!

If the revolutionary volcano had not yet overwhelmed the Residency, premonitory signs announced an approaching eruption. Every day new proclamations, calling on the population to undertake the holy war, were posted on the gates of palaces, mosques, and Brahmin temples; the rabble carried headless figures about the streets, dressed as European children and officers. In the early part of June certain ruffians, after having murdered a clerk of the Administration, made an attack on the police station—an unprecedented fact in the history of India—which was vigorously repulsed by the agents. A plot, implicating several members of the former royal family and an ex-Grand Vizier, was discovered, and the ringleaders imprisoned. Almost daily arrests and executions repressed these elements of disorder, but each day diminished the strength and prestige of English authority, which, in the end of June, was without influence beyond the limits of the Residency and of the Machi Bhowan.

This state of things was well known to the mutinous regiments stationed at Nawabganje, and they finally determined on attacking the Europeans in their last entrenchments. On June 29 the advanced posts reported the enemy's presence at Chinhat, a village some eight miles off. Sir H. Lawrence at once called a council of war, composed of the chief authorities of the garrison. The discussion was very sharp; for, as in the Punjab and at Delhi, the officers of sepoys loudly proclaimed their confidence in the men still remaining with their regiments. A civilian, in a manner and with an energy most offensive to the Chief Commissioner, is said to have contrasted the passive attitude of the garrison with that of the heroes of the last century, who, at the head of a mere handful of men, had conquered India for England. Colonel Inglis, of the 32nd R.A., whose name later on was gloriously connected with the defence, was the only one to deprecate any offensive operations. His advice did not prevail, and it was decided to attack the sepoys on the following day.

The expedition, some 600 men strong, of which 300 were Europeans, started on June 30, at dawn, under Sir H. Lawrence. Deceived by false reports, the general marched beyond the point fixed upon beforehand, and arrived unprepared in presence of the enemy, who was concealed in the jungle and behind the clumps of trees. The Europeans, though hard pressed, kept their adversaries in check, and the victory seemed assured, but treason was at work. The native drivers of the artillery cut the traces, tumbled the guns into ditches, and passed over to the sepoys, leaving the

300 Queen's soldiers exposed to a well-directed fire. Eye-witnesses have since declared that in this fight the artillery and cavalry of the sepoys were commanded by deserters, infamous traitors to their faith and to the flag of their country. Attacked on both sides by an enemy far superior in numbers, threatened in its communications with the Residency, the English force was obliged to retreat, abandoning almost all its dead and wounded, together with three guns. The heat, the failure of ammunition, and the want of cavalry were cruelly felt during the terrible hours of the retreat. Out of 300 soldiers of the Royal army, a third only reached the Residency. Sir H. Lawrence, worn out by fatigue and despair, was carried back on a gun. Fortunately the pursuers turned back at the iron bridge, in face of the fire of the batteries of the Residency and of the Machi Bhowan. Neglecting once more the opportunity, the rebels, instead of boldly following up their success, forded the River Gounti, and overran the Chowke, a wealthy quarter of the town, on whose inhabitants they levied heavy contributions.

The few hours' breathing time which followed the defeat of Chinhat enabled the English to repair, to some extent, the disasters of the day. Hitherto the enclosure round the Residency had been the foremost consideration in all plans of defence. It was a species of citadel in which a European garrison could always, as a last resource, find protection or a glorious death. Its incomplete entrenchments sheltered all the important stores of provisions and war material and the royal jewels,[1] valued at 80 lakhs of rupees. The decisive moment had arrived; the losses met with in the disaster of Chinhat made it necessary to diminish the extent of ground to be defended. Orders were given to evacuate the Machi Bhowan and to blow up its fortifications. This measure was carried out with as much skill as success, and the garrison of the ancient castle entered the Residency just as

[1] The transport of the Crown jewels from the palace to the Residency, which took place in June, exposed the honesty of men and officers entrusted with their removal to a trial which all could not withstand. Some worm-eaten chests fell to pieces on the way, and the precious jewels which were in them fell out, and were not all returned to the authorities.

the ramparts were shattered into atoms. During the night working parties had hastily completed, as far as possible, the defences of the place, but there had not been time enough to destroy the neighbouring houses that commanded the inner enclosure of the Residency, and the enemy at once took possession of them.

Events had indeed moved with startling rapidity. On the very morning that fire was opened against the Residency, very few of the Europeans who had taken refuge there understood the full extent of the disaster at Chinhat. The majority, accustomed to the abject submission of the Asiatic race, refused to see the situation in all its terrible truth.

The Residency at Lucknow stands to the north of the town, not far from the Char-Bagh, the Moti Manzil, the Chattar Manzil, and other royal dwelling-places. The vast undulating park contains the houses and bungalows reserved for the Resident and his numerous staff, as well as for the offices of different European administrations, such as the home, finance, and justice departments; that for the repression of Thuggee, the church, and the hospital. Under the pressure of events these buildings, whether public or private, had been united by incomplete entrenchments, palisades, and battlemented walls, the whole of which formed the fortified camp where the English garrison sought an asylum. The names of the various posts, of which we merely give the most important, Sikh Square, Mess Brigade, Martinière's School House, Gubbins's House, indicate the various elements of which the fortifications of the garrison were composed. Officers without regiments, magistrates, administrators, merchants, planters, clerks, loyal sepoys, Sikh soldiers, military pensioners, and, as only efficient force, the 32nd R.A., now reduced to 600 fighting men—in all, 927 Europeans and 765 native soldiers or servants. The ramparts of the Residency had also given shelter to the families of the civil and military officers and soldiers, about 200 women and 250 children. Amongst the latter were the juvenile inmates of the Martinière School.[1]

[1] The General Claude Martin, who was born at Lyons in 1732, and died at

The fortifications on the south-west front were unfinished, and, in some parts, scarcely commenced. The native *employés* of the administrations and the officers' servants who had left the Residency in crowds during the disastrous day of June 30, had not dared or had not been able to return on the following day, owing to the enemy's fire. The head of the Commissariat had been seriously wounded in the retreat, and at first there ensued terrible confusion in the distribution of food. The horses and cattle, deserted by those who ought to have attended to them, and maddened by hunger, broke loose and rushed wildly round the enclosure under a shower of bullets.

The besiegers pushed forward the works of their batteries with great activity, and by the end of the first week the place was completely invested by a circle of the enemy's guns. The great object of the attack was the east front of the Residency, the house of the Resident, and the Cawnpore battery. The position of the besieging batteries was generally very well selected, and in some places they were not two hundred yards from the lines of defence; a shelter of some sort was erected near each gun to which the artillery-men could withdraw, when the sentinels announced the approach of a projectile. The besiegers made good use also of the advantages offered by the ground, and sheltered their guns behind a wall or the corners of streets, only exposing themselves for an instant in order to discharge their pieces. Still, wherever the besiegers' guns could take effect, the sepoys' fire was promptly silenced. The houses round the Residency, which there had not been time enough to destroy, and which commanded the inner enclosure, were occupied by skilful marksmen, whose fire caused heavy losses to the English. An African eunuch belonging to the King made himself conspicuous from the first by his audacity and the accuracy of his aim. The losses caused by this man and his

Lucknow at the beginning of the century, left by will the greater part of a fortune acquired in the service of Indian princes of the good old time to the founding of large educational establishments at Lyons, Calcutta, and Lucknow. In memory of their benefactor, they received the name of 'La Martinière,' both in Europe and Asia.

companions in the British ranks were such, that a sortie was organised on July 7 to carry their formidable position. The house contained, besides sharp-shooters, some twenty individuals armed with bows and arrows, regular savages, fresh from the jungle. They were all bayoneted, but the expedition failed in its object, for there was no time to blow up the building, which was amost immediately re-occupied by the sepoys.

A few days before, a terrible blow had been dealt on the unfortunate garrison. On July 2, Sir Henry Lawrence was writing at a table in one of the rooms of the Residency, when he was wounded in the thigh by the fragment of a shell. A few hours previously, a projectile had exploded in the room, for the rebels pointed their guns with remarkable accuracy; but the noble-minded soldier, resisting the remonstrances of his staff, had refused to take refuge in another less exposed part of the building, which he had given up to the women and children. His wound was a very dangerous one, and he died from its effects on July 4, after having undergone the torture of amputation. His death was worthy of his life, and up to the last moment his thoughts dwelt on the necessary measures for perfecting and strengthening the means of defence.[1]

[1] Major Banks, in his diary, says that Sir Henry's last directions communicated to him after his wound were chiefly these:—

1st. Reserve fire; check all wall firing.

2nd. Carefully register ammunition for guns and small arms in store. Carefully register daily expenditure as far as possible.

3rd. Spare the precious health of Europeans in every possible way from shot and sun.

4th. Organise working parties for night labour.

5th. Entrench, entrench, entrench! Erect traverses. Cut off enemy's fire.

6th. Turn every horse out of the entrenchments except enough for four guns. Keep Sir Henry Lawrence's horse, Ludakee; it is a gift to his nephew, George Lawrence.

7th. Use the State prisoners as a means for getting in supplies, by gentle means if possible, or by threats.

8th. Enrol every servant as hisdar, or carrier of earth. Pay liberally—double, quadruple.

9th. Turn out every native who will not work, save menials who have more than abundant labour.

10th. Write daily to Allahabad or Agra.

The death of this respected chief was concealed as long as possible from his countrymen, whom it would plunge in the deepest grief, and from the enemies whose courage and hopes it would inflame. It was necessary, however, that the new authorities should be recognised. Sir Henry, thinking that, under the circumstances, it was more urgent than ever to place power in the hands of the most worthy, conferred on his death-bed the functions of Commissioner on Major Banks, his military secretary, who had been long acquainted with the politics of the kingdom, and gave the command of the troops to Colonel Inglis, of the 32nd R.A. The first of these nominations was against the strict rules of Anglo-Indian hierarchy, and provoked some discussions in the council of defence. But the good sense of the malcontents themselves soon put a stop to all objections. The moment was not suited for a dispute on points of etiquette, and public opinion moreover ratified the choice made by the late general.

At the battle of Chinhat, the effective of the sepoys' forces comprised the 13th and 48th B.A., the 4th, 5th, and 7th irregular regiments of the special Oude force, and a numerous cavalry. But from the very beginning of the siege the regiments which mutinied in the provinces betook themselves to the capital, and the ranks of the besiegers were swelled by nearly the whole forces of the Bengal and Oude armies, that is to say, by nineteen infantry and six cavalry regiments. The holy war, and the hope of pillage, had likewise attracted to the scene of events the greater portion of the troops in the service of the great vassals; and finally, the total mass of the sepoys, which in July amounted to almost 100,000 men, was increased by all the adherents of the former dynasty, by the eunuchs and the populace of the town. Fortunately for the English, dissensions—religious, political, and private—indiscipline and bad passions of all sorts,

11th. Sir H. Lawrence's servants to receive one year's pay; they are to work for any other gentleman who wants them; or they may leave if they prefer to do so.

12th. Place on Sir H. Lawrence's tomb no epitaph but this: 'Here lies Henry Lawrence, who tried to do his duty. No capitulation! no capitulation!'

existed in great force amongst their adversaries at Lucknow, as at Delhi. A putative son of Wajad Ali Shah, Prince Borjis Kadr, was raised to the throne, but never enjoyed more than nominal power. Besides this, an impostor, favoured by the priests, under the pretext of a divine mission, soon put himself forward as his rival. The authority of Wajad Ali's brother, who had been placed in command of the troops, was no longer respected. The officers, chosen by the soldiers, themselves appointed the generals. The latter often paid with their life the sweets of their short-lived dignity. European revolutionists are not the only ones who enjoy the privilege of decreeing victories and denouncing treason as the cause of shameful defeats, which are in reality the consequence of cowardice and insubordination. As to the peaceable citizens, they merely lived to obey, according to the Oriental expression. A reign of terror weighed upon Lucknow. Overwhelmed by taxes and exactions of all sorts, the bankers and merchants and all orderly people must certainly have regretted their late masters, who had always scrupulously respected property and justice.

On July 21 the besiegers made a general assault. From the early morning sentinels, stationed on the ruined tower of the Residency, had signalled numerous movements of the troops. At ten o'clock a mine exploded in front of the enclosure. Fortunately, the galleries had not been properly traced, and the attempt failed, leaving unharmed the works that had been threatened. At the signal given by this explosion, the Residency was enveloped in a circle of fire, and the sepoys advanced in compact masses to the trenches surrounding that portion of the lines of defence; but they were obliged to retire with heavy losses, before the well-directed fire of a detachment of the 32nd R.A., which held this position. Both attack and defence were not less vigorous at Times House, where the garrison was exclusively composed of loyal native soldiers, at Gubbins's House, and at the posts of Justice and Finance. Their want of success did not, however, discourage the besiegers; and the next day, whether by chance or design, all their efforts were directed against the weakest points of the place, more especially against Gubbins's House, which was commanded by buildings that there had been no time to destroy. Major Banks, whom Sir H. Lawrence had appointed his successor as Commissioner-General, was struck down dead by a bullet in the head, as he was watching the movements of the enemy on the roof of this house. He had fully justified the confidence reposed in him by his illustrious predecessor, and his death caused just and unanimous regret amongst the European garrison. After his demise there was no need of any civil authority, as the whole European population was placed under martial law. The post of Commissioner remained vacant, and Brigadier Inglis exercised, without control, the commandership-in-chief.

The results of these last days were satisfactory; the sepoys had courageously attempted a supreme effort, and not only had they been repulsed, but the losses of the garrison had not exceeded those in the early part of the siege (four killed and twelve wounded). It seemed now certain that the Residency could resist the attacks of the besiegers till help should arrive, and help was near at hand—a secret emissary had brought this good news.

On the evening of July 22 a strange scene, worthy of the pencil of a great artist, took place in the lower rooms of that very Gubbins's House, on the roof of which Major Banks had met a few hours previously with a glorious death.[1] 'The low room of the ground-floor, with a single light carefully screened on the outer side, lest it should attract the bullets of the enemy, the anxious faces of the men who crowded round and listened with breathless attention to question and answer, the exclamation of joy as pieces of good tidings were given out, and laughter at some of Angad's jeers upon the enemy. More retired would be shown the indistinct forms of the women in their night attire, who had been attracted from their rooms in hopes of catching early some part of the good news which had come in.' This messenger was the faithful sepoy Angad, whose name will be

[1] Mr. Gubbins, *The Mutinies in Oude.*

for ever associated with the defence of Lucknow. He brought the news of Havelock's marvellous success over the Nana and the re-capture of Cawnpore. The rainbow now appeared through the storm, and once again all hearts ventured to hope.

The change of the monsoon took place at this time, and proved of great assistance to the defence; the ground of the Residency was well drained, and the rains of the season, which purified the foul air and produced a temperature more favourable to European constitutions than the heat of summer, threw great difficulties in the way of the besiegers with regard to laying mines, making trenches, transporting guns and ammunition, and finally, in the movements of their troops. The month of July, however, did not come to a close without cruelly trying the garrison. Many officers had been killed, the hospital was thronged, and the feeble effective force of the 32nd was reduced by 170 men.

We shall not attempt to describe day by day the proceedings of besiegers and besieged. The painful and monotonous account would show the same faults, the same reverses continually recurring on the side of the former, the want of unity amongst the leaders, the ignorance of the officers; and the indiscipline of the soldiers prevented the success of any general attack. The fire of the besieged batteries was very accurate, but the artillerymen, in their puerile hatred of the European, neglected the fortifications, in order to aim their balls at the defenders themselves. Ladders were often wanting when an assault was to be given, and the mines, being badly laid, exploded under the very feet of the assailants. At the important moment the immense multitude, that had but a last effort to make in order to bury the handful of Europeans at bay beneath its overwhelming mass, lost heart, and did not put forth its whole strength. In the skirmishes that daily occurred, the adversaries fought hand to hand, and, in the style of Homer's heroes, mingled insults with their blows.[1] The labours of the Engineers, aided by

[1] Let us here recall the memory of a brave Frenchman, who succumbed in this struggle between civilisation and barbarism. The chances of an adven-

the self-sacrificing exertions of all, raised up barriers which the rebels found impassable. In vain did mines and projectiles destroy the fortifications. The wounded left their beds to seek the post of danger; a mutilated arm was no impediment to the handling of a musket. A rampart of stout hearts defended the breach till nightfall, when, favoured by darkness, the damage done was quickly repaired. Civilians, officers, soldiers—everybody worked, and only laid down the musket to take up the spade or the pickaxe. 'Entrench, entrench,' were Sir H. Lawrence's words when dying, and his orders, obeyed beyond the tomb, secured the general safety. A still more painful work was burying the carcasses of the horses and cattle already in a state of decomposition. It was necessary to descend into the very bowels of the earth in order to frustrate the operations of the enemy's sappers, and finally to bury the dead in the narrow graveyard. Biers were wanting, and the bodies were laid to rest in their last home sewn up in sacks. It was a sight at once sublime and horrible to see this handful of braves struggling against innumerable foes, with their ranks decimated by every sort of privation and disease.

The coarse rations, which satisfied the robust appetites of the men, were exceedingly trying to the delicate constitutions of women and children. Bread was entirely wanting. All bakers, without exception, had disappeared from the outset of the siege, and it was impossible to think of withdrawing men from the defence to employ them in baking bread. It was necessary to replace bread by 'chippatis,' a sort of cake cooked on the gridiron, very tasteless and difficult of digestion. Sugar, coffee, and

turous life had landed Duprat, an ex-non-commissioned officer of the Chasseurs d'Afrique, behind the fortifications of the Residency. The leaders of the mutiny, having an exaggerated idea of his military talents, if not of his courage, offered him enormous sums if he would join them, but he answered that not all the treasures of the world would induce him to serve a cause dishonoured by the blood of women and children. His refusal excited the rage of the sepoys to the highest pitch. 'Dog of Christian, we shall have you against your will,' said they to Duprat, who, as soon as he was recognised in the fray, was the object of all attack. These threats were finally carried into execution, and Duprat died from the effects of a wound in the shoulder.

tea were drawing to an end in the Government stores and in the private houses. A decoction of roasted grain took the place of coffee for the soldiers. In many families, as we have said, no servants had been able to return since the defeat of Chinhat; in others, they had deserted since the beginning of the siege, and the ladies of the family had to perform all menial offices. The danger was not less great, however, at the bedside of a sick child or by a kitchen fire than in the trenches; for balls, bullets, and fragments of shells were incessantly falling into every dwelling-place. Not a single corner of the place, however sheltered, was safe from the enemy's fire, and no one could count on his life being safe for more than five minutes.

Fighting, sentry duty, and working in the trenches, first under a burning sun, and later under torrents of rain, developed amongst the Europeans all the diseases peculiar to tropical climates—such as fever, dysentery, and cholera, which soon extended to the women and children. The hospital, overflowing with sick and wounded, possessed very few doctors and attendants. The air of the wards was noxious and pestilential. Swarms of flies, of filthy vermin, rats and mice, attacked in their beds the patients who were too weak to drive away these nauseous visitors, poisoned the sick and caused gangrene amongst the wounded. Scarcely a few cases of successful amputation can be mentioned. The courage of all, however, whether defenders of the breach, mothers, or young girls, was equal to the emergency. No one cherished the slightest delusion as to the consequences of a capitulation—capitulation meant death for the whole garrison, men, women, and children.[1] All were determined

[1] The Rev. Dr. Polehampton, one of the glorious victims of the siege, relates in his interesting journal that on being asked by Major Banks how he would advise a father and husband to act, in case the fortune of war caused the place to fall into the enemy's power, answered that it was a very difficult question to determine, but that for his part, were he certain that the last outrages were reserved for his own wife, he would not hesitate to kill her himself. Colonel Inglis afterwards asked me whether I thought his wife would be justified in killing her own children, rather than let them be murdered by the natives. I said, 'No: for children could but be killed; whereas we had been told that at Delhi young delicate ladies had been dragged through the streets, violated by many, and then murdered.' God forgive me if I gave

to perish under the ruins of the Residency; the only watchword was—'No capitulation.'

From the first days of the siege, the military leaders had felt that the only course of action open to the garrison was to keep behind the fortifications until the arrival of reinforcements strong enough to drive away the besiegers, or to cover the complete evacuation of the Residency. The appearance of the sepoy Angad, on July 22, awakened great hopes in the besieged; but the first half of the month of August was already over, and the messenger, who had started again with despatches on the day following his arrival, had not yet returned.

Other agents had left the entrenchments since Angad's departure. A sepoy of the 48th, for instance, left with arms and baggage, as if deserting. and carried away despatches under the plate of his musket. Some time afterwards, an old woman got out of the fortifications with letters, which she was to give to an agent in the town. These messengers never reached their destination. The besiegers subjected all whom they met in the streets or on the roads to a minute personal investigation, and the most infinite precautions were necessary to conceal letters. Written in Greek characters, on the finest paper, these letters were inserted in a quill sealed with wax at both ends. It need not be said that in case of discovery the messenger was immediately put to death. News was obtained more especially through the Sikhs, stationed in the work known as Sikh Square. They were in constant communication with those of their countrymen who had deserted to the enemy, and who constantly advanced close to the fortifications in order to relate how matters were going on, and entreat their former companions to imitate their example. According to them the place could never be relieved, and must fall before long. Events were not, however, to justify these prognostics.

Angad reappeared at length, safe and sound, on August 15.

wrong advice, but I was excited, and I know at the time I should have killed Emmie, rather than have allowed her to be thus dishonoured and tortured by these bloodthirsty savage idolaters.—*Memoirs of the Rev. Dr. Polehampton.*

He brought a laconic message from the Adjutant-General of the British forces, announcing that the troops would start on the following day, and arrive before Lucknow in four or five days more. The last paragraph instructed the besieged to operate their junction with the relieving army at any cost. The letter, dated Mangalwar, August 4, was already more than a week old, and Angad explained the delay by saying that he had been stopped by the sepoys and detained at the foreposts. As soon as he was set at liberty, he had retraced his steps, but the British tents had been struck, and he had found it impossible to reach the new camp.

This intelligence no doubt authorised great hopes; the liberators were only five days' march off—their arrival was imminent. But, on the other hand, the besieged were told to cut themselves a passage to the relieving forces. Could the attempt be made with a decimated garrison, encumbered, moreover, with so many women and children? Colonel Inglis's reply, which Angad carried off with him the next day,[1] described the dangers of the situation in

[1] To General Havelock.

Lucknow, August 16th, 1857.

My dear General,—A note from Colonel Tytler to Mr. Gubbins reached last night, dated Mungalwar, 4th instant, the latter part of which is as follows:—

'You must aid us in every way, even to cutting your way out, if we can't force our way in. We have only a small force.'

This has caused me much uneasiness, as it is quite impossible, with my weak and shattered forces, that I can leave my defences. You must bear in mind how I am hampered, that I have upwards of 120 sick and wounded, and at least 220 women and about 230 children, and no carriage of any description, not to speak of sacrificing twenty-three lakhs of treasure and thirty guns of all sorts. In consequence of the news received, I shall soon put this force on half rations. Our provisions will last us then till about September 10. If you hope to save us, no time must be lost in pushing forwards. We are daily attacked by the enemy, who are within a few yards of our defences. Their mines have already weakened our posts, and I have every reason to believe they are driving others. Their 18-pounders are within fifty yards of some of our batteries, and from their position, and our inability to form working parties, we cannot reply to them, and therefore the damage is very great. My strength in Europeans is now 350 and 300 natives, and the men dreadfully harassed, and, owing to part of the Residency having been brought down by round shot, many are without shelter. If our native forces, who are losing confidence, leave us, I do not know how the defences are to be manned. Did you receive a letter and plan from me? Kindly answer this question. Yours truly,

Inglis, Brigadier.

simple and veracious terms, though an involuntary error had slipped in amongst them. Provisions were not so entirely exhausted as Colonel Inglis affirmed. The work of victualling the place had been attended to by the civil authorities under Sir H. Lawrence, but the details were imperfectly known to the Commissariat. The stores still contained considerable quantities of grain when the final evacuation took place on November 29.

On August 27, eleven days after his departure, Angad returned with a letter from General Havelock, promising that the relieving forces should start in twenty or twenty-five days. A communication from General Outram,[1] brought a few days later by the same faithful and indefatigable messenger, certified that Havelock's promises would be scrupulously performed. At the appointed time, a well-equipped army had crossed the Ganges, and with God's help was soon to achieve the relief of the besieged. General Outram, on making known the good news, begged the garrison not to venture outside the lines, and to attempt no movement the issue of which might be uncertain, in order to lend assistance to the relieving troops.

In the preceding chapter we have had occasion to mention General Havelock's first efforts to succour the garrison of Lucknow, and the obstacles which in the month of August completely frustrated his indomitable energy. A short campaign sufficed to re-establish order in Bengal, and allow of the reinforcements despatched from Calcutta to reach Cawnpore. Towards the middle of September, Havelock, having assembled sufficient forces to hazard his heroic adventure, crossed the Ganges, without loss of time, on a bridge

[1] TO BRIGADIER INGLIS.

North Side of the River, September 20, 1857.

The army crossed the river yesterday, and all the material being over, marches to-morrow, and, under the blessing of God, will now relieve you. The rebels, we hear, purpose making a desperate assault upon you as we approach the city, and will be on the watch in expectation of your weakening your garrison to make a diversion in our favour as we attack the city. I beg to warn you against being enticed too far from your works when you hear us engaged. Only such diversion as you can make, without in any way risking your position, should be attempted.

J. OUTRAM.

of boats, at dawn of September 19, with all his troops. The expedition comprised a little more than 3,000 men,[1] under Havelock's orders; for Sir J. Outram, with the most chivalrous disinterestedness, had temporarily relinquished his own right to the command-in-chief. The passage of the river was not seriously opposed, and for the remainder of that day and the whole of the following one the English remained stationary on the bank to cover the transit of baggage and artillery. The start was made on the 21st, and towards midday the vanguard reached the village of Mangalwar, occupied by a rather considerable detachment of sepoys with six guns. The native troops were easily dislodged from this position, and General Outram, at the head of his cavalry, pursued the fugitives, stick in hand, as if he disdained to draw his sword against such adversaries. On the 22nd, after a fifteen miles' march, made under great difficulties and in torrents of rain, the little army encamped at Banni. The lesson of the previous day had not been lost on the enemy, and scarcely a few scouts were seen. On the 23rd a considerable body of sepoys was signalled in the neighbourhood of the Alumbagh. The resistance offered was not more vigorous than in the first fight, and the native forces speedily withdrew to the canal that protects the south side of Lucknow. The Alumbagh, a mosque surrounded by vast brick buildings, and situated in the midst of a large park surrounded by walls, was intended by Havelock to receive a part of the stores and assure communications with Cawnpore. The men were exhausted by the fatigue of marching over heavy ground; they needed rest, and a halt was made on the 24th.

The losses of the last skirmishes, amounting to a hundred dead and wounded, and the absolute necessity of leaving behind a strong detachment in the Alumbagh, made a very perceptible difference in the strength of the British troops, already so few in number at the best. But the aspect of this

[1] European Infantry, 2,388 men; European Volunteer Cavalry, 109; European Artillery, 280; Sikh Infantry, 340; Regular Native Cavalry, 59; total 3,176 men.

mere handful of men inspired confidence in the success of the undertaking. Privations, fatigues, the changes of the seasons had left their traces behind them; but the sombre expression of the eyes testified that neither fire, grape-shot, nor barricades would prevent the Queen's brave soldiers from penetrating to the Residency, where the garrison, though reduced to the last extremity, still raised on high the flag of Great Britain and of European civilisation!

On the 25th, after a prolonged conference of the generals, the British forces began decisive operations at eight o'clock in the morning. The attacking corps was divided into two brigades,[1] the first under Colonel Neill, the second under Colonel Hamilton, 78th Highlanders. Scarcely had the first brigade begun to march, than it was exposed to the fire of skirmishers hidden in the houses and gardens of the suburbs. These defences were carried, not without loss, and the two brigades effected their junction near the canal. The bridge over the canal (Char Bagh bridge) was defended by a battery of four guns, as well as by a numerous infantry stationed in the houses on the other side. A field battery, taking up position on the road, attempted to silence the guns of the bridge, but the European artillerymen were soon decimated by the plunging fire of the enemy, and the military leaders were obliged to have the obstacle carried at the point of the bayonet. Whilst a portion of the first brigade, covered by the trees and walls along the canal, opened a violent fire on the gunners of the bridge and the sepoys posted in the neighbouring buildings, the 5th Fusiliers, R.A., and the Madras Fusiliers charged the bridge and carried the houses, the defenders of which were all killed. Towards midday the first part of the operation had been successfully achieved, but yet how many difficulties

[1] First Brigade (under Colonel Neill): H.M.'s 5th Fusiliers; H.M.'s 64th and 84th; 1st Madras Fusiliers; Captain Maude's Battery; Major Eyre's Battery; Captain Barrow's Volunteer Cavalry; Captain Dawson's 12th Native Irregular Cavalry.

Second Brigade (under Colonel Hamilton, 78th): H.M.'s 78th Highlanders; Captain Brazyer's Sikh Regiment of Ferozepoor; H.M.'s 90th Light Infantry; Captain Olphert's Bengal Battery.

there still remained to be overcome before the Residency could be reached! The high street of Lucknow,[1] thoroughly Oriental in its character, too narrow in certain places to allow two elephants to pass abreast, and about two miles long, leads from the Char Bagh bridge to the gates of the Residency. There was every reason to suppose that this long thoroughfare was lined with barricades, and that the houses along the whole line would be occupied by determined and skilful defenders, such as had already been encountered at the bridge. General Outram, whose previous acquaintance with the city had made him perfectly familiar with its labyrinth of streets, advised marching on the Residency by bye-ways, to which General Havelock at once agreed. The guns captured from the enemy were thrown into the canal, and the Highlanders were stationed in the rear with orders to block the high street, and protect the passage of the baggage and of the wounded.

As soon as these arrangements had been made, the principal column took the outer road that runs parallel to the banks of the canal. When near the Sikander Bagh, however, the British forces, changing their route, marched

[1] Lucknow ranks amongst the most populous cities of the world, and it would be understating its population if we put it at 500,000 inhabitants. Everywhere in the streets there is a compact crowd, through which it is very difficult to make one's way, even when mounted on an elephant. In the midst of this ragged multitude there are, sometimes, scenes to be witnessed which recall the luxury of the India of good old times. A dignitary of the Court, dressed in white muslin, his head surmounted by an elegant turban adorned by a bird of paradise and a diamond brooch, advances on a richly caparisoned elephant, surrounded by tattered adherents armed with long guns, sabres, and shields; or else one meets a mysterious gilt palanquin, escorted by eunuchs with drawn scimitars, before which the crowd respectfully separates. When you pass by, seated on your elephant, it is easy, being on a level with the first and only floor of the houses, even without the help of the 'diable boiteux,' to penetrate into the intimate details of the life of the wretched households inhabiting them, whose whole worldly possessions consist in folding-beds and a few copper utensils. But what gives their special characteristic to the streets of Lucknow are the dark beauties in coquettish attire, who throng the balconies and windows, and whose intentions the most simple cannot misunderstand. Besides this, especially effeminate features, would-be fascinating glances and flowing locks, are the ensigns of a vice which cannot be mentioned in European countries, and which exhibits itself openly in this Indian Sodom.

straight on the Residency. This manœuvre had not been foreseen by the enemy, and the English approached the Moti Manzil, one of the numerous palaces of the King, close to the Residency, without meeting with any opposition. There the attacking columns found themselves exposed to the fire of a four-gun battery placed in the Kaiser Bagh, another vast royal abode, and to the well-directed fire of numerous skirmishers stationed in the barracks formerly occupied by the 32nd R.A. The English guns having vainly attempted to silence those of the sepoys, Havelock determined to leave the 90th and the heavy artillery under shelter in the courts and buildings of the Moti Manzil, in order to reinforce the rearguard. With the larger portion of his column, he sought a refuge from the tempest of shot and shell in a narrow gallery that unites two other royal dwellings, the Chattar Manzil and the Farhat Basch.

Unfavourable was the news received from the Highlanders who had been left at the bridge to guard the passage of the baggage. The enemy had soon reappeared in the houses near the canal, which had again to be carried by assault. Scarcely was this done, when a strong column of sepoys, with two guns, attacked the Highlanders from the high street. The guns were captured—one thrown into the canal, the other spiked; but after several murderous attempts, all hope had to be given up of dislodging the enemy from the buildings near the high street, of which they had again obtained possession. Fortunately, all the baggage had passed over by this time. The Queen's soldiers, seriously weakened by several hours' fighting, renewed their exhausted ammunition, and the rearguard followed the steps of the first column under a storm of bullets. At the junction of the outer road with that leading to the Bilkouska palace, whether by a lucky inspiration or an error on the part of the commanding officer, the route followed by the first column was abandoned, and a rapid movement was made on the left in the direction of the Residency. This manœuvre allowed of attacking in the rear the battery of the Kaizer Bagh, the shells from which were doing great execution among the principal body of the army. As soon as these guns were taken and spiked, the 78th effected its junction with the forces under Havelock.

The day was drawing to a close, the exhausted troops offered a picture of perfect chaos and disorganisation, the success of the undertaking seemed doubtful; to retrace their steps was out of the question, and if a rest were granted to the troops by allowing them to bivouac on the ground they had conquered, it would give the sepoys time to mass all their forces on the road to the Residency. A council of war, held at the last moment, decided on resuming operations without delay. Unfortunately, this time, the impetuous Havelock refused to listen to General Outram, who advised approaching the Residency by the interior of the palaces, and, notwithstanding the remonstrances of his colleague, persisted in taking the bull by the horns, and engaging the troops in the high street.[1]

The poignant anxiety with which the garrison of the Residency followed the different phases of the combat can easily be imagined. From the morning, the noise of the cannonade had reached the ears of the besieged, and towards eleven o'clock they perceived a great crowd of men, women, and children, encumbered with heavy baggage, crossing the bridge in hot haste. This decisive proof of the success of the attack was followed by a still more indubitable one. Armed men, cavalry, and sepoys in uniform were seen amongst the fugitives, who in their haste to fly did not attempt to cross the bridge, but forded or swam the river. The guns of the Residency fired on these fugitives, but the besieging batteries at once covered the place with shells, as if, in their rage at seeing their prey escape from their hands, the sepoys wished to take a last terrible farewell. At two o'clock smoke was seen to rise in the vicinity of the palaces, and soon afterwards a sharp fusillade was distinctly heard. The sentinel perceived European troops and cavalry marching in the direction of the Moti Manzil. Gradually the discharges of musketry drew

[1] See Documents, No. IV., 'Letter from Sir J. Outram to the Commander-in-Chief.'

nearer, and towards six o'clock the 78th Highlanders and the Sikhs were visible with the naked eye from the Post of Finance. They were seen to issue from the high street, and advance in quick time through the fire from houses and barricades, led by mounted officers. The besieged, dazzled, astonished, were still asking themselves if they were the victims of a delusion, when Generals Havelock and Outram arrived, and, dismounting, were raised on the shoulders of their men, and entered the place by an embrasure, a gate of honour which fate had reserved for the two heroes.

An eye-witness has thus described the appearance of the Residency at this eventful moment:[1]—

'Once fairly seen, all our doubts and fears regarding them were ended; and then the garrison's long pent-up feelings of anxiety and suspense burst forth in a succession of deafening cheers. From every pit, trench, and battery, from behind the sand-bags piled on shattered houses, from every post still held by a few gallant spirits, rose cheer and cheer—even from the hospital! Many of the wounded crawled forth to join in that glad shout of welcome to those who had so bravely come to our assistance. It was a moment never to be forgotten.'

The victorious troops were not less moved. 'Ere long, however, the gates were thrown open, and the stream of soldiers entered—heated, worn, and dusty; yet they looked robust and healthy, contrasted with the forms and faces within. Nothing could exceed their enthusiasm. The Highlanders stopped everyone they met; and with repeated questions and exclamations of "Are you one of them?" "God bless you!" "We thought to have found only your bones!" bore them back towards Dr. Fayrer's house, into which the general had entered. Here a scene of thrilling interest presented itself. The ladies of the garrison, with their children, had assembled, in the most intense anxiety and excitement, under the porch outside, when the Highlanders approached. Rushing forward, the rough and bearded warriors shook the

[1] Mr. Gubbins, *The Mutinies in Oude.*

ladies by the hand, amidst loud and repeated congratulations. They took the children up in their arms, and fondly caressing them, passed them from one to another to be caressed in turn.'

The victory, however, was not complete. In the murderous race which had the Residency for its prize, all the British troops had not reached the goal. A strong detachment of the 90th, R.A., had been left, as we have said, in the neighbourhood of the Moti Manzil, in order to lend assistance to the rearguard. Two heavy guns, ammunition, waggons, and numerous wounded were under its protection. All the houses close by were occupied by sepoys, and the English, who were without news of the second column that had rejoined the principal corps by a circuitous route, were obliged to abandon their guns and take refuge in a vaulted gallery of the Moti Manzil, in order to escape destruction. From the moment of entering the entrenchments, on the evening of the 25th, the critical position of this force had not escaped the attention of those in command. The leader of the first column, Colonel Neill, met with a glorious death, whilst retracing his steps in the dark with the intention of guiding these soldiers to the gate of the Residency. On the following day at dawn vigorous measures were taken to disengage the rearguard. Colonel Napier, who has since acquired European celebrity by the Abyssinian expedition, left the Residency with a strong detachment, and reached the portion of the Moti Manzil to which the 90th had withdrawn, without any very considerable loss. The two columns thus united spent the day of the 26th under shelter of the palace walls, and the following night, under cover of darkness, succeeded in crossing the spots which were most exposed to the fire of the sepoys, and in entering the Residency.

An irreparable misfortune cast, however, a cloud over the victory of the English. A young civilian had been entrusted with the charge of the wounded during the day, but, though well acquainted with Lucknow, he lost his way in the labyrinth of streets, and the convoy, with its escort, composed of a detachment of the 90th, was exposed to the most galling fire, on arriving in a square, known subsequently as the Litters' Square (Dhoolies' Square). Some brave and faithful bearers continued their route under a storm of bullets, and succeeded in bringing into the entrenchments the wounded confided to their care, amongst whom was Lieutenant Havelock, the general's son, dangerously wounded in the shoulder. The greater number of 'dhoolies' were, however, abandoned by their bearers, and fell into the hands of sepoys. Then ensued a scene of carnage worthy of the butcheries at Mirut and Cawnpore. The wounded and the soldiers of the escort were hacked to pieces with sabres, and then thrown into the flames. Nine able-bodied men and five wounded, who found a refuge in a side building of the Char Bagh, managed to defend themselves for a whole day against the horde of their assailants, and rejoined Colonel Napier's expedition in the night.

The successful and heroic defence of this little band worthily closes the series of operations on the part of the British army. The relief of the Lucknow garrison was not yet an accomplished fact; but, reinforced as it had just been, its situation could no longer inspire serious anxiety. The wished-for result had been obtained, and the telegraphic wires could at length transmit the good news to Calcutta.[1]

[1] SIR J. OUTRAM TO CAPTAIN BRUCE.

I hope you received my letter of the day before yesterday, telling you of our victory on the previous day at Alumbagh over hosts of enemies, and the capture of their guns as usual. Telegraph to the Governor-General from me as follows:—

'Yesterday, General Havelock's force, numbering about 2,000 men of all arms, the remainder being left in charge of the sick, wounded, and baggage, occupying the Alumbagh, forced their way into the city under serious opposition. After crossing the Char Bagh bridge, the troops skirted the city to the right, thus avoiding the enemy's defensive works prepared through the entire length of the main street leading to the Residency. Still much opposition had to be encountered ere we attained the Residency in the evening, just in time, apparently, for now that we have examined the outside of the defences, we find that two mines had been run far under the garrison's chief works, ready for loading, which, if sprung, must have placed the garrison at the mercy of the enemy. Our loss is severe; not yet correctly ascertained, but estimated at from four to five hundred killed and wounded.

'Among the former, Colonel Neill, Lieutenant Weld, 40th; Major Cooper, of the Artillery; Lieutenant Webster, 78th; Captain Pakenham, 84th; Lieu-

Havelock's troops had suffered terribly in the street-fighting, where they were exposed to invisible enemies. Since the passage of the Ganges, the British army, out of an effective force of about 3,000 men, had lost ten officers and 196 men killed, and numbered thirty officers and 339 men wounded; in all, dead and wounded, forty officers and 535 men. The casualties met with by the garrison during a siege of eighty-five days were still greater. On September 25, its effective force was reduced by one-half; and though originally amounting to 1,692 men, of whom 927 were Europeans and 765 natives, it presented a total of only 979 men, of whom 577 were Europeans and 402 natives. Forty-one officers and two civilians were among the dead. In this list, headed by the glorious names of Sir H. Lawrence and Major Banks, we cannot pass over in silence that of Captain Fulton, of the Engineers, who was entrusted with the work of the defence, and whose energy and peculiar talent contributed a large share towards the success of resistance.

tenant Bateman, 64th; and Lieutenant Warren, 12th Irregular Cavalry. Among the wounded: Colonel Campbell, H.M.'s 90th Foot; Lieutenant Havelock, Deputy Assistant Adjutant-General; Major Tytler, Deputy Quartermaster-General, and many others.

'To-day the troops are occupied in taking the batteries bearing on the garrison, which have been held till now, and continued occasionally to fire on the Residency. Since our junction with the garrison last night, many thousands of the enemy have deserted the city, and the late King's son and his court have fled to Faizabad.'

P.S.—Pray inform Lady Outram that I am all right. Lest any report should reach her that I am wounded, tell her that it is really the merest trifle—only a flesh wound in the right arm, which, though got early in the day, never incapacitated me for a moment. During the remainder of the day I remained on horseback, and scarcely feel it to-day. Don't mention anything about my wound in the telegraph to the Governor-General. John Anderson, the Fayrers, Gubbins, and Ogilvies, Banks's and Ommaney's widows, Mrs. Hayes and the Conners, and their families, in whom she is so interested, are all well. I send lists of the survivors of the garrison, which should be telegraphed first, and afterwards the other list of the dead should be given.—Sir James Outram' *Campaigns in India*, 1857–58.

CHAPTER VII.

BLOCKADE OF THE RESIDENCY—FIRST CAMPAIGN OF SIR C. CAMPBELL IN OUDE—RECAPTURE OF CAWNPORE.

Difficulty of evacuating the Residency—Change in the nature of the struggle—Attitude of the great chieftains of Oude—Man Singh—March of Sir Colin Campbell—Attack of November 16—Evacuation of the Residency—Death of Havelock—Sir C. Campbell marches on Cawnpore—Passage of the bridge over the Ganges—Return to Europe of the women and children belonging to the garrison of Lucknow—Recapture of Cawnpore.

THE military leaders of the forces assembled at Cawnpore in the middle of September, possessing no reliable information as to the condition of the Residency, and fearing that a few hours', a few moments' delay might compromise the safety of the place, had begun their march in the utmost haste, with the sole object of relieving the garrison at any price. The undertaking had succeeded so far, the liberators had forced their passage to the Residency through the tortuous streets of Lucknow, but that was all; the success of September 25 went no further. The following day the sepoys re-occupied most of the positions from which they had been dislodged the previous evening, and it was evident that there would be quite as much difficulty in forcing a passage out as there had been in forcing the passage in. It was no longer a question of leading battalions full of enthusiasm through showers of grape-shot, or across barricades, but of conducting an immense convoy of treasure and ammunition, with more than 400 women and children, sick and wounded to the number of 600, through the narrow streets of an Eastern town, under the fire of a numerous enemy. Such a responsibility might well alarm even so stout a heart as that of Sir J. Outram.

With noble abnegation, as we have seen, the honour of commanding the relieving forces had been given up to Havelock by Sir James Outram, who had fought as a volunteer in the foremost ranks since the passage of the Ganges. As soon as the expedition had been brought to a successful close by the old veteran, who, with such an indefatigable energy, had organised the first attempts to succour the besieged garrison, Sir J. Outram assumed the functions of 'commissioner.' Sir H. Lawrence could not have had a more worthy successor. The new functionary had already filled the office of Resident at the Court of Oude, and the bad state of his health had alone prevented him from organising English rule after the annexation, and thus, perhaps, solving the most thorny difficulties of the situation. On entering the Residency, Outram, under the impression that provisions were exhausted, at once took measures to procure the necessary means of transport for operating an immediate evacuation. The officers entrusted with these negotiations soon found out that not a single waggon could be obtained, but on the other hand, the Commissariat discovered in the State magazines stores of grain, the existence of which was entirely unknown to the military authorities.

Sir Henry Lawrence had provided for the future wants of the besieged in unlooked-for proportions. With order and economy, the amount of grain might still suffice for several months, even for the needs of the increased numbers of the garrison. The oxen used for the artillery and the ammunition waggons which formed part of the expedition, ensured a constant supply of butcher's meat. Sir J. Outram no longer entertained the idea of an immediate departure, and decided on awaiting behind the defences the arrival of the army at whose head Sir C. Campbell would shortly take the field.[1]

Once this resolution taken, it became necessary to profit by the disorder which the fighting of September 25 had caused amongst those works of the besiegers which were

[1] See Documents, No. V., 'Letters from Sir J. Outram to Sir C. Campbell.'

nearest the Residency. Outram's forces could hold a larger space of ground than the handful of soldiers under Inglis. By the end of September numerous and generally successful sorties facilitated the completion, before the end of the following month, of a system of defence capable of bidding defiance to the attacks of the sepoys. In the new entrenched camp, Bailey Guard, Fayrer House, and the hospital hitherto exposed to contact with the enemy, became central positions. The line of defence, protected on the north by the River Goumti, comprised to the east the Tarakoti and the palaces of Farhat Bagh and Chattar Manzil; on the south and west fronts, the old entrenchments were not sensibly modified, but more numerous defenders and a few new works secured them against the enterprises of the sepoys. The British forces, under the command-in-chief of Sir J. Outram, were divided into two corps; the first, under Colonel Inglis, was composed of the former garrison, reinforced by the Highlanders and the Madras Fusiliers, and was entrusted with the defence of the original lines. Havelock, at the head of the second corps, occupied the Tarakoti and the adjacent palaces.

These new positions became, during the remainder of the blockade, the object of the principal efforts of the besiegers, who, however, kept up an incessant cannonade against the old Residency. The palaces, which were built of solid masonry, furnished excellent quarters for the troops, but they were exposed to the fire of the batteries raised by the sepoys on the other side of the river; and, moreover, the besiegers could approach to the very foot of the bastions without being seen by the sentinels, thanks to the winding streets in the suburb. The fire from the batteries on the left bank could only seriously damage the top floors of the palaces, the gilt domes of which were riddled with shot when the English departed. The danger was greater on the side of the town, for the enemy took advantage of the position to push forward mining operations on a larger scale. The Engineers, under Colonel Napier, opposed all the resources of modern science to these subterranean attacks. On several occasions, the sappers of the opposite parties came face to face in the bowels of the earth.[1] The mines laid by the sepoys, though worked with marvellous tenacity, only resulted in destroying some portions of the palace walls and killing a few men in the English ranks.

We have already adverted in the previous chapter to the disunion which broke out almost from the beginning amongst the leaders of the mutiny. This state of things was much aggravated by the success of the English at the end of September. Sir J. Outram had been cognisant of the anxiety felt by the great land-owners, who had only joined the cause of the insurrection after long hesitation, and he had attempted to act on their fears, if not on their conscience.[2] In the first days of October, Rajah Man Singh offered General Outram a suspension of arms and an escort of 10,000 soldiers, if the latter would consent to evacuate the kingdom with all his forces. Man Singh's conduct in the different circumstances of the insurrection is a fair sample of that of most great nobles in Oude, and is, from this point of view, deserving special notice.

Rajah Man Singh did not belong to the ancient races of India. He was son and heir to a certain Burscham Singh, who built the fortress of Schahgange with the immense riches he had amassed as governor of the province of Sultanpore. From his youth upwards, he enjoyed considerable influence amongst the nobility of Oude. His intelligence, his courage, and the importance of the armed bands in his pay, soon placed him at the head of the Brahmin party, and he played a principal part in the unending strife which filled the provinces with bloodshed under the feeble rule of the last king. When the annexation took place, Man Singh, deprived of his influence at Court, exposed to claims at once

[1] The work done by the English sappers is without precedent in modern warfare. Twenty-one shafts, of an average depth of 11 feet, were dug, as well as 3,291 feet of gallery. The workmen on the enemy's side laid twenty mines against the palaces. Three exploded, and killed some few men; three exploded without doing any harm. Seven were countermined, and seven occupied by the English.—Napier's *Official Report to Sir J. Outram*.

[2] Letters from Sir J. Outram to the Secretary for Foreign Affairs and to Man Singh.

from his enemies, among his fellow-countrymen, and from the new authorities, withdrew to his stronghold of Schahgange, and did not reappear in public life until after the arrival of Sir Henry Lawrence. The latter, who was, as we have seen, desirous of conciliating the great proprietors, showed himself specially well-disposed towards the Indian chieftain. Whether out of gratitude for his kindness or from political perspicacity, Man Singh merely occupied himself, during the first months of the mutiny, in increasing his military strength, not, however, letting slip the opportunities of protecting those European fugitives whom chance brought into the vicinity of his domains. These friendly demonstrations did not prevent him from breaking his neutrality when Havelock re-crossed the Ganges in August to march on Cawnpore. The astute Indian, fully persuaded this time that the last hour of English rule in Oude had arrived, took part in the siege of the Residency at the head of his bands. The success of the relieving expedition soon dispelled Man Singh's illusions; and faithful to his habits of tortuous policy, he attempted to prove his goodwill to the Europeans without openly breaking with the insurrection.

The overtures he made were not such as a victorious general would even discuss; yet General Outram did not reject them with haughtiness. Other interests, besides those of politics, caused the utmost anxiety to the worthy Commander-in-Chief. The staff knew for a certainty that a number of English, both men and women, who had escaped from the massacre of Aurangabad, one of the most horrible blots on the cause of the sepoys, were confined in the prisons of the Char Bagh. Sir Mountstuart Jackson, his sister, Captain P. Orr, his wife and daughter, Miss Christian, the orphan daughter of the magistrate murdered at Sitapore, and Sergeant-Major Morton, after living whole months together in the jungle, without shelter against the burning sun or the tropical rains, and almost without food, had finally been given up to the rebel leaders, and were finishing their painful wanderings in the cells of the palace, almost within hail of the English sentinels at the Residency. Sir J. Outram tried every means of interesting Man Singh in the fate of these unfortunate persons, and went so far as to offer him several times a complete amnesty if he succeeded in obtaining their freedom. The antecedents of the Indian leader, and the kindness he had already shown towards European fugitives, lead us to suppose that his influence was not strong enough to prevail over the ferocity of his associates, and the negotiations proved unsuccessful. It is but just to acknowledge that Outram's kind heart led him not only to feel anxiety about the fate of his fellow-countrymen, but also to make his voice heard in the heat of the battle, in favour of the sepoys who had been driven into the ranks of rebels by blind terror, and who were relentlessly pursued by the fury of their former masters.[1]

The situation of the British forces during the blockade, painful and trying as it was, cannot be compared to that of the garrison during the siege. Coffee, tea, sugar, and rum had given out, and rarely made their appearance even on the tables of the highest officials. Medicines were coming to an end in the hospital, where chloroform had long been wanting; but the first necessaries of life were abundant. Sir J. Outram set the example, and scrupulously shared the hardships to which all were exposed.[2]

The incessant cannonade and the mines laid by the sepoys did not cause any serious damage to the works of the new lines, so that the general safety seemed sure and certain. Official information had been given that Sir C. Campbell was assembling considerable forces at Cawnpore, and would soon take the field. Though the place was carefully blockaded, intelligent and fearless messengers frequently managed to deceive the enemy's vigilance, and reach the detached

[1] See Documents, No. VII., 'Letter from Sir J. Outram to the Governor-General.'

[2] Sir J. Outram to Captain Bruce, Cawnpore:—

Lucknow Residency, October 21, 1857.

I trust you inform Lady Outram that I am well every time you hear from me. Tell her I cannot write to her, because, as our expensive cossids can only carry a 'quill,' private communications have been forbidden to others, and I cannot, in honour, take advantage to write privately myself.—Sir James Outram's *Campaigns in India*, 1857-58.

post of the Alumbagh, from whence it was easy to communicate with Cawnpore. At first, some anxiety had been felt as to the safety of the detachment left at the Alumbagh, but some slight works of defence had completely secured it from the enemy's attack. The position of this small garrison very naturally excited the envy of their comrades in the Residency, for besides the baggage of the army, the Alumbagh contained all the provisions brought by the relieving forces. Communications by semaphore were established between the Alumbagh and a tower of the Chattar Manzil, and at the decisive moment kept the garrison informed, hour by hour, of the events of the day. At length the long-expected news arrived.

On November 12, the arms of this old-fashioned telegraph, now superseded by electric wires, announced to the officer on guard at the tower of the Chattar Manzil that Sir C. Campbell had entered the Alumbagh, and a few hours later Kanou Ti Lal, an inferior clerk in an English Court of Justice, passed through the pickets of the sepoys, and confirmed the good news. The same messenger, accompanied by Mr. Cavanagh, a volunteer belonging to the garrison, re-crossed the enemy's lines on the following day, and after a journey, the touching and simple account of which the reader will doubtless peruse with interest,[1] brought to head-quarters information which greatly contributed to the success of the expedition. The last hour of their long trial had come for the garrison, but though they saw the signal of deliverance, they equally saw all the obstacles which would have to be overcome before their deliverance could be effected.

The view from the top of the signal-tower comprised a tract of country clothed with the most luxuriant vegetation, and interspersed with monuments characteristic of the richest Oriental art. As far as the eye could reach, were visible palaces, mosques, tombs of graceful or eccentric forms, groups of dark-foliaged trees and green meadows, through which meandered the capricious waters of the Goumti. In the

[1] 'Narrative of the Journey of Mr. Cavanagh through the Sepoys' Lines.' See Documents, No. VIII.

background, the Palace of Delight (Dilkouska), an ancient edifice built somewhat in the European style, was connected by the thick shade of a mango-wood with the fantastic building of the 'Martinière,' with its innumerable statues. A little nearer the river were the gilt domes of the Sikander Bagh and the flat-roofed tomb of King Gazi uddin Haïdar, known as the Schah Najif. The sepoys had made great preparations at this point for an energetic resistance. On the other side of the road was the two-storied building, flanked by four towers, known as the 'Happy Palace,' where the mess of the 32nd had formerly been situated. The windows were bricked up to three-quarters of their height, and the outer wall, protected by a wide ditch, was pierced with loop-holes. The walls still bear traces of the damage done by the fighting of September 25, and the building will play a no less important part in the military operations that were in preparation than on the first occasion. Nearer the Residency were the Tarakoti, or Royal Observatory, which was quite out of harmony with all these products of Oriental fantasy, by reason of its classic and elegant architecture; the Moti Manzil (Palace of Pearls), and the Chattar Manzil, the Royal hall, where the coronation of the kings took place. Finally came the Kaiser Bagh, a sort of Eastern Versailles, covering an immense surface with its courts, domes, and buildings of all sorts, and almost touching the outer entrenchments of the English. On the right was the grandiose fairy-like panorama of Lucknow, one of the most curious of Indian towns. The passions of men were about to blot this poetical picture with smoke and fire, leaving only ruin and corpses.

On his arrival at Calcutta, at the end of August, the new Commander-in-Chief, Sir Colin Campbell, had lost no time, as we have seen, in bringing all the matters connected with the army to the highest point of efficiency. The providential arrival of the China expedition at Calcutta, and the capture of Delhi, which set free a portion of the besieging forces, favoured his efforts, and in the course of October the troops destined to achieve the work so gloriously begun by Havelock were assembled at Cawnpore.

The expedition crossed the Ganges on October 30, and after four days' march, during which the enemy was rarely visible, rejoined the detachment encamped at the Alumbagh. The march proved full of emotions if not of combats. On the second day, the men of the 93rd Highlanders suddenly stopped, broke their ranks, disbanded, and fled right and left. For a few moments, the staff imagined it was some unexplained or inexplicable panic. The explanation was soon given; the Highlanders were flying before a swarm of wasps, to whose stings their bare legs offered an easy prey.

Sir C. Campbell, who had kept for himself the command of the second expedition against Lucknow, was detained at Calcutta by the necessities of the service, and only left the banks of the Hooghly at the very last moment, arriving at Cawnpore on November 3, after a rapid journey, which testified to his devouring activity and still youthful strength. On November 9 the general-in-chief joined the army corps encamped in the neighbourhood of the Alumbagh, under the provisional command of Sir Hope Grant, a general officer who had taken a most glorious part in the siege of Delhi.

It was not without anxiety that Sir C. Campbell left Cawnpore, which was threatened by the Gwalior contingent stationed at Calpi. But the fate of the Lucknow garrison had now, for five months, been the cause of most painful anxiety to every English heart, so that Campbell, leaving behind, under Brigadier Wyndham, a sufficient force for the defence of the place, determined to delay no longer the complete deliverance of the besieged. The troops composing this expedition amounted to 4,700 men and thirty-two guns.[1] In the ranks was, moreover, a detachment of sailors from the frigate 'Shannon,' commanded by Captain W. Peel, a worthy son of the illustrious statesman, whose name was already brilliantly associated with the siege of Sebas-

[1] H.M.'s 9th Lancers, 8th, 53rd, and 75th regiments from Delhi, very much reduced; 93rd R.A., 1st Madras Fusiliers, 2nd and 4th regiments Sikh Infantry, and also detachments of the 5th, 23rd, 64th, and 82nd H.M.'s Foot; two batteries of artillery, 401 men of the Naval Brigade 900 cavalry, 3,200 infantry, 200 sappers—total, 4,700 men.

topol. These new enemies excited the curiosity and terror of the natives to the highest point by their appearance. Popular rumour represented them as amphibious monsters, as broad as they were long, always harnessed to their guns. They had been obliged to leave at Allahabad the 68-pounders which were brought from the 'Shannon,' in consequence of their having found it impossible to procure the necessary cattle for their transport, and had replaced them by 24-pounders and 8-inch howitzers.

The object of these operations was no longer to rejoin the besieged at any cost, but a much more difficult undertaking yet was necessary, to occupy the whole ground between the Alumbagh and the Residency, a distance of more than four miles, in order to protect the departure of an immense convoy of wounded women, children, and treasure. There was no hope of dislodging (except under a delay of several days) an enemy, ten times superior in number, from the streets, squares, and byways that had been crossed at double quick march on September 25. Sir Colin Campbell, in accordance with the opinions expressed by Outram, determined to make a circuit on the right of the Alumbagh, and to advance on the Residency through the parks and palaces which stand on the bank of the Goumti.[1]

The Palace of Delight (Dilkourka), and the buildings of 'La Martinière,'[2] the selected basis of the contemplated

[1] See Documents, No. IX., 'Plan of Attack by Sir J. Outram.'

[2] The palace of 'Constantia,' built by General Martin, stands close to the buildings of 'La Martinière.' It is difficult to guess what this gigantic assemblage of brick and mortar was intended for, even after visiting it minutely. Two circular one-storied galleries are connected with the principal pile of buildings, which is surmounted by a series of small pavilions and terraces superposed in the style of a Chinese pagoda, and profusely adorned with every kind of statues, shepherds *à la* Louis XIV., Chinese figures, Roman emperors, Greek sages, &c. &c. The mortal remains of General Martin rest in the vaults of the palace, and are contained in a white marble sarcophagus. Four painted cardboard statues, representing sepoys in scarlet uniform, and in an attitude of conventional grief, guard the approaches of the monument. A bust of white marble, placed in a niche in the wall, represents the general, and surmounts a tablet, on which is engraved the following inscription:—'Here lies Claude Martin. He was born at Lyons, A.D. 1732. He came to India a private soldier, and he died a major-general.'

operations, were taken from the sepoys on November 14, after a vigorous struggle of several hours. During the attack, the English left wing took up a position on the canal to protect the Alumbagh, where the military magazines were, from any offensive movement of the enemy. The next day the defence of the Dilkourka and 'La Martinière' was fully organised, and the sappers made a temporary road through the parks in the direction of the junction of the canal and the Goumti. At this point, the canal offered few difficulties to the passage of troops and artillery, for the sepoys, who expected to be attacked by the Cawnpore road, had destroyed all the bridges and barred the canal on the side of the town; in the whole extent of the parks its bed was almost dry.

On the morning of the 16th, the attacking columns left 'La Martinière,' and marched straight on the Sikander Bagh, where the sepoys were assembled in great numbers. This edifice was composed of a two-story building, defended by a wall of solid masonry, which in its turn was protected at the four corners by semi-circular bastions. Skirmishers stationed in a serai and in the neighbouring villages completed the defence of the Sikander Bagh. A field-battery, advancing through violent volleys of musketry, opened fire on the outer line of enclosure, whilst the English infantry dislodged the enemy from the surrounding positions. But the strength of the walls defied all projectiles, and, after more than an hour's ineffectual cannonade, it was decided to attempt an assault through a narrow breach on the east side of the wall. Whilst the 93rd Highlanders were carrying out this audacious plan, the 4th Sikh regiment, supported by several companies R.A., were forcing the principal entrance. In presence of this double assault, the terrified sepoys descended from the upper stories, and crowded into a space too narrow to allow them to use their arms. This compact and terrified mass was literally slaughtered by the bayonet. After the fight, the Sikander Bagh offered a ghastly sight, such as the eye of man has rarely contemplated; more than 2,000 dead bodies were piled up in a space of 120 square yards. The victors advanced in pools of blood almost up to their knees.

The ensuing attack on the mosque known as Schah

Najif encountered equal difficulties. The strong enclosure of the edifice proved impervious to light artillery, so Captain Peel brought up two of his guns nearly to the foot of the wall, just as if he had meant to board an enemy's ship from the quarter-deck of the 'Shannon.' But though large masses of the wall fell down, the breaches, which were filled up with rubbish, remained inaccessible. Success seemed more than doubtful, when someone thought of using Congreve rockets. The effect of these engines, which were thrown with the greatest precision, was decisive and almost immediate. Some volunteers got over the wall into the enclosure, by means of trees, and perceiving through the smoke the rearguard of the sepoys in full retreat, opened the gates to the besiegers without meeting with any resistance.

During these operations the cavalry was protecting communications between head-quarters and the Dilkouska, and the left wing was guarding the Alumbagh against any hostile return of the sepoys. The garrison of the Residency, on its side, had not remained inactive, and had taken all the buildings between the Chattar Manzil and the Moti Manzil. In the evening, the latter palace, and that of the mess of the 32nd R.A. (the Happy Palace), alone separated Sir Colin Campbell's forces from Outram's. The successive checks met with that day, and especially the disaster at the Sikander Bagh, had filled the sepoys with terror. The buildings of the mess of the 32nd were evacuated at nightfall, notwithstanding their formidable strength, and only a hundred men remained in possession of the Moti Manzil. But the guns of the Kaiser Bagh and the batteries placed on the left bank of the river, commanded in several places the road between these two buildings and the Residency, so that the English, on the following day, could advance but slowly in the teeth of a galling fire. When Outram and Havelock left their entrenchments to meet Sir C. Campbell in the afternoon, they were met by a hail of grape-shot from the defenders of the Kaiser Bagh, and several aides-de-camp were wounded close to them.

The instructions with which the two generals returned

from this interview cast a veil of sadness over the transports of joy which the victory had caused amongst the garrison. It was decided to evacuate the place within twenty-four hours; the general-in-chief gave formal orders to that effect. The men, who had defended these ruins for five months with so much energy and constancy, were now to abandon as fugitives, and the sepoys would profane, the precious remains placed in the graveyard of the Residency. Such humiliation filled every heart with deepest grief. The chiefs of the garrison, acting as the mouthpiece of their soldiers' feelings, endeavoured to change the decision of the Commander-in-Chief, but they could merely obtain a final delay of twenty-four hours.

Though communications had been established between the relieving forces and the garrison, the decisive operation was not even begun. In the first place, Sir C. Campbell had to escort an immense convoy of women, children, sick, and wounded from the ruins of the Residency, and when this task had been fulfilled, other and most important interests demanded his utmost attention. Chance, or the incapacity of its leaders, had detained the Gwalior contingent up to this moment inactive at Calpi. In a few hours' march, however, along a road without obstacles, it could, if not occupy the bridge over the Ganges, at least take up a position close at hand, and prevent any approach to it. A simple forward movement on the part of the rebel corps would suffice to place the Commander-in-Chief between them and the mutineers of Lucknow, and thus deprive him of all communication with India, isolating him in a country devastated by war, where every village was a fortress. Fortune, which had hitherto smiled on the attempts made to succour the Lucknow garrison, now perhaps held in reserve some immense disaster. There was every reason, it is true, to believe that the Kaiser Bagh, like the Sikander Bagh or the Schah Najif, could be carried by assault, but would the results be such as to justify the attempt? The English force was merely an advanced guard, without even a reserve to fall back upon. The men had been under arms and exposed to the enemy's fire for five days; it was impossible to occupy the whole of the town. Above all, a skilful pilot ought not to run the slightest risk of a failure, which would involve the loss of the women and children whose safety had already cost so many generous efforts, so much bloodshed. Having regard to these powerful considerations, Sir Colin Campbell remained deaf to the entreaties of his colleagues, and persisted in the order for the immediate evacuation.

On November 19, at midday, the women and children left the Residency. All means of transport had been put into requisition—litters, native carts, European carriages (the latter bore many traces of the siege)—wheels, cushions, frames were riddled with bullets. The horses of these miserable conveyances presented no better appearance. Having been confined to the stables for five months, uncared for, and almost without food, the wretched beasts could scarcely use their legs. The Commander-in-Chief had provided for the security of the convoy with anxious care; shelters and trenches had been established along the unprotected parts of the route, and it reached head-quarters without a single accident. In the evening it arrived at Dilkouska, where, at the mess of the 9th Lancers, the poor creatures were regaled with fresh bread and butter, of which they had been deprived for so long. That same night the departure of the sick and wounded was also successfully accomplished. Sir C. Campbell had justified the trust reposed in him by his country; and to the glory won on the battlefield, he added the yet purer glory of restoring to England some four hundred women and children.

Military operations were not slackened whilst the measures necessary for rescuing the garrison were being carried out. On the day following the junction of the English forces, the Naval Brigade opened fire with its big guns and Congreve rockets against the Kaiser Bagh, whilst within the fortifications the last preparations for retreat were hastily made. More than 200 pieces of artillery were spiked, and thousands of cartridges and projectiles were thrown into the wells. But in order to conceal ulterior movements from the enemy, the ruined ramparts and buildings of the Residency were not blown up. The stratagem succeeded beyond all hope; the sepoys, up to the last moment, imagined that hostilities would be resumed, and continued to fire on the English positions some hours after they had been completely evacuated. In the middle of the night of the 22nd, the outposts of the Residency fell back upon head-quarters. Sir James Outram, on horseback, sword in hand, surrounded by his staff, was the last to leave the Baillie Guard; but one noble figure was missing.

Though he had long been suffering from dysentery, General Havelock had nevertheless taken an active share in the late military operations. When Sir Colin's victory had assured the safety of his companions in misfortune, yielding to the advice of the doctors, he had retired to the Dilkouska for change of air; but his constitution had been worn out by the labours, anxieties, and privations of the last six months, and he expired on November 24 in the midst of the women and children for whose safety he had devoted himself. Fortune, which had reserved this last consolation to the old general on his death-bed, had not always been favourable to him.

For forty years an officer in active service of the Queen's army, Havelock had laboriously gained his rank step by step in the military hierarchy. His strength of character and his talents, overlooked in obscure regimental positions, had never obtained for him the favour of a special command. When he was called, by right of seniority, to the honour and responsibility of supreme authority, the situation was of immense gravity. A terrible crisis was shaking British rule in India to its foundations. The leader who left Allahabad, in the early part of July, at the head of a handful of men, was expected to unite the audacity of a partisan to the prudence of a tried tactician; a single check or defeat might cause dreadful and incalculable consequences. It was not only a question of the usual dangers and fatigues of warfare; every species of privation and suffering, famine, a pitiless sun, tropical rains had to be met and endured.

Havelock, by his success over the Nana's multitudinous followers, taught the British soldier not to doubt of victory, whatever the number of his opponents. In the same way he struck terror into the rebels, secured the fidelity of the natives still serving with the colours, and opened the way for the glorious campaign which Outram first, and afterwards Sir C. Campbell brought to such a glorious conclusion. Death, which struck down Havelock in the most glorious moment of his life, did not take him unawares. His Christian resignation is apparent in the farewell words he addressed to Outram, his old companion in arms and glory:[1] 'I have always ordered my life so as to look death calmly in the face.' Notwithstanding the suddenness of his end, Havelock had had time to receive the reward with which the Government recognised his first success, and Sir C. Campbell conferred on him, in the Queen's name, the Cross of Knight Commander of the Most Noble Order of the Bath. England

[1] We think it proper to place under the eyes of the reader a fragment of official correspondence, which gives a correct idea of the chivalrous character of these veterans of the Indian army. The date of the letter makes it plain that Havelock's expedition, and the battle fought by his troops on September 25, are what is here alluded to :—

'Not less deserving of the Victoria Cross, in my opinion, is Lieutenant Havelock; and I trust I may, without giving offence, beg you, as my friend and comrade, as well as my official colleague, not to allow the name of this gallant officer to militate against his just claims. Under the tremendous fire of guns and musketry which the enemy directed across the Char Bagh Bridge, Lieutenant Havelock, with the Madras Fusiliers, stormed the bridge, took the guns, and cleared the street sufficiently to allow of the troops in the rear closing up. I cannot conceive a more daring act than this forcing the bridge, and the officers who led the Fusiliers on that occasion, in my opinion, *most richly deserve promotion*; but hazardous as was their position, they being on foot, and therefore not readily distinguishable from their men, risked little comparatively with Lieutenant Havelock, the only officer on horseback, who cheered the men on, and became the target of the enemy's musketry. I shall feel truly delighted to learn that you accept my recommendation of this brave officer, and I shall deeply regret having divested myself of the command during the advance on Lucknow, if (from what I must regard as a morbidly sensitive delicacy) you withhold from Lieutenant Havelock, because he is your relative, the reward to which, as a soldier, he has so unmistakably established a just claim.'—*Sir J. Outram to General Havelock,* October 12, 1857.

However great his paternal disinterestedness, Havelock, as everyone will understand, yielded to this appeal, and demanded for his son a recompense, which was granted without difficulty.

has since paid her debt of gratitude, by granting a baronet's title and a pension of 1,000*l.* per annum to Havelock's son, a gallant officer, twice wounded during this campaign.

Other losses cast a feeling of gloom over the rejoicings caused by victory. The English casualties had been very great; there were 122 killed and 414 wounded, of whom ten officers killed and thirty-five wounded. The Artillery, the Naval Brigade, and the 93rd Highlanders had suffered more especially in the fighting which took place since leaving the Alumbagh on November 16.

A few hours after Havelock's death, head-quarters were removed to the Alumbagh, where two days were spent in completing the last preparations for departure. The general-in-chief did not intend taking the road to Cawnpore with all his army. The evacuation of the Residency was a serious blow to British prestige, and it was of the highest importance to retain a footing in Oude. By holding the Alumbagh, the return to Cawnpore was shown to be merely a temporary measure, and the sepoys were made to feel that the fate of the kingdom would soon be decided by a new campaign. Besides being easy of defence, the Alumbagh offered the advantage of rapid communications with Cawnpore; in fact, in this position the British forces held the enemy more completely in check than if they had been shut up in the Residency or in the Kaiser Bagh.

On November 27, the army began its retrograde movement with an immense convoy, covering a space of some nine miles in extent. The suddenness of this retreat was about to be justified by the events which immediately followed. Scarcely had the march begun, than the dull vibration of the atmosphere which, to military men, indicates distant discharges of artillery, became perceptible. Deep anxiety weighed heavily on the whole army, when the tents were pitched in the neighbourhood of the bridge of Banni. Doubt was no longer possible; a sharp cannonade was heard in the direction of Cawnpore. Orders were given to strike the tents next morning at dawn, so as to reach Cawnpore, a distance of more than thirty-six miles, in one march.

During the entire route discharges of artillery were uninterrupted, and towards three in the afternoon Sir C. Campbell learnt, by direct information from the scene of action, of the disasters which had befallen Brigadier Wyndham.

This general, who had been entrusted with the defence of Cawnpore against the combined forces of the Nana and the Gwalior contingent, being informed on November 25 of the enemy's approach, had imprudently marched out to meet him with a detachment of about 1,000 men. The sepoys, twenty times superior in number, and entrenched, moreover, behind the bed of a torrent, successfully repulsed the attack. After three days' continual fighting, the English were obliged to withdraw to their fortifications, leaving the native town, the magazines, and the tents of the army in the hands of the enemy. All the war material was burnt, and on the night of the 28th the flames of an immense conflagration, which lighted them on their way, told Sir C. Campbell's dismayed soldiers of the victory won by the sepoys. The triumphal return of the deliverers of the Lucknow garrison was threatened by an immense disaster. Sir C. Campbell, who had foreseen the danger from the very day on which he had opened the campaign, lost no time in preparing to remedy it.

Notwithstanding its apparent rigour, fortune had not quite deserted the British cause. By an unlooked-for and inexplicable chance, the enemy, though aware of the evacuation of Lucknow, had not, as might easily have been done, established batteries to command the bridge over the Ganges and its approaches. At night, the heavy guns of the Naval Brigade were disposed in such a manner as to prevent the sepoys from repairing this oversight. On the morning of the 29th, an infantry brigade, the cavalry, and the light artillery were able to cross the bridge without opposition, and to take up their position on the road to Allahabad, thus securing communication with Calcutta and the interior. In the following night, the remainder of the artillery, the wounded, the women and children crossed in their turn; the passage was not over before sunrise on the 30th. The generals of the enemy, who had at length perceived their mistake, tried in the day to destroy the bridge by cannon shots and fire-ships; it was happily too late.

The rapidity of Sir C. Campbell's movements had triumphed over all difficulties. The precious convoy was in safety on the right bank of the Ganges, under the protection of British bayonets, in the midst of the ruins that had witnessed General Wheeler's disasters. 'Here ended our sufferings,' writes one of the heroines of the siege; 'here, from the very bottom of our hearts, we could thank the merciful Providence who had protected us among so many dangers, and had not allowed us to meet with a fate similar to that of the women and children whose innocent blood was shed at the fatal station of Cawnpore.' The most delicate part of the general-in-chief's mission was not finished as long as the women and children remained in his keeping, so that during the days following the passage of the Ganges he devoted all his energies towards assembling means of transport. On December 3 the convoy started for Allahabad, where a flotilla of steamers, prepared beforehand, was lying ready to convey them to Calcutta.

Seven weeks later, on January 30, the European population of the City of Palaces was agitated by a true patriotic emotion. The ships were decked with flags, salvoes of artillery were fired as on gala days; the Governor-General the authorities, all the white inhabitants of the town were waiting on the banks of the river for the arrival of the victims rescued at Lucknow, whose deliverance excited unanimous and almost delirious rejoicing. But when a long black-robed procession of widows and orphans appeared, with emaciated bodies and thin faces, the acclamations of the crowd gave way to a deep and painful silence, and all eyes filled up with tears. Notwithstanding previous trials, fortune was not yet appeased, and the steamer 'Ava,' that was conveying to Europe the greater number of the women and children from the Residency, was wrecked on a rock in the Red Sea. If no lives were lost, yet the sea swallowed up many precious remembrances which had been saved from the enemy's fire.

As soon as the departure of the convoy relieved Sir C. Campbell from the greatest responsibility that ever rested on a military man, he took immediate measures for wresting Cawnpore from the troops of the Nana and his allies. Whilst the last preparations were being made, the sepoys were not inactive, and kept up a continual fire on the British advanced posts. On the 5th an attack on the pickets of the left wing was only finally repulsed after two hours' fighting. On the morning of the 6th Sir C. Campbell had made all the dispositions necessary to begin the attack.

The army of the sepoys, some 25,000 men, with 40 guns, comprised two corps perfectly distinct by their composition and their base of action. The left and the centre were composed of the regiments of the Bengal army and of the troops of the Nana, commanded by his brother, and had its line of retreat in the direction of Bithour; that of the Gwalior contingent, which formed the right wing, was distributed in the direction of Calpi. The left of the sepoys, stationed in the former European cantonments, from whence it seriously threatened General Wyndham's positions, was easy of defence, thanks to the obstacles of all sorts which covered the ground. The centre, established in Cawnpore itself, was flanked by the houses built along the Doab Canal, which also protected the vast plain where the camp of the Gwalior contingent was situated. The position of the sepoys presented this weak point, that communications between the wings and the centre and *vice versâ* could only take place slowly and with difficulty through the narrow streets of the town. The canal, which covered their centre and right wing, was the key to the position, and by attacking it vigorously the Gwalior contingent might be dislodged before reinforcements had time to arrive from the centre or the left. Two bridges crossed the canal, one in the neighbourhood of the town, the other about three miles off. Sir C. Campbell's army numbered 5,000 infantry, 600 cavalry, and 50 guns.

On the morning of the 6th General Wyndham opened a violent fire from the entrenchments in which he was blockaded, in order to make the sepoys believe that an attack on their left wing was intended. A brigade under Colonel Greathed threatened the centre of the town, avoiding any serious engagement, whilst, during this time, the mass of the army was concentrating on the left. Already, at daybreak, Sir Hope Grant, at the head of some cavalry, with field batteries, had marched upon the bridge furthest from the town. The principal body, which, owing to the broken ground, had succeeded in concealing its movements, deployed on arriving at the first bridge, and the decisive attack immediately began. The outposts of the sepoys were thrown back on the other side of the canal, and the bridge carried by the 53rd R.A. and a Sikh regiment. The victorious assailants, debouching into the plain, continued to drive the sepoys before them, and in an hour's time took possession of the camp of the Gwalior contingent. The surprise was so complete, that guns, harnessed waggons, and messes in course of cooking for the soldiers, were left among the tents. The Naval Brigade, under Captain Peel, took a most glorious part in this action, and his heavy guns, which the sailors dragged forward by main force, were seen in the first rank of the skirmishers. The Gwalior contingent was, moreover, attacked in its retreat by the cavalry and the light artillery, which, after a delay caused by the treachery of their guides, had finally crossed the second bridge without opposition. The rout became complete. The sepoys threw away their arms to run the more easily, and finally, despairing of escaping on the high road from the sabres and lances of the troopers, took to the jungle and the open country. The pursuit continued for the space of fourteen miles, and only ceased when no more enemies were visible.

As soon as he was master of the camp of the Gwalior contingent, Sir C. Campbell lost no time in completing the success of the day. He despatched several regiments under General Mansfield, the chief of his staff, against the left wing of the sepoys, which hitherto had taken no share in the fight. Protected by the inequalities of the ground, the troops of the Nana, deserting their camp, were able to escape without losing a single gun, and to retreat to Bithour. The rebels were so completely discouraged that they made no attempt to defend the fortress of the Nana, but pressed forward towards the Ganges, and were about to cross it, when they were overtaken, on December 9, by an expedition sent in pursuit under Sir Hope Grant. The sepoys dispersed immediately without offering any resistance, leaving fifteen guns in the hands of the English. Already, on the 6th, seventeen pieces of artillery had fallen into the possession of the latter. After this easy victory Sir Hope Grant's column occupied the stronghold of Bithour without striking a blow. Immense treasure is said to have been found in its wells.

This expedition closes the first series of Sir C. Campbell's operations against the mutineers. For nearly a month each day had been a day of battle for the English soldiers. Means of transport were wanting, as all available ones had been employed in conveying the women and children to their destination. The important position of Cawnpore had been recaptured, and was henceforth safe from attack; so that the Commander-in-Chief could at length allow his men the rest they so well deserved, and prepare the operations on a grand scale, which were to re-establish British authority in Oude and Rohilkund.

CHAPTER VIII.

INSURRECTION IN CENTRAL INDIA.

The great Mahratta dynasties—Siraji Peischwah—The dynasties of Scindia and Holkar—The Rajpoot princes—The Pandaris—The Rohillas—The English infringe the native right of adoption—State of the public mind in Central India and Rajpootana—Mutiny at Gwalior—Scindia remains faithful—Mutiny at Indore—Holkar remains faithful—Massacre at Tansi—Mutiny of the native troops at Nacirabad, Neemuch, Joudpore, &c.—The Nizam of Hyderabad—Mutiny at Aurangabad—Relief of Mhow—Expedition of the Anglo-Indian forces into Malwa.

It still remains for us to follow the different phases of the insurrection in the central provinces of India, where the great Mahratta dynasties and the Rajpoot princes retained a semblance of sovereign power. In order to explain the condition of the country, it is necessary to define in some detail the relations between the British authorities and the native sovereigns. The generic name of Mahratta (*Mah*, great; *rat*, country) is given to the entire population of that large portion of Hindostan to the south of the Nerbudda, known under the name of the Deccan.[1] The origin of the

[1] At the beginning of the insurrection, the population of the native states whether allied or tributary, can be estimated in round numbers as follows:—

The Rajah of Mysore	3,000,000
The Nizam	10,000,000
The Guickhowar	2,000,000
Bhopal	5,000
Kotah	6,500
Bondi	2,500
Travancore	6,000
Cochin	2,000
The princes of Rajpootana, of Joudpore, Jeypore, Oudeypore, Bikanir, Tessalmir, and others; the Mahratta princes Holkar, of Katyarat, of Guzerat, &c.	15,000,000
The dominions of Scindia	4,000,000
Total	34,022,000

Mahrattas is lost in the night of ages, but they rose to no importance before the chaotic period that preceded the overthrow of the throne of the Moguls, and then only, thanks to the enterprising spirit of the clever adventurers who founded the dynasties of Sivaji, of the Peischwah, of Scindia, and of Holkar.

The first on the list of these adventurers, Sivaji,[1] of the tribe of Bhosch, acquired great influence over the populations of the Deccan by his talents, martial and political. At strife during his whole life, with varying success with the generals of Aureng-Zeb, fortune finally crowned his efforts. Recognised as Rajah of Sattarah by the Emperor of Delhi, at his death in 1680 he left to his heirs a compact little kingdom and considerable treasures, and to his co-religionists the secret of those sudden and rapid expeditions

Deccan, from the Sanskrit *Duxun*, signifies south, and was originally applied to the country lying south of the Nerbudda and Mahanuddee rivers, consisting of the five principal divisions called Drawed, Carnatic, Telingana, Gondwana, and Maharashtra. 'Europeans,' writes Grant Duff, 'have adopted the Mahommedan definition, and the modern Deccan comprises most of Telingana, part of Gondwana, and that large portion of Maharashtra which extends from the Nerbudda to the Krishna.'

The Nizam, Hassan Gangu, the first King of the Deccan, was an Afghan of the lowest rank, and a native of Delhi. He farmed a small spot of land belonging to a Brahmin astrologer, named Ganga, who was in favour with the King, and having found accidentally a treasure in his field, he had the honesty to give notice of it to his landlord. The astrologer was so much struck with his integrity, that he exerted all his influence at court to advance his fortunes. Hassan thus rose to a great station in the Deccan, where his merit marked him out among his equals to be their leader in their revolt. He had before assumed the name of Gangu, in gratitude to his benefactor; and now, from a similar motive, added that of Brahmani (Bramin), by which his dynasty was afterwards distinguished.—*The History of India*, by the Hon. Mountstuart Elphinstone, *Appendix*.

[1] Sivaji was in his youth entirely under the influence of his mother. She was a woman full of religious enthusiasm, a common enough occurrence amongst the Mahrattas, and imagined herself to be in intimate connection with the Deity. The goddess Bowhani, the protectress of her family, had, she believed, revealed to her the future grandeur of her son and the end of the Mussulman rule in India. Her words and example had a considerable share in the labours and fortune of this extraordinary man, who at his death was regarded by his co-religionists as an incarnation of the Divinity; for during his life he had been an example of all the virtues--wisdom, courage, and piety.

which, one hundred years later, were to strike a fatal blow at the power of the Mogul sovereigns. The successors of Sivaji did not inherit the qualities of the founder of the dynasty. Entirely given up to the dissipations of the harem, they left the supreme authority in the hands of their ministers, who soon became the real rulers. One of these 'maires du palais,' Ballaji Wischwanath, received the title of 'Peischwah' (leader) in 1708 from Shao, Sivaji's grandson, and was himself succeeded by his sons and grandsons. This heredity conferred supreme power in the Mahratta confederation on the family of the Peischwahs, and the sovereign, *de facto*, transferred his residence to Poonah, leaving at Sattarah the descendant of Sivaji, surrounded by all the vain pomps of royalty.

During the whole course of the eighteenth century, the Mahratta dynasty constantly increased in power, took a successful and profitable share in all the wars which convulsed the land in the last stages of the Mogul empire; and, at one time, it seemed probable that the empire of India would pass from the hands of its Mahommedan conquerors into those of the Peischwahs. Towards the middle of last century, the confederation comprised the greater part of the Deccan, between the Nerbuddah and Krishna rivers, the provinces of Berar and Cuttack, and the whole of Western India, except the Punjab and Moultan. Its military strength amounted to 210,000 cavalry and 96,000 infantry, and its annual income to 17,000,000*l.* sterling.

This was the real period of dual government in India. Adventurers attained the highest rank in a few years. Bonslah seized upon the district of Berar; the Guickhowar (shepherd), Holkar, and Scindia founded the dynasties which still occupy the thrones of Guzerat, Indore, and Gwalior. But these upstart kings recognised the suzerainty of the descendant of Sivaji, shut up though he was in his harem of Sattarah, just as the great Mussulman princes, the Nawab of Bengal, the Viceroy of Oude, and the Nizam of Hyderabad were proud to bear the title of viceroy of the sovereigns of the house of Timour. Let us add, that in this vast confederation, based on fraud and violence,[1] the chiefs never recognised any reciprocal system of rights and duties binding on all alike. Independent of each other and merely connected by the feeble link of feudal suzerainty, first to the descendants of Sivaji, and then to those of the Peischwah, the Mahratta princes always settled their quarrels by force of arms, and thus prepared the way for the success of the East India Company. The power of the Peischwah was not destined long to survive that of the Emperors of Delhi, and disappeared from the scene a few years afterwards. The Peischwah fell into the hands of the English in 1815, and, in return for his abdication, received a considerable pension; he died in 1852 at Bithour, near Cawnpore. The cowardly and cruel share taken by Nana Sahib, the adopted son of the last Peischwah, in the events of the mutiny, has already been described.

The family of the Scindias, which after that of the Peischwahs played the most important part in the struggles of the Mahratta confederation against the Mogul Emperors, was not of any great antiquity. The first Scindia whose name is recorded by history, Ranoji Scindia, made his appearance in the household of the Peischwah, in the character of Keeper

[1] Certain customs of the Mahratta princes were evidently intended to keep alive the love of warfare and pillage amongst their subjects. Up to the present day, on the great feast of the Duserah, instituted to commemorate Ram Chandra's victory over the giant Rawan, they march out of their palace in state, surrounded by their guards, in the midst of discharges of artillery. In a field of wheat, already chosen and marked out for destruction, the Maharajah dismounts from his elephant, gathers a handful of corn, and the crop, which is given up to the suite, is trodden down by the feet of the horses and torn up by their riders. Let it be noted that the Mahrattas, though belonging to the Hindoo religion, take part in all the great Mussulman feasts, and also observe the days of mourning and abstinence of the Moharam, which are set apart for the celebration of the death of Hussein, the Prophet's grandson. Finally, amongst the extraordinary customs of Indian courts, we must mention the encouragement of regicide, which was long prevalent at that of the Zamorin of Calicut. It was an understood thing there that on a certain day of the year, any one who could assassinate the sovereign became his legitimate successor, and at the fatal date the Zamorin used to encamp outside the town, in the midst of his guards, in order to escape the danger of a would-be murderer.

of the Royal Slippers. Tradition relates that Baji Rao, who succeeded his father as Peischwah in 1720, on coming out one day from an audience with his suzerain, found Ranoji Scindia asleep in the ante-room, still, however, clasping to his breast the royal slippers confided to his guard. The Peischwah, feeling that a servant who, even when asleep, was so careful of his charge, must possess some rare qualities, at once enrolled Ranoji Scindia in his body-guard. The rise of this humble servant was rapid and brilliant: at his death he left 'jhagirs' (feudal properties) worth more than 120,000*l.* sterling a year. Madhoji Scindia, his second son and successor, a man of great talent and wonderful energy, raised a considerable body of troops, and introduced European arms and discipline into their ranks, with the assistance of some French officers, amongst whom we may name MM. de Boigne and Perron. His military power gave him the first rank amongst the Mahratta princes; he took an active and successful part in all the great events of his time, whether political or military. He was recognised as an independent prince by the English in 1793, and died soon after, leaving a royal inheritance to his adoptive son, Daoulah Rao Scindia. The latter prince joined the Mahratta League against the English in 1805, but was soon forced to conclude a disastrous peace by the victories of Sir A. Wellesley and of Lord Lake. The relations between the Company and Daoulah Rao Scindia continued on a friendly footing until 1818, when, the Pandaree war threatening to convulse the whole of India, the Government obliged him to sign an offensive and defensive alliance, and to apply the revenues of some of his provinces to the maintenance of a body of troops commanded by Anglo-Indian officers. This was the origin of the Gwalior contingent, which, as we have seen, figured so prominently in the mutiny. Daoulah Rao Scindia died in 1827, and was succeeded by an adopted son, who died in his turn, in 1843, without leaving either direct or other descendants. His widow, the Begum Tara Baï, in conformity with the customs of the country, and with the permission of the British authorities, adopted a child of eight years, named

Bhagirah Rao, whose maternal uncle, Mamou Sahib, was appointed regent of the kingdom. This temporary arrangement was soon disturbed by internal intrigues.

Since the peace of 1817, the Gwalior contingent had merely been employed in expeditions which, though nominally for police purposes, were little more than brigandage. Abundance of bread and idleness, to use the Indian proverb, had given rise to discontent and indiscipline. Scattered about in various fortresses, they had, under the old sovereign, always refused to accept reductions or vacancies in their ranks. The weakness of the new Government gave both chiefs and soldiers the opportunity of insisting on, and increasing their pretensions, and the whole army gathered together in the vicinity of the capital. Under pressure from these Asiatic pretorians, the Begum withdrew the regency from Mamou Sahib, and replaced him by Dada-Khas-Ti-Wallah, an Indian of low extraction, and in no way connected with the young sovereign. From the beginning, the new Regent assumed a position of hostility towards the English, and discharged all the officers who were favourable to them.

The tranquillity of Central India, and of the neighbouring territories annexed to the dominions of the East India Company, was seriously threatened. Moreover, at this very time, the anarchy which overspread the Punjab after the death of Ranjit Singh caused great trouble to be anticipated in the north of India. The Governor-General, Lord Ellenborough, resolved to settle matters in Gwalior before the Sikh question should attain its full development. The Begum was called upon to dismiss the new Regent and reduce her army, whilst increasing by way of compensation the special Gwalior contingent. On her refusal, the British troops passed the Chambal in the beginning of December, 1843. The following days were consumed in fruitless negotiations, and on the 27th the Company's army defeated the Mahratta forces in a great pitched battle at Maharajpore. The contest was sanguinary and stubborn, and cost the victors 800 dead and wounded. The next day, Tara Baï sent a deputation to the Governor-General to make her full submission, and soon after she came herself to the English camp with the young Maharajah, and confirmed the pacific words of her envoys. Towards the middle of January, a new treaty restored the throne of Scindia under the protectorate of England. All the native troops were disbanded, with the exception of the Gwalior contingent, which was organised on a different basis, and considerably augmented, whilst a diplomatic agent, accredited to the Court, exercised henceforth a preponderating influence over the internal affairs of the country.

The story of the rise and fall of the Holkar dynasty greatly resembles that of the race of Scindia. Mulhar Rao, the founder of this family, which came next in importance in the history of the Mahratta confederation, was of humble origin, and belonged to a caste of shepherds. He was born at the end of the 17th century, at Hull, a small village in the Deccan, whence his descendants took the name of Holkar. If we are to believe contemporaries, extraordinary signs announced his future destiny. It is said that, having fallen asleep in the fields when quite a child, his mother found him watched over by an enormous *cobra di capello*, which was shielding the little sleeper from the rays of the sun with its head and neck. Mulhar justified these prognostics, and having enlisted under the banner of the Peischwah, from being a simple soldier he rose to the highest rank amongst the Mahratta chieftains. Inferior, as a politician, to his contemporary Madhoji Scindia, he possessed to a much greater degree the qualities of a warrior. Generosity was his dominant characteristic, and if a soldier displayed bravery by his side in the combats in which he never spared himself, he would exclaim, with enthusiasm, 'Fill the shield of this hero with rupees.' Mulhar Rao died in 1765, at the age of seventy-nine, leaving as the only heir to his greatness a son scarcely of age, whom history represents to us in most sombre colours.

The story goes that this youthful satrap found a malicious pleasure in hiding scorpions and other venomous insects in garments, which he would then offer to fakirs, or in vessels full of rupees, out of which he would graciously invite beggars to take handfuls. This evil-natured young man died in a fit of madness, and was succeeded on the throne by his mother, Alahaya Baï. Her rare virtues place her in the category of those great queens whose lives form the most precious ornaments of European history. In the course of these sketches, we have already come across Sultanas who gave proof of virile qualities, and long before 1857 the weaker sex had played a conspicuous part in the annals of India, where, before the Begum of Oude and the Ranee of Jansi, other women had wielded with distinction the supreme authority, and amongst these the first place belongs to Alahaya Baï.

This remarkable sovereign took a truly regal view of the duties and responsibilities of the Crown, and was accustomed to say, when her ministers demanded the infliction of severe punishment: 'Let us take care, mere mortals that we are, not to destroy thoughtlessly the work of God.' Indefatigably active, she defended with the utmost ardour the interests of humble village functionaries or small farmers, and her entire life was given up to prayer and good works. She rose before daylight, performed her devotions, listened to readings from the sacred books, and then distributed alms to Brahmins and food to beggars. Then followed several hours of work in her study. After a frugal lunch came other prayers and a short rest; the Queen finally went to the 'durbar,' where she presided over the council of ministers till the evening. On her return to her apartments, Alahaya Baï retired very late to rest, after devoting the last portion of the day to affairs of state or religious meditations.[1] We borrow these

[1] Alahaya Baï was very unhappy in her old age. The melancholy death of her only son, Malee Rao, has been noticed. She had besides one daughter, Muchta Bhye, who was married, and had one son, who died at Mhysir. Twelve months afterwards his father died, and Muchta Bhye immediately declared her resolution to burn with the corpse of her husband. No efforts that a mother and a sovereign could use were untried by the virtuous Alahaya Baï to dissuade her daughter from the fatal resolution. She humbled herself to the dust before her, and entreated her, as she revered her god, not to leave her desolate and alone upon earth. Muchta Bhye, although affectionate, was calm and resolved. 'You are old, mother,' she said, 'and in a few years will end your

details almost literally from Indian chronicles; they would apply equally to those pious princesses who still live in the memory of Europe, for in all latitudes the existence of choice spirits is characterised by the same virtues and habits. The success of Alahaya Baï as a sovereign was thorough and complete; she succeeded in giving to her subjects that rare benefit in those troublous times in India—absolute peace, both internal and external. This glorious episode in the dynasty of the family of Holkar never again repeated itself, and after a long and severe struggle, the heir to the throne of Indore was obliged to renounce his independence (1817) and, like his Gwalior neighbour, accept the position of a vassal of England.

By the side of these two great relics of Mahratta power, there still remained in 1857 many small independent native states, about which we must say a few words. The district known as Rajpootana, and comprised between Central India and the North-West Provinces in one direction, and the states of Guzerat and Holkar in the other, is extremely interesting. Often devastated, but never conquered by Mussulman invaders, it always preserved a species of independence. Even in the palmy days of the Mogul Emperors, the Rajpoot population paid tribute to the Court of Delhi with great reluctance, and for short periods only. This portion of India contains magnificent scenery, and is not less interesting from an historical point of view than from its natural conformation. The Mahommedan historians, who

pious life. My only child and husband are gone, and when you follow, life, I feel, will be insupportable; but the opportunity of terminating it with honour will then have passed.' Alahaya Baï, when she found all dissuasion unavailing, determined to witness the last dreadful scene. She walked in the procession and stood near the pile, where she was supported by two Brahmins, who held her arms. Although obviously suffering great agony of mind, she remained tolerably firm till the first blaze of the flame made her lose all self-command. But after some convulsive efforts, she so far recovered as to join in the ceremony of bathing in the Nerbudda, when the bodies were consumed. She then retired to her palace, where for three days, having taken hardly any sustenance, she remained so absorbed in grief that she never uttered a word. When recovered from this state, she seemed to find consolation in building a beautiful monument to the memory of those she lamented.—Major-General Sir John Malcolm, G.C.B., *A Memoir of Central India.*

have related the struggle between the Court of Delhi and the races of Central Asia, are full of accounts of proud Rajpoots perishing sword in hand, after giving their families and treasures as a prey to the flames. Every hill is crowned by a dismantled castle, and every castle has its legend. Other ruins recall monastic establishments almost similar to the convents of Europe, where Jaïn or Buddhist priests were maintained by the piety or remorse of powerful rajahs. Numerous rudely-sculptured stones representing a horseman extending his hand towards a kneeling woman, indicate the places where widows, who devoted themselves to 'suttee,' had ascended the funeral pile in order to rejoin their husbands.

The origin of this custom, almost entirely discontinued in our day, is lost in the night of ages. To explain it, one is obliged to admit, like a certain traveller of the last century, that Indian women having got into the habit of poisoning their husbands, the Brahmins, to stop this practice, made suttee a religious obligation.

If, in 1857, European influence had rooted out suttee from Rajpootana, as in other parts of India, it had not been equally successful in repressing another custom equally barbarous and equally prevalent, viz., female infanticide. Amongst Rajpoots the pride of birth assumes the most extravagant proportions, and though most noble families modestly trace their descent from the sun or the moon, not all stand on the same footing; and a *mésalliance*, or an unmarried daughter, was a dishonour alike to connections and relations. Moreover, the custom of the country obliged the family of the bride to expend immense sums in public feasts, presents to the priests, &c., on the occasion of a wedding. These few details give the key to this criminal practice, which before the mutiny was still in vogue in the harems of Central India, and often occasioned serious difficulties between the native powers and the Company's agents.

Before acquiring relative influence over these vast and wild territories, besides meeting with opposition from the local authorities, the English had been obliged to overcome strange and formidable enemies. In the first place came the Pandaris, whose organisation and excesses recall the free companies and the brigands who desolated Europe in the worst days of the Middle Ages. They belonged to no special caste. Their hereditary chiefs, generally of Pathan extraction, enrolled under their banner bandits and vagabonds without distinction of caste or religion. Soldiers who had been dismissed from the service of native princes, thieves, assassins, the vilest scum of India, found a refuge and means of existence in the Pandari bands. The life of these bandits had no object but theft and pillage, and they exercised their infamous trade on an immense scale, sometimes on their own account, sometimes paid by princes, whose auxiliaries they became in their intestine wars.[1] The outrages committed

[1] It is said that in the early years of this century, the Rajah of Bhopal, who was then at war with his Nagpore neighbour, having declined the assistance of the Pandaris, they offered their services to the Rajah of Nagpore. The latter prince, wiser than his adversary, accepted their proposals, and the Pandaris ravaged so cruelly the territory of Bhopal, that twenty-five years after an English traveller found traces of their devastation. The 'durrahs' (bands) comprised 2,000 or 3,000 horsemen, armed with sabres and lances, some with matchlocks. They were famous for the rapidity of their movements. In case of necessity, the Pandaris marched forty and even fifty miles a day, keeping up their strength and that of their horses by spices and stimulants. The mystery which surrounded their expeditions was not less remarkable. The whole gang bore down in forced marches on the province marked for destruction, and on arriving at their destination, divided into small bodies, thirsting all of them for bloodshed and booty. The hands and feet of women were cut off, in order to obtain the ornaments they wore, and the most horrible tortures were practised upon the inhabitants to make them disclose the spot where their treasures were hid. As soon as the work of devastation was accomplished, the bandits retired as rapidly as they had appeared, preceded by numerous droves of cattle, and laden with spoil of all sorts, leaving behind them a desolate country and smoking ruins. When they were once again safe back in their haunts, they proceeded to divide the booty, first putting aside the share of the government whose auxiliaries they were for the moment, and, when the expedition was on their own account, that of their chief. In certain bands, the chief's share was a quarter; in others, he had a right to the elephants and certain objects previously determined on. As soon as the spoil was divided, the camp was turned into a vast fair, which was attended by crowds of the people of the country. The Pandari women, who accompanied their husbands on their expeditions, managed the sale, whilst the bandits were gambling frantically or were deep in carouse. These saturnalia went on till the booty came to an end, and it was necessary to fill by pillage the purses emptied by

by the Pandaris in Rajpootana and the neighbouring districts gave rise in 1817 to a campaign full of difficulties for the British troops. The most formidable chiefs were, however, killed in the struggle, or ended their days in prison. A few years later, the population had forgotten even the name of these bandits, who had been for so long the terror of the country.

In default of the Pandaris, other warlike races of Central Asia, such as the Rohillas, were ready to lend an energetic assistance to the mutineers. Amongst the adventurers who thronged to the standard of the Mogul Emperors were certain tribes from the neighbourhood of Cabul and Candahar, known under the above name. Their services were rewarded by grants of lands, which were situated for the most part in the fertile plain watered by the Ramganga before its junction with the Ganges, and known as Rohilkund. Favoured by the events that followed the death of Aureng-Zeb, the little colony achieved its independence. The Rohillas differed from other Indian tribes by the fairness of their skin, their warlike qualities, and their skill in the arts of peace. Whilst anarchy was desolating the whole of India, these emigrants, who were governed with the utmost wisdom by their own chiefs, escaped the general disaster. In the midst of this prosperity, which still endears to the Rohillas the memory of their Afghan rulers, the Nabob Vizier of

dissipation. The ravages committed by the Pandaris in Central India in 1817–18 were followed by a desperate struggle, which severely tried the endurance of the British troops. Most of the chiefs fell in battle, or expiated their crimes in prison. As to the mass of the bandits, who were not to be distinguished from the general population, they were obliged from this time to earn their bread by peaceful trades. Repressive measures were so effectually carried out, that five years afterwards Sir J. Malcolm, a high Government official, was able to write that even the name of Pandari was forgotten in the very districts where formerly the mere mention of it was a cause of terror. The death of Chiton, one of the most formidable chiefs, who had commanded a 'durrah' of 8,000 horsemen, was attended with rather unusual circumstances. Tracked on all sides, he had disappeared for several days without leaving any traces, when his horse was discovered, saddled, and peacefully feeding in a meadow. The neighbouring jungles were immediately searched, and his lacerated body was found with the head untouched; a tiger had surprised him asleep, and had made an end of the terrible Pandari.

Oude, Sujah Dowlah, cast covetous glances on his neighbour's territory, and found an accomplice in Warren Hastings, then Governor-General, who, in return for an indemnity of half a million sterling, engaged to assist him with the British troops in the conquest of Rohilkund. When informed of these designs, the Rohillas proposed to purchase their independence, but Warren Hastings refused their offer, and Rohilkund became a prey to war and all its attendant horrors. More than a hundred thousand persons are said to have left the country in order to seek a refuge beyond the Ganges from the tyrant to whom they had been consigned by a shameful bargain, and the rich province which had tempted Sujah Dowlah's cupidity became the poorest in his dominions. But the Rohillas did not disappear from the face of India; and we may suppose, from the fervour with which they embraced the cause of the mutineers in the Central Provinces, that they had not forgotten the crime committed against them in the preceding century by the highest representative of the Company.

Before the mutiny, Rajpootana was divided into two distinct categories of native states—small independent states, as Alwar, Tonke, Bikanir, &c., and those far more numerous and powerful states which were bound to England by offensive and defensive alliances. Among the latter were Jeypore, Joudpore, Burtpore, Kotah, Oudeypore, Malwa. Every allied prince had at his court an English agent who, under pretext of diplomatic privileges, assumed an overwhelming share in the internal direction of the country. An agent of the Governor-General for Rajpootana, who resided the greater part of the year at Mount Abou (150 miles from Joudpore),[1] was the immediate head of all these missions, and in his hand was concentrated all their correspondence. The native princes, on their side, kept certain 'vakils' (representatives) in attendance on the English agent, who were

[1] The station of Mount Abou, situated on the highest peak of the Aravelli chain, 5,000 feet above the sea, is a great resort for Europeans in Central India during the heat of summer. For the Hindoos it is a favourite place of pilgrimage, and the temple of Mount Abou in point of architectural magnificence is only inferior to the Tarje of Agra.

charged with the defence of their political interests in all diplomatic matters. The system on which the relations between the Company and the States of Central Asia was regulated differed in no way from the ordinary one, and a plenipotentiary sent by the Governor-General had the direction of a staff of secondary agents, who resided at the courts of Holkar, Scindiah, and other princes. We will here mention that in Central India, as in Rajpootana, the English agents were selected from the *élite* of the Civil Service or the army, and usually justified the choice of the Indian Foreign Office by the influence they acquired over the native sovereign, and by their intimate acquaintance with the concerns of the country.

The disturbances which, in the month of May, 1857, began to agitate the North-West Provinces and Oude, found a prompt and terrible response in Central India. The system of confiscation, disguised under the name of annexation, on which the Company had embarked since Lord Dalhousie had been at the head of affairs (1849), caused all the more aversion and distrust among the natives, that in several instances it had infringed the right of adoption, one of the fundamental bases of the Brahmin religion. 'A son, whether legitimate or adopted, by performing funeral rites in honour of the dead, delivers his father from hell,' says the great Indian legislator. In certain districts, adoption by the chief widow is as valid as any that the deceased husband might have made. Amongst a polygamous people it is astonishing to find adoption playing so great a part in royal inheritances, and yet the history of India is there to attest that the harem does not always ensure direct descendants. There are but few of the princely families of India who do not owe their present position to the fictitious paternity of adoption.

Under the Mogul Emperors the principle of adoption, having finally passed into an established custom, merely entailed very heavy succession duties. This tolerant policy was continued by the Company, which, in its early days, was desirous of following the traditions of its predecessors as far as was consonant with its own interests. But, in 1849, the contrary system came into vogue, notwithstanding the conscientious and disinterested opposition of certain high Anglo-Indian officials.[1] In default of direct and legitimate

[1] It is customary, in the Indian Council, for members to give their opinion in writing on important questions. The *résumé* of a minute, dated February 10, 1854, and drawn up by Colonel Low, on account of the annexation of the principality of Nagpore, will be read with interest:—

'If Great Britain shall retain her present powerful position among the states of Europe, it seems highly probable that owing to the infringement of treaties on the part of native princes and other causes, the whole of India will, in course of time, become one British province; but many eminent statesmen have been of opinion that we ought most carefully to avoid unnecessarily accelerating the arrival of that great change; and it is within my own knowledge that the following five great men were of that number, namely:—Lord Hastings, Sir Thomas Munro, Sir John Malcolm, the Hon. Mountstuart Elphinstone, and Lord Metcalfe.

'When I went to Malwa, in 1850, where I met many old acquaintances, whom I had known when a very young man, and over whom I held no authority, I found these old acquaintances speak out much more distinctly as to their opinion on the Sattarah case, so much so that I was on several occasions obliged to check them. It is remarkable that every native who ever spoke to me respecting the annexation of Sattarah, asked precisely the same question, What crime did the late Rajah commit that his country should be seized by the Company? Thus clearly indicating their notions, that if any crime had been committed our act would have been justifiable, and not otherwise. That the annexation of the Punjab, for instance, had not been regarded as a wrong, because the chiefs and people had brought it on themselves, but that the extinction of a loyal native state, in default of heirs, was not appreciable in any part of India, and that the exercise of the alleged right of lapse would create a common feeling of uncertainty and distrust at every durbar in the country.

'Colonel Lowe, in his minute, dwelt upon the levelling effects of British dominion, and urged that, as in our own provinces, the upper classes were invariably trodden down, it was sound policy to maintain the native states, if only as a means of providing an outlet for the energies of men of good birth and aspiring natures, who could never rise under British rule. He contended that our system of administration might be far better than the native system, but that the people did not like it better; they clung to their old institutions, however defective, and were averse to change, even though a change for the better. "In one respect," he said, "the natives of India are exactly like the inhabitants of all parts of the known world; they like their own habits and customs better than those of foreigners."

'After that Lowe turned to the discussion of the particular case before him. He contended that the treaty between the British Government and the Sah Rajah did not limit the successor to heirs of his body, and that, therefore, there was a clear title to succession in the Bouslah family, by means of a son adopted by either the Rajah himself or by his eldest widow, in accordance with law and usage. The conduct, he said, of the last prince of Nagpore had

heirs, the Supreme Government annexed in 1849 the principality of Sattarah in Central Asia, founded by the great Sivaji: at the death of Ragofi Bouslah in 1853, the territory of Nagpore, and towards the same period, at the death of Gangadhar Rao, the dominion of Jansi, and of Sambahlpore, &c. The principality of Kerowli was more fortunate, and, thanks to the antiquity of its royal house, it escaped the general confiscation. The succession of the Rajah of Kerowli gave rise, however, to sharp discussions, and the rights of the adoptive son of the last prince to the paternal dominions were not recognised without considerable hesitation.

These systematic attacks against the most deeply-rooted religious prejudices of the native population excited perhaps greater indignation than if the European conquerors, putting forward no right but that of the strongest, had brutally dispossessed the deceased princes in their lifetime. Moreover, not all of the Maharajahs, Rajahs, and great vassals accepted the gilded but heavy chain imposed by the new suzerain, with the same resignation as Holkar and Scindiah. Some of them, with a pride which must be taken into consideration, refused to play the part of 'rois fainéants,' or of richly paid pensioners. Among the latter was the Ranee of Jansi, Lackschmi Baï, a clever and energetic woman, who took an active and prominent share in the events which followed. Such of the Rajpoot princes who had preserved their independence, feeling themselves threatened in their hereditary rights, were longing for the oppor-

not been such as to alienate this right; he had been loyal to the paramount state, and his country had not been misgoverned, there had been nothing to call for military interference on our part, and little to compel grave remonstrance and rebuke. For what crime, then, was his line to be cut off and the honours of his house extinguished for ever? To refuse the right of adoption in such a case would, he alleged, be entirely contrary to the spirit, if not to the letter of the treaty. But how was it to be conceded when it was not claimed; when it was certain that the Rajah had not exercised his right, and there had been no tidings of such a movement on the part of his widow? The answer to this was, that the Government had been somewhat in a hurry to extinguish the Raj without waiting for the appearance of claimants, and that if they desired to perpetuate it, it was easy to find a fitting successor.'—Sir John Kaye's *History of the Sepoy War*.

tunity to take up arms against their European conquerors, of whose power and resources they, in their presumptuous ignorance, could form no idea.

The lower classes shared to a great degree these hostile sentiments. The poorer Hindoos, bound to the Procrustean bed of caste—street-sweepers or masons, sons of masons or of street-sweepers, fathers of street-sweepers or masons, with no worldly goods but a hovel open to every wind, a few earthen pots, and some wretched garments—were incapable of comprehending the benefit which accrued to them from the intervention of Europeans in the affairs of the State. To these outcasts of humanity, what mattered order in the finances, a better administration of justice, the development of public works, roads, canals, railways, &c. The Indian, says an eminent Anglo-Indian official, with great truth, has this point in common with other men, that he prefers his old customs to foreign innovations. Resigned to their fate, without wants or hopes, the inferior castes, by a very natural feeling recalled the good old times when suttee and infanticide flourished in the land—even the Thugs, those curses of India, came in no doubt for a share in these naïve regrets. Do we not see the peasants in certain parts of Europe cast a halo of glory over the feats of the smugglers and robbers now suppressed by the strong arm of the law?

It is useless to dilate upon the state of anxiety which was common to all the small European colonies in Central India, as soon as the first outbreaks occurred at Mirut and Delhi. Even in the most important stations the white population never reached more than an insignificant number. The regiments belonging to the native contingents were formed on the irregular system, and contained at the most four or five English officers. A political agent, one or two secretaries, and a chaplain were the only civil authorities. No words can describe the horror of the position of these few English families lost in the middle of India, and separated by immense distances from European bayonets, among which alone they could find a secure refuge. Premonitory signs of the storm began to appear on the horizon. What an amount of hatred lay under the insolent and sullen obedience with which the orders of a European master were received, whether addressed to the soldiers or delivered in the 'durbars!' The servants, formerly so submissive, performed their domestic duties with murmurs and complaints. It was not merely for the Europeans a question of the evils which war entails, when carried on between civilised nations, where the conqueror respects infancy and weakness; the massacres at Delhi and Cawnpore showed clearly enough that wherever the mutiny triumphed, the women and children were irrevocably doomed. Whether from indecision, want of cordial understanding among the rebels, or a providential delay in the development of the crisis, the rising at Mirut was not immediately followed in the stations of Central India.

Several weeks' agony was reserved to the European residents of Gwalior, Indore, Jansi, &c.; they were able to follow —and with what breathless interest!—the opening phases of the contest, the concentration of European troops at Kurnaul, the adhesion of Sikh Rajahs, the victory of Sir H. Barnard under the walls of Delhi. For a few moments even the news of the capture of Delhi, the capital of the insurrection, filled every heart with joy in the station of Gwalior. Short and bitter delusion! The tide of revolt was rising, ever higher and higher. To the general consternation the good news was contradicted by telegram on the morning of the following day.

That same evening, June 14, at nine o'clock the alarm-gun announced that the two infantry regiments of the contingent were in open revolt. It had long been impossible to doubt of the sinister intentions of these two corps, which, like the sepoys of the Bengal army, were recruited from the Brahmins and Rajpoots of Oude. Their officers, eleven in number, vainly attempted to recall the men to their duty; several were killed by the rebels, and the others obliged to fly. The European houses were then sacked and pillaged, but the atrocities committed were less than might have been expected.

Maharajah Scindiah, who occupied the throne of Gwalior under British protection, in a recent journey to Calcutta had had the opportunity of personally appreciating the strength of European civilisation. The diplomatic agent at Gwalior, Colonel Macpherson, was conversant with the languages and customs of Asia, and had acquired great influence over the prince. In short, whether from political tact or philosophic resignation, the Maharajah had, loyally and without reservation, accepted the position of a vassal of England. On the first symptoms of a rising, some of the women and children took refuge in Colonel Macpherson's apartments in the palace of Scindiah, and the prince showed both will and power to protect them. By a tacit infringement of the treaty he had in his pay several hundred of those faithful Mahrattas, who had been the glory and greatness of his ancestors. These soldiers served as escort to the Resident and to the European families who had clustered round him, and conducted them in safety within the walls of the fortress of Agra. A few ladies who lived in bungalows some distance from the palace, or who for other reasons had been unable to reach the Resident, escaped from the nocturnal researches of the assassins, owing to the devotedness of Mouza, the major-domo (Khansommah) of one of the officers, who deserves that 'history should record his name!' After great dangers and frightful hardships, these poor creatures, who were secretly protected by Scindiah, succeeded also in reaching Agra.[1]

The other regiments of the contingent soon followed the example of their companions in the capital, but in the midst of these disorders, Colonel Macpherson, even from Agra, still continued to exercise great influence over Scindiah's conduct. In obedience to the councils of his politic mentor, the Maharajah undertook by threats, by entreaties, and by timely gifts of money to direct the movements of the insurgent troops, so as most effectually to subserve the plans of the English. Thus it happened that the contingent did not

[1] See Documents, No. X., 'Account of the Escape from Gwalior of Mrs. Copeland and some other English ladies'

join the rebels under the walls of Delhi, and did not arrive at Cawnpore in time to hamper the first operations of Havelock. It was only after long hesitation that the Gwalior forces took up their position at Calpi, and marched from thence on Cawnpore. We have already related their successful attack on General Wyndham's corps, and their defeat by Sir C. Campbell, on his return from the first expedition to Lucknow in the beginning of December.

The occurrences at Gwalior were followed at an early date by the revolt of Holkar's contingent. On July 1, two regiments belonging to it attacked the Residency, which was occupied by Colonel Durand, the temporary agent at the Court of Indore. A European battery was quartered at the station of Mhow, some twelve miles off, but before any assistance could arrive, the victory of the sepoys was complete, and had been stained by the murder of thirty-four officers, women, and children, and by the pillage and destruction of the European dwellings. Notwithstanding the defection of his troops, the Maharajah remained faithful to his word. His intervention secured the escape of Colonel Durand and his family. Moreover, with a courage worthy of his race, Holkar did not shrink from resisting the insurrection. Being asked, in an interview with the leaders of the revolt, to place himself at their head, and fight under the walls of Delhi for the religion of his fathers, Holkar nobly answered that his faith and the faith of his ancestors had nothing in common with that of murderers who had shed the blood of women and children. On the evening of July 1, a mutiny broke out in the native regiments stationed at Mhow. The colonel and adjutant of the 23rd B.A. were slain by their soldiers, but the other officers with their families took refuge in the fort, where, protected by the European battery, and by incomplete fortifications, they awaited in relative security the arrival of a relieving force.

The success of the mutiny in the minor stations was not less great than in the capitals of Scindiah and Holkar. At Jansi, the victory of the sepoys was accompanied by a horrible slaughter, which, in the number of victims, was only surpassed by the massacre at Cawnpore. The local authorities and some English families, among whom there was an exceptional number of children, sought shelter in a fort, which was in no condition to resist, and where they were immediately besieged. Provisions soon gave out, and Major Skeene, the district superintendent, had the weakness to listen to the proposals of the emissaries sent by the dethroned Ranee, who had placed herself at the head of the revolt. As at Cawnpore, a convention was signed which guaranteed the life of the Europeans, but the Ranee, not less than the Nana, was thirsting for the blood of the foreign conquerors. The capitulation had the same results as at Cawnpore; the prisoners were all massacred with unheard-of refinements of torture in the early part of June.

On May 28, the Nacirabad brigade, composed of a native battery of artillery, and of the 15th and 31st B.A., mutinied, and marched towards Delhi, after sacking the station. The 1st Lancers, B.A., who were quartered at Nacirabad, protected the escape of the officers, without, however, acting vigorously against the rebels, and the victims were few in number. The results of this skirmish were in all respects less serious than might have been feared. The important fortress of Ajmir, containing the public treasure, and a well-stored arsenal, escaped from the hands of the insurgents by the opportune substitution of a local battalion in the place of the companies of the 15th, which had hitherto been garrisoning it. On June 3, at Nimach, a native battery of artillery, the 72nd B.A., and the 7th of the Gwalior contingent, followed the example of the other disaffected regiments. The Joudpore contingent, having driven away its European staff, attempted to surprise the station of Mount Abou, where numerous European families had taken refuge. But the attempt failed ignominiously, thanks to the resolute attitude of the inmates of the military hospitals, some thirty British soldiers. The mutiny of the 52nd at Jabbalpore was followed by a curious correspondence. After deserting in a mass, the regiment addressed a collective letter to their colonel, in which the titles of Lord of Mercy, Pearl of the Age, &c.,

were lavishly bestowed, and ended by saying that they had deserted only because the havildar major had announced the speedy arrival of a regiment belonging to the Madras army, with orders to disarm, and then to massacre them. This document discussed at length the question of money, demanding pay up to the day of their sudden departure, and proposing that the goods left in the cantonments should be sold in order to defray the price of the muskets carried off by the sepoys. We shall go no further in this list of the regiments that proved false to their colours; let it suffice to state that with the exception of the fortress of Ajmir, Mhow, and Saugor, where some officers had taken refuge with their families, by the end of July not a trace of English rule remained in the vast districts comprised between the Nerbudda and the North-West Provinces. At this point disasters were to end, thanks to the loyalty of the Madras and Bombay armies, and to that of the Nizam of Hyderabad.

The spirit of mutiny had not penetrated thoroughly into the army of Madras. A regiment of regular cavalry alone gave signs of disaffection, and was disbanded without exciting any emotion among its brothers in arms. The Bombay army, which drew its recruits from the same classes of the population as the Bengal army, offered a far more favourable field to the spirit of revolt. Being much nearer to the scene of action, by the very fact of its position it was more exposed to the intrigues of conspirators. But, in its ranks, discipline was never relaxed, and the concessions to prejudices of caste and religion never attained the extravagant proportions they had assumed in the sister Presidency. During the first weeks, however, of the insurrection, there was reason to fear an explosion which would have led to most disastrous consequences. By the end of July, severe examples, and more especially the arrival at Bombay of regiments returning from the Persian expedition, put an end to this state of things, and crushed out any thought of revolt. But whatever the loyalty of the mercenaries belonging to the Madras and Bombay armies, the spread of sedition could only be checked if the Nizam of Hyderabad, whose dominions separate

Central India from the Madras Presidency, remained faithful to the treaties he had signed.

The kingdom of the Nizam, situated between 15° and 21° of north latitude and 75° and 81° of longitude, comprises the best part of the Deccan, and numbers amongst its provinces the romantic kingdom of Golconda, the diamond mines of which, after supplying for centuries the theme of Oriental poetry, are scarcely worked at the present day. The country is composed of tableland, averaging 1,800 feet above the sea-level, and enjoys a salubrious and temperate climate, such as is rarely met with in India; the soil, which is extremely fertile, yields as much as two crops of rice a year. The capital, Hyderabad, contains with the suburbs about 250,000 souls, and outside the walls rise the vast buildings of the English Residency. It is said that when, in 1795, there was a question of beginning the edifice, Major Kirkpatrick, the then Resident, ordered the plans of the ground necessary for the construction to be drawn up on an immense scale, and presented them in full 'durbar' to the Nizam, who, on inspection, absolutely refused the desired grant, the English agent was retiring, very far from satisfied, from the interview, when the Prime Minister said smilingly to him, that on seeing such immense sheets of paper, which far surpassed in size the most complete native maps of the kingdom, the Prince had been alarmed, thinking that the largest part of his dominions was demanded of him, and that plans on a smaller scale were certain to meet with a more favourable reception. This advice was followed, and no more trouble was experienced.

The family, which still occupies the throne of Hyderabad, goes back to very remote antiquity. Without attempting to pierce the darkness of Indian genealogies, we may stop at Killick Khan, better known as Azaf Jah, one of Aureng-Zeb's most illustrious generals, who was wounded in the shoulder at the siege of Golconda, and died in consequence. A native historian relates the fact in the following simple and touching words:—'In the year 1686, during the siege of Golconda, Killick Khan was struck by a shot from a zambarouk (rampart-gun), which shattered his arm. The energy of the wounded man was so great that he returned to his tent on horseback. The Grand Vizier was at once sent to him by the Emperor, and arrived just as the surgeons were at work, but was nevertheless allowed to see the patient. Killick Khan conversed calmly with the royal messenger, praising the skill of the operation, and pouring out coffee with the hand that still remained to him. Nothing was spared to save this precious life, but fate had ordered it otherwise. After three days' agony, the brave soldier drank the sherbet of death, brought by the messenger of the All-Powerful.

Ghazi Uddin the First continued the glorious traditions of his father, and Aureng-Zeb, in order to perpetuate the remembrance of Ghazi's noble conduct at the siege of Bijapore, wrote with his own hand among the imperial records: 'The fortress of Bijapore has been taken, thanks to the bravery of our dear and loyal son, Ghazi Uddin.' The greatness of the family, however, only reached its full height under his son Mir Kammar Uddin, who, in 1713, received from the Emperor Feroz Shah the title of Nizam Ulmuck (leader of the State) and the vice-royalty of the Deccan, and the Fouzdari of the Carnatic.

The empire of Aureng-Zeb was now falling to pieces on all sides, and during the forty years that followed his death, his debauched and imbecile successors vied apparently with one another in incapacity and weakness. A Persian conqueror crossed India and forced the gates of Delhi, whilst the invasions of the Afghans completed the work of devastation. The warlike tribes of Rajpootana shook off the Mohammedan yoke. Mahratta adventurers carved out principalities for themselves in the heart of the empire. The viceroys and high dignitaries merely retained a nominal connection with the Court of Delhi; from time to time they placed offerings at the foot of the throne or sent to solicit honorary titles, but they ceased to be functionaries revocable at the pleasure of the great Mogul. Finally, the rivalry between France and England broke out even in these remote parts of Asia. The future heir of the King of kings now appeared on the scene, and intervened actively in the quarrels of the native princes.

The greatness of Nizam Ulmuck arose triumphant out of this period of confusion, and he died on the throne of the Deccan in 1748. Almost immediately European influence made itself felt for the first time at the Court of the Nizam, in the person of the Marquis de Bussy, the cleverest lieutenant of the great Dupleix.[1] This brilliant representative of the France of the eighteenth century acquired such an influence over the sovereign of the Deccan and his ministers, that in 1753 he obtained the cession of the four northern 'sirkars.'[2] The revenues of these provinces were to pay for the maintenance of French battalions or others commanded by French officers under Bussy's orders. This was the first offensive and defensive alliance with any European Power, the first step on the road which was to lead England to the conquest of the finest portion of India. Orders from his superior, M. de Lally, forced Bussy to leave Hyderabad in 1758, but the Nizam only let his friend go after a scene of heartrending farewell. His departure struck a terrible blow at French influence in India, and it may be said with every appearance of reason that had De Bussy remained at Hyderabad and been able to develop the system which he had initiated, the success of England would neither have been so prompt nor so decisive. All his compatriots did not follow him, however, and till the end of the century the Nizam kept in his pay French soldiers, whose number continually varied, and who were for a long time commanded by a soldier of fortune, a certain M. Raymond.

One can understand that the chief object of English diplomacy at Hyderabad should have been to get rid of these dangerous auxiliaries. Its efforts were finally successful,

[1] 'As to M. de Bussy, if I had another like him, I can promise you that matters in this part of India would have been settled more than two years ago.'—*Dupleix to M. de Machault*, Oct. 16, 1753.

[2] The four northern 'sirkars,' formed by the provinces of Mustaphanaggar, Ellore, Rajahmandri, and Chicacoli, secured to the French supremacy over the whole length of the coast of Coromandel, from Medapilly to the pagoda of Juggernaut, a distance of more than 600 miles.

and by a treaty signed on July 8, 1798, the Nizam engaged to dismiss and place in the hands of the English all the French officers and soldiers who were still in his service. To be just, we must add that this treaty was executed without unnecessary severity, and that our countrymen had no reason to complain of the behaviour of the winners in this diplomatic game. French influence was thus for ever ruined.

In touching a period of our history, which cannot be thought of without regret, if not without remorse, we still have the consolation of remembering that it was one of our countrymen who devised the secret of the conquest of India. 'The man who first saw that it was possible to found a European Empire on the ruins of the Mogul monarchy was Dupleix. His restless, capacious, and inventive mind had formed this scheme at a time when the ablest servants of the English Company were busied only about invoices and bills of lading. Nor had he only proposed to himself the end. He had also a just and distinct view of the means by which it was to be attained. He clearly saw that the greatest force which the princes of India could bring into the field would be no match for a small body of men trained in discipline and guided by the tactics of the weak. He saw also that the natives of India might, under European commanders, be formed into armies, such as Saxe or Frederic would be proud to command. He was perfectly aware that the most easy and convenient way in which a European adventurer could exercise sovereignty in India was to govern the motions and to speak through the mouth of some glittering puppet dignified by the title of Nabob or Nizam. The arts, both of war and policy, which a few years later were employed with such signal success by the English, were first understood and practised by this ingenious and aspiring Frenchman.' [1]

When the English entered upon the inheritance of Bussy and Raymond at the Court of the Nizam, they did not accept all the military institutions in existence there. Among the

[1] Babington Macaulay, *Critical and Historical Essays*, vol. iv.

regiments, formed on the European model, were two battalions composed of and commanded by women, to which French politeness had given the name of 'Zaffar palthans' (victorious battalions). These amazons on foot or 'gardennis' (doubtless a corruption of gardes) were specially employed in escorting the ladies of the harem and guarding the interior of the palace. 'It is not a rare thing,' says a traveller, 'to meet with sentinels in the corridors, a gun in one arm and a baby in the other, or to find them cowering in a corner occupied with still more maternal cares.'

In 1857 the last traces of India of old days had long disappeared, and the contingent which formed the chief basis of the Nizam's military forces was composed of four cavalry regiments of 600 sabres each, of eight infantry regiments of 800 men, and of four batteries of artillery. This contingent, which was always on a war footing, and ready to take the field, was remarkable for its cavalry, which was mounted on Deccan horses, the best race in India. The Anglo-Indian staff attached to the service of the Nizam comprised eighty-four officers and thirty non-commissioned officers, or quarter-masters. We have already often pointed out that service in the contingents, which conferred higher position and pay, was much sought after by Anglo-Indian officers. Let us add, to complete these details, that though the budget of the kingdom amounted to 2,500,000*l.* sterling, there was invariably a deficit in the annual accounts, and that twice during the thirty preceding years the English Government had been obliged to use vigorous measures in order to re-establish order in the Nizam's finances. The Nizam was nevertheless possessor of considerable treasures, and the finest jewels in India had little by little found their way into his coffers; amongst the most valuable one heard of, an uncut diamond of 375 carats, and supposed to be worth 7,000,000 fr. Certain customs, peculiar to the country, tended to increase the Nizam's fortune beyond all limits. He was by law the heir to all his subjects, and at the death of any rich man the fiscal agents at once took possession of his goods. It was only by a special favour that the natural heirs inherited.

At the beginning of the mutiny a new reign had just commenced at Hyderabad, where Azafuddanlah had only ascended the throne a few months previously on the death of his father, Nacir Uddanlah (March 1857). Like all Oriental princes, the new sovereign had hitherto lived remote from affairs in the reclusion of the harem. He could, however, scarcely be ignorant of the harshness with which Lord Dalhousie, a few years before (1852), had exacted the cession of three important provinces in payment of his father's debts. He was, moreover, known as a man full of religious fervour, and much inclined to surround himself with fakirs, astrologers and sorcerers, those invariable hangers-on of an Eastern Court.

England was destined nevertheless to meet with faithful allies at Hyderabad. In the first place there was an old man eighty years old, Schanisch ul Oumra, the maternal great uncle of the young Nizam, and the head of the religious party, over which he had great influence. This Moslem Nestor, in the course of a long life, had formed a just estimate of European might. Sincere faith, absolutely devoid of fanaticism, allowed free place in his heart to the instincts of humanity, and he had been horror-struck at the cruelties which, from the outset, had disgraced the cause of the sepoys. Against the entreaties and advice of his family, the old man invariably in the durbar took the side of peace and conciliation, of which the State minister, Salar Jung, was also an active and devoted partisan. Bound by his education and sympathies to European interests, the latter remained always faithful to them, and not even the daily threats of assassination to which he was exposed succeeded in intimidating him.

The condition of things at Hyderabad was very precarious, notwithstanding the goodwill of the Prince and of the Prime Minister. The lower classes, little better than ignorant savages, were governed by fanatical 'moulvis,' always ready to preach the holy war. The contingent, the oldest force of its kind, was organised and recruited like those of Holkar and Gwalior, which had so promptly embraced the cause of the insurrection. Besides his contingent, the

Nizam kept in his pay bands of mercenaries, Afghans; Rohillas, Arabs, on whose fidelity it was not safe to rely. To so many elements of danger, the English authorities could only oppose some few troops, stationed in the cantonments of Secunderabad (five miles distant). The Presidency of Madras, the only one from which any assistance could be expected, having sent all the troops it could dispose of to Bengal, the expectation of speedy reinforcements could only prove a vain delusion.

The news of the capture of Delhi by the insurgents arrived at Hyderabad after many delays, and at once occasioned great excitement in the population. On the very next day, proclamations more violent than usual were posted on the mosques, inciting the people to revolt, and launching insults at the Prince and the Minister who persisted in upholding the cause of the impure Christian conquerors. These exhortations soon produced an armed attack against the Resident's house. On July 17, bands of fanatics, led by a professional bandit named Toura Baz Khan, marched on the residency, but the skilful disposition taken by the military authorities, and the loyalty of one battery of the contingent, which unhesitatingly fired on the rioters, promptly put down the outbreak. The hopes inspired by this first success were fully justified. The mercenary troops, satisfied with their regular pay, and feeling that there was nothing to be gained by a change, resolutely backed up the Government. Salar Jung's skill and the Nizam's passive fidelity staved off any serious crisis till the day when the fall of the temporary throne raised at Delhi re-established European prestige.

The contingent, however, had not been entirely proof, as a whole, against the appeals to mutiny. On July 13 the 1st irregular cavalry regiment of this force, in garrison at Aurangabad, refused to march. The prudence of the officers succeeded in averting danger until the arrival from Bombay of a small body of troops under Major-General Woodburn. The Governor of Bombay, Lord Elphinstone,[1] had perceived

[1] In his youth, Lord Elphinstone, then a handsome, dashing captain in the Life Guards, had been looked upon with favour by Queen Victoria. To prevent

from the beginning the importance of the occurrences at Mirut and Delhi, and had undertaken the work of repression with rare activity and great energy. The speedy return to India of the troops employed in the Persian expedition was partially due to his initiative. Moreover, though plots discovered at Poonah and Ahmedabad had revealed serious ramifications of the mutiny in the very midst of the Bombay army, Lord Elphinstone, like the illustrious dictator of the Punjab, did not hesitate to sacrifice his personal safety to the common welfare, and all the troops that disembarked a Bombay were at once sent on to Central India. This abnegation was rewarded by the timely arrival at Aurangabad of forces necessary to put down all attempts at mutiny.

General Woodburn's column, composed of one European battery and two squadrons of the 14th Dragoons, was strong enough to meet the emergency without striking a blow, but things did not turn out as well as was expected. The operation of disarmament was not performed with sufficient energy, and failed, the disaffected taking to flight before it was resolved to use artillery against them. A few days afterwards, General Woodburn resigned his command for reasons of health, and was replaced by Brigadier Stuart, B.A. Every moment was precious. Above all it was necessary to relieve the garrison at Mhow, before the rains should have swollen the rivers and made the roads impassable. Chance favoured Stuart, and though the season was far advanced, his troops were able to accomplish their long march without delay or great fatigue. By August 2 the relief of Mhow had been effected.

The rains began to fall early in the month of August, and necessitated the suspension of military operations. This

a girlish caprice from hampering negotiations for the marriage of the sovereign, the ministers sent the Scotch nobleman into honourable exile by appointing him Governor of Madras. His talents and affability won immense popularity for him, and on his losing a large portion of his fortune by speculating, the Court of Directors, in recognition of his services, gave him the governorship of Bombay, which he was still holding in 1857, and in which he gave proof of eminent faculties. On his return home, Lord Elphinstone, worn out by the climate and overfatigued, died a few hours after being honoured by a private audience with the Queen.

enforced rest was employed in preparing the way for the success of the next campaign in Central India. Mhow afforded an excellent basis for future operations, and it was of the highest importance to secure it from the attacks of the enemy. The defences of the old fort were considerably increased, and communications with the coast were secured by re-establishing the telegraphic and postal services. Finally, every effort was made to bring together the camp-followers and the means of transport, which in India are requisite for an army in the field. The end of the rainy season, that is to say, the first days of October, found Stuart's little army ready to march, but, though reinforced by the 86th R.A., and a strong column of the Hyderabad contingent, it was still not strong enough to take the bull by the horns, and penetrate into the centre of the revolted districts. Besides which, the enemy dispersed in every direction, and bands of Rohillas traversed the province of Malwa, exercising their depredations almost within sight of the outposts at Mhow.

The province of Malwa is formed by the possessions of the Princes and Rajahs who were formerly allied to the Company, or, more properly speaking, were its vassals. It contains many large towns, noticeable by the number, the wealth, and the industry of their inhabitants: Dhar, Noli, Mandasore, Mahidpore, Oujein, Sita, Mhow, Indore. The products of the soil are numerous and varied, including amongst other things the 'papaver somniferum,' from which opium is made. The culture of this plant requires immense care and constant irrigation. The fields sown with it are generally found in the neighbourhood of villages; and, however extensive, are divided into small portions separated by high ridges, which need water day and night. The Malwa opium is very highly valued by Chinese consumers, and though the monopoly of the trade is in the hands of the English Government, the culture of the poppy is a source of considerable wealth to the country. When the new crop is despatched to the Bombay market, even the princes of European finance would be astonished by the enormous scale on which transactions are carried on by the bankers and Parsees of Mhow and Indore. Owing to the ignorance and rapacity of the small native governments, English influence, which is still a new thing in these districts, has as yet been able to do but little towards facilitating communication. The rivers, all equally devoid of bridges, are impassable in the rainy season, and the roads, which exist in a state of nature and are cut up by sloughs, offer serious obstacles to the development of the natural resources of the country.

In the month of October, 1857, anarchy, as we have said reigned supreme in Malwa, which was overrun in every direction by armed bands. It was a matter of urgency to repress this brigandage, and the campaign opened by the siege of Dhar, an old fortress belonging to the Rajah of the same name, which had been taken possession of by a body of Rohillas amounting to several thousand men. After a week's siege, on November 1 the breach was pronounced practicable, and the English entered the place, which the enemy had evacuated in the night, without meeting with the slightest resistance. Stuart's cavalry was sent in pursuit of the fugitives, but only succeeded in bringing back a dozen prisoners, the nature of the ground having favoured the escape of the rest. A few days later the Rohillas of Dhar were reinforced by their junction with the mutineers of the Mahidpore contingent, and the whole body was overtaken and defeated in several bloody encounters, which took place in the village of Rawal and before the town of Mandasore. Bad news from Neemuch prevented this success from being followed up.

Stuart was warned, on November 23, that the Europeans who had recovered possession of Neemuch after the departure of the sepoys were threatened by armed bands, numbering ten or twelve thousand men, under the orders of a chief called Hira Singh. The provisions and ammunition of the garrison were drawing to an end, and resistance could not long be maintained. Stuart at once started for Neemuch. Scarcely had he begun to march, than a considerable force of infantry and cavalry was seen in the distance. Hira Singh's army had come out to meet the English column.

The engagement, which began immediately and ended by the rout of the Indians, was one of the hardest fought in the campaign, and cost the English a hundred in killed and wounded. Two or three hundred Rohillas, who had taken refuge in a neighbouring village, renewed the struggle on the following day, refused to surrender, and perished heroically to the last man in the flames. This victory secured the safety of the Neemuch garrison, and the expedition once more took the road to Indore, where the news of their success had already preceded them. It enabled the Maharajah to disarm his contingent, which had been in a state of insubordination, bordering upon open revolt, since the month of July. The tranquillity of the capital was secured by this means; the English marched in on December 15 without striking a blow, and were received by Holkar as friends and almost as deliverers.

On this expedition the English had been confronted by the soldiers of the India of former days: bands of partisans, Rohillas, Mekranis, Klayatis, which, badly disciplined, armed with matchlocks and blunderbusses, could offer no serious resistance to Enfield rifles and Anglo-Indian artillery. The Rohillas and their allies displayed nevertheless in the highest degree the qualities peculiar to warlike and fanatical races, for whom death has no terror. In action the chiefs would challenge the officers among their adversaries to single combat; fanatics would issue from the Indian ranks, discharge their arms, and come dancing and gesticulating to seek death at the point of the English bayonet. Without pity for themselves, the Rohillas respected neither dead nor wounded. The bodies of soldiers and officers were constantly found on the battle-field literally hacked to pieces, and the heads figured as trophies in the enemy's camps. Terrible reprisals were inflicted, and constant executions of their prisoners marked the advance of the troops.

The Malwa expedition was not followed by a long rest for the troops. A new and brilliant campaign in Central India, destined to give the death-blow to the insurrection, opened in the early part of the new year under the auspices of Sir H. Rose, a general recently sent out from England.

CHAPTER IX.

SECOND CAMPAIGN OF SIR C. CAMPBELL IN OUDE—CAMPAIGN OF ROHILKUND.

The mutiny at the end of 1857—Capture of Fattigarh—The Governor-General decides on a second and immediate expedition against Oude—Sir J. Outram at the Alumbagh—Military forces of Sir C. Campbell—Nepaul and Jang Bahadour—First day's march—Preparations for defence—Sir J. Outram on the left bank of the Goumti, from the 6th to the 9th of March—Occupation of La Martinière and the first line of defence—Death of Sir W. Peel—Operations of March 10 on both banks—Interview of Sir C. Campbell with the Maharajah Jang Bahadour on March 11—Capture of the Begum Kothie—Death of Major Hodson—Capture of the little Tinambarah and of the Kaiser Bagh—Last days of the siege—Police regulations—Lord Canning's proclamation—Noble conduct of Sir J. Outram—Lord Ellenborough and Lord Canning's proclamation—Revulsion in public opinion in England—Sir J. Outram—Change in the nature of the struggle—Insurrection in Rohilkund—Koër Singh—The English are defeated at Indgespore—Expedition against Rohilkund—Death of Brigadier Adrian Hope—Night marches—Capture of Schahjahanpore—Death of General Penny—Attack of the Ghazis—Panic in the English rear-guard—The Moulvi's attack on Schahjahanpore—Sir C. Campbell retires on the Ganges.

We left Sir C. Campbell at Cawnpore, after the defeat of the Gwalior contingent, waiting for the return of the waggons which had conveyed the women and children of the Lucknow garrison to Allahabad. Fortune had favoured the first efforts of the new Commander-in-Chief; the capture of Delhi, and the uninterrupted success of Sir J. Lawrence in the Punjab, had considerably dispelled the clouds hanging over the political horizon. England's victory was no longer doubtful, but there was still much to be done before the authority of the Company could be re-established in the whole extent of India. At the end of the year which had witnessed the outbreak of the mutiny, the seat of war lay in three different localities. On the right bank of the Ganges, among the semi-independent states of Central India, a few native princes had remained loyal, but the insurrection had penetrated into the country, and the work of repression had scarcely begun. On the left bank of the Ganges was the kingdom of Oude, with a warlike population of ten millions of inhabitants, covered with impenetrable jungles and bristling with 400 fortresses. Finally, there was the province of Doab, between the Jumna and the Ganges, and that of Rohilkund, between the Himalaya and the Upper Ganges.

In the Doab, the revolt was headed by the Nabab of Farrackabad, who, with the help of a strong garrison of sepoys, held the town from which he derived his name, and the neighbouring fort of Fattigarh. Farrackabad and Fattigarh, which are not far from Agra, half-way between Allahabad and Delhi, not only command all the communications through the Doab, but two roads, one to Bareilly, the other to Lucknow, start from a bridge of boats under the very guns of the fortress. After Allahabad, the most important position for securing communications between Bengal and Central India was Fattigarh. Although after the capture of Delhi, a column under Colonel Greathed had moved along the great trunk road from Delhi to Cawnpore, the enemy had immediately reappeared in his rear, and this march had produced no more effect on the population than a ship ploughing through the waves does on the sea.

In Rohilkund, a fertile and level country, inhabited by a warlike race of Rohillas full of traditional hatred towards the English, all trace of European supremacy had vanished since the month of July. A native chieftain, Bahadour Khan, had established at Bareilly a government which was accepted everywhere in the province. As long as the districts bordering on the Upper Doab were in the power of the insurgents, communications between Bengal and the North-West Provinces could not be said to be re-established. As to the Gwalior contingent, which had taken refuge at Calpi after its defeat before Cawnpore, it had met with such losses in men and artillery that for the moment it had ceased to be formidable. Besides which, at the first hostile demonstration, it would certainly have retreated into the interior, where pursuit was impossible. A strong garrison at Cawnpore was sufficient to prevent any offensive movement on its part, and to secure permanently communications between Cawnpore and Allahabad.

The convoy entrusted with the care of the women and children of the Lucknow garrison returned to Cawnpore on December 23. The next day three columns, under Colonel Seaton, Brigadier Walpole, and Sir C. Campbell, took the field in order, by a concentric march on Fattigarh, to drive back the numerous bands belonging to the Doab. On January 2, the expedition commanded by Sir C. Campbell, which had, the previous evening, crossed the iron bridge over the Kalli Naddi (black river), found itself suddenly in presence of the forces of the Nabab of Farrackabad, composed of four regiments of the Bengal army, of a numerous body of cavalry, and of eight guns. Driven from a village where they were strongly entrenched by a furious charge made by the 52nd (R.A.), the sepoys at first retreated in good order, but on being attacked by the British cavalry under Sir Hope Grant, they fled ignominiously, abandoning their guns, and reached their camp, situated under the batteries of the fort of Fattigarh, in a state of the greatest confusion.

The panic did not end there. Chiefs and soldiers hastily assembling all their most precious valuables, crossed the bridge over the Ganges to take shelter in Rohilkund or Oude. On January 3, Sir C. Campbell took possession both of the town of Farrackabad and of the fort of Fattigarh, without meeting with any resistance. The flight of the sepoys had been so sudden, that the factory established by the Company for the manufacture of artillery trains, together with immense stores of wood, were found untouched in the fort. The decisive blow had been struck earlier than had been intended, and the detachments under Seaton and Walpole, which were to have co-operated in the taking of

Fattigarh, only arrived at head-quarters on January 5, after the victory had been won.

The forces assembled at Fattigarh under the orders of the General-in-Chief amounted to 10,000 men, of whom 1,800 were cavalry, and this allowed of the immediate invasion of Rohilkund and the reduction of Bareilly. Thus, the end of the fine season was still available for the re-establishment of the Company's authority in its ancient provinces, whilst in another direction the Madras and Bombay armies might be employed to wrest Central India from the hands of the insurgents. There was every reason to hope that before the great heats came on, the insurrection would be put down everywhere but in Oude, against which it would be time to act in the autumn.

This plan, which would have spared the army the losses and fatigues of a summer campaign, was made to yield to political considerations. From Allahabad, where he had transferred the seat of government, Lord Canning insisted that his authority should be re-established at Lucknow without delay. Politicians declared that the fall of the capital of Oude, by causing discouragement in the ranks of the rebels, would be promptly followed by the submission of the whole kingdom, and of the still rebellious districts in the North-West Provinces. No thought was given to the possibility that the bands driven out of Lucknow might very well organise a guerilla warfare on both banks of the Ganges, a warfare especially formidable in India, where even in regular operations the immense distances to be covered present almost insurmountable difficulties. Sir Colin Campbell's army, though sufficient to enable him to undertake with success an expedition against Rohilkund and Bareilly, was not strong enough to warrant an immediate attempt at reducing Oude, and considerable delay must necessarily occur before the reinforcements sent from Calcutta and a train of artillery from Agra could arrive at head-quarters. Adopting, though perhaps unwillingly, the plans of the Governor-General, Sir C. Campbell took up his position at Fattigarh, from which point he could at one and the same time direct the concentration of troops on Cawnpore, maintain order in the re-conquered territories, and hold in check the rebels of Rohilkund and Oude.

For one whole month the General-in-Chief, whilst in his quarters at Fattigarh, was exposed to the unanimous attacks of the Anglo-Indian press, which applied the name of 'Cunctator' to him. The new Fabius was not, however, completely inactive, but concealed the secret of his future operations under preparatives which seemingly pointed to the immediate invasion of Rohilkund. An expedition advanced to the banks of the Ramganga river, and, under the eyes of Sir Colin, began to rebuild the iron bridge which had been destroyed. A body of rebels stationed in a neighbouring village was dislodged after an obstinate resistance. At the end of January information of the departure from Agra of the long-expected siege-train under strong escort was received at head-quarters. Sir Colin Campbell, being now certain of its arrival, lifted the mask, and, leaving Fattigarh on February 1, arrived after a four days' march at Cawnpore.

The news from Oude, though couched in pompous and emphatic language, full of the high-flown metaphors characteristic of the inhabitants of India, announced the firm resolution in high and low to defend their independence vigorously. It is very difficult to get any clear idea of the events which were passing in the capital. No Court journal of Lucknow is there, as at Delhi, to reveal the secret of the humiliation and sufferings of the Begum Hazrat Mahal and of the King Borjis Kadr. It is probable that sharp political and religious disputes often broke out in the councils of the native government. Stationed on the advanced post of the Alumbagh, the last spot of Oude territory remaining to the English, General Outram had several times in his possession proofs of the difficulties which overwhelmed the highest Court dignitaries. A communication from the Begum's Prime Minister, Scherif Uddanlah, described the situation somewhat in the following terms:—'It is impossible to recount the violence and brutalities practised on the inhabitants of Lucknow by the durbar and the soldiery. Ruined and terrified, all would wish for the restoration of English rule, if they were not convinced that the European soldiers would massacre the women and children without mercy. Having lost all hope, they say to themselves: "Let us die like men!" Formerly the Company was a lover of justice, and under its sway its subjects enjoyed order and peace: now it is only animated by a spirit of vengeance, and the only thing left for us is to perish to the last man.'

Sir J. Outram met these exaggerated fears by replying, with much truth, that in his proclamation of September 20 he had promised a free pardon to all who, having been compelled to join the insurgents, should lay down their arms. Many months had elapsed before Scherif Uddanlah had chosen to appeal to his mercy: nevertheless, his life and that of his family would be spared if they presented themselves in the English camp. Outram even went further in his generosity. Hearing that two English ladies were still detained captives at Lucknow, he offered to exchange the numerous native prisoners at the Alumbagh for them. But, however great his willingness and his fears, Scherif Uddanlah was no more able to restore the two ladies than to come to the English camp himself.

These peace negotiations went on in the midst of constant fighting, and Outram, by the way in which he resisted for four months the attacks of an army, more than 120,000 men, against the Alumbagh, added another admirable page to the already illustrious record of his military exploits.[1] The

[1] Strength of the enemy on January 26, 1858, as ascertained by Captain Alexander Orr, of the Intelligence Department:—

Thirty-seven regiments of sepoys, including Oude force	27,550
Fourteen regiments of new levies	5,400
One hundred and six regiments of Najeebs	55,150
Twenty-six regiments of regular and irregular cavalry	7,100
Camel corps	300
Total	95,500

ARTILLERY.

Guns of all sorts and calibres, not including wall pieces, and the guns brought from Futtehpore, 131. Number of artillerymen unknown. The above is ex-

British not only occupied the gardens and the mosque of the Alumbagh, but, from the nature of the case, were obliged to hold an immense extent of ground, and the circumference of the entrenched camp might be reckoned at eleven miles.[1] The garrison, some 4,000 men,[2] had not only to defend ill-

clusive of the armed followers of the talookdars and zemindars still at Lucknow on January 26, amounting, at the lowest calculation, to 20,000 men, exclusive of the armed budmashes of the city and exclusive also of four or five regiments that fled to Lucknow from Fattigarh with from three to five guns, amounting certainly to not less than 3,000. The total aggregate of hostile forces at Lucknow, on January 26, was not less than 120,000 men of all arms. Since that date, several of the Zemindaree troops have left; but their place has been much more than supplied by the regiments ordered in from the district.—Sir J. Outram's *Campaigns in India*, 1857–58.

[1] Length of lines from picket to picket, enclosing the position defended by 1st Division :—

	Yards.
Jellalabad to Alumbagh	4,400
Alumbagh to left front village	2,600
Left front to left rear village	3,900
Left rear village to rear picket	2,400
Rear picket to Jellalabad	5,500
Total yards	18,800

Or a total of 10 miles and 1,200 yards.

[2] Strength of the division commanded by Sir James Outram at the Alumbagh :—

Corps.	Details. Europeans.	Natives.
Artillery	332	108
CAVALRY.		
Military train	221	—
Volunteer cavalry	67	—
Irregular cavalry	3	40
Oude irregular cavalry	1	37
INFANTRY.		
5th Fusiliers	526	—
84th Foot	431	—
75th Foot	355	—
78th Highlanders	439	—
90th Light Infantry	591	—
1st Madras Fusiliers	411	—
Ferozepore regiment	5	295
Madras Sappers	4	110
27th Madras Native Infantry	9	457
Total	3,395	1,047
Grand total, Europeans and Natives	4,442	

—Sir J. Outram's *Campaigns in India*, 1857–58.

defined positions against adversaries thirty times as numerous, who at any moment might attack any of the extreme points, but was obliged to move out of the fortifications whenever the enemy threatened the communications with Cawnpore. Attacks became more determined and more frequent during the latter part of February. The provisions that were accumulating in Outram's camp revealed to the inhabitants of Lucknow the nature of the danger threatening them, and, with the fury of despair, they attempted, by destroying the magazines at the Alumbagh, to avert the vengeance which they foresaw would follow the arrival of Sir C. Campbell. It would be useless to give a detailed account of the attacks against the English positions: let it suffice to state that a last assault made, on February 26, on the fortress of Jellalabad by a body of native troops, amounting to at least 20,000 men, proved once again the superiority of a handful of Europeans over a host of Indians. This victory, which fitly crowned the noble defence made by Outram at the Alumbagh, only occurred a few days before the entry into Oude of a third expedition, which, in less than five months, was to force its way through the gates of Lucknow.

The army which, in the latter part of February, was assembled in the neighbourhood of Cawnpore, under the orders of Sir C. Campbell, was the most formidable ever known in India. It comprised four infantry divisions (two brigades by division, three battalions by brigade), commanded by Major-Generals Sir J. Outram, Sir Edward Lugard, and Brigadiers Walpole and Franks. The latter division, then employed in restoring order in the neighbouring districts, was not to rejoin head-quarters under the walls of Lucknow before a certain date. The cavalry was led by Sir Hope Grant, and the artillery and engineers by Sir Archdale Wilson, the victor of Delhi, and Brigadier Robert Napier, of the Engineers, who had figured prominently in the defence of the Residency at the second siege. The English army, some 25,000 men strong, of whom two-thirds were Europeans, was formed of the veterans who had been victorious at Delhi and in the two expeditions against Lucknow. In its ranks, for instance, were the 9th Lancers, the 73rd and 93rd Highlanders, the 1st Fusiliers, B.A., the 2nd Madras Fusiliers, the Sikh Ferozepore Regiment, and the Naval Brigade. The officers were worthy of their men, and the names of Sir William Peel, Brigadier Adrian Hope, Lieut.-Colonels Tombs and Turner, of the Artillery, and Major Hodson, of the cavalry, already occupied a glorious place in the military annals of Great Britain. Adjutant-General Norman had already given proof, in the same capacity, of exceptional talents at the siege of Delhi, and Colonel Mansfield, the head of the staff, who had recently arrived from England, with Sir Colin Campbell, was well known for his dashing exploits on the battle-fields of the Crimea. To these forces we must add a body of Goorkhas under the Rajah of Nepaul, Sir Jang Bahadour, who was to join the English at Lucknow and lend its aid towards reducing the place.

Nepaul comprises the fertile valleys that extend between the higher and lower Himalaya from the latitude of Delhi to the confines of Bengal. The population consists of Goorkhas, descended from the Rajpoots, who conquered the country about the fourteenth century and settled there. The Company, owing to a system of ill-defined frontiers, got into difficulties with Nepaul, and the campaigns of 1815–16 seriously compromised at their outset the prestige of European armies. General Ochterlony's[1] brilliant operations soon restored victory to the side of England, and the war was ended by a treaty of peace which, besides bringing about an important rectification of frontier, won for the latter an ally whose loyalty has never failed since. The devotedness of the Goorkhas in the Company's service and their admirable behaviour at the siege of Delhi have already been noticed.

In 1857 the life of Sir Jang Bahadour, Prime Minister of the crowned puppet who, in name at least, wore the crown of Nepaul, had been one of strange and sinister adventures. A nephew of the Prime Minister Mahtabar Singh, he began

[1] See Documents, No. XI., 'General Ochterlony.'

his career as subahdar (captain) in the Nepaulese army, and soon after, in order to finish his education, he started on his travels to the various courts of India. At Delhi and Gwalior he acquired the reputation of being a gallant cavalier and of enjoying a constant run of good luck when throwing the dice or making wagers in cock-fights and athletic games. After increasing his patrimonial fortune by more or less legitimate means, Jang Bahadour was employed in the secret diplomatic service of Nepaul; but the Company almost immediately put an end to his missions in foreign parts, and he was sent back to his own country by the Anglo-Indian police. On his return to Katmandow, the capital of Nepaul, war was being openly waged between the favourite Sultana and the Prime Minister. Faithful to the worship of beauty, Jang Bahadour took the side of his sovereign, and even went so far as to kill his own uncle one day on the threshold of the royal palace. The grateful princess conferred on the murderer the command of the army, and the musket which had opened to him the road to power was destined to be the means of preserving his influence at a future date. It is said that, on meeting with resistance in a sort of Nepaulese Parliament, he surrounded the hall with his guards and shot fourteen of his adversaries with his own hand. This *argumentum ad hominem* established the authority of the new Maharajah on so firm a basis that he started off at once to visit the Great Exhibition of 1851. The chronicles of the fashionable world in London and Paris unanimously concurred in praising the jewels, the cashmeres, and the social successes of the Indian 'lion.'[1] We must do him the justice to say that he appreciated at first sight the strength and resources of European civilisation, and returned to his dominions determined on cultivating friendly intercourse with his powerful neighbours. The latter, moreover, dazzled

[1] The clever pencil of Cham himself illustrated the visit of the Indian prince to the coulisses of the Opéra at Paris, with, we hope, more humour than truth, by representing him, on his entrance, clad in splendid cashmere and resplendent with jewels, and, on his departure, dressed in a fireman's boots and helmet.

by his brilliant reception in Europe, gave their sanction to his crimes and usurpation by conferring on him the Cross of Knight Commander of the Most Honourable Order of the Bath, and consequently the title of Sir Jang Bahadour. At the beginning of the mutiny the Maharajah took refuge in a prudent neutrality, but immediately after the siege of Delhi he offered to fulfil the conditions of his offensive and defensive alliance with England. His offer was only accepted after long and unreasonable hesitation. A body of 12,000 Goorkhas, with strong artillery, commanded by the Maharajah in person, was to second Sir C. Campbell's operations.

The expedition against Oude, which had long been in preparation, at a great expense, was carefully provided, by a skilful commissariat, with all the comforts and luxuries indispensable to Europeans when fighting in the trying climate of India, and we may estimate at one hundred thousand the number of servants, syces, coolies, merchants and black milkmaids (the *vivandières* of the country) who followed the troops. 'As soon as we had advanced a few miles from the Ganges, not only the broad road, but the broad track at each side of it, was thronged by an immense and apparently illimitable procession of oxen, hackeries, horses, ponies, camels, camp-followers on foot or riding, trains of stores, elephants, all plodding steadily along in the burning sun under the umbrella of dense clouds of white dust. What an infinite variety of sights and sounds! What a multitude of novel objects on every side! What combinations of colour, form, and of sound! As we jogged along, half-choked and baked, in our inglorious chariot, with a syce, running as *avant-courier*—shouting all kinds of mendacious assertions as to our rank and position, as a sort of moral wedge to open the way for us—I, for one, looked with ever-growing wonder on the vast tributary of the tide of war which was surging around and before me. All these men, women and children, with high delight, were pouring towards Lucknow to aid the Feringhee to overcome their brethren. The sight gave me a notion of the old world times, when nomad tribes came from east and north to overrun and conquer. These people carried all their household wealth with them. Their houses were their tents; their streets, the camp-bazaar; their rules, the bazaar-kotwal; their politics, the rise and fall of rice and such commodities. The old men, perhaps, had been with Lake, or had followed Scindia or Holkar; the young men could talk of the Punjab or Scinde; the children were taking up their trade with the campaign of Oude. Bred in camps, but unwarlike, for ever behind guns and never before them,—the aptitude of myriads of the natives of Hindostan for this strange life is indicative of their origin, or, at all events, of the history of their country for ages. Most of those people are Hindoos from Bengal or the North-West Provinces. Some are from Central India. Few of them are Mussulmans, except some domestic servants. The huge-limbed Afghan, with his enormous turban and fair complexion, toils alongside his camel, which is laden with dried fruits; the Sikh, whose whiskers are turned up and tied in a knot on the top of his head, protects the precious hairs from the contamination of the dust by tying a handkerchief under his jaws, and is marching with a light, cat-like tread on his long thin sinewy legs to join his comrades; the fat bunneah hurries on in his bamboo-car to see his store-tent pitched, leaving his dependents to make the best of their way after him; the wives of the bunneahs who sit astride the tiniest of donkeys, with their toes almost touching the ground, several children in their arms and across their loins, and such a heap of bags and baggage, that all that may be seen of the creatures that carry them is a disconsolate face, long ears, a ragged, mangy tail, and four little black hoofs, bent outwards, with fetlocks quivering at every step; the shrewd-looking, slender Madrassee, in a turban of the grandest dimension, and a suit of fine muslin or of gaudy stuff, sits grinning and laughing with a select circle of his own set on "master's elfent;" whole regiments of sinewy, hollow-thighed, lanky coolies, shuffle along under loads of chairs, tables, hampers of beer and wine, bazaar stores, or boxes slung from bamboo poles across their shoulders. Now comes a drove of milch-goats and sheep, which your servant announces as "master's mess buckree." A flock of turkeys is destined to fatten for Her Majesty's regiment; and this long line of camels presents side views of many boxes of beer, pickles, potted meats, and soda-water for the use of the officers of another equally fortunate corps. Monkeys, held captive on the backs of camels or ponies, chatter their despair or fear at every jolt. Parrots scream from recondite and undiscoverable corners of hackeries or elephants. Tame deer pant and halt in their ungenial march; and crowds of pariahs precede, accompany, and follow the march, which presents also some exemplars of their more favoured domesticated compeers, each with a domestic attached to them.'[1]

The reduction of the capital of Oude was not an easy matter, even for so formidable an army as that of Sir C. Campbell's. All that could be effected by the perseverance and skill of an enemy, in no wise devoid of these qualities, had been done to strengthen the place. The army, which loyalty, the love of independence, religious fanaticism, or thirst for bloodshed and pillage retained under the flag of the Begum and her son, amounted to more than 120,000 men, recruited from rebel sepoy regiments, new levies, volunteers and the armed followers of the great vassals. The immense circumference of Lucknow, a town of seven or eight hundred thousand souls, forbade Sir C. Campbell, with a force of 25,000 men only, to think of investing it and undertaking the operations of a regular siege. He could no more, then, than in November, attempt to traverse the whole length of an enormous city, intersected by narrow streets, in which vast palaces were converted into formidable fortresses. This new attack had necessarily to be made like the preceding ones, on the right and in the neighbourhood of the Goumti.

Three distinct lines of defence were there: the first or outer line, formed chiefly by the portion of the canal which was full of water, and was consequently safe from attack, was carried along the dry banks of the said canal to the

[1] W. Russell's *My Diary in India*, 1858–59.

river, in the shape of a rampart with a parapet, flanked with semicircular bastions. The second, or middle line, covered the Little Tinambargh, the mess-house, the palace of the Begum and other buildings, which in previous assaults had been the scene of severe fighting. The besieged had taken advantage of the course of a ravine, and had opened a wide trench crowned by works of defence at the points unprotected by any natural obstacle. The third line was composed of the series of palaces, courts, and gardens enclosed by walls, known as the Kaiser Bagh, which constituted the real citadel of the system. The front of these positions, which continued to fire during the evacuation of the English troops in November, was protected by works the strength and relief of which resembled a permanent *enceinte* more than fortifications hastily thrown up on the spur of the moment. On the other fronts, the doors and windows were walled up and loopholed, the streets and squares were provided with barricades, and commanded by artillery, but no fresh works were erected. The extent of the city round the Kaiser Bagh seemed of itself to be sufficient protection against an attack on that side.

In front of the first line, the curiously constructed buildings and the walled park of La Martinière were held by a considerable body of sepoys, protected by outer works, some of which were rather formidable. The radical weakness of this system of defence was the want of any effective works, capable of preventing the occupation of the ground on the left bank of the river. Guns of long range, planted on the other bank of the river, could enfilade or take in reverse the greater part of the first line. Sir C. Campbell perceived at once this capital error, and lost no time in taking advantage of it.

After some sharp skirmishing, in which the outposts of the sepoys were dislodged from the Dilkouska and lost a gun, Sir C. Campbell left the camp of Bantara, and established himself on March 2 in the plain before the palace, his right resting on the Goumti, and his left on the Mohammed Bagh. The nature of the ground in the rear compelled him to place his camp within range of the bastions along the canal, but means were found to avert the danger from that quarter. Counter-batteries were placed at the extreme points of the camp, which answered the fire of the town, and in the two following days all action was confined to a rather ineffectual artillery duel. Meanwhile, provisions, ammunition, and heavy guns, were being hastily brought up by the military trains; the sappers were secretly collecting materials necessary for throwing two bridges over the Goumti, and on the evening of the 5th, Frank's division, in pursuance of orders, rejoined head-quarters.

On the 6th, Sir C. Campbell's whole design became at length apparent. At daybreak, an army corps, composed of the 1st Infantry division under Brigadier Walpole, of a cavalry brigade under Brigadier Sir Hope Grant, and of five batteries of artillery under Brigadier Wood, marched towards the two bridges of boats thrown in the night over the Goumti. The original deliverer of the Lucknow garrison, the vigilant defender of the Alumbagh, General Outram, had been appointed commander-in-chief of this expedition, which was to figure most prominently in the operations of the siege. While Sir C. Campbell was forcing a passage through the ramparts of the town, Sir J. Outram was to advance on the left bank, close all means of escape and assistance on that side, and pour volley after volley on the east and north faces of the fortifications.

This plan of attack took the leaders of the sepoys completely by surprise. A few skirmishers, scattered about in the high grass which covered the plain, would have proved a very considerable hindrance to the works of the pontooners and to the passage of the troops. This obvious precaution was neglected; both operations were successfully completed, and the expedition reached the left bank without striking a blow. The native authorities soon perceived the importance of Outram's movements, and in the course of the same day bodies of cavalry were sent to re-occupy the lost ground. Their attack was easily repulsed, and the English continuing their march northwards, encamped for the night near the village of Chinhut, where the disastrous combat which heralded the first siege of the Residency had occurred. A demonstration against the pickets made by the sepoys on the following day met with no better success, and did not even interrupt the labours of the men, who were laying down platforms for the heavy guns which were momentarily expected. The siege batteries were intended to act first of all against the Chukkur Kothi (Yellow House), a palace with parks and gardens, belonging to some great chief. It was defended by a strong garrison and by field works, and might be considered as the key to the position of the besiegers on the left bank.

The convoy of heavy artillery, eight 24-pounders and three 8-inch howitzers, arrived on the 8th, and on the following morning decisive operations began. A column of infantry, marching northwards, cleared the surrounding villages, and took up its position on the road to Faizabad. whilst Outram led the chief attack. After a short cannonade, the 1st Bengal Fusiliers, some companies of the 93rd Highlanders and a Sikh regiment, stormed the Yellow House,[1] and took possession of the Badschah Bagh, another royal residence, which was defended by works of some importance, and was the last refuge of the besieged on the left bank. The object

[1] The fight was stained by an episode of infernal cruelty. After the walls had been perforated in all directions with shot and shell, so that it seemed impossible for the little garrison to have escaped, a detachment of Sikhs rushed into the house. Some of the sepoys were still alive, and they were mercifully killed; but for some reason or other, which could not be explained, one of their number was dragged out to the sandy plain outside the house; he was pulled by the legs to a convenient place, where he was held down, pricked in the face and body by the bayonets of some of the soldiery, whilst others collected fuel for a small pyre, and when all was ready, the man was roasted alive! There were Englishmen looking on—more than one officer saw it. No one offered to interfere! The horror of this infernal cruelty was aggravated by an attempt of the miserable wretch to escape when half burned to death By a sudden effort he leaped away, and with the flesh hanging from his bones, ran for a few yards ere he was caught, brought back, put on the fire again, and held there by bayonets till his remains were consumed. 'And his cries, and the dreadful scene,' said my friend, 'will haunt me to my dying hour.' 'Why didn't you interfere?' 'I dared not, the Sikhs were furious. They had lost Anderson, our own men encouraged them, and I could do nothing.'—W. Russell's *My Diary in India*, 1857-58.

of Sir J. Outram's expedition was at length attained, and his heavy guns could now rake the defences of La Martinière and the first line of the enclosure.

The cannonade which, on the morning of the 9th, overwhelmed the defences of the Yellow House gave the signal for action on the right bank to Sir C. Campbell. Early in the day the naval brigade poured shells and Congreve rockets on the defenders of the parks and buildings of La Martinière, and towards two in the afternoon the position was carried at the point of the bayonet by four regiments of Sir Edward Lugard's division (the 42nd, 53rd, 90th, and 93rd R.A.). The fire from Outram's batteries began to produce some effect upon the defenders of the outer line; the sepoys in crowds hastened to leave the entrenchments and parapets. Profiting by their panic, Brigadier Adrian Hope, at the head of the 42nd Highlanders and the 4th Punjab Infantry, attacked the portion of the fortifications resting on the Goumti. At the same moment, a man dripping with water was seen to climb up the bank under a storm of bullets; it was the brave Lieutenant Butler, of the Bengal Fusiliers, who had swum across the river to bring news of Outram's success on the left bank to his companions on the right.[1]

[1] Colonel Seaton, commanding 1st Madras Fusiliers, to Lieutenant-General Sir J. Outram, G.C.B :—

17th November, 1858.

My dear General,—May I bring to your notice one of the officers of my regiment—Lieutenant Thomas Butler. I hear so much of this young lad's gallantry, that I firmly believe there are few who would not rejoice to see him in possession of the Victoria Cross. I have made him write the enclosed memorandum. The modesty with which he puts his interview down on paper is quite characteristic of the little fellow. I hear you said more to him :—

Conversation between Major-General Sir J. Outram, G.C.B., and Lieut. T. A. Butler, 1st Madras Fusiliers, on March 16, 1858.

Q.—Is your name Butler?

A.—Yes, sir.

Q.—Are you the officer who swam the Goumti the other day (March 9, 1858)?

A.—Yes, sir.

Sir J. Outram.—Well, sir, it was a most gallant thing, and I have spoken to Sir Colin Campbell on the subject, and you may depend upon it you will not be forgotten.

Reply of Sir J. Outram :—

My dear Colonel,—The above memorandum furnished to you by Lieutenant

The dash of the English overcame all obstacles, and they spread themselves along the ramparts. At nightfall the besiegers were masters of all the outer line from the river to the neighbourhood of Banks's House. This great success had been obtained without any very great losses, but unfortunately amongst the wounded was Captain Peel.

Sir W. Peel, to give him the title he had won a few months before under the walls of Lucknow, had been hit in the thigh by a bullet. Though the wound was a serious one it gave no cause for anxiety, yet the brave sailor, worn out by hardships, could not resist the trials of a long convalescence, and succumbed soon after to an attack of small-pox. A younger son of the illustrious statesman who inaugurated the system of free trade in England, he had justified exceptional promotion by exceptional services at Sebastopol, and more recently in India. The worthy successor of the great sea-captains who have made the fortune and glory of England, he had, during the second expedition against Lucknow, attacked the citadels of the place with his guns, in the same way in which he would have brought into action his own frigate, the 'Shannon,' in presence of an enemy's ship. His great merit, his courage, and the qualities of his mind and character had won for him the sympathies of his comrades, who believed him to be destined to attain the highest honours. So that one of the

Butler correctly gives the substance of what passed between that officer and myself on the occasion referred to. But my impression is, that I must have expressed myself more strongly, for I regarded what he had done as one of the most daring feats achieved by any individual throughout the campaign. I mentioned the circumstance to Lord Clyde, who was, I believe, as much struck with it as I was myself. I also noticed it in my memorandum, which was published with the Chief's despatch.

I, myself, would have recommended Butler for the Victoria Cross, had I not thought that, to do so, would be irregular, the act being performed when we were under the Chief's immediate command. But I had hoped that my notice of it in my 'memorandum' would secure the Cross for him; and can only conclude that it escaped his Excellency's recollection. I still hope, therefore, that if you brought it to his Lordship's notice, he may be induced to obtain the Cross for that gallant young soldier.

Very sincerely yours,

J. OUTRAM.

—Sir J. Outram's *Campaigns in India*, 1857–58.

most influential writers of the London press was fully justified in saying with regard to his death, that 'England would never know the full extent of the loss she has made in the park of La Martinière.'

The day after gaining possession of the park and buildings of the Yellow House, Sir J. Outram pursued his triumphant course on the left bank, drove the besieged out of the suburbs, which they defended inch by inch, and successively passed the iron and stone bridges over the river. But the whole extent of the ground won could not be held without dangerously extending the English lines, and it was deemed sufficient to occupy the approaches to the iron bridge, thus interrupting all communication by means of the latter between the town and the outer world. The heavy artillery which had been used to capture the Yellow House was now transferred to other batteries, where they had a better command of the defences of the second line and of the Kaiser Bagh. On the right bank of the Goumti, the Lugard division gained possession of the buildings known as Banks's House towards mid-day on March 10. This placed the principal works of the outer line in the hands of the English, and they were enabled to make use of the palaces and gardens between Banks's house and the Kaiser Bagh, instead of having to throw up trenches against the middle line of defence.

During this part of the siege, the regular course of operations consisted in using the axe or the heavy guns to effect an approach through the buildings and enclosures, and, as soon as the passage was practicable, in leaving to the infantry the care of finishing the work begun. Howitzers placed in the rear, whose position was changed, according to the necessities of the moment, seconded operations by their vertical fire. But as Sir C. Campbell was desirous, above all, of sparing the blood of his soldiers, he would not allow them to occupy any buildings which had not first been under the fire of his heavy guns, or to hold positions communication with which was not perfectly secure.

During the whole morning of the 11th, the batteries on

both banks of the river showered shot and shell on the last defences of the city. Before mid-day the English occupied without resistance the Sikander Bagh, where the severest fighting during the last assault had occurred. It seemed as if the sepoys, mindful of the past, had not dared to defend a palace which was still so full of bloody memories. The courts of the Sikander Bagh were one vast charnel-house, and the skeletons of sepoys who had been partially buried, or had been dug up by jackals, were met with at every step. The victors did not expose themselves for long to the terrible sights and the foul smells of this abode of horror, but continued their forward march. Towards the end of the day, the mass of buildings known as the Begum Kothi (palace of the Begum) still resisted the fire of the heavy guns. Whilst his lieutenants were waiting for the moment when bayonets could take the place of artillery, Sir C. Campbell was presiding over a peaceful *fête*, in which European luxury vied with Asiatic pomp.

The Rajah of Nepaul, Sir Jang Bahadour, who that very morning had, after long delay, arrived at the English camp, intended visiting the General-in-Chief at four in the afternoon. At the hour named, a double line of Highlanders in full dress guarded the approach of the gala-tent, richly furnished with gilt seats, soft carpets, and silk and velvet hangings, where Sir C. Campbell, surrounded by a brilliant staff, was expecting the arrival of his official guests. The grave countenance of the English general, and the roar of the cannon, gave a strange character to this display of luxury, and recalled at every moment the desperate fighting going on in the interior of the town. After more than a quarter of an hour's delay, the Maharajah of Nepaul made his entrance to the sound of martial music, to the immense relief of Sir C. Campbell, who could scarcely repress his impatience. The Rajah's helmet and breast were glittering with gold and jewels, while the costumes of his officers were not less gorgeous than his own. As soon as the ceremonies of presentation were over, the General-in-Chief and his guests took their seats, and the interpreters began to deliver the usual formal speeches. Suddenly a strange figure came like an apparition to recall the brilliant assembly to the realities of the moment. A tall officer, his boots and clothes covered with dust, broke hastily through the line of Highlanders, and advancing towards Sir C. Campbell, announced in a low voice that the Begum's palace was in the power of the besiegers. The good news was soon made known to all. Unable to find words to express their feeling, the Maharajah and Sir C. Campbell grasped one another's hand; the durbar was at an end, and the interpreters were obliged to keep their harangues to themselves. The Asiatic prince remounted his richly caparisoned elephant; the veteran general, free at length from all bonds of etiquette, leaped on his horse with the ardour of a young man, and rejoined the brave soldiers, who once again had deserved well of their Queen and their country.

According to official accounts, the combat, the successful termination of which had put so abrupt an end to the interview between the two allies, was the severest of the whole siege. After a bombardment of eight hours, the breaches being judged practicable, an assault was ordered at three points. Brigadier Adrian Hope, lifted on the shoulders of his Highlanders, was the first to enter the palace, revolver in hand, by the window of a room, the defenders of which took to flight in the most cowardly fashion. The two other columns, composed of Highlanders and Punjabees, entered almost at the same time. The sepoys soon recovered from their first surprise, and defended themselves with desperate energy from court to court, from building to building, from room to room. Alive, or wounded, they were all mercilessly bayoneted, and after the fight the palace offered the most hideous spectacle. In its chambers of horrors, the wadded garments of the dead caught fire, and piles of corpses were burning, emitting nauseous odours; more than 500 bodies were thrown into the deep ditch surrounding the palace, a vast tomb unwittingly constructed by the sepoys for themselves.

The English losses would not have been considerable, if Major Hodson, one of the heroes of the siege of Delhi, had not been numbered among the dead. The smell of powder, curiosity, the hope of Oriental treasures attracted the bold guerilla chief to the scene of action, and the bullet of a sepoy concealed in the corner of a room cut short his glorious career. The *lex talionis*, the hand of God, struck him down. Posterity must overlook the slaughter of the Delhi princes, and place on Hodson's brow a crown without thorns! Boundless grief was felt by the formidable cohort of wild horsemen of whom he was the idol, and for many years doubtless popular legends will celebrate in the depths of Asia the feats of this Anglo-Indian Cid.

On March 12, the forces of the Maharajah of Nepaul (9,000 men and 24 guns) made their appearance, and attacked that portion of the outer line beyond Banks's House which still remained in the hands of the besieged. On the right, Frank's division took the place of Lugard's, worn out by three days' fighting under a burning sun, and the Engineers and Artillery prepared to storm the Little Tinambargh. To protect the artillerymen from the musketry fire of the sepoys, the guns were placed behind walls, through which projectiles were launched against the defences of the beautiful mosque. By March 14 the cannon had done its work, and Russell's brigade (the 10th R.A. and the Ferozepore Sikh regiment) entered the Little Tinambargh without meeting with any great resistance. The massacre which followed the capture of the Begum's palace had probably alarmed the defenders of the sacred edifice, for they fled in crowds towards the Kaiser Bagh, into which the victorious Sikhs entered pell-mell with them. The host of the besiegers soon invaded the courts, the gardens, the kiosques, and the palaces. A few mortally-wounded native soldiers were gasping out their last breath at the foot of statues or by the side of fountains; others, concealed in remote hiding-places, sold their lives dearly; stores of powder and ammunition, strewed about carelessly, exploded from time to time, but all serious resistance had ceased, and pillage and rapine succeeded to fighting.

The victory had been so complete, so unexpected, that no

measures had been taken to maintain discipline. What a prey was this, now given up to brutal soldiers, this Oriental Versailles, in which generations of kings had accumulated treasures upon treasures! The lust of gain inflamed all minds. Satan seemed to be displaying all the riches of earth to the dazzled eyes of the conquerors, and hell to have let loose its demons. Some crowned their heads with marabout feathers, birds of paradise, or grotesque turbans, draped themselves in Cashmere shawls, gold brocades, or costly muslins, and strutted about with fans of peacock feathers in their hands, or contemplated their bronzed features in hand glasses hitherto only used by beautiful Sultanas. Others seized upon hautboys and trumpets, from which they drew the most infernal sounds, or tried with their rough fingers to play the musical instruments of the ladies of the harem. The more brutal ripped up with their bayonets the sofas, the embroidered cushions, and smashed with their guns the chandeliers, the Chinese vases, and the most precious articles of furniture. Plunderers ran through the halls and corridors, discharging their muskets into the locks of the doors, searching every corner; and often reappearing with handfuls of necklaces, bracelets, pearls, and precious stones sufficient for a king's ransom. At the gates of the palace, the scene was still more horrible. The camp followers, attracted by the hope of pillage, crowded by thousands in the neighbouring streets. Eager, yet half afraid, they watched for the moment to take part in the orgie, as a flock of vultures waits till an eagle has glutted himself ere they venture to gorge themselves with the remains of the victim. The Kaiser Bagh was completely despoiled and stripped to the bare walls. The whole night long an uninterrupted string of coolies, syces, and servants passed from the camp to the palace, from whence they returned staggering under the weight of pillows, mattresses, and utensils of all sorts.

We must here mention a sad episode which happened during the day. Some of the princesses and their women had taken refuge in a casemate, and had sustained no harm from the bombardment. After the assault the soldiers broke open the doors of their asylum, and, dimly perceiving human forms in the darkness, discharged their arms, and killed a young deaf and dumb prince and two waiting-women. An officer who arrived at this moment fortunately perceived the mistake, stopped the firing, and conducted the poor Begums and their attendants to a place of safety.

The sepoys had left the Little Tinambargh and the Kaiser Bagh in such haste that their losses were comparatively inconsiderable in both assaults. But towards evening there to be a further abundant effusion of blood. About 400 natives had taken refuge in magazines used to store old machines, and consequently known as the engine-house. The buildings were surrounded by the 10th R.A., and all their defenders slain to the last man. The success of March 14 was not as decisive as it might have been if, after the capture of the Kaiser Bagh, Sir J. Outram had seized the iron bridge and prevented all egress from the town. But the General-in-Chief had given strict orders not to attempt any offensive operation on the left bank if it entailed the loss of a single man. The works which defended the bridge were still intact, and a sharp fusillade announced that it was held by a numerous body of defenders. There was no hope of carrying it without bloodshed, and Sir J. Outram, who was as observant of discipline as he was brave, remained inactive, and lost the opportunity of completing the victory.

General Outram's task on the left bank was now done, and the next day he again crossed the river on a bridge of boats with his brigade to direct the operations intended to drive out the besiegers from the posts they still occupied in the town. On the 16th he traversed the buildings of the Chatter Manzil at the head of his men, now reinforced by two regiments, and carried one after another, almost without fighting, the ruins of the Residency, the head of the iron bridge on the right bank, the Machi Bhowan, and the Great Tinambargh.[1] The besieged left the town in

Doctor Russell relates in his journal an act of unheard-of barbarity which

crowds by the stone bridge; but this way of escape was soon closed to them by the English troops, which had remained on the left bank under the orders of Brigadier Walpole. The fugitives retraced their steps, and fled towards Rohilkund; others sought a last refuge in the very heart of the town or in the park of the Mousa Bagh. Whilst their last positions in Lucknow itself were being wrested from them, the sepoys, in order to create a diversion, made a desperate attack on the Alumbagh, which was easily repulsed by the defenders of the entrenched camp, with the vigorous assistance of the Nepaulese. On the evening of the 16th the English were in possession of the whole quarter of the town situated on the river, and the besieged were completely cut off from all communications with the other bank.

Fighting continued nevertheless, and the following days furnished fresh examples of the fantastic courage and capricious strategy of the Indian race. The same sepoys who had deserted formidable positions in the most cowardly manner would conceal themselves behind trees or bits of walls to wait for the passing by of European soldiers, and sacrificed their lives without regret in order to satisfy their thirst for vengeance. Without definite object, without chance of victory, or, at most, of safety, the Begum and her son, actuated, no doubt, by the same feeling of attachment to their home which had detained the King of Delhi in the tombs near his capital, had withdrawn to the Mousa Bagh, a palace surrounded by a vast park at the north-west extremity of the town, beyond the suburbs. These representatives of the native dynasty were protected by 6,000 faithful soldiers, most of them horsemen, and twelve guns.

On March 19 Sir J. Outram made his dispositions for

avenging history ought to record. After the Fusiliers had got to the gateway, a Cashmere boy came towards the gate, leading a blind and aged man, and throwing himself at the feet of an officer, asked for protection. That officer, as I was informed by his comrades, drew his revolver, and snapped it at the wretched suppliant's head. The men cried 'shame' on him. Again he pulled the trigger—again the cap missed. Again he pulled, and once more the weapon refused its task. The fourth time—thrice had he time to relent—the gallant officer succeeded, and the boy's life-blood flowed at his feet, amid the indignation and outcries of his men.

attacking the Mousa Bagh. A frightful accident had happened the day before to his brigade. Nine waggons full of powder and ammunition had fallen, on the 16th, into the hands of the English. By accident or by carelessness, whilst the powder was being thrown into a well, in accordance with orders given, the waggons caught fire simultaneously, and in the explosion 2 officers and 30 sappers were killed, and many wounded.

The attack against the Mousa Bagh was not wholly successful. It had been hoped that, whilst the positions were being attacked in front by the infantry, the natives would disperse and be intercepted by various bodies of cavalry, which were intended to operate on the flanks of the principal column. This anticipation was not realised. A single detachment of 300 Lancers arrived in time to pursue the native forces in their retreat. The ground being intersected by ravines, the Begum and her horsemen escaped with little loss but that of their guns.

An engagement took place two days afterwards in the very heart of the city, where the Moulvi, the Mohammedan leader of the insurrection and the Begum's rival, still maintained himself with 1,500 of his adherents, in fortified buildings. The struggle was a hard-fought one, and artillery and mines had to be resorted to before the rebels could be dislodged from their last stronghold. Amongst the victims of the skirmish was the Begum's prime minister, Scherif Uddanlah, whose dealings with the English the reader has perhaps not forgotten, and who had long been an object of suspicion and jealousy to the Mohammedan party. The unfortunate hostage was murdered by his jailers towards the close of the combat. Like European revolutionists, Asiatic savages strove to drown the bitterness of defeat in the satisfaction of their murderous instincts.

The last great centre of the mutiny to the east of the Jumna was now in the hands of the English. This great success was not appreciated at its true value by the Anglo-Indian press, which, without taking into account the immense circumference of the town and the numerical weakness of the British troops, bitterly reproached the Commander-in-Chief for not having destroyed the insurgent army within the walls of Lucknow. Such undeserved criticism could not, however, detract from the importance of the results obtained, nor from the merits of the troops and their leader. Sir C. Campbell, with true strategic insight, had at once discovered the weak point of the place. In his attack on the left bank of the Goumti he had, for the first time in the history of warfare, employed guns of long range, without having recourse to preliminary works, for the bombardment of a town, an example which, alas! has not been forgotten since. In the operations on the right bank, when exposed to the dangers of street fighting and obliged to force his way through fortified buildings defended by ditches and strong barricades, he had no less judiciously used his artillery to batter these strongholds before attempting to storm them with his infantry. During twelve days of almost consecutive fighting, the English losses had amounted to 500 killed and wounded; 3,000 corpses of natives were buried. The success was as complete as circumstances would allow, the denunciations of envious minds ceased of themselves, and England rewarded with a peerage the veteran general who, in less than six months, had twice earned laurels in the capital of Oude.

A last satisfaction was still in reserve for Sir C. Campbell. Two English ladies, Mrs. Orr and Miss Jackson, had been hid for some months in the harem of a darogah (a functionary of the court). An officer, on being informed of their hiding-place, rescued them by force, and brought them safe and sound to the English camp.[1]

After the victory measures were immediately taken to prevent plundering. An order of the day forbade the soldiers to leave the camp, and ordered the officers to keep strict watch over the proceedings of their numerous native

[1] Their companions in misfortune, Sir M. Jackson, Captain Orr, and Sergeant Morton, were no longer in the power of their barbarous jailers, and but imperfect details are known of their sad end. See Documents, No. XII., Deposition of the Grave-diggers who buried the Bodies of the Prisoners.'

servants. The same instructions enjoined on the brigadiers, in default of a sufficient staff of chaplains, to make all the necessary arrangements for enabling Catholics among their men to be present at divine service. We intentionally give this detail; it proves that, in the depth of Asia, in the midst of absorbing occupations, the English generals preserved the deep religious feeling which so eminently characterises their nation, and which the God of battles had just rewarded by His most precious favours.

On their side the civil authorities were doing their utmost to re-establish order. From the moment in which Lucknow was occupied by the English army, the power of the Commander-in-Chief over the town had ceased, and had passed entirely into the hands of the Chief Commissioner. The capital of Oude had been for a short time the scene of the most horrible licence and brigandage, as not only the victorious troops, but also the numerous camp-followers, had given the reins to their passions. Sir J. Outram, with the able assistance of a small but energetic staff, succeeded in evolving a semblance of order out of this chaos. A native police force was organised. At certain points (thanahs) permanent judges gave summary sentences, which were executed without delay. Public criers, preceded by a tam-tam, went through the streets, striking terror into the culprits by proclaiming aloud the punishments reserved for thieves and murderers. All who lent their help to the cause of order were rewarded by a free pardon or liberal gifts of money. The wretched inhabitants began to return to their homes and resume their ordinary occupations. The first shop to be opened was one where essence of rose was sold. Let us not too severely condemn the sensuousness of Asiatics; under similar circumstances in Europe the wine-shop would doubtless have taken precedence over that of the perfumer.

The most active efforts on the part of the police were not sufficient to restore tranquillity to a kingdom which for months had been convulsed by revolutionary agitation. The moment had now come to take a great political decision. From Allahabad, where he had established his head-quarters,

Lord Canning determined on announcing his intentions towards Oude in a proclamation the effects of which were not only felt in India but also in England, where it almost caused the fall of the Tory Ministry then in power.[1]

In its original shape this document, which was forwarded to Outram at the beginning of the siege of Lucknow, stated that all land-owners in the kingdom, with the exception of six designated by name, were to be deprived of their possessions. Life and liberty was guaranteed to those rebels who had had no share in the assassination of English prisoners, and who would make their submission at once. More favourable conditions would only be granted as the Governor-General should think fit; he was, however, disposed to show leniency towards such as would lend their assistance against agitators and intriguers. Whoever had protected British subjects during the recent events had claims on the Government, which would meet with full acknowledgment.

Such vigorous measures could be viewed only with disfavour by a man who, like Sir J. Outram, felt strong and generous sympathy for the natives. With all the dignity of a faithful public servant, he unhesitatingly opposed the publication of the document sent to him, and pleaded the cause of the vanquished in an eloquent letter which deserves a brief notice:—

'Was it not adding injustice to injustice to confiscate the possessions of all the landowners who, though badly treated by the settlement of 1856, had only taken up arms when all vestige of English rule had disappeared? Such severity would drive the great nobles to organise a guerilla warfare in their own lands, which it would require long and ruinous efforts to subdue. If their estates were restored to them in their entirety, they would rally at once and for ever to the Company's rule, and become the most ardent defenders of the cause of order.'

Lord Canning yielded so far to this appeal, which was conspicuous alike for its generosity and its political common sense, as to add a paragraph to his proclamation, de-

[1] See Documents, No. XIII., 'Proclamation of the Governor-General.'

fining more clearly the favourable conditions offered to those who would lend their assistance to the European authorities. To do more than this, and make greater concessions whilst the kingdom was still full of armed bands, was, in the opinion of the Governor-General and his council, an act of weakness and not of clemency.[1]

The proclamation of 'Clemency' Canning, to use the derisive epithet bestowed on him by the Anglo-Indian opposition, assumed the proportions of an act worthy of Nero or Tiberius in the correspondence from Calcutta. No less exasperation was felt in England. Lord Canning belonged to the Whig party, and had been appointed to the Government of India by the preceding administration. The Ministry remained unmoved in presence of the first outbreaks of public opinion against their political adversary; but Lord Ellenborough the President of the Board of Control, had not forgotten that a few years before (1843) the Court of Directors, alarmed by his bellicose tendencies, had brutally torn from his grasp the sceptre of India. The Tories, with a few strokes of the pen, might now strike a heavy blow at the Court of Directors by attacking a functionary who enjoyed their full confidence, and win popular sympathy for the Ministry by condemning a policy which called forth the deepest reprobation on all sides. The opportunity was too tempting a one, and Lord Ellenborough was unable to resist it. The English statesman remembered only the injuries which the ex-Governor-General had to complain of, and the secret committee, or rather the minister himself, gave formal expression to its official blame in a despatch which Lord Canning could only answer by sending in his resignation. The general tenour of it was as follows:—

'However conciliatory were the secret instructions sent by the Governor-General to his agent in Oude, the population of India was merely aware of the bare fact of a proclamation which confiscated the estates of all the land-owners in the kingdom, except those of six

[1] See Documents, No. XIV., 'Correspondence between Sir J. Outram and the Governor-General.'

favoured individuals. The great nobles who were thus despoiled would naturally harbour the deepest aversion to English rule. Oude had never been conquered; contrary to all treaties, annexation had overturned a dynasty which for many years had been faithful to the English, and had dispossessed a Government feeble and corrupt enough, no doubt, but which, in the eyes of the natives, represented the national party. Far from treating the chieftains of Oude as loyal enemies, they were being punished in a way almost unexampled in history. Hitherto the victors had chastised the few and spared the many. Lord Canning had followed different principles. What could be expected from such extreme severity? Public order and confiscation rarely go together, and the Indian Government had aroused a feeling of hatred which even the lapse of time would be powerless to assuage.'

This official reprimand did not remain, according to custom, buried for months under piles of ministerial papers, but by a calculated publication the secret of it was at once divulged. The effect of this indiscretion was as sudden as unforeseen. The strong good sense and the straightforwardness of the English people were revolted by such proceedings; politicians and influential papers alike ceased to lament the fate of the great land-owners in Oude; everyone's sympathy was transferred to Lord Canning. It was instinctively felt that never had any agent engaged in a foreign country on a difficult mission acquired greater rights to consideration from his chiefs and his fellow-citizens. Supplied with imperfect information by his advisers, calumniated by those he governed, he had yet courageously withstood a terrible storm, and, unmoved amongst the most trying events, had given way neither to weakness nor to anger. Thanks to him, and to him alone, a military insurrection had not become a war of races; thanks to him, the English Government was innocent of the butcheries which had occurred in India. If the Cabinet was dissatisfied with Lord Canning, and wished to recall him, they ought to have done so boldly, but to resort to stratagem, and to cause by an insolent reprimand the resignation of a high official, was unworthy of honourable men. Moreover, in the critical position of affairs, was it opportune to show that the highest representative of English authority beyond seas was, after all, a simple clerk, whose fate depended on the caprice of the Sultan who presided over the Board of Control? Finally, it was encouraging the residue of the mutineers to prolong the struggle, and would paralyse the victors in the moment of victory to declare that before and after the annexation the great chieftains had had just cause for complaint. The last and most powerful consideration still remained: it was the grossest error to assimilate the land-owners in Oude to the same class in Europe. Landed property, in the full meaning of the word, had never existed, and did not exist actually in the kingdom. The greatest nobles were mere tenants, who held their lands on varying conditions from the Government, which alone was the real proprietor of the soil. All of these powerful vassals had not been equally maltreated by the settlement of 1856, and many of them had requited the favour shown them by the English authorities by the blackest ingratitude. Others had acquired their estates by fraud and violence; almost all, in short, had taken up arms to defend their feudal rights and privileges, and to keep alive centres of anarchy in every corner of the kingdom.

All these arguments were made use of by Lord Canning's friends in the papers and in Parliament, and soon produced a complete revulsion in public opinion. The cause of the absent Governor-General was won. The debate on Lord Ellenborough's manifesto in the House of Lords gave the Ministry a majority of nine only. After four nights' debate in the House of Commons, Lord Derby and his colleagues only escaped a vote of censure by accepting Lord Ellenborough's resignation.

The parliamentary crisis had resulted in forcing public opinion to declare itself on Indian affairs: the trial had been made, and Lord Canning's victory left no doubt as to the popular wishes and sympathies. In the first days of the mutiny England, full of anxiety for its magnificent dependencies beyond the seas, and stricken in its dearest affections, had given way to transports of rage and fury, only too well justified, alas! by the frightful massacres which took place in India, and even the wisest had been obliged to keep silence in the presence of the appeals to vengeance and extermination which were heard on all sides. After the victory, however, England soon felt ashamed of the first excess of her grief. The nation who has so often assisted with its sympathy revolutionists against kings on the Continent of Europe had been obliged to resort to an immense number of executions, confiscations, and all the violent measures so often imposed on governments, under pain of abdication, by the follies of demagogues or the inopportune awakening of the spirit of nationality. What were the prisons and the galleys of the King of Naples, so eloquently denounced by Mr. Gladstone, by the side of the wholesale slaughters at Delhi and in the Punjab? Could even the Czar's confiscations in Poland be compared to the summary measure which had stripped all the land-owners of Oude of their possessions? Hitherto we have never grudged our sympathy to the best Government India has ever enjoyed, and we recall these truths in no bad spirit. May henceforth the recollection of the necessary severity which clouds the history of India in 1857 prevent the English from listening to the declamations of a false philanthropy when judging unfortunate nations who are bound to punish without mercy, not wretched barbarians deluded by superstition, but thieves, incendiaries, and assassins.

The return of public opinion to sentiments of moderation, if not of mercy, was, still more than the debates in the two Houses of Parliament, a triumph for Lord Canning. The reader has not forgotten that at the first outbreak of the mutiny neither violence nor calumny had caused him to forget the claims of humanity or the duty he owed to the natives of India. Let us add, moreover, that the proclamation which had excited so much anger was, in reality, nothing but a bubble phantom put forward to intimidate the great chieftains of Oude. Secret instructions of the most conciliatory character were given to the Chief Commissioner, whose liberty of action was practically unlimited. The pacification of the kingdom was now to depend exclusively on the intelligence of this high official and on his skill in managing the Indians. The lessons of experience had not been lost on the Governor-General and his council, and the idea of extending to Oude the system of village communities and equal territorial rights, which had been the first cause of the rising in the North-West Provinces, was relinquished. What advantage would be gained by depriving of their estates an aristocracy to whom the population had just given such marked proofs of attachment? The decree of confiscation, when rightly interpreted, allowed of regulating the rights and duties of the great proprietors, and giving to the taloukdars of the kingdom a position similar to that of the zemindars of Bengal. In return for certain judicial privileges, the great proprietors would naturally become responsible for order, and for the enforcement of the law within the limits of their domains.

Before Lord Ellenborough's despatch reached Calcutta, the re-establishment of order was already far advanced. By granting them new title-deeds, the Chief Commissioner had already confirmed in the possession of their former properties such members of the native aristocracy as had cast themselves on his mercy, and had promised to co-operate loyally with the Government. The work of pacification did not fall to the lot of Sir J. Outram. Mr. Montgomery, Sir J. Lawrence's able coadjutor in the Punjab, whose gallant conduct when the sepoys were disarmed at Lahore must not be forgotten, had been appointed to the post of Chief Commissioner at Lucknow. Under his management there was no fear that the mistakes which had exasperated the inhabitants of Oude against their new masters at the beginning of the annexation in 1856 would be repeated.

Mr. Montgomery's predecessor, the illustrious General Outram, had left Lucknow in the early part of April to take his place at Calcutta as a member of the India Counci

Unfortunately, the Government did not long enjoy the services of this eminent man. His health and strength, exhausted by forty years' residence in tropical climates, had given way under the tremendous hardships of the recent campaigns, and his doctors soon ordered him to leave India for Europe, where he succumbed at the age of sixty.[1] To dwell at greater length on the career of this illustrious soldier would be to outstep the limits of these sketches. In taking a last farewell of this noblest figure of contemporary history in India, it is important to note that though he was ever and everywhere the defender, *sans peur et sans reproche*, of the oppressed, he never allowed himself to be persuaded by those idealists who claim the Government of India for India and by India, the assimilation of the conquered to the conqueror, the equality of dark skins and white skins. The proconsul of a victorious Power, an Englishman, and a thorough Englishman, Outram cared for the natives as a kind master cares for his servants, as a great king cares for his subjects. Though generally parsimonious in the extreme to men who distinguish themselves in India, England paid in full her debt to Sir J. Outram. He successively received the rank of lieutenant-general, the Grand Cross of the Bath, and the title of baronet, with a pension of 1,000*l.*, with reversion to his wife and son. Finally, a bronze statue was raised in a public square near the Thames Embankment to this valiant knight.

[1] Outram died at Pau, March 14, 1863. The birthplace of Henry IV. was worthy of receiving the last breath of this Bayard of India. He was buried at Westminster Abbey, and the Government defrayed the expenses of his funeral.

The author enjoyed the honour of personal acquaintance with General Outram, and desires to offer a deserved tribute to his amiable qualities and to his keen and humorous wit. With regard to the latter, here is a short anecdote which simply illustrates the life of English residents at the native courts. In March, 1855, I was the guest of Outram, at Lucknow, and the first time I sat down to table with him, he asked me half seriously, half in joke, 'Well, V——, would you have any objection to be poisoned?' 'Undoubtedly, Sir James,' I replied, very much astonished. 'Then mind what you are at here, for they have tried it already on me more than once.' Our water was, I perceived, kept carefully locked in a bottle. This precaution made me feel that the general's words were based on fact, and notwithstanding the abundance and

The success which attended the Chief Commissioner's negotiations with the great chieftains of the kingdom did not, however, justify the authorities in suspending military operations and concentrating the troops in their summer quarters. If strategic movements on a large scale were no longer necessary, partial and continual expeditions could alone consolidate the results of diplomacy. In April 1858, the mutiny entered on its last phase; in the European meaning of the word, there was no longer either a hostile army or an organised resistance on the left bank of the Ganges. But Oude, Rohilkund, and the provinces of Azimgarh, were full of armed bands, and of fugitive sepoys, fighting under the flag of independence, if not, rival leaders such as Mahaddi, Hucaïn, the Moulvi, the Begum and her son, Bahadour Khan, Koër Singh. Hostilities, in this shape, resembled the warfare waged by the English in the first years of the century against the Mahrattas and the Pindarees. The rapid movements of the enemy and the heat of the season were so many formidable difficulties in the way of the European soldiers, who were no longer, as formerly, assisted by a well-disciplined native army.

These repressive measures did not merely aim at destroying the numerous bands of marauders. The country was in a state of complete disorganisation, and it was necessary above all to amend or rather to reconstruct the whole administrative machinery. The native community, by its very nature, escapes the immediate influence of political events. The dull, resigned character of the Indian is little inclined to trouble itself with thoughts of the future, and, for a long time, the masses who had been quite unmoved by the first successes of the mutineers, could not believe that the

the delicacy of the dishes, I cannot pretend that I allowed free play to my appetite.

These criminal practices against the lives of English residents are still common in India. At the moment that we write these lines, Mulhar Rao, the Guickhowar of Baroda, is being brought before a court-martial, accused of attempting to poison Colonel Phayre, the English political agent at his court. The preliminaries of the trial are exciting great interest in India, and the proceedings will doubtless be reported by the European papers.

power of their foreign rulers, which had existed for a century, was seriously threatened. The laws of England, which were put into execution by men who were lenient, enlightened, and tolerant in matters of religion, were not regarded with any great aversion by the natives. Ten months of anarchy, however, gave rise to doubts, and at the very time when the defeated rebels were dispersing on all sides, the population began to believe that the last hour of the Company's reign (raj) had arrived. This revulsion of feeling showed itself not in desperate risings or in determined resistance, but in useless agitation produced by the general disorganisation of affairs, and more especially by the suspicion which naturally follows when confidence is shaken. Recent events had not overturned England's supremacy, but had paralysed or destroyed her means of action, and awakened doubts in all minds as to the stability of the future. After the great struggles round Delhi and Lucknow, the provinces of India resembled a country devastated by an earthquake, where the convulsions of nature have been succeeded by a sudden calm. Everywhere traces of the disaster could be seen in damaged crops, broken milestones, and ruined buildings. No less confusion had been occasioned in the native minds; and the poor wretches, who had suffered all the evils of anarchy, asked themselves if the return of their European masters would not be followed by bloody vengeance and ruinous taxation.

In such a state of things, it was highly necessary to reap the fruits of victory without delay. On the other hand, it was urged, and not without reason, that a summer campaign under the pitiless rays of a May sun would be fatal to the English soldiers, who, moreover, were too few in number to completely surround the rebel bands. Would it not be preferable, instead of exhausting the troops by incessant expeditions, to wait for the winter, at which time the reinforcements expected from home would enable a decisive blow to be struck? The period during which the operations were possible was very limited. In the rainy season which follows immediately on the summer, and never sets in later than

June 5, the troops could not keep the field, and, *nolens volens*, would have to withdraw to their stations. These considerations were fully weighed and discussed at Allahabad in lengthy interviews between the Governor-General and the Commander-in-Chief. Finally, policy outweighed strategy, and it was decided to pursue the enemy to his last stronghold at once.

Rohilkund, which, since the capture of Delhi, had become the principal centre of the insurrection on the left bank of the Ganges, perpetually recalled to mind one of the most disgraceful acts of English diplomacy. We have already related the ignominious transaction by which Warren Hastings, at the end of last century, sold this fertile province to the Nabob Vizier of Oude for a considerable sum of money. Rohilkund possesses a territory containing some 150 miles square, from its northern frontier to the confines of Oude on the south; from the Ganges on the west to the mountains of Nepaul on the east. It is a country of plains watered by numerous rivers, that run almost parallel to the Ganges, into which they fall south of Farrackabad. Its only defence against invasion are some very primitive fortresses, a few jungles, and groups of mango trees. The capital, Bareilly, covers a large extent of ground, but is not even enclosed by a wall, and only the erection of considerable works could have put it into a condition to sustain a siege.

Ten months had already elapsed since Rohilkund had shaken off the Company's yoke. On May 31, a mutiny broke out in the brigade stationed at Bareilly, but there was little bloodshed to deplore; the European officers and their families escaped almost all, and found shelter in the sanitarium of Nyni Tal, among the Himalayas. The example set at Bareilly was immediately followed at Schahjahanpore, the second town in Rohilkund, by the 29th B.A., but the sepoys confined themselves to getting rid of their officers without doing them any harm, and all vestige of English authority disappeared from the province.

The insurrection soon lost its military character. In July, the mass of the sepoys marched to the assistance of the

King of Delhi, and power passed into the hands of an ambitious old chieftain, Bahadour Khan. Formerly a magistrate (sudder amin) in the Company's service, and in that capacity in receipt of a pension from the Board of Directors, he became the leader of the movement, and gave proof of great energy and remarkable power of organisation. Assuming at once all the prerogatives of supreme rank, he caused coins to be struck in his name, and imposed his rule on the country by means of his agents, who collected the taxes and administered justice. The European prisoners, the wealthy natives or those suspected of sympathy for England, were the victims of his revengeful spirit and his rapacity, but he took care to conceal his misdeeds under legal forms. Owing to its distance from the principal scene of action, Rohilkund escaped repressive measures until the day when the fall of Lucknow brought into the dominions of Bahadour Khan the greater part of the fugitives from Oude, some 20,000 sepoys in all, besides numerous armed bands. The former included both soldiers and their leaders, the Moulvi and the Begum and her son.

As before said, the English Government, notwithstanding the risks of a summer campaign, had resolved on active operations, and towards the end of March the army was divided into expeditionary columns. Six thousand Europeans and two thousand five hundred natives were left at Lucknow, under Sir Hope Grant. Cawnpore, Allahabad, and Benares were protected by small garrisons. Sir E. Lugard, at the head of his division, turning southwards, marched on Azimgarh to destroy the bands of Koër Singh. The Commander-in-Chief with 8,000 men, of whom 6,000 were Europeans, undertook the reconquest and pacification of Rohilkund. Sir C. Campbell's plan was interfered with at the outset by a considerable check inflicted on the English forces in the south.

Koër Singh has already been mentioned as one of the chieftains who figured prominently in the first events of the mutiny. At the head of his feudal bands, and the brigade that mutinied at Dinapore, he had for a long time interrupted all transit on the Great Trunk Road, and had become a source of terror to the European inhabitants of the districts of Lower Bengal near the Ganges. Koër Singh was defeated several times, and withdrew in consequence to the confines of Nepaul, but he was known to be still in arms. So formidable was he considered, that a price of 25,000 rupees was set on his head. When Sir C. Campbell evacuated Gorrackpore in order to reinforce the army with which it was intended to reduce the capital of Oude, Koër Singh immediately re-appeared in the field, and directed himself towards the south. Colonel Milman, the military head of the station of Azimgarh, marched out with a portion of the garrison (300 men) on March 24, to meet the rebels. After an engagement of outposts, in which the English came off victorious, Colonel Milman, who had only recently landed in India, seeing himself surrounded by numerous enemies, did not think it prudent to continue the struggle. He began to retreat, but did not succeed in reaching Azimgarh without the sacrifice of some portion of his baggage. On the following day, Koër Singh's forces blockaded the place. A first reinforcement was despatched from Benares, and, on April 5, a detachment under Lord Mark Kerr forced the lines of the besiegers.

The precarious condition of Lower Bengal had not escaped Sir C. Campbell's attention, and as early as March 29, the Lugard division marched from Lucknow in a southerly direction. Sir Edward Lugard succeeded in relieving Azimgarh almost without striking a blow, and Koër Singh, relinquishing his prey, hastened towards the Ganges. Two columns were at once sent in pursuit of the fugitives, one from the east the other from the west, in the hope of surrounding them in the angle formed by the junction of the Gogra and the Ganges. The detachment from the East, under Colonel Douglas, overtook Koër Singh and his men after a forced march of five days. A warm engagement followed, in which the old guerilla chief was defeated and severely wounded. Even in this extremity, he did not lose courage; boldly retracing his steps, he eluded the column which was arriving from the west, and crossed the Ganges at

Ballah Ghaut, in spite of the steamers sent from Ghazipore and Patna to prevent his passage.

Once on the right bank of the river, Koër Singh soon reappeared in his hereditary dominions of Indgespore, at the head of his bands, which, though somewhat weakened, were still very numerous. His return to the scene of his first exploits threatened to revive the yet scarcely extinguished spirit of mutiny in Lower Bengal. The rich districts of Patna and Bihar, the principal centres of the opium culture, were devoid of any means of defence; the road from Indgespore to Calcutta was merely protected by the feeble garrisons of Arrah, Ranniganje, and Barrackpore. Great was the terror felt by the civil and military authorities of the capital. The 6th R.A. was hastily despatched by train from Calcutta to the assistance of the threatened districts. The Naval Brigade, which was about to rejoin the 'Shannon,' then lying in the Hooghly, received orders to suspend its march. The necessity of these precautions was soon shown by a considerable check inflicted on the English troops.

A portion of the garrison of Arrah, a station close to Indgespore, left its entrenchments on the night of April 22, to march against Koër Singh. This little expedition, about 300 men strong (150 of the 35th R.A., 50 sailors, and 100 Sikhs), and two guns, misled by inaccurate information, perhaps ill-served by its reconnoitring parties, was overwhelmed by numbers in the jungle. Captain Lebas, who commanded the expedition, was killed, the two guns fell into the hands of the rebels, and a third only of the detachment succeeded in reaching Arrah in safety. This was the last success won by the brave old partisan. He is said to have died in this affair of the wounds he had previously received. His death deprived the insurrection of one of its most active and most intelligent leaders. After his decease, his adherents (2,000 sepoys and 5,000 or 6,000 armed men), far from taking advantage of their recent success to overrun the province, relinquished active operations, and confined themselves to throwing up entrenchments in the midst of the jungles of Indgespore, thus giving full time to the English forces to arrive on the scene of action.

The Lugard division had left Azimgarh some weeks previously, and was slowly marching in pursuit of the rebels, in the teeth of many difficulties, caused by the nature of the ground, the climate, and the scarcity of provisions. On May 8, after crossing the Ganges, it reached the neighbourhood of Indgespore. The following day, the positions held by the native forces since the death of Koër Singh were carried at the point of the bayonet by the men of the 35th who took a terrible revenge for the death of their comrades. That same day, the little town of Indgespore was occupied by main force, and the discovery of a cannon foundry in full activity explained how it was that the rebels were in possession of a very considerable artillery. This success, however, did not suffice to restore peace to Bihar. The bands, though beaten, were not destroyed; they dispersed among the neighbouring jungles, which Koër Singh, himself a devoted sportsman, had preserved for his bear hunts. The struggle proved a long and arduous one, and the natives displayed all the energy of despair. At one time, hidden in the heart of impenetrable thickets, at another appearing under the walls of Arrah and Buxar, favoured, moreover, by the complicity of the country people, the Hindoo guerillas long defied the efforts of their victorious adversaries. This campaign, though totally devoid of glory, tried to the utmost the endurance of the English soldiers. Exhausted by the sun, by fatigue, by privations, even the most hardy lost their sleep and their appetite; and Brigadier Douglas, in an official document, stated that a whole regiment of the Royal Army, the 84th, was incapable of active service. The work of pacification could only be completely carried out by constructing a network of military roads, which should open up easy communications through the vast jungles, so long the hunting-ground of Koër Singh, and now the last hiding-place of his partisans.

The first operations against Rohilkund were not successful. Brigadier Walpole's column, which had left Lucknow in the early days of April, arrived on the 14th in front of a small earth-fort situated in a dense jungle, and known indifferently as Rhadamon or Ronya. A native force of from four to five hundred held the place and its environs. An assault was at once ordered without any preliminary bombardment, though a siege train was attached to the expedition. The detachments of the 42nd Highlanders and the 4th Punjab regiment, selected for this operation, were met by such a deadly fire that they stopped in confusion. The big guns were at once brought forward to retrieve this check, but the fort was not invested on all sides, and it was evacuated in the night by the garrison. This badly managed affair cost more than a hundred killed and wounded. Amongst the dead was the Hon. Adrian Hope, Colonel of the 93rd Highlanders, one of the heroes of the two assaults of Lucknow, who was mortally wounded as he was trying to re-establish order in the attacking column. By his dashing bravery and his military talents, he had obtained great notoriety in the army, and his loss was all the more deplored that he had been killed in an insignificant action, which might have been avoided by a little prudence and strategy. Resuming its march, the Walpole division arrived on April 21 in sight of a body of the enemy, which was defending a bridge of boats over the Ramganga. The cavalry and light artillery attacked the natives with such impetuosity that the latter fled in hot haste, leaving them in possession of the bridge. Rohilkund now lay open to the invaders. A few days later, Sir C. Campbell joined the Walpole division with reinforcements, thus swelling its numbers to 10,000 men, and under his personal direction the campaign entered on its period of activity.

His plan was not to pursue an intangible enemy through Rohilkund, but to destroy the last effective forces of the insurrection by enclosing the fugitives of Lucknow, whether sepoys or armed bands, within a circle of iron. The season, the natural aptitude of Indians for a guerilla warfare, and the capricious strategy of their leaders, offered great obstacles to a complete success. How was it possible to foresee the movements of an enemy who recognised no supreme head? How was it possible to baffle the unaccountable manœuvres of adversaries who passed with the rapidity of lightning from ignominious cowardice to the most heroic courage? In the eyes of the Rohilkund chieftains, the whole art of war consisted in flying before the adversary, stopping when he stopped, and falling upon him with the swiftness of an arrow at the first symptoms of retreat. The motive, too, of the warfare had undergone certain modifications which we must point out. The former campaigns, when the English fought against the forces of the Emperor of Delhi, of the Mahratta princes, or the Maharajah of Punjab, which, if not regular armies, were at least regularly commanded, as soon as the opposing forces were defeated, one yoke was substituted for another, and the population passed without resistance under the rule of the conqueror. Ten months of anarchy had revived the religious fanaticism, the hatred of race and the spirit of independence among the Rohillas, so that the English were certain to meet with ill-will, if not armed resistance.

The month of May is the hottest month in the year, and there are few hours in the day when Europeans can brave the burning rays of the sun without danger to life; the time for operations was strictly limited. In these parts of the East, the marvellous mechanism of nature is regulated by unchangeable laws. On June 5, at the latest, the rainy season sets in in the north of India. In the rear were terrible enemies: the Ganges, the Rumgunga, and all the rivers would, at a fixed period, overflow their banks, inundate the roads, and turn the whole country into an impassable swamp. Under pain of seeing the English army perish in the bogs or beneath the floods, it was necessary that active operations should be over, at latest, by the last week of May. Let us add, that the spirit and discipline of the troops were no longer what they had been in the early days of the campaign, when all hearts were inflamed by love of their country and of humanity. Pillage and plunder acquired by the sword are fatal to all martial virtues. Certain accidents sustained by convoys, certain disappearances of treasure chests could not be all attributed to carelessness or chance. Many an officer, many a soldier who concealed priceless jewels beneath his uniform, was longing to return home and rest, and performed his duties with remissness, if not with discontent.

Two columns were directed to second the operations of the principal body. Brigadier Jones's corps, of about 4,000 men, started from Rourki, in the middle of April, and moved in a southerly direction, pushing back the rebels upon Bareilly. Another column, commanded by General Penny, was advancing on the east, and should have joined the main body between Shahjehanpore and Bareilly. A day was fixed for the concentration of the troops, their marches had been regulated in advance; but it is only under the shadows of night that Europeans can thread their way through these fiery regions. The weariness and fatigue of these long and incessant marches were calculated to enervate the stoutest hearts.

he three English columns advanced toilfully, in the midst of all these trials, in search of an intangible enemy. The boldest of the rebel chiefs—the Moulvie, the Begum, and Prince Firoz Shah—showed themselves only to disappear again; as if they wished to leave the task of combating their enemy to fatigue, privation, and the heat of the sun. In the English army the troops were almost brought to wish that the foe would somewhere offer a serious resistance. On April 30, Sir Colin Campbell entered Shahjehanpore without striking a blow; where vendors of sweetmeats and beggars were the sole representatives of the population. The following day was spent in placing the town jail in a condition of defence. Sir Colin Campbell left there a garrison of 600 men under Colonel Hall; and the moving column was again in motion on May 2. Two days afterwards General Penny's brigade joined the main body at the rendezvous appointed between Shahjehanpore and Bareilly; but a fatal accident had saddened their march.

On May 1, at the first glimmer of daylight, General

Penny, accompanied by the magistrate of the district, advanced along the road at the head of the column, when some indistinct figures were seen a little in front. A sudden flash lit up the horizon, followed by a fearful report. A squadron of Carabineers dashed rapidly forwards, and made short work of the ambuscade; but not without loss to themselves. General Penny's body, stripped of its clothes, and literally hacked to pieces by sabre cuts, was found on the spot lately occupied by the enemy. The veteran officer, wounded probably in the arm by the first discharge, had not been able to restrain his frightened charger, which carried him into the hostile ranks, where he met his death. The movements of the detachments coming from Rourki were not less regular than those of the column which had been deprived of its leader; and, on May 5, Bareilly was attacked on the north and on the east by the combined forces of Brigadier Jones and Sir C. Campbell.

The capital of Rohilkund is composed of a thoroughfare more than two miles long, intersected by narrow streets. Round the town, country houses surrounded by gardens, clumps of trees, and cultivated fields formed a species of suburb. Beyond this first enclosure stretched immense plains which, though cut up here and there by nullahs (ravines), were favourable to the operations of cavalry, an arm in which the rebels were very strong. The road from Shahjehanpore to Bareilly, by which Sir C. Campbell's troops had to advance, is crossed by a river, with steep and easily defended banks. The forward movement began on May 5 at dawn, and after a cannonade which did little harm, the English effected the passage of the river, the bridge over which their adversaries had not even taken the trouble to blow up. The information possessed by the staff was very meagre, and a belt of trees and sugar canes prevented the positions held by the defenders of the town from being minutely reconnoitred.

The suburbs were being slowly traversed when a vanguard composed of Sikhs, told off to search the ruined houses, were received by a galling fire, and fell back in hot haste. About a hundred Ghazis (Moslem fanatics) issued from the broken walls, and came bounding forward like panthers, shouting, 'Bismillah Deen' (for God and the Faith), covering their heads with a leather shield, and brandishing their formidable 'tulwars.' Their leader, notwithstanding a perfect hail of bullets, arrived to within a few feet of the English lines, where he was struck dead by a musket shot. Sir C. Campbell passed a few moments later over the scene of this sharp encounter, and most fortunately escaped a great danger. Seeing one of these fanatics lying a few steps off across the road with his tulwar in his hands, the position of the body and the brightness of the eyes caused him some suspicion, and he ordered a Highlander, who was by chance near him, to finish the Ghazi. The bayonet did not penetrate the thickly-wadded tunic of the impostor, who, jumping up, rushed at the General. At the same moment a Sikh, with one blow of his sabre, struck off the head of the Ghazi, as easily as he might have done that of a poppy. Not a man of the valiant cohort survived their defeat. A hundred and thirty-three corpses were counted after the action; and although *bhang* and opium might, without doubt, have played an important part in this heroic and foolish enterprise, history cannot speak of the affair without a word of eulogy and regret for these Indians. They were, for the most part, grey-bearded men; all wore turbans and waistcloths of green, the colour dear to the Prophet; and on the little finger was a silver ring with a stone, on which was engraven a long text from the Koran. A few minutes after, a body of rebel cavalry, which fell on the rear, threw confusion into the enormous convoy of carts and camp-followers attached to the English army. The sick and wounded officers, carried in palanquins, and among others Dr. Russell, escaped the sabres of the *sowars* (horse-soldiers) only by a miracle.

That eminent writer has given in his 'Journal' a graphic account of this episode in an Indian battle; and the reader will, no doubt, be pleased with the following extracts therefrom:—

'The delay, or rather the halt of the column where I was, lasted some time after this. Every moment the heat became more fearful. More than one European soldier was carried past me fainting, or dead. Major Metcalfe had kindly given me two bottles of French wine of the Chief's. I gave a cupful to one of those poor fellows who was laid down by my dhooly, getting it down his mouth with difficulty, for his teeth were partially set; his tongue sticking in his throat. He recovered a little —looked at me and said, "God bless you!"—then tried to get to his feet, gave a sort of gasp, and fell down dead. The crush on the road had become tremendous. The guns were beginning to move. Every moment a rude shock was given to the dhooly, which threatened to hurl it down the bank; so I told the bearers to lift me, and carry me off to a small tope in the field on my left, which seemed to be a quarter of a mile away, and certain to give us shade. The field was covered with camp-followers, who were plucking the grain and salads, with which the country appeared to abound all over. But it turned out that the tope, which after all was a very small cluster of bamboos and other trees, was much farther than I thought, and was by no means very umbrageous. Here my dhooly was placed close to Baird's; the bearers went inside among the bamboos, and squatted down to smoke or sleep. . . . Around us just now there was no sign of the British troops in front. They had dipped down into ravines, or were at the other side of the high road. Here and there were clouds of dust, which marked the course of cavalry. Behind us were the columns of the rear-guard and of the baggage. But the camp-followers were scattered all over the plains, and the scene looked peaceful as a hop-gathering. There is a sun, indeed, which tells us we are not in Kent. In great pain from angry leech-bites and blisters I had removed every particle of clothing, except my shirt, and lay panting in the dhooly. Half an hour or so had passed away in a sort of dreamy, pea-soupy kind of existence. I had ceased to wonder why anything was not done. Suddenly once more there was a little explosion of musketry in our front. I leaned out of my dhooly, and saw a long line of Highlanders, who seemed as if they were practising independent file-firing on a parade ground, looking in the distance very cool, and quiet, and firm; but what they were firing at I in vain endeavoured to ascertain. A few native troops seemed to be moving about in front of them. . . . A long pause took place. I looked once or twice towards the road to see if there were any symptoms of our advance. Then I sank to sleep. I know not what my dreams were, but well I remember the waking. . . . There was a confused clamour of shrieks and shouting in my ear My dooly was raised from the ground and then let fall violently. I heard my bearers shouting "Sowar! Sowar!" I saw them flying with terror in their faces. All the camp-followers, in wild confusion, were rushing for the road. It was a veritable *stampedo* of men and animals. Elephants were trumpeting shrilly as they thundered over the fields, camels slung along at their utmost joggling stride, horse and tats, women and children, were all pouring in a stream, which converged and tossed in heaps of white as it neared the road—an awful panic. And, heavens above! within a few hundred yards of us, sweeping on like the wind, rushed a great billow of white sowars, their sabres flashing in the sun, the roar of their voices, the thunder of their horses, filling and shaking the air. As they came on, camp-followers fell with cleft skulls and bleeding wounds upon the field; the left wing of the wild cavalry was coming straight for the tope in which we lay. The eye takes in at a glance what tongue cannot tell or hand write in an hour. Here was, it appeared, an inglorious and miserable death swooping down on us in the heart of that yelling crowd. At that instant my faithful syce, with drops of sweat rolling down his black face, ran towards me, dragging my unwilling and plunging horse towards the litter, and shouting to me as if in the greatest affliction. I could scarcely move in the dooly. I don't know how I ever managed to do it, but, by the help of poor Ramdeen, I got into the saddle. It felt like a plate of red-hot iron; all the flesh of the blistered thigh rolled off in a quid on the flap; the leech-bites burst out afresh; the stirrup-irons seemed like blazing coals; death itself could not be more full of pain. I had nothing on but my shirt. Feet and legs naked—head uncovered—with Ramdeen holding on by one stirrup-leather, whilst, with wild cries, he urged on the horse, and struck him over the flanks with a long strip of thorn—I flew across the plain under that awful sun. I was in a ruck of animals soon, and gave up all chance of life as a troop of sowars dashed in among them. Ramdeen gave a loud cry, with a look of terror over his shoulder, and, leaving the stirrup-leather, disappeared. I followed the direction of his glance, and saw a black-bearded scoundrel, ahead of three sowars, who were coming right at me. I had neither sword nor pistol. Just at that moment, a poor wretch of a camel-driver, leading his beast by the nose-string, rushed right across me, and, seeing the sowar so close, darted under his camel's belly. Quick as thought, the sowar reined his horse right round the other side of the camel, and, as the man rose, I saw the flash of the tulwar falling on his head like a stroke of lightning. It cleft through both his hands, which he had crossed on his head, and, with a feeble gurgle of "Ram! Ram," the camel-driver fell close beside me with his skull split to the nose. I felt my time was come. My naked heels could make no impression on the panting horse. I saw, indeed, a cloud of dust and a body of men advancing from the road; but just at that moment a pain so keen shot through my head that my eyes flashed fire.'

The mass of armed men whom Dr. Russell had just seen approaching along the road easily put to flight the rebel cavalry, and re-established order in the rear of the English army. The day was drawing to a close, and the soldiers, exhausted by fatigue and heat, were encamped on the field of battle by star-light. The struggle was resumed next day; the intelligence was always insufficient and contradictory; it was evident the besieged were quitting the town in crowds. On the other hand, the reports of the spies spoke of crenelated and undermined battlements, still strongly occupied. Sir Colin Campbell, always sparing of the lives of his men, contented himself with covering the town with the fire of his powerful artillery. Brigadier Jones, on the eastern side, imitated the example of his chief; and these delays in the assault permitted the rebel bands to evacuate Bareilly without serious loss. The next day, a mere military promenade gave to the English as prize possession the capital of Rohilkund. They found there a great quantity of cannon and munitions, but the principal prey, as at Lucknow, had slipped through the hands of the English. Bahadoor Khăn was already far from Bareilly, and, still worse, the Moulvie had been for some days threatening Shahjehanpore.

Scarcely had Sir Colin Campbell passed that town on his way to Bareilly, than the Moulvie presented himself under its walls at the head of 6,000 or 8,000 men and 12 guns. The small English garrison, unable to sustain the contest, abandoned its stores, and concentrated its strength on the prison, which had been surrounded by weak defensive works. The town, left to the rebels, was immediately stripped of everything. This bad news reached head-quarters on the night of the capture of Bareilly. To march to the relief of the threatened garrison without arranging for the defence of the chief seat of English authority in Rohilkund, was to lose all the fruits of victory; Sir Colin Campbell was obliged to satisfy himself at the moment with despatching a relieving force, consisting of a picked brigade under Brigadier Jones. That officer performed his mission with as much energy as good fortune.

Starting from Bareilly on May 8, he succeeded in breaking through the lines of the Moulvie, who tried to prevent his passage, and reached the English entrenchments on the 11th. Three days of forced marches over a parched soil, under a burning sun, had exposed the expedition to great sufferings, and many of the men died of sunstroke by the way. The arrival of this reinforcement did not effect the complete relief of Shahjehanpore. The Moulvie, recovering from his first surprise, or better informed as to the numerical weakness of the column under Brigadier Jones, reformed his lines of investment. On May 15 the rebels attempted to carry the English positions by main force, and, when foiled in the endeavour, withdrew from the immediate neighbourhood of Shahjehanpore. Sir C. Campbell's return a few days later completed the success. Full of anxiety for the fate of Shahjehanpore, the General-in-Chief had not waited to finish the works intended to secure the safety of Bareilly, but had set out, on May 14, for the former town, which he reached in five days, after handing over the military command of the province to Brigadier Walpole, with whom he left a considerable body of troops.

The rainy season was at hand; the Ganges was rising rapidly. The expedition against Rohilkund had succeeded as far as was possible. English supremacy was re-established in the two principal towns; all traces of Bahadoor Khan's authority had vanished, and though there were still a great many rebel bands in arms on the frontier of Oude, their movements could inspire no serious alarm.

On the other hand, since his arrival in Rohilkund, Sir C. Campbell had been unable to keep up any communication with the different bodies of the army, whose operations he had to direct in various parts of India. The most imperious necessity recalled him to the seat of Government, and forced him to leave in other hands the care of completing his task. But being desirous above all things of securing the success of his lieutenants, the old general unhesitatingly left all his European troops behind him, and journeyed towards the Ganges, escorted solely by some squadrons of irregular cavalry and a detachment of Beloochees (native infantry).

The sufferings experienced in the recent marches surpassed all that had been hitherto endured. The thermometer in the tents, even when provided with 'taths,' stood at 116° Fahrenheit. As the Moulvie and his bands had not yet left the neighbourhood of Shahjehanpore, success depended on the rapidity of the advance, and the day's march was often one of twelve hours. 'The men gasped like broken-winded horses as they drew their breath,' says an eye-witness. During the last march but one the scouts suddenly perceived a body of troops on the horizon, and an attack seemed imminent. Happily it was diverted to the attack of a convoy on its way to Shahjehanpore, under the protection of the

80th Regiment of the Royal Army. Sir Colin Campbell took advantage of this circumstance, and sending back the native troops with the convoy, continued his retrograde march with the European regiment. On the last night, a hot wind storm—the veritable simoom of the desert—swept over the little column, and threatened to swallow it up in its clouds of fiery dust. This was the last and greatest trial. The wind abated towards morning; and, on May 25, the troops began to cross the Ganges.

'I really believe that if the dust-storm had lasted half as long again, the result would have been fatal to most of the column. It was the same evil wind that smote Lake's corps in his awful march to Cawnpore at precisely the same period, and just fifty-four years ago.

'The "devil's breath" was upon us. If I could describe it, I should shrink from reviving the recollections of that "mauvais quart d'heure," which was in its horrible fervour worthy of the name which is translated by the above epithet. I crawled back to my dooly into a bed of burning sand, and there I lay exhausted. For hours we marched on. Oh! what delight at last to wake up in the midst of a stream of bright clear water, to see beyond its banks another broader still. I had been borne over the Rumgunga in a sort of dreamy consciousness, and even the pangs of thirst could not awake me. But now I was in the midst of water, my dhooly was at rest in a shallow stream like some small island, and the waters rolled over the sandy bed with a gurgling, pleasant song, away, under, and through the legs of my bed, and then came old Sukeeram, and taking up the grateful draughts in a gourd, held them to my parched lips. Then, with the hollow of his hand he dashed the dimpling surface of the current on my head and face. I could fancy how the sun-smitten earth drinks in the first autumn showers. All around me, above and below, the native camp-followers, syces, bazaar-people were rolling in the river, and puffing and blowing like so many porpoises. We were in a branch of the Ganges, and beyond us, across a long low waste of sand-banks, rolled the main body of the sacred river. Nor were the poor fagged British soldiers less delighted, if they were not quite as demonstrative in their joy, when they beheld the water, and bathed their aching heads and legs in the stream. Presently, sitting over his horse's shoulder with an air of fatigue, as well he might, came Sir Colin himself, with a few of his staff. His clothes and face were covered with dust, his eyes were half filled with sand, and, indeed, I scarcely recognised him for a moment, when he drew up to speak to me. "Futtehguhr is only four miles away," said he, "we'll be there in an hour and a quarter." And after a minute or so more spent in talking of the night we had passed, he rode his horse, which had not lost its time in the water, across the stream, and went on. If any of the Senior United Service or of 'the Raj' Seniors could have seen the dirty, jaded men who followed the General, they would have required much faith to believe they were staff officers.

'We jog on over the wide sand-banks of the broad bed of the Ganges, cut here and there into deep nullahs and dry water-courses, and covered with coarse grass, which will soon be under water.' [1]

[1] *My Diary in India in the Years* 1858–59, by W. H. Russell.

CHAPTER X.

SIR HUGH ROSE'S CAMPAIGN IN CENTRAL INDIA—LAST DAYS OF THE MUTINY.

Sir H. Rose—March on Saugor—Capture of the fort of Gurakota—Passage of the defile of Madanpore—Siege of Jansi—Arrival and defeat of Tantia Topee—Assault of Jansi—Departure from Jansi—Capture of Kounch—Excellent behaviour of the Gwalior Contingent—March on Calpi—Battle of Golowli—Capture of Calpi—Defeat of Maharajah Scindiah at Bahadourpore by Tantia Topee—Death of the Ranee of Jansi—Capture of Gwalior—Summary of Sir H. Rose's campaign—The situation in June 1858—End of the Honourable East India Company—The last campaign in Oude—Tantia Topee and his allies—Sir C. Campbell—Approximate loss of the natives.

WHILE Sir Colin Campbell was pursuing the work of conquest in the kingdom of Oude, and the English army was forcibly penetrating, for the third time in six months, to the heart of the capital, the columns we left at Mhow, on their return from a successful expedition in the district of Malwa, did not remain idle, and their deeds were not inferior, either in danger or fatigue, to those of their comrades who were combating on the left bank of the Ganges. The object was to push back the revolted sepoys, and the bands holding Central India, upon that great river, so as to get them between two fires. The country, bristling with forts, destitute of roads, intersected by rivers and torrents, offered almost insurmountable difficulties to military operations, especially when directed against an enemy with whom the entire population was in league. In this part of India, the war was not merely a mutiny but a national up-rising. Though thegreat princes, the Nizam of Hyderabad, Scindiah at Gwalior, and Holkar at Indore, had remained faithful to the English, the latter had irreconcilable enemies in the dispossessed rulers and the warlike population. The

Indian, it has been said, rarely thinks of the past or of the future, and the lessons of experience are no more unanswerable arguments to him than they are to the European. The fall of Delhi, and the success of the English at Lucknow, had not even yet demonstrated to the chiefs and people the superiority of regular armies, however weak numerically, over undisciplined hordes. Sustained by religious and military enthusiasm, to the very last the whole population clung to the national cause with a fervour productive of many heroic acts of devotion. We must also add that Tantia Topi, the principal adviser of the Nana and of the Ranee of Jansi, who were the chief leaders of resistance, showed an energy and military talent such as were not possessed by the veteran officers of the Bengal army, to whom the King of Delhi entrusted the command of his troops.

As has already been said, a general recently arrived in India had received the direction of the military movements intended to complete the work of pacification, and to drive back to the Ganges the armed bands and the revolted regiments of Central India. During the foregoing events, the names which appear in the first ranks of the armies and councils of England were those of soldiers of fortune, or statesmen who had reached the summit of the hierarchy only after a prolonged struggle. Outram, the two Lawrences, Nicholson, Sir C. Campbell himself were the authors of their own success, and owed nothing to the advantages of family. Fortune, however, reserved a glorious share in the great Indian drama for a member of the English aristocracy. The record of the birth of the general who brought to a successful issue one of the most brilliant campaigns of the war, is to be found in the peerage, and, what is more, he had never been mixed up in any way with Indian affairs.

Sir Hugh Rose, a son of a former ambassador of England to Berlin, entered the army in 1820, and rose step by step to the rank of major, without having seen any military service except in the repression of some disturbances in Ireland. Towards 1837, Major Rose, becoming weary of a garrison life, had himself placed on the unattached list, and family influences procured for him the position of Consul-General at Beyrout. The events of 1840 brought the new agent into prominence, and from Syria he passed as first secretary to Constantinople, where he was acting representative of England when the difficulties broke out which soon after resulted in the Crimean War. Major Rose, now a colonel by seniority, took an active part in the campaign, without giving up his diplomatic career, and as commissioner represented English interests at the French head-quarters before Sebastopol. His services had just been rewarded by promotion and the cross of K.C. of the Bath when the mutiny broke out. At his own request Major-General Sir Hugh Rose, to give him his new title, was sent to Bombay to assume the command of the army, intended for the reduction of Central India. This choice naturally excited much sharp criticism in the Anglo-Indian public, and the claims of a 'Griffin' to a command of such importance were freely discussed. The soldier-diplomatist was, however, a born general, and was to justify the trust reposed in him by the home authorities by unparalleled energy and first-class military talents.

Towards the middle of December, a high dignitary belonging to the Anglo-Indian Government arrived at Mhow simultaneously with Sir H. Rose. Sir Robert Hamilton had been, for many years, the agent of the Governor-General in Central India, where he had acquired great influence over the native princes. He was intimately acquainted with the people and customs of the country, and by his advice the first measures of the authorities were skilfully directed towards restoring all their former prestige to the native rulers. Well-timed severity secured Holkar's power against the defection of his soldiers and subjects, and when the expedition set out on its task of reconquest, it left behind a firm and grateful ally. The little force which, under the pompous name of the Army of Central India, started, early in January 1858, to relieve the Europeans shut up in the fortress of Saugor, met at first with no obstacles.

It advanced through the dominions of the Begum of Bhopal, one of those superior women who appear from time to time like a star in the sombre annals of India. She, as well as her royal brothers of Indore and Gwalior, fully gauged the all-powerful resources of European civilisation, and during the mutiny she remained scrupulously faithful to the treaty which bound her to her powerful neighbours. The well-cultivated fields of the tiny kingdom breathed an air of universal wealth and comfort. The capital, Bhopal, possessed straight, clean streets, well lighted at night, with a steamer on a small lake close by. To complete this likeness to Europe, the Princess Royal was married to an English officer, Victoria and Albert fashion, as the dark-skinned dowager pointed out triumphantly. On leaving Bhopal, military operations began by an attack on Rhatgarh, a native fortress, perched on a rock, like an eagle's eyrie. The defence was not a vigorous one, and after a few days' siege, the garrison evacuated the place under cover of darkness. As soon as day broke, the English cavalry pursued the fugitives, whose rear-guard they cut to pieces. Amongst the spoil were found lances surmounted by painted wooden heads, stained with blood, made to represent Europeans, both men and women, in features and complexion. We must not omit a horrible detail: long tresses of hair, the fineness and colour of which showed that it must have belonged to some of the poor victims slain at the outset of the mutiny, were discovered fastened on the lances. The capture of Rhatgarh opened the road to Saugor, without endangering the communications with Indore. On February 3, the deliverers appeared before the fortress where so many English families had found shelter in the day of trial. Amongst the defenders of the place was the 31st B.A., the only native regiment which had remained faithful to the laws of military honour, or, as the Indian expression puts it, to their salt, without being obliged to do so by the fear of punishment.

The primary object of the campaign was now reached, and there only remained to exact vengeance for the massacre at Jansi, on the spot itself where it had taken place, which had plunged so many English families into mourning. Before marching forwards it was, however, necessary, in order to secure communication with Bombay, to reduce the fortress of Gurakota, 25 miles to the east of Saugor, and then held by the 51st and 52nd, B.A. It was situated on a high promontory between two rivers, and was so well guarded by nature that, in 1818, after a siege of three weeks, an Anglo-Indian force of 11,000 men only succeeded in penetrating within the walls, by granting an honourable capitulation to the defenders. The expedition, under the personal command of Sir Hugh Rose, arrived at Gurakota on February 11, and though the day was far advanced, proceeded at once to drive the sepoys and their allies from their positions in front of the fort. Twice the rebels bravely charged the batteries which were mowing down their ranks, but on being repulsed with loss, they retired to the fortress or dispersed in the neighbourhood. Next day a breaching battery opened fire, and did such execution that the sepoys abandoned all idea of resistance. The fort was evacuated in the night, and on the following morning it was occupied without resistance by the 3rd European Fusiliers, B.A. The cavalry of the Hyderabad contingent was sent in pursuit of the retreating enemy, whose rear-guard they overtook, bringing back a great many prisoners and some booty. Sir H. Rose's victory was incomplete, but the position of the fortress was so well chosen, that it would have required a much more considerable force than he could dispose of to invest the place entirely, and prevent the garrison from escaping into the dense jungles covering the hills on the south. The object of the expedition was, however, obtained, for the enemy had lost a fortress formidable from its natural defences, and abundantly supplied with ammunition and provisions, where the rebels on their return from their forays would have found a secure refuge.

The English troops re-entered Saugor on February 17. Their two months' campaigning had taught them what difficulties and privations would be entailed by any further advance into the interior. The districts between Saugor and Cawnpore having been for ten months in a state of complete anarchy, offered no means of providing provisions for the army. Even at the time of the return from Gurakota miserable natives, driven to it by hunger, had been seen picking up the remains of the corn left by the horses and beasts of burden. Sir Hugh Rose attended with the greatest care to the organisation of the expeditionary force. The sick and wounded were left in the hospital of Saugor. All supplies necessary for the siege-train were renewed, and a few pieces of artillery added. The troops exchanged their usual uniform for one more adapted to the climate, the heavy baggage was stored in magazines in the fortress of Saugor, and finally, the provisioning of the active portion of the army was provided for by establishing a line of military trains in communication with Bombay. Lord Elphinstone, the Governor of the Presidency, was not less careful for the comfort of the men than the general himself, and attended to the sending of the convoys with an unflagging zeal, which greatly contributed towards the success of the campaign.

The English forces recommenced operations on February 27, and the very first night of their march plainly showed the feelings of the population. Their movements were signalled to the enemy by fires on every hill. The native troops occupied the defile of Malthoun, forty miles north of Saugor, in the heart of the Vindhyas chain, the natural difficulties of which had been skilfully augmented. But, on this occasion again, the leaders, exclusively preoccupied as they were with the defence of a single point, scarcely fortified the neighbouring pass of Madanpore, which offered an approach to Jansi, through the territories of the Rajah of Schahgarh, who had joined the insurrection some time before. Having captured the small fort of Barodia, situated between the two passes, Sir Hugh Rose undertook to force that of Madanpore. A feigned attack on the pass of Malthoun called off the attention of the allied chieftains, whilst the principal body of the English army marched on the defile of Madanpore. At daybreak, the 3rd European Fusiliers B.A. and the infantry of the Hyderabad contingent advanced to dislodge the enemy's outposts from the wooded heights which they occupied, whilst the main body, preceded by artillery, appeared at the same instant at the entrance of the pass. The skirmishers, concealed in the jungle, and a battery placed at the other end of the defile, showered such a storm of bullets on the English, that the artillerymen had to shelter themselves behind their guns. Sir H. Rose had his horse wounded under him, and the forward movement was arrested. The check was but a momentary one. Some cannon belonging to the Hyderabad contingent shelled the defenders of the pass, and the English troops made a charge with decisive effect. The natives dispersed, and the pass of Madanpore was carried by assault. The victory was completed by the dragoons of the Royal Army and the cavalry of the Hyderabad contingent, who galloped through the defile, and pursued the enemy for a distance of several miles.

The natives, in their discouragement, successively abandoned the fortresses of Seraï, Marowa, Tel Bihat, and that of Banpore, the residence of the Rajah of the same name. The possession of these strongholds secured the re-establishment of English authority in the district, and Sir H. Rose resumed his forward march. On March 17, the English troops effected the passage of the Betwa without firing a shot. That same day, the 2nd Brigade, which had been detached from the main body for some time, achieved an important success by capturing the formidable fortress of Chanderi, situated on the left bank of the Betwa. The defenders of the place showed great resolution and skill. A mine, which was fired just as the column was to begin the assault, made great havoc in the ranks of the 86th R.A. The news of the capture of Chanderi was received by Sir H. Rose the day after the passage of the Betwa. Feeling certain from this that his forces would soon be at their full complement, he continued his advance on Jansi.

The Indian Government attached the greatest importance to the speedy reduction of this town, rightly considering it the stronghold of the insurrection in Central India. Minute care had been taken with the defence of the place: the trees round the town were cut down, the walls and houses, so placed as to be of any advantage to the attacking forces, were levelled with the ground. The old citadel, which commanded the town, was completely armed and repaired, and the flag of the Ranee was displayed on one of the towers. The town, in a circuit of four miles, was defended by a loop-holed wall 25 feet high and flanked at intervals by bastions provided with heavy guns. The final preparations for the defence were being made when the English arrived, and native workmen were still seen putting the last touches to a battery on the wall. All these posts were held by a garrison of 11,000 men, composed of rebel sepoys or warlike tribes, and inspired by the presence of the Ranee of Jansi, a courageous and bloodthirsty woman, one of the principal authors of the massacre in the month of June, and who, as such, could hope for no mercy.

There were other dangers to be apprehended besides those from the town itself. It was vaguely known that Tantia Topee, one of the most formidable and clever leaders of the rebels, had left Jansi some time before to go in quest of assistance. His errand acquired great importance from the presence of the Gwalior contingent at Calpi, where it had come to recruit after its defeat at Cawnpore early in December by Sir C. Campbell. The conflict was beginning under terrible difficulties, but Sir H. Rose was not a man to flinch. He had instinctively divined the secret of victory in Asiatic warfare, and his first proceedings showed a master-mind.

It was soon recognised that before attempting to make a breach in the outer wall of the fortress, which was defended by three lines of solid masonry, it was necessary to capture the town, and Jansi was accordingly invested on March 22. The next day four breaching batteries on the right, which had been finished on the evening of the 24th, opened fire. Steward's brigade, which had just taken the fort of Chanderi, reached head-quarters that same day. This reinforcement was all the more important that a company of Sappers R.A. and a considerable amount of artillery were attached to it. With their help Sir Hugh Rose was able to complete the attack on the left. On March 26 two supplementary batteries, placed on heights commanding some of the works of the fortress, gave a fresh impulse to the attack. Although the town and its fortifications were exposed till the end of the month to a terrible fire, the resistance offered by the besiegers never slackened. The example of the Ranee sustained the courage of her subjects; the women and children showed themselves on the ramparts in the midst of the soldiers, to whom they brought food and drink. The English had been obliged to employ most of their artillery in silencing the fire from the town, and the breaching battery, consisting only of two guns, had little effect on a wall of remarkable solidity.

The sufferings of the besiegers had almost reached the limit of human endurance. Since the passage of the Betwa, sixteen days before, the troops had scarcely been able to snatch a few hours' rest; the horses were always saddled and bridled at the picquets. Besides this, the terrible summer season had set in; the men, from morn till night, were exposed to the fiery rays of the sun, and that among granite rocks, which refracted the heat like so many furnaces. When in action, officers and soldiers only escaped apoplexy by causing the Chistis (water-carriers) to pour the contents of their masacks (skins) on their heads. Terrible though the position of the besiegers was, it was about to become still more so. On March 31 the semaphores placed on the heights round the camp gave warning of the approach of numerous armed bodies. On being carefully examined, they turned out to be a force of 20,000 men. The Gwalior contingent, calling itself the army of the Peischwah, and reinforced by hordes of fanatics, under Tantia Topee, was advancing by forced marches to the relief of Jansi.

In presence of this great danger, the English general never faltered. A worthy successor of Clive, Wellesley, and all the illustrious soldiers whose courage and skill gave India to England, Sir H. Rose put a bold face on the matter, and fortune rewarded him by success. If the operations of the siege were once interrupted, the besieged would regain courage and would prolong their resistance. Sir H. Rose decided not to withdraw a single man from his lines of attack, and to march against Tantia Topee with two incomplete brigades, amounting to about 2,000 men, of whom not even the half were Europeans. On learning towards nightfall that a strong column of the Peischwah's army was advancing on the north front of Jansi, he modified his original plan, and sent the first brigade to bar their passage. This movement, thanks to the darkness and to the nature of the ground, passed unperceived by the enemy. Encouraged by the small numbers of the English forces, which his vanguard had easily ascertained from the heights occupied by it early in the day, Tantia Topee had passed the Betwa, and pitched his camp a short distance from the English tents. During the night the sentinels could plainly hear the challenges and insults hurled against them by their adversaries. The besieged followed with deep interest the different incidents of the day from the top of the towers and walls. As the evening drew on their hopes of speedy deliverance showed themselves by bonfires, discharges of musketry and artillery, cries of joy, and beatings of drums and tamtams.

At daybreak the English outposts fell back on the main body before the Peischwah's army, which advanced in one long line, with such extended wings as to threaten to outflank Sir H. Rose's feeble brigade. The English infantry received orders to lie down, and the horse artillery, opening a well-directed fire, carried death and confusion into the enemy's ranks. The decisive moment had arrived. Sir H. Rose, followed by a squadron of dragoons, and Captain Prettyjohn, at the head of some light cavalry belonging to the Hyderabad contingent, rushed headlong, one on to the right wing, the other on to the left of their adversaries. Their example was immediately followed by the infantry, who made a charge with the bayonet. This heroic conduct decided the fortunes of the day. When the smoke round the guns lifted, a handful of English dragoons were seen in the midst of an affrighted multitude, flying in hot haste towards the second Indian line, commanded by Tantia Topee. The latter body was provided with formidable artillery, and had taken up its position about two miles from the scene of the first combat, on rising ground surrounded by jungle. The operations of the second English brigade had been equally successful.

While Sir H. Rose and his dragoons were laying about them like ancient paladins in the very thick of the Peischwah's hordes, the first brigade had routed the native column which the evening before had directed its march to the north front of Jansi, and was about to bear down upon the reserve of the English army. The fiat of the God of battles had gone forth. The first line of the native forces had given way; their right wing was turned; the troops that had not been engaged were thrown into confusion by thousands of fugitives, who hampered their movements. Tantia Topee wisely resolved on retiring, covered by his artillery. The nature of the ground, cut up by ditches and strewn with blocks of granite, and the overpowering heat of the day, protected the natives in their retreat, and they were able to recross the Betwa, leaving, however, seventeen guns and 1,000 dead behind them. The English forces, and especially the cavalry, had suffered severely. No prisoners had been made on either side. Meanwhile the defenders of the town had not remained idle: constant discharges from the ramparts in the early part of the day had seemed to announce a sortie on a great scale; but the result of the battle, which was being fought before their eyes, and the phases of which they were able to follow, filled all hearts with despair. The growing discouragement could be perceived by the slackening of the fire from the place, and when the English troops re-entered the camp, the silence of the night was only broken by the reports from the breaching battery, which still continued its work of destruction.

Profiting by this state of feeling, Sir H. Rose, with happy decision, made use of the favourable opportunity to strike a decisive blow. The siege batteries had continued their fire uninterruptedly, and on the evening of April 2 the breach was pronounced practicable. The assault was fixed for the following day. At three in the morning the 86th R.A. and the 28th B.A. stormed the breach with no great loss. The troops told off to assist the storming column, the 3rd European Bombay Fusiliers and two companies of native sappers, met with more difficulties in the attempt to escalade the walls. One of the detachments, while advancing over open ground by the light of the moon, was decimated by the fire of the besieged before reaching the foot of the ramparts. Once there, the ladders were found to be too short, others were not strong enough, and broke. The undertaking seemed desperate, when some officers of the Engineers, hoisted up by their men, reached the top of the wall, where they were soon followed by their soldiers. The struggle was one of the fiercest, and was still uncertain, when the shouts of victory raised by the storming column were heard in the distance, and the besieged, giving way, fled in all directions. The two corps effected their junction, and marched towards the palace by way of the main street. Before they could get there the artillery of the citadel where the Ranee had taken refuge opened fire on the heart of the town, causing a conflagration of the buildings near the palace, and it was through flames and projectiles that the besiegers arrived at the royal abode.

The entry was vigorously defended. An explosion of powder, which occurred when the English were debouching through the great gate, caused many deaths in their ranks. The sepoys were driven from room to room, and the magnificent palace, one of the glories of Indian architecture, soon offered a terrible scene of murder and pillage. Towards the middle of the day the English troops, who had been fighting since dawn, took a short rest. To this halt succeeded a bloody combat. About fifty body-guards of the Ranee had taken refuge in the stables, where they were all slain to a man. Meanwhile, fighting was still going on in the streets and houses. Like the Rajpoots of olden times, the inhabitants threw their wives, their children, their treasures, into the wells, into which they leapt themselves after burning their last cartridge. Outside the town there occurred several terrible episodes. Some hundreds of fugitives who had escaped over the outer wall were surrounded on rising ground by a body of cavalry, and were all mowed down by discharges of grape-shot from a native battery B.A., notwithstanding their entreaties and heart-rending cries.

Fighting, which ceased at night-fall, was resumed the following day. One after the other, the cannon foundry and the elephant park of the Ranee fell into the hands of the English. The Princess, with 500 adherents, had taken refuge in the citadel the day before. At one time it was thought that, in order to escape from her enemies, she had ascended a funeral pile and perished in the flames, like the Indian widows of yore. The Ranee, however, did not wish to succumb unrevenged by a useless suicide, and when all hope of resistance was lost, she evacuated the fortress. An officer who, on the morning of April 6, ventured in the neighbourhood of the citadel, found the gates wide open and the garrison gone. The English cavalry sent in pursuit of the Ranee only succeeded in cutting to pieces a few badly mounted horsemen of the escort.

Next day an assembly of armed men and sepoys entrenched in the houses of Lane Bagh, in the centre of the town, resisted for several hours the troops sent to dislodge them, and the losses on both sides were considerable. This was the last fighting of the siege, and from this moment the smoking ruins of Jansi were no longer defended. In this six days' battle the English lost 300 killed and wounded, about 15 per cent. of the troops engaged. Among the dead was Colonel Turnbull, who was mortally wounded in the attack on the palace. He was a distinguished officer, and had shown great skill in directing the artillery in the battle of April 1. Of the eight officers of Engineers attached to the expedition, only two escaped safe and sound. The losses of the besieged were much greater: inside the walls, more than a thousand bodies were burnt or buried. Large stores of food and ammunition fell into the hands of the conquerors; the citadel alone contained more than fifty guns of various calibres. The search made immediately after the victory for the remains of the unfortunate victims of June 1 proved successful. The bodies had been thrown pell-mell into a ditch outside the town, close to the spot where the work of murder had been done.

Since his departure from Mhow, fortune had constantly smiled on Sir H. Rose's undertakings. He had advanced on the very heart of Central India without a check, and had wrested their most formidable strongholds from the allied natives by main force. Always and everywhere he had disconcerted his adversaries by the rapidity of his movements and the vigour of his blows. The capture of Jansi, though it placed almost the last refuge of the insurgents in his hands, did not complete the work of repression. A halt was, however, absolutely necessary. Losses in battle, combined with fatigue and privations, had reduced immensely the brigades designated by the pompous title of Army of Central India. Sir Hugh Rose granted a well deserved rest to his troops, and spent the greater part of April in preparing for ulterior operations.

The allies, on their side, were not idle. Though worsted in a hundred encounters and deprived of their fortresses, chiefs and soldiers alike, with the heroic determination we have been called upon to admire nearly at every page of these sketches, were still resolved to try the fortunes of war. The valiant Ranee, Tantia Topee, Rao Sahib, the Nana's brother, had united their forces, and the army of the Peischwah was rapidly reconstituted under the walls of Calpi where, for ten months, the flag of the mutiny had floated. The fortress of Calpi, situated on the right bank of the Jumna, which, as before said, commands the road from Jansi to Cawnpore, was the last stronghold of the insurgents. Its fall would at once re-establish direct and easy communication between Sir C. Campbell's army and the troops in Central India.

Before resuming active operations, Sir H. Rose was

obliged to diminish still further his small force by leaving a sufficient garrison at Jansi, and on April 26 he reappeared in the field. Since the middle of the month, small flying columns had been scouring the country and taking possession of the tiny forts scattered over it, in order to clear the road between Jansi and Calpi. The season and the nature of the soil were most unfavourable to the movements of the troops. The ground, cut up in all directions by deep ravines and calcined by the summer sun, bore no trace of vegetation. At the bivouacs, the wretched oxen and horses were lucky if they received meagre rations of branches and dry leaves; the wells were almost dry, and what little water they yielded was bad. The heat of the day had become so frightful that, as far as possible, the soldiers were not exposed to the rays of the sun, and all marching was done at night. The sufferings of Sir H. Rose's soldiers were not less than those their brothers in arms were enduring at the same time in Rohilkund under Sir C. Campbell. A few hours of unrefreshing doze (sound sleep was impossible, from howling dogs, jackals, and beasts of burden chewing their cud and jingling bells with every move of the head), and then another march and a battle. We marched most of the night; and how long the hours seem in night marches! The infantry were fatigued before they started, but they began to try hard to bear up against it. In the first halt they sit down and are soon asleep, then they awake, nod off again, and awake again several times. The bugle sounds, and they are up and off again; but before a second halt is sounded, they begin to fall out, and must be carried in 'dhoolies.' An occasional joke passes off among the older campaigners, and the hopes of meeting the foe keep up their flagging spirits.

The sun rises, and then the heat and clouds of white dust well-nigh overpower them, and the men begin to cry out, almost hysterically, for water. Water! but the bag is empty; and they look round imploringly and keep on a little longer. By-and-bye, a village and a large tope of trees is seen, and then the 'bheesties rush off for water, and the men expect a halt.' Long-continued excitement like this soon begins to tell upon the best of them; a shadowing of delirium begins to show itself; there is a nervous restlessness and a wild glare from the dry red eye, and awful vengeance is vowed against the foe! Men begin to talk of home, and cool shady places and brooks, as the hot air begins to blow over them, parching up every drop of moisture in the body; and dogs rush past with great raw wounds in their backs, like sabre cuts, caused by the sun, howling for water and shade; the patient camel cries and grunts, and the intelligent elephant tries to rut the raw soles of his feet, and big tears trickle from his eyes as the advance continues; at length the head of the column has halted; there is a village, and the men are blessed with ample shade and water for a time!

In the midst of these trials the English forces were steadily advancing on Calpi, but the difficulty of procuring water in sufficient quantity prevented Sir H. Rose from concentrating his forces on one point, and giving to his movements their usual rapidity. The allies, by taking up a position under the guns of the fortress of Kounch, forty miles south-west of the fort of Calpi, shortened by one-half the march of their adversaries. Conspicuous among the native cavalry was the Ranee at the head of a body of Amazons. On learning their approach, Sir H. Rose assembled his two brigades on May 5, ten miles from the fort. The day before, the 93rd Highlanders had joined head-quarters. Though their effective force was very small, yet it almost filled up the gap made by the garrison left at Jansi. On May 6, the day being already far advanced, Sir H. Rose attacked the front of the enemy's positions at the head of the first brigade and of the Hyderabad contingent, whilst the second brigade executed a flank movement on the left. The allies did not wait for the result of this double manœuvre, and fearing that their communications with Calpi would be cut off, they beat in retreat after a short artillery engagement. The town and fortress of Kounch offered no resistance. The only serious fighting occurred when the English troops pursued and attacked the rear-guard. The Gwalior contingent, who had been ordered to protect the retreat, extorted praises from the victors by their firm attitude, and kept up the high reputation they had acquired during the campaign.

Their infantry, drawn up in a line of skirmishers two miles long, connected by groups of from thirty to forty men, saved the Peischwah's army from an immense disaster. These fine soldiers retreated for several hours in good order, keeping up a steady fire, and only hastening their steps when the English cavalry and artillery appeared on their flanks. The victors lost few men in the engagement by the enemy's fire, but suffered greatly from fatigue. They had begun to march at midnight, and the pursuit did not cease till nine the next evening. The thermometer stood at 120° in the shade, and the sun made many victims in the ranks. Three times the General-in-Chief came very near having a sun-stroke. Stopping at the foot of a tree, he was obliged to have buckets of water thrown on his head in order to prevent congestion of the brain. The allies left about 600 dead and nine guns on the battle-field.

Even after this trying day, Sir H. Rose gave his troops only a few hours' rest, and next day at dawn they started for Calpi. On leaving Kounch, the English force deviated from the straight line of march, Sir H. Rose having been informed that the allies had raised many obstacles on the road from Jansi to Calpi. This change had the advantage of placing the expedition in communication with a detachment sent by Sir C. Campbell to operate on the left bank of the Jumna. The latter body was composed of several companies of Sikhs, of the 88th R.A., and of the Camel Corps—that is to say, infantry mounted on dromedaries—under Colonel Maxwell.

Before any successful operation could be effected, the Peischwah's army, like a phœnix, rose from its ashes. The citadel of Calpi, with its well-stocked arsenal, was held by a garrison composed of the Gwalior contingent, the remains of the Bengal regiments, and bands of Rohillas, the whole recently reinforced by the cavalry of the Rajah of Bandah, and, according to an official document, amounting to 20,000 men in all. The Ranee of Jansi and Tantia Topee had sworn to defend to the death this last stronghold of the mutiny, and to win heaven by destroying the infidels.

The citadel of Calpi, situated on the right bank of the Jumna, stands on a rock outside the town, from which it is separated by a line of precipices. On the town-walls, numerous temples surrounded by ditches played the part of detached forts. The outer line of entrenchments was formed by fortifications, armed with heavy guns, beyond which extended fields intersected by deep ravines. Ground of this nature not only opposed great difficulties to any offensive operation, but also facilitated sorties on the part of the besieged by furnishing them with all kinds of covered ways. Tantia Topee skilfully turned the natural advantages of the soil to the utmost account, and being fully aware that the sun was his best ally, never began his attacks until the middle of the day, when the heat was at its fiercest.

Sir H. Rose concentrated his two brigades at Golowli, to the south-west of Calpi, on May 19, and was joined on the following day by a rather strong force from Colonel Maxwell's detachment, some companies of Sikhs, and of the 88th R.A., and the whole Camel Corps. Colonel Maxwell, with the rest of his forces, was to second the attack by bombarding the fortress from the left bank of the Jumna, where he was stationed. The arrival of this reinforcement enabled the operations of the siege to be commenced at once. Sir Hugh's left rested on the road from Bandah to Calpi, and his right reached the ravines in the immediate neighbourhood of the Jumna. On May 22, towards ten in the morning, strong hostile columns debouching by the road to Bandah attacked the English left, and the contest became a severe one. Whether, owing to a secret information or to a fortunate inspiration at the last moment, Sir H. Rose considered this engagement as a mere feint, and altered nothing in his previous arrangements, refusing to withdraw a single man from the forces composing his right wing. This determination decided the fate of the day.

Suddenly, as by magic, the long line of ravines on the right of the English appeared bristling with guns, which showered grape and balls, while sepoys, emerging as it were from the bowels of the earth, covered the English battalions with a storm of bullets. The sharpness of the attack, the great number of the assailants, and the heat of the sun then straight overhead, overpowered Sir H. Rose's most energetic men. The ranks wavered, and the enemy, encouraged by the sight, advanced with demoniacal yells. One moment's hesitation and the battle was lost. But Sir H. Rose had already provided for the danger, and the Camel Corps, setting off at full galop, arrived on the scene of action just as the English artillery was about to fall into the hands of the victorious allies. The soldiers dismounted, and led by General Stuart, sword in hand, fell on the sepoys. The effect of this charge was decisive; it checked the natives in their triumphant advance, and caused them to fly ignominiously after a short resistance. The cavalry, by taking part in the fight at the right moment, captured a great many guns and a considerable amount of baggage, in spite of the difficulties of the ground. The Ranee, who was looking on at the head of her Amazons, lost her tents, and was obliged to spend the night in the open air at the foot of a tree. During the struggle Colonel Maxwell poured a continuous artillery fire into the town and citadel from his position on the left bank of the Jumna.

Discouraged by the events of the day, their ranks decimated by the English fire, the allies evacuated the place in the night, and the following day it was occupied by the English without resistance. All that was found there showed that a prolonged resistance had been contemplated. There were buildings and tents sufficient to house a great number of troops; there were smithies and cannon foundries in full activity. The arsenal was overflowing with stores of all sorts—such as saltpetre, sulphur, coal, cartridges for muskets and cannon, surgical instruments and medicines pillaged from the magazines at Cawnpore and Agra. Finally, an immense quantity of official documents was discovered, among others, one proclaiming Nana Sahib the sovereign of all the land south of the Jumna. On May 24, the troops celebrated the Queen's birthday in the midst of the trophies of the previous day's victory. Never had a more precious gift been offered to a beloved sovereign by devoted and brave soldiers. How much suffering, however, clouded this day of rejoicing! Sir H. Rose's two brigades were almost in a state of dissolution. The staff existed merely in name, its head was lying delirious on a sick bed; Sir H. Rose's constitution was being slowly undermined by fever, after having been severely tried by three sunstrokes; the chaplain had gone mad. The officers, all of whom were wounded or completely worn out, stood in the utmost need of seeking strength and health in the salubrious climate of Europe.

After so much fatigue and so many hardships, it might have been supposed that the task of the little army of Central India was at length accomplished. A flying column, under Colonel Robertson, composed of troops of all arms, had been sent in pursuit of the natives. The reports of the spies gave rise to the belief that Tantia Topee and his companions were moving towards the Ganges, and that after crossing it, they would take refuge in Oude, where there could be no thought of following them. Deceived by this reassuring intelligence, Sir H. Rose was preparing to leave the army, after conveying by an order of the day his thanks to his faithful companions in danger and fatigue for their devotedness and good discipline, when an event which occurred a few days previously threatened to wrest from the English all the fruits of the campaign.

On leaving Calpi, Tantia Topee and the Ranee had advanced on Gwalior by forced marches, instead of flying to the jungles of Oude from the relentless vengeance of their enemies. In order to bar their passage, Maharajah Scindiah marched out at the head of his troops, on May 30, as far as Bahadourpore, some nine miles from Gwalior. He was deserted by the bulk of his troops, who passed over to the enemy, and taking to flight with his body-guard, he crossed the Chambal and arrived safe and sound at Agra. By a bold stroke, the men, who only a few days earlier were despairing fugitives, their last battle fought and lost, had become masters of Scindiah's treasures, of the wealth of his adherents and of a well-stocked arsenal.

Tantia Topee at once proclaimed his master, Nana Sahib, Scindiah's successor, and rewarded the treachery of the Gwalior troops by considerable gifts of money. In a short time this Indian Mithridates, by an unexpected turn of fortune, saw himself at the head of an army of 20,000 men, and in a position to withstand the efforts of adversaries exhausted by innumerable hardships.

The column sent from Calpi in pursuit of the fugitives soon perceived that they were marching on Gwalior instead of retreating to the Ganges, and, in order to avert serious danger in that direction, Sir H. Rose despatched some of his forces under Brigadier Stuart to the help of the Maharajah. The reinforcement did not arrive in time, and the disaster which befell Scindiah at Bahadourpore was soon known at Calpi. Tantia Topee's success gave every reason to anticipate grave complications. Holkar's contingent, carried away by this example, might turn against their leader, and take possession of Indore in the name of the mutineers. Where were the forces strong enough to prevent the Mahratta population of the Deccan and of Hyderabad from joining the standard of the heir of the Peischwah? Once again the English supremacy in India was seriously threatened.

The military authorities of Northern India, on learning Scindiah's defeat, hastened to despatch help to the scene of danger. The 3rd European Bengal Fusiliers were at once sent from Agra to the Chambal, and a column employed in Bandelkhund, under Brigadier Smith, received orders to march northwards. Brigadier Robert Napier hastily left head-quarters at Cawnpore with reinforcements, and took the road to Gwalior by way of Calpi. On June 6, Sir H. Rose, calling on his men for a last effort, quitted the banks of the Jumna to rejoin his advanced guard.

During these last marches the English troops experienced the worst sufferings of a summer campaign in India. 'As we passed along, we saw several camels, bullocks and tatoos, which had fallen dead from the heat, but there was no decomposition going on—they seemed to be drying up like mummies in this intensely powerful sun. Scores of poor sepoys, who could go no further, had taken off their belts and horrible red cloth coats, and lay down gasping in any morsel of shade; others, jaded and worked up to intense nervous irritability, were dragging themselves along—limping onwards with drooping heads, or staggering with a gait like an idiot, a paralytic, or a drunkard.'

On June 16, the two brigades effected their junction at Indorki, on the banks of the Sinde, and, in the evening, Brigadier Napier, with his corps, joined head-quarters. This officer-general, who had taken a glorious share in both the sieges of Lucknow, and who was to distinguish himself still more in the Abyssinian war, assumed the command of the second brigade, vacant by the placing of Brigadier Stuart on the sick list. Brigadier Smith and the column sent from Agra advanced on their side to invest the place on the north and south.

There had been no time to repair the ruined fortifications of the citadel of Gwalior, which owed to its position the name of the Gibraltar of India, and the allies had confined themselves to fortifying the heights round the town. The Ranee of Jansi personally superintended the works of defence, and fought to the end with heroic courage. As to Tantia Topee and his colleagues, according to their usual tactics they took to flight on the approach of danger.

Three miles to the east of the fortress and the citadel were the cantonments of Morar, where Scindiah's contingent with the European officers commanding it had been formerly stationed. On the morning of June 17 Sir H. Rose perceived that Morar was occupied by a considerable portion of the native army; an engagement immediately followed, which proved a mere artillery duel, till one of the English brigades, turning the right flank of the natives, the latter beat in retreat through the camp, hard pressed by their adversaries. The retreat became a total rout on the arrival of Sir H. Rose's other brigade, which very opportunely appeared at the further end of the cantonments; but the artillery and cavalry, owing to the nature of the ground, were unable to complete the victory by pursuing the enemy. The day was marked by one of those terrible episodes so common in Indian warfare. Fifty sepoys, who stood at bay in a ravine, defended themselves to the last against the Highlanders by whom they were surrounded. Not a man issued alive from this modern Thermopylæ.

The result of the encounter seemed to presage a speedy and decisive victory; the entry of the troops into Gwalior was imminent, and a wise policy seemed to demand the giving some guarantee that the object of the expedition was merely the restoration of a faithful ally to his throne. It was necessary that Scindiah should make his appearance among the English on their entry into Gwalior, in order to reassure the population against any fear of annexation. The Maharajah had already been some days with the column sent from Agra to assist in the reduction of the place, and was at once summoned to head-quarters. Brigadier Smith's column, which was advancing from the south, arrived on the evening of the affair at Morar at Kota Ki Seraï, on the little river Omrar, seven miles from Gwalior. Beyond the village the road winds between hills, until it issues into the plain, in the midst of which Gwalior is situated. An encounter between advanced posts had taken place that morning. The enemy's vedettes having been seen on the other side of the stream, two squadrons of the 8th Hussars R.A. and a small body of infantry were ordered to make a reconnaissance. They were soon met by the fire of a masked battery, which the Hussars carried by a dashing charge, only retiring after spiking the guns and on the approach of very superior forces. Some native cavalry, on advancing to attack the Hussars, were overthrown, and perished almost to a man, trodden down under the horses' feet. On this occasion, according to a report, the Ranee of Jansi, who disappears henceforth from the scene, was among the dead. Let us accept popular rumour, without too minute investigation, and assume that the valiant Ranee met with her death on the heights of Gwalior, whether by ball, shell, or sabre cut. It seems only appropriate that the modern Semiramis should be slain fighting at the head of her Amazons in a cavalry engagement.

In the affair of the 17th it had been made pretty clear that Brigadier Smith was in presence of the bulk of the allied forces, and Sir H. Rose, deviating from his line of operations, joined his lieutenant. On the morning of the 18th the native leaders entered into action with an impetuosity which was of short duration. The 86th R.A. deployed on the right in lines of skirmishers, the 71st R.A. in the same order, followed by the main body, composed of the 95th R.A. and the 10th and 25th B.A., dislodged the allies from their positions on the heights, and drove them as far as the last ridge overlooking the plain of Gwalior. Considerable forces of horse and foot were seen to issue from the town, and to form in confusion in the neighbouring fields. Notwithstanding the exhausted condition of his troops, and the lateness of the hour, Sir H. Rose determined to strike a decisive blow. His cavalry continuing to advance, descended into the plain, and the allied troops fled at their approach, without attempting the slightest resistance. In the evening the victors occupied the town and the palace. The next day Scindiah re-entered his capital in triumph at the very time a detachment of the 25th Native Regiment B.A. was completing the victory by the capture of the fortress of Gwalior. Some fifty sepoys and armed natives had taken refuge in the ruins, and, with the dogged heroism characteristic of the Indian race, resisted to the last.

On June 29 Sir H. Rose placed the command of the army in the hands of Brigadier Napier, and set out for Bombay, after successfully conducting one of the most brilliant campaigns that any general can boast of. At the head of two small brigades he had traversed Central India from the banks of the Sipri to those of the Jumna, meeting at every step with an enemy ten times superior in number, with citadels which were at least formidable from their natural defences, and with populous towns animated by the most hostile sentiments. Besides all this, the climate from the very beginning had thrown almost insurmountable obstacles in his way. Everywhere, and always, victory had been on his side; everywhere and always he had changed defeat of the enemy into a complete rout by the rapidity and the determination of his movements. After five months of daily fighting, the English flag at last floated on the walls of Calpi, and the object of the campaign seemed attained, when the revolt of Scindiah's troops compromised the results of so much labour and hardship. Sir H. Rose's military talents, ever fertile in resources, did not fail him in this emergency, and by immediately taking the field, with exhausted and badly-equipped troops, he prevented Gwalior from becoming a second Delhi, and receiving into its walls all the malcontents of India. By his capacity for enduring fatigue, by his presence in the very thick of the battle, by his care for his soldiers, he succeeded in winning from them the most boundless devotion, and his name deserves a foremost place among those of Anglo-Indian captains. Once again fortunate England—and here we may be allowed a feeling of envy—had put the right man in the right place by entrusting to a military diplomatist the command of the adventurous expedition sent against Central India.

In June 1858 a year had scarcely elapsed since the outbreak of the mutiny, and though the smouldering embers still emitted flames, no serious conflagration was to be feared. In Bengal, in Central India, and in the North-West Provinces, the sepoys no longer existed as an organised army; they had disappeared without a single military genius of any sort having appeared in their ranks, and without showing any conspicuous bravery on the battle-field, with the exception of some few picked regiments. The principal leaders who still resisted, Tantia Topee, Beni Madho, Prince Firoz-Shah, and the Begum of Oude, now only thought of saving their heads from the vengeance of the conquerors.

Thousands of bewildered fugitives were scattered over the country, attacking small forts, and disappearing on the approach of the first horseman sent in pursuit. After the capture of Calpi and Gwalior, deep discouragement fell upon the rebels, who saw themselves threatened on all sides. A new enemy now appeared: the vanquished carried about with them in their belts and turbans the rich spoils of Jansi, Calpi, and Gwalior, and the rapacious inhabitants attacked these richly laden vagabonds who neither dared to fight, to halt, nor to disperse.

In all the vast extent of India, the kingdom of Oude alone had not yet acknowledged European supremacy. The capital, it is true, was in the hands of the English. Communications were secured by a chain of military posts, and before the rains had made the country impracticable even to the natives, the English columns scoured it in every direction. But a deep feeling of hostility existed among the inhabitants, whose proud and warlike character and sincere attachment to their feudal institutions predisposed them to try the chances of a guerilla warfare. It was necessary, in order to secure a lasting peace, not only to conquer the country, but also to occupy it militarily, diminish the power of the great chieftains, and disarm the population. The task reserved for the English army was more wearisome than dangerous. Nothing was to be feared from the enemy in the open field. The only checks to be apprehended in the multifarious operations which would necessarily follow, even when carried on in the heart of unexplored districts, would be checks due to imprudence or want of skill, as in the expeditions of Rhadamoa and Indgespore.

The lessons of experience clearly pointed out the way to avoid danger in the future, and to prevent the respite afforded by the rainy season from being used to recruit and organise the rebel forces. It was of the highest importance to let it be known by all, chiefs and soldiers, that the war was no longer one of dispossession and extermination, and that all means of safety were not denied to them. The English authorities were fully alive to the exigencies of the moment. We have already had occasion to notice the revulsion of feeling that had taken place in England on the question of India. The secret instructions of the Court of Directors, couched in a spirit of moderation, if not of clemency, fully in harmony with the kindly dispositions of Lord Canning, provoked no serious opposition among high Indian functionaries. Even in the army itself there was no longer any very fervent wish to prolong a contest where no mercy was shown to the conquered and no glory redounded to the conquerors. With the exception of a few fanatics, all the authorities, civil and military, began faintly to grasp the immense distance which separates assassins from rebellious but honourably-minded men, and ignorant soldiers from rebellious leaders. Political good sense was making itself heard, and people began to feel that though in the eyes of Asiatics clemency borders closely on weakness, there are yet certain thorny situations in which to pursue a war of extermination to the bitter end and to exasperate one's adversaries by merciless punishments, is both a mistake and a crime.

This conciliatory policy found an able interpreter in the new Commissioner-General of the kingdom, a man admirably fitted to carry it out. Skilled in the management of the natives, Sir R. Montgomery took advantage of the respite furnished by the rainy season to soothe and propitiate them. Some landowners, important from their birth and their wealth, came to make their peace at Lucknow; others, in their secret correspondence, made it clear that they were only held back from imitating their example by the fear of violence from their neighbours. Dissensions broke out among the mutineers, and one of their most formidable leaders fell in an insignificant quarrel. The Moulvie was shot in an encounter with the partisans of the Rajah of Powayne. The victor is said to have cut off his enemy's head, and sent it to the nearest English commissioner with a request for the promised reward. By a curious piece of trickery the price of blood was withheld, because the Rajah was already dead before the head was cut off.

In the midst of all these negotiations, and whilst small expeditions, which were generally successful, were going on, the rainy season came to a close, and the moment for resuming active operations arrived. Before Sir C. Campbell reappeared at the head of his troops an important event had been chronicled by contemporary history. We allude to the substitution of the Queen's Government for that of the East India Company. We shall be able more fully to appreciate this change by studying the reforms, not very considerable, however, introduced into Anglo-Indian institutions by the vote of Parliament. For the moment, we shall confine ourselves to saying a few words regarding the effect produced on the native population by the nominal change of rulers.

The proclamation in which Queen Victoria announced to her new subjects that she was about to assume the sceptre of India heretofore wielded by the Honourable Company was worthy of the sovereign of the great nation, which as yet, alas, is the only one in Europe capable of reconciling respect for the past with liberal institutions. Certain parts of the preamble to the new charter of India were calculated to please and conciliate the natives. All thought of future aggrandisement was formally disavowed. All treaties and engagements, all the rights of the native princes, were to be scrupulously respected. A Government which was swayed by feelings of pure Christianity could not but have broad notions of religious toleration, and extend an impartial protection to all sects. Her Majesty's representatives bound themselves to respect the rights of the natives, especially that of property, so dear to a people like the Indians, who think so much of living and dying on the paternal acres. Liberal conditions of pardon, more liberal than those mentioned in Lord Canning's proclamation, were offered to all who would lay down their arms before the end of the year. 'May the Almighty God grant to us and to our representatives the strength to carry out the wishes which we make from the bottom of our heart for the well-being and prosperity of our Indian people.' So said, with touching modesty, the pacific conqueror to whom her faithful Parliament had just offered 150 millions of new subjects.

On November 1, 1858, a memorable date in modern annals, Queen Victoria's proclamation, translated into twenty languages, promulgated simultaneously in the great centres and in the remotest stations of the vast empire, announced that the Bill of the Parliament had come into force. Universal rejoicings took place on that day from Cape Comorin to the heights of the Himalaya; prayers were offered alike in churches, temples, mosques and pagodas; salvoes of artillery were fired; the military bands played their most joyous airs, and military displays were general. In the port of Bombay, on the Indus, the Ganges, the Irrawaddy, hundreds of ships were gaily decked with flags. In the evening, the accession of Queen Victoria to the throne of the Great Mogul, and the last day of the Honourable East India Company's rule, were celebrated by banquets, followed by many toasts and copious libations, by brilliant illuminations, and by fireworks. These proofs of loyalty, given by the European community to a beloved sovereign, were also an expression of triumph after a struggle for life and death which had lasted more than a year.

The native population made fewer demonstrations, and only the enlightened spirits among them understood the real meaning of the great political change they were witnessing. Having been accustomed to the rule of invisible masters secluded in the depths of the harem, the Indians had never comprehended the mechanism of the foreign Power whose yoke they bore. We think we are justified in stating that the defunct Company, whose magnificent funerals had just taken place, had always been thought of by the great majority of its subjects as an antiquated Begum, living in grand style beyond the seas. The Begum had paid her debt to nature; there was no reason for rejoicing or for wonder. But change and novelties are as attractive to the Indian as to the European. The actual sovereign engaged in the most solemn terms to respect the rights and religion of her new subjects, she offered a full pardon to the rebels who had not yet laid down their arms. Her reign opened directly after a terrible struggle, in which European authority had asserted itself on a hundred battle-fields; the native press, the public orators, and addresses covered with thousands of signatures welcomed simultaneously the august heiress of the East India Company.

After being present at the ceremony of November 1, by the side of the Governor-General, Sir C. Campbell lost no time in resuming the offensive, and left the same evening to take the chief command of the several expeditions intended to re-establish definitively European supremacy in Oude. The main body left Beylah on November 8. It was provided with considerable supplies for siege operations, with a view of shedding as little English blood as possible in the reduction of the petty forts that were to be met with at every step. Other columns, under Brigadiers Troup, Walpole, and Hope Grant, were to act in concert with Sir Colin, and combine their movements so as to enclose the insurgents in a circle of iron.

The great war was over; and a detailed account of the marches and counter-marches of the troops in pursuit of an invisible enemy would offer little interest. The most renowned strongholds fell in a few hours under the fire of Sir Colin's guns, but an impenetrable jungle was within easy reach of the ramparts, and the darkness of night favoured the retreat of the garrisons. In the morning, the only trophies remaining to the English were battered buildings, a few unserviceable pieces of artillery, and some provisions. The leaders would often at the last moment betake themselves by one gate to the English camp, in the hope of saving their life and treasures, whilst, by the opposite one, the entire garrison would hurry to join the standard of the nearest chief. The natives, who were masters in the art of deceit, sought to gain time by feigning to negotiate. The son of Beni Madho, one of the most determined opponents of English rule, wrote to head-quarters, disavowing his father's conduct, and claiming the latter's confiscated lands for himself. The population was evidently in heart on the side of its hereditary masters. On the approach of the foreign columns, the villagers fled from their houses; the most vague, the most contradictory information was supplied to the staff. How strange was the attachment of these poor creatures to rulers who had never known any law but that of their own passions and interests!

All material advantages were on the side of the English. Their absolute supremacy was enforced in the neighbouring villages by detachments of police and troops; little by little order was re-established; the taxes began to be collected; the most prominent leaders, such as the Rajah of Anrethie, Man Singh, and his brother, Rutber Singh, made their submission. All armed bands had retired from the districts on the left bank of the Ganges. Towards the end of November Beni Madho and his many thousand partisans were driven by main force from the fortress of Dondla Khera, a highly venerated sanctuary on the banks of the sacred river, which he had sworn to defend to the death; but the wily fugitive left no trace of his flight. The reports of the spies affirmed that he had been seen at the same day and at the same hour in four different places. The first object of the expedition was now accomplished, and Sir Colin Campbell marched on Lucknow. Though the losses inflicted by the enemy were light, yet the endurance of the soldiers had been severely tried; for several days in succession they had to march twenty-four miles at a stretch.

In the beginning of December, more reliable and circumstantial information was forthcoming. It was ascertained that Beni Madho had taken refuge in the district of Bareitch, on the confines of Nepaul, and that the Begum of Oude and the infamous Nana Sahib were in his camp, sharing his good and evil fortunes. The hope of at length seizing the author of the Cawnpore massacre revived the general courage, and the pursuit was undertaken with immense ardour, but the most secretly planned expeditions, the boldest enterprises resulted in failures. A rear-guard in full retreat, which soon disappeared in the direction of the unhealthy territory of Nepaul, was just caught sight of and nothing more. The difficulties of the ground and the complicity of the peasants placed insurmountable obstacles in the way. The limits of the known world seemed to have been reached. Maps and guides were both wanting; two or three English officers, formerly in the service of the King of Oude, had a few years previously ridden through the scarcely inhabited country, but they knew absolutely nothing of its topography. It was necessary to make one's way through swamps and torrents, over precipices and through primæval forests, where traces of wild beasts were to be met with at every step.

On December 25, the English forces celebrated their Christmas in sight of the glaciers of the Himalaya; the Dhawalaghiry, and Mount Everest, the highest peak in the world, were visible on the horizon, some leagues off, while the enemy, who refused either to fight or to submit, was making for the neutral territory of Nepaul. A romantic episode ended this romantic campaign. On the last day of the year, certain information was received that Beni Madho and his allies were encamped a short distance from the Rapti, a river separating Oude from Nepaul; and Sir C. Campbell could not refrain from attempting a surprise. That evening, the entire camp was set in motion; 150 elephants, intended to carry five foot soldiers each, were standing ready to start; a battery of horse artillery and the entire force of cavalry completed the expedition. A lantern borne by the elephant at the head of the column was to direct the march in the midst of darkness. Sir C. Campbell, who had been seriously hurt a few days previously by a fall from his horse, insisted nevertheless on taking the command himself. All these efforts proved fruitless: the wily chieftain escaped once more from his adversaries. Next morning, the Hussars alone succeeded in overtaking the last of the enemy's cavalry, as they were crossing the Rapti, and in exchanging sabre cuts and pistol shots in single combats with the Begum of Oude's sowars. The rebels managed to reach the territory of Nepaul, and once there, they could afford to rest in relative security till the native government should grant permission to pursue them.

Sir Jang Bahadour was not chivalrous enough to take in hand the cause even of his own race, when it was hopeless, and on hearing of the treasures the chiefs carried with them on their wanderings, he soon sent his troops in pursuit. In the early part of February an English brigade, after following the fugitives without intermission through the wildest parts of Nepaul, took from them their last guns, fifteen in number. Beni Madho was soon afterwards killed in an encounter with the Nepaulese forces. By the month of April the armed bands were entirely destroyed. Those among them who refused to lay down their arms, perished by fever or by hunger. The Nana and his brother succeeded in eluding the vengeance of the English, but they are both supposed to have been carried off by illness in 1859.[1] The English

[1] At the time of going to press, the last news from Calcutta announces that the prisoner taken at Gwalior, whose capture excited such interest and curiosity both in India and in Europe, is not the real Nana Sahib. The fate of the arch-murderer is still enveloped in mystery, as is shown by the following letter:—

'Sir—In your paper of Monday, the 16th, you have quoted from the *Delhi Gazette* a statement made by one Sheodul Singh, who died a year ago, at his native village in the Azimgurh district, that Nana Dhundut Punh died of Serai fever in the Nepaul jungles, and that he (Sheodul) was one of the number who took part in the performance of the funeral obsequies. Sheodul Singh may very possibly have done this, for the personal obsequies were duly performed with all the usual ceremonies; but, nevertheless, Nana did not die—his funeral obsequies were a feint. In the autumn of 1859, Nana was encamped with his brother Bala Bao and Debi Bux Singh, the ex-Rajah of Gonda, and with a considerable army under his command, at the foot of the Nepaul mountains, near the entrance of a pass. There they remained for some time, but at length the movement of the British troops in search of them rendering their position dangerous, they broke up their camp, and, entering the pass, retreated entirely through Nepaul, until they arrived within the confines of Chinese territory. They then fixed their quarters, after crossing a large river, at a village or town named Tharwaria, close upon the frontier. Before they left the plains, however, the three chiefs had their funeral rites performed, lest, as they gave out, they should never return to the Holy Ground of Hindustan. This gave rise to the report which prevailed very universally at that time, but which was not believed by the inhabitants of our own provinces, who were in the habit of passing to and from Nepaul, and with whom I came in frequent contact, that Nana was dead. My informant was a man who was taken prisoner

had the good sense to cease the pursuit of a mother who had but defended the legitimate or fictitious rights of her son, and the Begum of Oude was allowed to live at Khatmandou, the capital of Oude, without being further disturbed.

The remainder of the insurgents on the right bank of the Ganges were as hardly treated by fortune as those on the left bank. After his defeat at Gwalior, Tantia Topee escaped for a long time from the numerous columns sent in pursuit of him, and even the defection of the Rajah of Bandah and of other powerful chieftains, who had hitherto adhered to the cause of the mutineers, did not shake his courage; and for many months, in company with his lieutenant Man Singh, of Gwalior, he pursued his vagrant course in the most widely separated districts of Central India, from Gujerat to Jeypore, from Jeypore to the neighbourhood of Agra. Treachery finally triumphed over his inexhaustible resources. Man Singh made his submission in April 1859 to Major Meade, and, in order to save his head, betrayed the secret of his leader's hiding-place. After a few days' confinement, Tantia Topee was brought before a court-martial, and executed on April 15, 1859, at Sipri. The calmness of the Indian chief did not fail, either during the trial or at the moment of death, and he died with heroic courage. Though we quite admit that, with the certain proofs of his complicity in the massacre of Cawnpore before them, the authorities could not do otherwise than to condemn him to death, we must none the less pay a tribute of admiration to

by a party of the Nana's scouts in November 1859, and carried off to the camp, where he was kept in irons. Being of a good caste, he was employed in menial offices about the person of the chiefs, and accompanied them in their march through the mountains. In June 1860, aided by some of the natives in the country, he made his escape, and returned to his own house, a few miles on the British side of the Nepaul frontier, leaving Nana Sahib safe within the Chinese territory and in perfect health. The description given by the man of the nature of the Chinese boundary, and of the dress and appearance of the inhabitants, was, I was informed by good authority, quite correct. A curious part of the man's statement, and one that may be of importance in the inquiry now going forward, was that the chiefs at the time of performing the funeral rite each cut off a finger, and that these little members were burned and the funeral obsequies solemnly performed over them as representatives of their whole bodies.—B.——, Calcutta, November 19, 1874. To the Editor of the *Englishman*.'

this truly remarkable character. At Cawnpore, on the Betwa, at Kounch, Calpi, and Gwalior, Tantia Topee gave indications of a political genius, full of audacity and fertile in expedients. If he can be reproached with holding aloof from the battlefield, his courage at the last showed that death possessed no terrors for him.

By January 1859 the work of repression was completely finished, and in the whole extent of India there was no enemy capable of exciting the alarm of the European authorities. The Anglo-Indian empire had, we must acknowledge, proved both its strength and its resources; Delhi had fallen, Havelock and Outram had relieved the garrison of Lucknow, before a single soldier or officer sent from England had disembarked on Indian soil. Sir Colin Campbell, however, played a glorious part in the events which followed, and fully deserved the elevation to the peerage, with the title of Lord Clyde, with which a grateful Government rewarded his services. When he arrived at Calcutta, in September 1857, final success entirely depended on the military talents of the new Commander-in-Chief; a single false step, or even a partial success, might once again compromise the fate of India. No fault, no imprudence was committed by Sir C. Campbell, and if he can be reproached with slowness at the outset, we must take into consideration the difficulty of acting with precision under the circumstances. The climate, the immense distances, and the fact that he was a free agent neither as regarded time nor the scene of operation, were all against him. The Lucknow Residency had to be relieved at any price. A delay, even of a few days, might have occasioned a second Cawnpore massacre. Sir C. Campbell's first efforts were crowned by victory, the trophies being the women and children whom he rescued from the ruins of the Residency, and whose fate Europe was watching with the most painful anxiety. The occupation of the Doab, the second expedition against Lucknow, the taking of Bareilly and the last campaign in Oude, commanded by the General-in-Chief in person, were accomplished without a single serious check. Though neither at Lucknow nor at

Bareilly were the effective forces of the insurrection destroyed at a single stroke, the blows dealt were none the less mortal. In the multifarious operations he was obliged to carry out, Sir C. Campbell did not perhaps always estimate his own strength and the weakness of his adversaries at their true value. But before criticising the methodical prudence which characterised all his proceedings, we must remember that he was not sent to India to play the part of a guerilla leader, who is always expected to risk his life and his cause. His position was a higher one. As General-in-Chief, he had to direct the movements of a great regular army, and his first duty was, above all, to place nothing at the mercy of chance. What mattered the greater or less duration of the conflict, if success was eventually to follow! The prudence which marked all Sir C. Campbell's plans was as conspicuous in the open field as in the sieges of towns and in the heat of battle. Full of the most paternal solicitude for his men, he invariably spared his battalions by a judicious use of his artillery. His second expedition against Lucknow (March 1858), in which, by the employment of heavy guns, he reduced a town of more than half a million souls in eight days with inconsiderable loss to himself, a town defended by every resource which despair could suggest to the enemy, may be considered a model of street-fighting. If one is to judge of the merits of a leader by the severity of blows he dealt to his adversaries, Sir C. Campbell would rank among the most illustrious captains of history. Never were any enemy, any mercenaries guilty of violating the code of military honour, punished more unsparingly than were the sepoys of the Bengal Army.

By January 1859, the cadres of this once powerful organisation only contained a small number of disarmed regiments, closely watched by powerful European garrisons. The remainder had disappeared in the storm, leaving no living traces, but a few hundred native soldiers, who had been transported to the Andaman Islands, two or three thousand prisoners in the gaols of India, and five or six thousand sepoys who, by good luck, by chance, or by unusual clemency on the part of the victors, had succeeded in reaching their homes or losing themselves in the mass of the native population. The number of native soldiers and officers belonging to the Bengal Army or to the various contingents, who in little less than a year fell on the battlefield, were executed, or perished by wounds, privations, or illness, can be computed at more than 120,000. It is impossible to give any approximate idea of the losses sustained by the native population which took part in the struggle, and it would be below the truth to estimate these losses at the same figure as those of the sepoys. More than 200,000 natives forfeited their lives in consequence of the risings at Mirut and at Delhi. Yet even confronted by this vast loss of lives, and these streams of human blood, impartial history must still recognise that India did not pay too dearly for the triumph of the foreign rulers, who alone could give her order, peace, and progress.

CHAPTER XI.

CAUSES OF THE MUTINY—END OF THE EAST INDIA COMPANY—THE NEW CHARTER OF INDIA.

Attitude of the Anglo-Indian population during the crisis—The native population and the Mutiny—Causes of the Mutiny—Retrospective glance on the East India Company—Unpopularity of the Company in England—The new Bill relative to India before Parliament—Religious ferment in England—Reforms in the military institutions of India—The Staff Corps—The India Council—The Legislative Council—The High Courts—Rewards granted to native princes—The finances of India—The problem of castes.

BEFORE summing up the causes which produced the Mutiny, and the changes in the government which followed, we must pay a just tribute to the noble conduct of the European population during this memorable crisis. The history of India in 1857 offers a strange and terrible phenomenon. In a single day the work of a hundred years was overturned by the revolutionary storm. A formidable army, in which not only crime but indiscipline was unknown, abjured in a few hours the laws of military honour, stained its weapons with the blood of its officers, their wives and children, and turned the undisputed masters of yesterday into the proscribed of to-day. European families who had retired to rest at night under the care of obsequious servants, found themselves, on awaking, surrounded by ferocious enemies. Roads and by-ways, on which a woman or a young girl had hitherto been able to travel in all security, became infested with rapacious and blood-thirsty marauders. Without previous warning, without preparation, a few handfuls of English, lost in the heart of India, far from all help, were exposed for months to mortal dangers. Everywhere the storm was valiantly withstood; and here we do not allude to the Cannings, the

Lawrences, the Outrams, the Nicholsons, the statesmen or the soldiers who won for themselves undying glory, but to the English *bourgeoisie*, if we may use this term, whom necessity had scattered over India in the public service or in undertakings of a private nature, to the almost defenceless communities, who for many weary, heart-breaking days were surrounded on all sides by thousands of sepoys, aided by the scum of the great towns and the riffraff of the prisons, to the modest officers, planters, railway engineers, whose courage and presence of mind often averted an impending outbreak. At Cawnpore, at Saugor, at Lucknow, men, women, and children braved all the horrors of a long siege and a pitiless warfare with the most heroic energy. Facts like these, which were of daily occurrence, speak eloquently in praise of that branch of the Anglo-Saxon race inhabiting India. this terrible juncture, civil and military authorities, officers, soldiers, planters, merchants, women and children, all did their duty, and deserved well of their country. Never before had the superiority of the white man over the black, of the Caucasian over the Asiatic race, asserted itself so triumphantly.

To what degree did the native population take part in the struggle, to which side their hopes and wishes incline? Difficult though the problem be, we shall attempt to solve it, at least approximately. If it is difficult to form a correct idea of public opinion among the compact and enlightened nations of Europe in moments of great political excitement, it is far more so in India, where the population is an aggregation, not a fusion of races. Religious affinities, which alone unite the inhabitants of the vast Indian continent, scarcely soften down the characteristic differences between them. The Moslem of Oude is quite as distinct from the Moslem of Bengal as the Turk is from the Greek, and the Hindoo of Amritsur from his co-religionist of Benares, as the Frenchman from the German. Without passing the bounds of probabilities, we may safely assert that the Hindoos felt towards their foreign rulers those feelings of jealousy, if not of hatred, which always exist between the weak and the strong, the conquered and the conqueror. Further than this we will not go.

In fact, in this strange land patriotism does not exist; the feeling of nationality, of independence finds no echo in the population. The political notions of the Indian, which conceive nothing higher than mere despotism, are the same from the sovereign to the humblest subject. Whether from apathy or resignation, each man is satisfied with his lot, and, desirous of no change, obeys the master whom Providence has set over him, whatever be his creed or the colour of his skin. The fanaticism and bloodthirstiness of which the adepts of the Koran gave so many proofs during the struggle can easily be explained. Before the conquest of India, the sons of the Prophet had never submitted to Christian and for the first time they had to bend their necks to the yoke in a land where everything reminded them of the recent and now vanished glory of their race. Is it to be wondered at that they could not forget their degradation, and should have attempted one last effort to rid themselves of masters separated from them by every distinguishing characteristic: religion, custom, and colour?

English supremacy in India is maintained under circumstances almost unknown in history. The nineteenth century alone has seen sixty or eighty thousand foreigners impose their laws on two hundred millions of subjects, with whom they have no social connection, and whom they govern merely by the superiority of civilisation over barbarism. It was far otherwise in the days of the Mogul conquerors, whose inheritance has been seized by the English. The victorious Moslems accepted up to a certain point the customs and laws of the vanquished Hindoos. India became their second country, in which they made their home. Marriages between the various royal families united different creeds on the throne. Hindoo ministers became the depositaries of the power of the Moslem princes, and *vice versâ*. The outburst of religious passions and persecutions, it is true, often gave expression to the antagonism of races, but a calm soon followed the storm, and peace was speedily restored at least on the surface. The magnificent ruins, which still attest the grandeur of the Mogul Empire, reveal the love of the conquerors for their adopted country.

English rule follows a diametrically opposite policy. The European master carefully preserves his nationality in all its exclusiveness, has no points of contact with his subjects, and is separated by an impassable barrier from the natives he has despoiled. He knows nothing of the interior life of his very servants—their hut is a sacred spot, whose threshold none dare cross. In the large towns, the native banker, if he is wealthy, possesses, it is true, a fine house adorned with every European luxury—pianos, bronzes, and pictures—where, from time to time, he offers to the European community nautch-dances or banquets, of which he never partakes. Nevertheless, he himself dwells in a hut, sleeps on a pallet-bed, and eats with his fingers, as did his forefathers. The gulf is still more perceptible in the country, where the great landowners and the foreign authorities only meet on rare occasions at hunting-parties. In this way, England loses a most important element of governmental strength.

Formerly, the Mohammedan dynasties rewarded those who deserved well of the Empire by gifts of fiefs and lands, and common interests bound the great territorial nobles to the Court of Delhi. Now, humiliated when not crushed by the levelling character of English rule, the native aristocracy has no motives, either of gratitude or of self-interest, for supporting the Government. Outside public or private business, both in the great centres and in the provinces, the white population only mixes with the higher native classes at nautch-shows, at sports, or at evening promenades. As to the lower strata of society—the masses—they know nothing of their rulers, and scarcely differ in any way from their primitive ancestors. As we have often said, the beliefs and customs of Europe have not penetrated into the native community, and modern civilisation has passed over the soil of India without making any impression on it, as the sun's rays pass over the earth.

Even taking into consideration the many divergencies between the English and the natives, the Mutiny of 1857 cannot be called a national movement in the full sense of the word. The semi-independent states of Central India, the North-West Provinces and the Kingdom of Oude, from which chiefly the Bengal Army was recruited, alone took an active share in the insurrection. The population of Bengal, of Madras, and of Bombay remained neutral, almost indifferent, and only bandits and thieves joined the rebels. The inhabitants of the Punjab rose as one man to fight for England; the veteran Sikh regiments, strengthened by fresh levies, covered themselves with glory at the siege of Delhi. Lastly, though the observance of treaties is not a distinguishing feature of the Indian race, the native princes, who still possessed considerable political power, adhered almost all with remarkable steadfastness to the English cause. Under the influence of his minister, Salar Jung, the Nizam maintained order in his dominions, and preserved the Presidency of Madras from the spread of disaffection. Holkar and Scindiah steadfastly resisted the threats of their own soldiers, who had raised the standard of revolt. The Rajah of Pattyalah, and the other chieftains of the confederate Sikh States, made common cause from the outset with the Anglo-Indian authorities, and placed troops and treasure at their disposal. Nepaul took an active, if not decisive, part in the third expedition against Lucknow. Facts of this kind prove that the events of 1857 had nothing of the character of a patriotic movement, and that the Mutiny had no claim to be considered a war of independence. Had it been otherwise, had India's two hundred million inhabitants risen in one and the same spirit of revolt against their invaders, the European population would have perished down to the last child in less than a month, overwhelmed by the multitude of their assailants.

Are we to connect the Mutiny with the religious prejudices of the sepoys, and admit that, alarmed at the progress of Christianity, they took up arms to defend their faith, which they believed to be seriously threatened? If the fear of an enforced and speedy conversion had really been the reason which roused the soldiers of the Bengal Army, the Mutiny would have soon spread to the army of Bombay, and especially to that of Madras. The Presidency of Madras is the one in which the Christian propagandism is most successful, and where the greatest number of converts are made. The strength of religious passions is such amongst Indians that the movement would have assumed a national character, which it never did. It is quite as fallacious to ascribe the crisis to the intrigues of the native princes. The thousand inquiries, instituted after the English victory, brought to light neither documents nor correspondence to justify the belief in dark plots between the native courts and the rebellious regiments. It results from all this that the latent state of indiscipline of the Bengal Army, and a mad panic produced by the spirit of caste, are the only assignable causes of the outbreak of the Mutiny in the first instance.

Formerly, caste was the basis of Indian law and religion; now caste has become all-powerful, and absorbs both law and religion. Nothing can be well imagined more subversive of discipline than the influence of the Brahmins, as it made itself felt for many years in the ranks of the Bengal Army. We may well be surprised that any military institutions should have resisted this radical source of weakness for the space of a century. In the eyes of his comrades in the regiment, a Brahmin is not only a man of illustrious blood, whom a caprice of fate has placed in the ranks, but a superior being whose favour they court and whose anger they dread. The relations between a native officer and a high caste soldier are still more difficult. How dare the former give orders to or inflict punishment on this living incarnation of Brahma, at whose feet he prostrates himself, and who, by a word, may condemn him to everlasting torments? As to the European officer, Brahminical doctrines assign him a social rank far inferior to that of the most degraded Indian, lower even than the street-sweeper or the corpse-bearer: his breath, his very shadow pollutes the men over whom he exercises paramount authority! If we remember that this sacred order has wielded supreme authority in India for two thousand years, in spite of revolutions and dynastic changes; that its members are united among themselves by the indissoluble bonds of hierarchical order, and by the fraternity of the clan, it is not difficult to perceive that a horrible explosion would one day necessarily result from the many inflammable materials existing in the ranks of the Bengal sepoys. The introduction of greased cartridges into the army was the spark which fired this formidable mine. The annals of India are not the only ones which record unlikely events, currents of error and madness which, at certain fatal periods, overwhelm our poor humanity! Does not European history relate that, out of a reformist banquet of small *bourgeois*, there arose a movement which, in 1848, swallowed up one respected throne, and threatened others at Berlin and Vienna?

The terrors of the spirit of caste are the only adequate explanation of the mixture of passion and weakness which characterised the Mutiny. Instantaneous outbreaks occasionally take place in bodies which have long been ready for the infection of poison. In others, on the contrary, its action becomes apparent but slowly, and slight external circumstances suffice to arrest its progress. The Bombay and Madras armies, where military discipline triumphed over the spirit of caste, escaped the contagion. On the other hand, some regiments which had remained faithful under trying circumstances suddenly gave way to temptation, as if under the influence of a sort of malaria, mutinying at the very time when success was impossible, and when revolt could only lead to dishonour and death. A panic is a disease which spreads of itself, and against which there is no remedy but uprightness and firmness of character. Lord Canning and his skilful coadjutors had the merit of discerning the real state of things: they perceived that India, as a whole, was not imbued with the spirit of disaffection, and that, without laying themselves open to the accusation of folly or credulity, trust might be placed in certain portions of the population. In the Punjab, Sir John Lawrence, who was intimately acquainted with the national character, did not give his Sikh regiments time to be corrupted by idleness, but kept them in the path of duty by the energy and opportuneness of his measures. He sent off his Punjab auxiliaries to Delhi, whether veteran soldiers or new levies, with as much apparent security as if they had been English troops. His confidence was amply justified, and during the whole siege the Sikhs showed the firmest zeal and loyalty. There can be no doubt that without the assistance of these valiant allies the European forces, tried as they were by the murderous climate, could not have succeeded in their task. If, instead of obeying this inspiration of genius, the impulse of fear and anger had been allowed to triumph, the struggle would speedily have become a war of races, and an impassable gulf, which neither bloodshed nor multitudes of victims could have bridged over, would have separated for ever the English from their subjects. The statesmen who understood the real nature of the Mutiny, and saw clearly that the question was not one of national independence nor of religion, but exclusively one of caste, earned thereby imperishable rights to the gratitude of England. In order to clear up all doubts on the subject, we shall here give a summary of the declaration made before a Parliamentary Commission by one of the most prominent actors in the insurrection.

'The Mutiny,' says Sir J. Lawrence, 'was the explosion of fanatical passions in a demoralised army, and at once attracted to itself all the impure discontented elements of the country. Nowhere was it a war of religion or of race. It is noticeable that the native troops took part in all the operations which followed the outbreak at Mirut. Another native element was substituted for the insurgent regiments, and the names of the new levies showed the extent and the resources of the Anglo-Indian Government—Theend's Horse, Moultanee Horse, Punjab Guides, &c., &c. And we may venture to say that England's power over the races of India received a new and brilliant confirmation by the events of 1857. As to the King of Delhi, whatever part he took in subsequent proceedings, nothing shows that he had entered into a serious conspiracy, intended to cause the revolt of the

Bengal Army. The Mutiny is the work of the army, and it cannot be attributed to anterior and external intrigues, though ambitious and discontented persons made use of it for their own purposes. The deciding cause of the Mutiny was the introduction of greased cartridges; the examination of several hundred letters written by or to sepoys leaves no doubt on this point.'

Whatever was the nature and the cause of the Mutiny of 1857, the East India Company was not destined to survive it. Up to that time the concerns of India had never excited much interest in England. The loquacious traveller, newly disembarked from a Peninsular and Oriental steamer, amply satisfied the curiosity of his audience in a single afternoon by the recital of some bits of family news, the description of a tiger hunt, or by the communication of a few culinary recipes. To this apathy succeeded, almost without transition, the most feverish, the most devouring anxiety. England, maddened by the terrible occurrences in India, gave way to incoherent transports of rage and despair, and the whole burden of this anger fell, in the last instance, on the ancient corporation which, in name at least, was responsible for recent events. The public voice unanimously demanded that the Government of India should be withdrawn from such unskilful and feeble hands, and we have seen that the reign of Queen Victoria was inaugurated in India on November 1, 1858. Whilst considering the dethronement of the East India Company, the impartial observer cannot but remember the glorious part it has played in modern history, and it will not be out of place to examine a little the accusations which caused its fall.

The obvious fact which appears in every page of these sketches is surely this: that English rule in India can only be maintained by the help of a force at once imposing and devoted, differing from the native population in customs, language, and belief, and occupying all the strategic positions of the country. Now, we must remember that the year before the Mutiny, the Home Government, hard pressed by the needs of the Crimean war, had reduced the effective forces of the Royal Army in India lower than they had been in the early part of the century, and this in spite of the immense increase of annexed territory, and against the energetic protests of the Court of Directors. Just before the outbreak there were scarcely 3,000 European soldiers to be found in the North-West Provinces, Oude and Bengal taken together. Hence the necessary counterpoise to the sepoys and the indigenous population was wanting, and a few days were sufficient to sweep away the last vestige of British power. In the Punjab, on the contrary, after a short struggle, victory remained with the representatives of the Company. The spirit of disaffection among the sepoys was not less rife at Lahore than at Delhi, but in Ranjit Singh's former kingdom more than 10,000 European soldiers were quartered in the neighbouring stations of Peshawur, Lahore, Sialkote, and these imposing forces were equal to the task of repressing the revolt.

At the same time that we do full justice to the skill and the indefatigable energy with which Sir John Lawrence and his staff carried out the work of repression in the Punjab, it is impossible not to ascribe the greater part of their success to the number of soldiers at their disposal. This indisputable fact warrants our saying that if the authorities of Oude and of the North-West Provinces had had at their command a certain number of English regiments, the spirit of disaffection would have remained latent among the native forces stationed at Delhi and Lucknow, and that, if any outbreak had occurred, the sepoys' triumph would have been of short duration.

Is it not equally unjust to throw the exclusive blame of the immense expansion given to the Anglo-Indian territory during the last twenty years on the rapacity and ambition of the Company?

It is a difficult matter to believe that all the statesmen who contributed to the formation of the Indian Empire obeyed the same impulse and followed identically the same system with the same success. Yet history proves that all their labours have had the same result. Clive, Warren

Hastings, Wellesley, Bentinck, Dalhousie, all added a certain number of provinces to the original possessions of the Company. The identity of the results reveals a deep-seated permanent cause stronger than the will of statesmen, which has constrained them to alter their individual opinions, and has furnished unexpected, and often little desired, solutions to the problems they were called upon to solve. In the interest of truth, and at the risk of wounding prejudices popular even in England, we here intend to take a retrospective glance at the conditions under which less than ten years before the annexation of the Punjab, England's firmest ally in the crisis of 1857, had taken place.

The kingdom founded by Ranjit Singh on the right bank of the Sutlej, far from exciting the jealousy of its European neighbours, was the object, on their part, of a sympathy which is easy to explain. Under the impression that the most formidable dangers which might at any moment threaten the empire would come from the north and from the vigorous Mohammedan races on the other side of the Indus, the English statesmen had seen with marked favour the rise of a Hindoo power, forming a natural barrier against the invasions of the mountaineers of the Indian Caucasus and the tribes of Central Asia. The kingdom of Ranjit Singh was the work of one man. After his death, the only vestige of his power was an army left without a hand to rule or a head to guide it; and, against their wish, the English were obliged to treat the heirs of the Lion of the Punjab as they had done the lieutenants of Aureng Zeb's successors. Their goodwill towards the kingdom of Lahore was so real that, when the victory of Sobraon (1846) placed the Punjab at their mercy, the Governor-General preserved by treaty the native government.

The Crown had passed to a child, and the attempts to govern in his name led in 1849 to another dangerous war. Twice had the Sikh power exposed the European masters of India to perils as great as the possible invasions of the Afghans or the Persians, against whom it had been expected to act as a barrier. Here was an additional proof of the short-sightedness of human previsions; the difficulty could only now be solved by cutting the Gordian knot with the sword, and incorporating the Punjab into the Anglo-Indian territory.

This example is a demonstration of the obstacles which constantly hindered the success of the most carefully concerted and thoughtfully considered plans of Anglo-Indian statesmen, and, to a certain degree, exonerates the Company from the accusation of a capricious policy and insatiable ambition. Again, it is quite unfair to reproach the Bengal Government with having caused the mutiny of its native troops by inopportune measures. The introduction of greased cartridges, which proved the final and decisive cause of the outbreak, was rather a fiction cleverly made use of by the disaffected than a reality. Were not these cartridges found in the pouches thrown away by the sepoys on the battle-fields? Only one error, but that a tremendous one, was committed by the Company. Its highest representatives placed too great confidence in an army of mercenaries who, it is true, had been faithful for a century, and its officers failed to discern the spirit of mutiny and rebellion which was smouldering in the ranks. The European conquerors forgot the lessons taught by Oriental history, which at every page exhibits revolted armies overturning powerful empires. The infatuation of civil and military authorities led to one of the greatest catastrophes ever experienced by England, and to the disappearance of the East India Company, even to its name.

The causes of the Mutiny, and the errors for which the Company was justly blamed, had little influence on the hostile sentiments felt towards the latter in England. By a strange effect of the power of words, the scapegoat demanded by public opinion scarcely existed in point of fact. For many years, the share taken by the Company in the government of India had been reduced to the smallest proportions. The modifications made in the original charter during the debates presided over by Pitt had, since 1784, placed all the real management of affairs in the hands of the counsellors of the Crown. The name of the Company was merely retained in the administration of India, in order to deprive the ministers of the means of influence and bribery which they might have found in the patronage of special, civil, and military services. From this time, the paramount authority of the sovereign in the domain of politics was legally established, and the members of the Court of Directors, the highest expression of the Company's power, became mere advisers of the minister, known as the President of the Board of Control. Such unimportant personages were they in reality, that their wishes could easily be overruled by sending secret instructions from the Crown to its agent, the Governor-General.

The political revolution was accomplished, and in all the revisions of the Indian Charter that followed, the changes made were exclusively in the commercial rights still retained by the Company. In 1813, it lost the monopoly of the India trade; in 1833, that of the China trade. At the last renewal of the Charter in 1853, the commercial question was finally settled, and the Bill of the Parliament encroached upon the last privileges of the Company by taking from the Directors the disposal of Civil Service appointments, which henceforth could only be obtained by passing an examination.

The Mutiny cut the thread which, for seventy years, had held the sword of Damocles suspended over the head of this venerable corporation. A blind and insatiable desire for revenge was added to the popular jealousy and instinctive ill-will to which it had been exposed at every important period of its existence. Public opinion, under the influence of a sort of mirage, caused the weight of its anger to fall on the dual government which presided, at least nominally, over the affairs of India. In reality, there only existed the two governments which must always co-exist—the Government of India and the Government of England. The East India Company, as a political power, had collapsed more than fifty years before. No formal recognition of this fact, it is true, had taken place. The acts of the Anglo-Indian authorities were still in its name, and its seal was still affixed to the instructions and orders sent by the President of the Board of Control to his agents beyond sea.

This was enough to cause, though not to justify, the public indignation against the whole system, and to determine the fate of the victim. How was the culprit to be discovered, when responsibility was shared by two bodies? Fictions such as these, anomalies unworthy of a century of progress and order, ought to be abolished. Whigs and Tories, disciples of Exeter Hall and free-thinkers united for once in loudly demanding the dissolution of the Company, and this universal cry of 'Delenda est Carthago' showed that its days were numbered.

In December 1857, a communication from Lord Palmerston, always eager to pander to popular passions, at that time Premier, informed the Court of Directors that a Bill was to be introduced into Parliament with the object of investing the Crown with the immediate government of India. This warning, which indicated their speedy ruin, caused the Court of Directors to abandon the attitude of passive dignity which they had assumed in face of the outbursts of public opinion, and to reply somewhat as follows, in a letter dated December 31.

The Directors expressed their surprise that the Ministry should have taken the initiative of so sweeping a measure, without previously inquiring into the causes of the Mutiny and the errors of the Government. The destruction of a great institution, which had rendered good service in the terrible crisis just passed, had been determined on even before the revolt had been completely suppressed. In spite of the appeals of a rebellious soldiery, the chiefs of the native states had remained loyal, and the mass of the population neutral, if nothing more. Could a more striking testimony have been given to the solidity of, and the benefits conferred by the original institutions? At the opening of Parliament, in February, the first protest was followed by a petition in which all the reasons in favour of the Company were exposed with unexampled clearness.[1]

[1] The petitioners demanded, in the first instance, that an inquiry should be instituted as to their past conduct, the causes of the Mutiny, and the measures taken for its suppression. The most complete harmony had existed between

The document had not long to wait for an answer, and towards the middle of February, Lord Palmerston submitted to Parliament the new Bill for the better government of

the representative of the Crown and the Company. To pretend that a minister could govern more successfully without the help of the Court of Directors was to assert the strange theory that experienced, honest, and responsible advisers hinder the action of authority. It was not less absurd to repair the mistakes of the past, by suppressing the inferior branch which by the very fact of its subordination was the least responsible for official errors. The directors did not wish to decline their share of responsibility in the acts of a well-intentioned government, whose conduct deserved praise, and could fearlessly abide the verdict of history. But it was useless to shut one's eyes to facts, and the threats hurled at the Company were calculated to produce a very bad effect on the native population. The changes proclaimed necessary and opportune by the Ministry would lead to the belief that a radical alteration was contemplated in the existing political system. The people of India might well fear that the new government, ceasing to hold the balance fairly between the various races and religions, might abandon the wise traditions of impartiality and respect for prejudices and habits from which its predecessor had never departed. If this were to happen, a general rebellion would break out. Owing to the reputation for toleration enjoyed by the Company's representatives, this had not been the case, even when soldiers, maddened by religious passions, had risen in open mutiny. There were further dangers to be apprehended. The English were inflamed by feelings of ardent and still unquenched hatred against the natives. The new theory was that India should be governed with a view to the greater benefit of European interests. Her former masters had never made any difference between their subjects, and their fall foreshadowed the triumph of an opposite system. All these considerations pointed to deferring the decision of the questions under discussion till the public feeling should calm down under the influence of time, and then changes in the government could no longer be ascribed to the sad events which had recently occurred. Any amelioration, any reform made even at their own expense, in the interest of the public, would be welcomed with pleasure by the petitioners. They were ready to lay down their power without a murmur when convinced of the possibility of providing India with a better government than its actual one. But how was it possible to do this?

No minister of the Crown could assume the direction of Indian affairs without being assisted by experienced advisers capable not only of furnishing him with information on special matters, but of exercising in addition a sort of moral control, and acting as a counterpoise to the pressure of exclusively English interests. If the Council did not serve this purpose, it became a mere sham! What Council would possess the influence of the historic Court of Directors! Councillors appointed by the Crown offered no guarantee of an independent spirit. Subject to the influence of Parliament and of party feeling, they would be unable to preserve that happy independence which allowed the Court of Directors to reward ability and eminent services in India by advancement. A good system of government for the latter country must necessarily unite three requisites: a council independent of the minister's will, the control by that council, apart from the ministers, over the officers and despatches of

India. The first clauses decreed the transfer of the political powers, the rights and the possessions of the Honourable East India Company to the Queen's Government. As the recognised sovereign of India, Her Majesty delegated her authority to a president and a council of eight members. The president was to enjoy the same privileges and powers as the other Secretaries of State, and on almost all questions his veto was to be absolute. The members of the Council were to be chosen from English subjects who had served the Crown or the Company, or who had resided fifteen years in British India. The Council was invested with the powers formerly divided between the Board of Control and the Court of Directors, and its members could only be dismissed by a royal decree consequent on a vote of Parliament. No modification was made in the services or the patronage of India.

the Home Department, and finally a council in which all the special branches of Indian administration were represented, and which, therefore, could not have fewer than eighteen members, like the Court of Directors. If the latter were found to possess all these conditions of efficiency, they prayed Parliament not to abridge the duration of their power.

As to the reproach so often made against the Anglo-Indian authorities of dual government and want of real responsibility, was it in any degree founded? Did the Court of Directors possess executive power? It could safely be said that no branch of the Home Department possessed such, in the usual meaning of the word. The executive power resided, and rightly so, in India. As matters were constituted, the Court of Directors filled the functions performed by Parliament in the constitutional scheme. To examine and revise past acts, to lay down principles, and send out general instructions, to give or refuse their sanction to the important measures submitted to their approbation, such were in short the rights and duties common to both sections of the central government. Work of this description was beyond the strength of one man—would it then increase the vigour of the Government to simplify it by destroying its most potent spring of action? The unenlightened public considered the responsibility of the Government of India was less than that of the ministerial departments, because of the co-existence of the Court of Directors and the Board of Control. The merest explanation would dissipate this popular error. The central administration of India was doubly responsible by the Minister and the Court of Directors, but, as in all departments of the State, the representative of the Crown took the initiative in or sanctioned all the acts of his coadjutors. The petitioners wound up by praying Parliament to spare in any case the civil and military officers who had contributed so much to their success, and demanded not to appear before their judges until preliminary inquiries had been made.

In this new shape, said the partisans of the Ministry, the old tree was relieved of its parasitical branches, and for the future the Home Government would be exclusively responsible. The logic of events demanded this reform. The Queen's Army being now called to take a larger share in the defence of India, it was but just that the powers of her Government should be increased in direct proportion to the development of her military forces. The accession of a new ruler could not fail to calm the ill-will and opposition existing both in England and India against the former Government. The adherents of the Court of Directors, on the contrary, pointed out the imprudence of selecting the actual troublous times for effecting a radical change in the Anglo-Indian institutions. The proposed reforms invested a single member of the Cabinet with a dangerous and almost unbalanced power; from every point of view, a dual government was preferable to the despotism of one man. Would not the irresistible pressure of public opinion lead the Minister of the Crown to enforce measures more conformable to European than to native wishes? Finally, how could the Indian Mohammedans accept a sovereign who bore amongst other glorious titles that of Defender of the Faith?

Lord Palmerston's Bill was not destined to pass. Though voted after a three nights' debate on February 18, it shared the fate of the Ministry, who went out in the following sitting on a question of home policy, caused by Orsini's attempt on the life of Napoleon III. The mere thought of the slightest concession to a foreign prince roused all the latent fire of British pride, and the Whig Cabinet was succeeded by a Tory one. Lord Ellenborough took the place of Mr. Vernon Smith at the Board of Control, and the second reading of the India Bill was fixed for April 22. During this interval the new Ministry drew up an India Bill on a more liberal basis, in which the number of the members of the Council was fixed at eighteen. Nine of these, representing the multifarious branches of the Anglo-Indian service, were to be elected by all who had resided or served in India for the space of ten years; five other members were to be elected by the five great centres of English commerce and industry, and four by the holders of 1,000*l.* India Stock or 2,000*l.* of shares in Indian railways.

This liberal but complicated Bill, by attempting to conciliate all opinions, pleased none, and the Ministry were warned in time to modify their work. Lord Ellenborough was not to be the author of Anglo-Indian reforms; in consequence of unreasonable disputes with the Governor-General, he handed over the presidency of the Board of Control to Lord Stanley. A recent voyage to India had enabled the new Secretary of State to study on the spot the intricacies of Indian administration. Possessing a practical turn of mind, he set to work earnestly, and brought out in July a Bill, both just and well considered, which conciliated with rare ability former rights and future interests, and of which we shall reproduce here the most salient features.

A Secretary of State and a Council of fifteen members were to compose the Supreme Government of India. Eight of the fifteen must have served or resided fifteen years in India. The Council, in the first instance, was to be appointed jointly by the Crown and the Court of Directors, and afterwards, alternatively by the Crown and the Council itself. The members who were named during good behaviour were to receive a salary of 1,200*l.*, and none but the President could be a member of Parliament. The Secretary of State assigned to each councillor a special department, but all official documents had to receive his signature. He or his representative had a double vote on every question, but within certain limits, his opinion was sufficient in most discussions to counterbalance that of the majority. As the successor of the former secret committee, the minister retained the privilege of sending and receiving despatches, which were not communicated to the Council. The local authorities had still the patronage in civil and military matters, but that originally belonging to the Court of Directors was divided between the Crown and the Council; commissions in the Artillery and the Engineers had now to be obtained by competition. Other clauses determined the transfer to the Crown of the fleet, army, possessions, claims and debts of the Company, with the exception of India Stock; handed over to the Secretary of State the control of Indian receipts and expenditure, and decreed the non-liability of the Indian budget for the expenses of wars undertaken for other than Indian interests.

Lord Stanley's Bill, which was drawn up in a real spirit of conciliation and progress, could not but please all parties, and in spite of opposition from Lord Palmerston, who asked that the number of councillors should be reduced to twelve, and their appointment vested exclusively in the Crown, it surmounted victoriously the perils of a third reading in the Lower House on July 8. A few days later, the Bill was discussed in the House of Lords, where Lord Ellenborough attempted, but in vain, to substitute his own Bill for that of Lord Stanley. Unfortunately, the Lords Spiritual were unable to refrain from taking a part in the debate. One of the Archbishops gave vent to the imprudent wish that the contemplated reforms might bring about the speedy conversion of the population of India, and called upon the Government to tolerate no longer the system of caste. Such a challenge from such a quarter might, if reproduced by the native press, have produced a terrible effect in India. Lord Stanley instantly met the danger by asserting once more that the policy of the Anglo-Indian Government was one of toleration. 'England's vital interests, the very existence of her power in India, demands that her representatives should abstain from all religious intervention, and grant impartial protection to all sects and all creeds. The Government could do no more fatal nor inconsistent act than lend its aid openly and actively towards converting the natives from their belief, however false and superstitious it might be.'

This wise declaration was all the more needed that religious passions, which are always powerful in England, were then at their height. The fanaticism of the Exeter Hall party, over-excited by recent victories, gave vent to the wildest declamations. The time had come to display the banner of the Cross and throw open the towns, the bazaars, the country districts to missionary effort. The Bible was henceforward to be the text-book in native schools. No further favour, no toleration of idolators and pagans! total withdrawal of subsidies and support from native priests and temples, the suppression of the system of caste, of the Indian laws and holy days. India was to be delivered over to Christianity bound hand and foot. The display of energy, and a firm action on the part of the Government, would cause the docile Indian to submit to give up a proscribed faith, and to accept the doctrines of the Gospel instead of those of the Koran and the Vedas. Fortunately for England, her statesmen were not blinded by religious mania, and Lord Stanley's words were a pledge that the new Government would not be less tolerant than its predecessor.

On August 2 the India Bill received the Queen's sanction, and the ancient and glorious corporation disappeared from the scene of politics. On September 1, the dispossessed Directors held a last meeting, in which they won great applause by the dignity with which they accepted their fate. They still watched with fatherly care over the interests of their agents, and one of their last acts was to grant a considerable pension to Sir John Lawrence in recognition of his eminent services.

The reform inaugurated by Lord Palmerston possessed the great advantage of freeing the Government of India from obsolete forms, devoid of all significance, and the Delusion which associated all previous success with the Company's rule was quite as pernicious as the one which attributed to it every past reverse. The fiction of the Company did more harm in England than in India, as it weakened the Government, caused little interest to be felt in the affairs of India, and led both Crown and Parliament to overlook their own responsibility, and throw on their coadjutors the blame due in the first instance to themselves. It was time to put an end to a two-headed organisation, which prevented anything like real responsibility. But the reform touched none of the essential elements of a good government. It was of little moment whether the members of the India Council were selected by the holders of India Stock or otherwise; whether their acts were sealed or not with the arms of the Company. Yet such were the principal alterations made by the new Bill.

The essential machinery of the system remained much as it had been left after the great debates of the past century. The new India Committee was invested with all the power of the Court of Directors. The number of councillors was slightly modified, but the weight of the Council depended less on this than on the reputation and attainments of its members. The first appointments were very satisfactory, and were made from among the former servants of the Company, whose past offered a guarantee for their future services. Almost at the head of the list were the names of Sir John Lawrence, the successful dictator of the Punjab, and of his skilful coadjutor, Sir Henry Montgomery. The former members of the Court of Directors were also widely represented in the new council.

The reform to which Lord Stanley gave his name has already victoriously withstood the test of time, and the last fifteen years have amply proved its prudent character and the necessity which existed for it. Influenced by the spirit which ought to preside over all innovations among a great nation, it spared all well-tried institutions or recognised services, and merely suppressed a name—though a great one.

The modest Company of Merchants, which, by the enterprising spirit and the political and military genius of its agents, created an empire of two hundred million subjects beyond sea in the centre of Asia, has acquired eternal right to England's and even to India's gratitude. Its haughty but just and civilising rule kept peace for more than fifty years between a creed of exclusiveness and one of extermination, induced hereditary sects of priests, soldiers, thieves, and assassins to live together in harmony, and conferred the most entire liberty of worship on a country which had hitherto been a prey to religious wars and persecutions. As a last favour, fate had allowed the ancient corporation to continue in power long enough to carry out the work of repression victoriously, if not radically, almost without help from Europe. For all these reasons, the merchant company, whose magnificent inheritance H.M. Queen Victoria acquired in 1858, deserves a high place in modern history. The work of the great politicians and illustrious soldiers who built up the glory and fortune of 'Old John Company,' to give it its familiar nickname, is no ways inferior to that of the Cæsars, the Charlemagnes, the Napoleons. The rare good fortune which favoured the founders of English greatness in India had extended to their successors. Time, which has not spared the labours of great conquerors, seems inclined to leave the Anglo-Indian Empire undisturbed, and, hitherto at least, there is no reason to believe that, in the hands of the powerful Queen of Great Britain, it is exposed to any danger.

Local institutions did not pass through the great crisis of 1857 as easily as the supreme government. In the first place, out of the immense Bengal Army only eleven regiments remained, which, owing to special circumstances, to feelings of loyalty or to fear, had remained faithful to their colours. The contingents of the native princes had all disappeared in the storm, except that of the Nizam of Hyderabad. It was necessary to reorganise the whole of the military forces of India. Experience had shown the full extent of the error committed by the Company in basing its power on a body of mercenaries; but at the same time it had once more exhibited the important part necessarily played by native soldiers in military operations. Superior as a fighting animal, according to the picturesque expression of Sultan Hyder Ali, irresistible on the battle-field, the European finds it hard to support the fatigue of marching and the trying climate. Ignorant of the many languages of Asia, he is not able to perform the ordinary services of camp life; and a native force is the indispensable complement of an European one. If the budget of India could suffice to maintain an army of a hundred thousand English soldiers, numerous native forces would still have to be employed. On the other hand, recent events proved that the population was a stranger to the feelings of nationality and independence, and therefore did not suffer from the pressure of the conquerors. The masses in India easily resigned themselves to a foreign rule which respected their religious prejudices, and secured order and peace to the land. In short, the matter for consideration was not how to hold down two hundred millions of recalcitrant subjects at the point of the bayonet, but how to maintain order in an immense territory, guaranteed by the weakness of its neighbours from all external danger, and inhabited by docile races long accustomed to obey. The only solution to the problem of military reorganisation was the augmentation of the European and the reduction of the native forces.

Circumstances had taken the initiative of these reforms. In order to meet the exigencies of the war, considerable reinforcements had been sent from England, and for some time the effective force of the Royal troops in India amounted to more than 110,000 men. Reductions were made later on in the number of European troops serving in India, which finally have been fixed at fifty-two infantry and eleven cavalry regiments, besides considerable artillery. The nine Fusilier regiments in the pay of the Company, with the artillery belonging to the latter, were incorporated into the Royal Army.[1] The troops actually serving in India are only 17,000 men more than in 1857. The counsels of experience were equally considered in the reorganisation of the native armies. The Bengal Army has been reconstituted on a small scale with the loyal regiments and new levies, while important reductions have been made in those of Bombay and Madras. The total number of native forces now amounts to 137 infantry and forty cavalry regiments, besides a few troops stationed in Central Asia.[2] The effective force of a

[1] See Documents, No. XV.

[2]

	INFANTRY.	CAVALRY.
Bengal	49	19
Madras	40	4
Bombay	30	7
Punjab	12	6
Contingent of Hyderabad	6	4
Total	137	40

All the artillery, except a few Sikh batteries, is now commanded by Europeans.

cavalry regiment is fixed at 500 sabres, that of an infantry regiment at 700 bayonets. The native army, which does not muster 120,000 men, is inferior nowadays to what it was at the beginning of the century, and is not even half as strong as in 1857. It can safely be affirmed that in no country are the military forces so disproportionate to the population as in India. In reality, the native army, which is reduced to its lowest figure, is a mere skeleton, and the ranks would have to be increased in order to carry out the most insignificant expedition; such an increase is, however, a very easy matter. The irregular system has preponderated in the work of reorganisation. The regimental staff for cavalry and infantry regiments is uniformly composed of seven officers, viz., a commander, a sub-commander, wing officer, a second wing officer, an adjutant, a quartermaster, two lieutenants, intrusted with the general service, and wing subalterns.[1] The rules of promotion by seniority, for native soldiers alone, have been abolished, and the new system gives the commander summary power to reward or punish.

We still have to consider the most important reform which was ever made in Anglo-Indian military institutions. We have often had occasion to point out the attraction felt by officers in the Company's service for civil and military functions other than regimental, and among the original causes of the Mutiny can be cited the spirit of discontent and apathy existing in the regimental staffs. To remedy this state of things, Anglo-Indian officers have been formed in each Presidency into a body, incorrectly enough known as the 'Staff Corps,' whose members must choose, on entering the service, between a purely civil or a purely military career.[2]

[1] The Anglo-Indian regiments are divided into two wings or battalions.

[2] Independently of the Civil Service, properly so called, India offers to the English people a magnificent field of military, political, and administrative appointments, where a well-educated man can, if not make his fortune, at least obtain considerable emoluments. Thus on July 1, 1874, the Staff Corps of the three Presidencies was composed as follows: 219 general officers, of whom 22 were on the active list; 184 officers on the staff or in purely military posts; 1,027 in native regiments; 397 filling civil or political functions; 133

Another important innovation makes promotion in the Staff Corps to depend on a fixed term of service, and not on seniority alone, as was formerly the case. Four years' service in one of the Staff Corps gives the rank of captain; twenty years, twenty-six years, thirty-one years, those of major, lieutenant-colonel, colonel. After thirty-eight years' service, a colonel may retire on full pay to England, where, by right of seniority, he may reach, if his life is prolonged, the highest military dignities. For the rank and file, promotion proceeds on entirely different principles, and is conferred at will by the Commander-in-Chief, independently of rank. There is nothing to prevent the most eccentric regimental arrangements, such as giving the command of a corps to a captain, and thus placing lieutenant-colonels and majors under his orders. The pecuniary position of regimental officers has been considerably ameliorated, and their pay is quite on a par with that of their equals in rank employed in civil functions, or on the staff proper. An ensign or a cornet of the Royal Army (from whence all the Indian Staff Corps are supplied) receives on joining the native regiment the rank of lieutenant and a supplementary pay of 100*l.* The pay of a lieutenant-colonel commanding a regiment is as much as 1,750*l.*

The establishment of the Staff Corps, which was principally intended for the improvement of the regimental staffs, can only be considered an experiment, and fifteen years' experience has shown its many drawbacks. The reformers, who rightly desired to respect the former organisation, and all vested rights, and who were, moreover, influenced by the brilliant results of a mixed administration in the Punjab, forgot that the work of force is finished in India, and that there is no longer a foot of territory to be gained by arms. Under present circumstances, the mission of the soldier-statesman, equally fitted to lead an army or to complete the work of conquest, who played so prominent a part in Indian

in the police; 61 in public works; 232 in departments of the posts and the studs; 161 on sick leave; 90 superior officers, doing general duties; 66 retired lieut.-colonels living in England with a pay of 1*l.* a day.

history, has come to an end. To the rule of the sword must succeed an administration more in harmony with the wants of the country. Nevertheless, the number of military men who receive civil appointments tends to increase more and more, and will, doubtless, in a few years amount to half that of the effective of Anglo-Indian officers. Yet the young man who, on being admitted into diplomacy, or into the administration, bids an eternal farewell to the noble profession of arms, will none the less pass through all ranks, till, if life be given him, he returns to end his days in England, with the rank of a general officer. Grades won by the pen, far from the battle-field, cannot fail to weaken the prestige which till now has surrounded the higher grades of the English Army.

From a purely military point of view the reforms have not produced entirely satisfactory results. The system of promotion at will, exclusively for regimental grades, if we may still use the expression, has never been adopted in any regular army. Even allowing that the Commander-in-Chief resists all private influence, and promotes the most deserving with a view to the interest of the service alone, yet one of the principal causes of weakness in the old Bengal Army is not thereby obviated, viz., the absence of intercourse between the European officer and the native soldier. Promotion in the corps itself can only be the exception in cadres of seven officers, and the latter must consider their regiments as mere stations which they will have to leave at a moment's notice. Moreover, unfilled vacancies, which was pointed out in 1857 as one of the immediate causes of the Mutiny, have reappeared in the regimental staffs. From one cause or another, from illness, from absence on leave, or from occupying posts on the military staff, the seven European officers are very rarely present at the same time with their regiments. Lastly, the peace enjoyed by India for the last fifteen years, and the system of grades acquired by a stated period of service, have destroyed the proper proportion between the superior and inferior grades. For thirty regiments of regular cavalry, the Anglo-Indian Army numbers eighty superior officers, and for 115 infantry regiments, 407. These weak points of the new organisation are not irremediable; the definitive separation of the civil and military services, and fixed qualifications for promotion in the army, would doubtless prove sufficient to complete the military reforms brought about by the terrible events of 1857.

We have still to consider the changes among high Anglo-Indian officials, which almost immediately followed the transfer of the Company's possessions to the Crown. The title of Governor-General was replaced by that of Viceroy. The Viceroy, members of the Indian Council who are not selected from the Indian Service, and the Governors of the presidencies of Madras and Bombay, are appointed by the Queen. Members of the Indian Council belonging to the Indian Services and the Commanders-in-Chief hold their functions from the Secretary of State for India. The Viceroy appoints, with the Queen's authorisation, the deputy-governors. Up to 1859, all the decisions of the Indian Council were taken collectively, but at that time Lord Canning, overwhelmed with business, assigned to each member, in the interest of the public good, the direction of the department with which he was best acquainted. Only measures of great importance were reserved for the examination of the Governor-General and his Council. This division of labour received legal sanction by an Act of Parliament in 1861. At the head of the Government of India in our day is a Cabinet, the prime minister of which is superior to his colleagues in authority and social rank, and who exercises absolute control over their actions.

At the time of the Mutiny, the Indian Council was composed of two members drawn from the Indian Civil Service, of one member belonging to the native army, and of a fourth, chosen from the cleverest barristers in London, whose office was to give a legal form to the acts of the Council. But as money matters occupied the first place amongst the difficulties of the crisis, the post of legal member which had become vacant was conferred on a distinguished financier, Mr. T. Wilson. Since then, the need of legal knowledge having been felt, a new member has been added to the Council. Each of the councillors receives a magnificent salary of 8,000*l.* Under the Company's rule, in case of the absence or death of the Governor-General, the senior member of the Council became his temporary successor. At present the viceroyalty is exercised *ad interim* by the Governor of Madras or the Governor of Bombay, according to seniority.

The Indian Legislative Council, which completes the constitutional machinery of the empire, has also undergone certain modifications, and is composed of twelve members, of whom at least six are chosen, not from either the civil or the military services, but from the principal merchants and planters, or from high-class natives. Similar councils exist at Madras and Bombay. Finally, the supreme courts of the three presidencies, which till the Mutiny had exercised their authority independently of the Company, have been amalgamated with the native supreme courts (saddar uddanlat), and now bear the name of high courts. They are composed of judges, taken from the Indian Civil Service and the English bar, before whom English and native barristers plead. To give an idea of the magnificent prizes offered to followers of the law, it will be sufficient to say that judges of the High Courts receive from 5,000*l.* to 6,000*l.*, and that famous barristers at Bombay and Calcutta make from 8,000*l.* to 12,000*l.* per annum.

Administrative and military reforms were not the only pressing exigencies of the moment. Events had amply justified the policy of conquest and annexation which was followed during the last twenty years of the Company's rule; for if the sepoys had found a Tippoo Sahib, or a Ranjit Singh in British India, the struggle would have assumed proportions too vast even for England's strength. The native princes who held their thrones under her protectorate remained loyal, for they had measured the chances of the revolt with great political judgment, and had been able to estimate England's resources and the weakness of her adversaries at their real value. With a few exceptions, they felt that the triumph of the sepoys would be full of danger for their own authority, and that if the English were defeated, their thrones would soon give way beneath the blows of a lawless soldiery. It was both just and politic to take into account intelligent loyalty such as this, and to give marked proofs of confidence to the friends in adversity. The means of reward was ready at hand.

We have already mentioned the confiscations disguised under the name of *post-mortem* annexations, which became part of the Company's system after Lord Dalhousie assumed the management of affairs. It was determined to put a stop to all such proceedings, by granting to the native princes the right of adoption in the fullest meaning of the word. In default of direct descendants, every native prince above the rank of 'jaghirdar' was allowed to perpetuate his power by adoption according to Hindoo customs if he was a Hindoo, or, in other cases, according to the laws of his race, as long as the real or fictitious representative of the family remained faithful to the treaties and engagements which bind him to the English Government. This restoration of the ancient common law of India facilitated relations between the suzerain and her vassals, by completely reassuring the native princes as to the transmission of their hereditary rights. The measure was equally well received by the native population, which had been irritated by seeing the European conquerors tread under foot the religious custom of adoption. The Nizam of Hyderabad, the Rajah of Pattyalah, the Maharajah of Nepaul, and the confederate Sikh chieftains were rewarded for their services by an increase of territory, which in most cases was a mere restitution. Finally, the alliance between the two parties was cemented by the institution of an order of chivalry, the Star of India.[1]

On November 1, 1861, in a solemn assembly at Allahabad, where European luxury vied with Oriental pomp,

[1] The Star of India is divided into three classes:—

1st. The Knights Grand Commanders, G.C.S.I., twenty-five in number, of whom fifteen are natives and ten Europeans.

2nd. The Knights Commanders, K.C.S.I., fifty in number.

3rd. Companions, C.S.I., to the number of a hundred.

Lord Canning, acting as Grand Master of the Star of India, invested with the insignia of the Order the Maharajahs of Gwalior and Pattyalah, the Ranee of Bhopal, and the Rajah of Rampore, all of whom by their loyalty had deserved well of England. On the same day was held high festival at the old castle of Windsor. The august lady who, thanks to the admirable system of the balance of power, bears a sceptre worthy of Charlemagne in her feeble hands, without sinking under it, conferred the Grand Cross of the Star of India on the veteran Sir C. Campbell, now raised to the peerage as Lord Clyde, on Sir John Lawrence, and on Lord Harris, Governor of Madras during the Mutiny. Besides this, later on, and by degrees, all the civil and military officers who distinguished themselves in 1857 became Companions of the same order.

The financial history of the Company offers the picture of a daily struggle between receipts and expenditure, and only by incessant efforts could the local revenues be made to suffice for the maintenance of the civil and military services which were necessary to preserve and develope its dominions beyond seas. These budget difficulties are easily explained. On one side, a civil and judicial administration, Staff Corps and troops, sent from a distance at great expense, and bringing along with them the habits and wants of another hemisphere; on the other, a primitive system of taxation, borrowed from the traditions of the great Moguls. In a word, the expenditure of a European Government had to be defrayed by the budget of an Asiatic one. The state of affairs grew worse after the Mutiny. The military budget, from eleven and a half millions sterling in 1856–57, increased to twenty millions in 1857–58. The European forces were raised to 112,000 men, and the native forces, including the Bombay and Madras Armies, the new levies and the Sikh regiments exceeded 300,000 men. Two years had elapsed, and there seemed no reason for anticipating any reduction in the amount of military expenses. Europeans continued to arrive in great numbers, and the local government was at the end of its resources.

Under these circumstances, the Legislative Council, faithful to old-fashioned economical ideas, enormously increased the import duties, and established taxes on the exportation of the principal articles. Fortunately, the deficit in Indian finances had attracted the notice of the Home Government, and the latter, desirous of securing for the Calcutta authorities the advice of an experienced financier, appointed, as we have already said, Mr. James Wilson to the vacant post in the Indian Council.

Up to 1859, the revenue of India had remained fixed within stereotyped forms, and was drawn almost exclusively from three sources: the land-tax, the salt-tax, and the opium monopoly. The land-tax forms the real basis of the Indian budget, and its proceeds yield more than both the other branches of the revenue together. It is intimately connected with the fundamental principles of the administration, and any alteration in this principal source of the wealth of the State would assume the character of a political question. It has already been stated that, though more moderate under the Company's rule than under that of the great Moguls, the land-tax weighed very heavily on the rural population. The English officers who found a refuge in the huts of the natives during the Mutiny, and were in a position to judge the life of the ryot, almost all agreed as to his extreme misery. Similar considerations of humanity forbade any great increase in the salt-tax, which is specially burdensome to the lower classes. The produce of the opium monopoly entirely depends on the demands of China, and the Government cannot possibly exercise any influence over it.

When Mr. Wilson, whose short and brilliant career we intend briefly to relate, arrived in India, the temporary triumph of obsolete doctrines had already borne fruit. Trade and commercial transactions were paralysed, the public revenue scarcely yielded a slight surplus; far from being averted, the crisis daily became more threatening. The new arbiter of Indian finance perceived the urgent necessity of creating fresh sources of revenue, and of introducing the system of direct taxation. In February 1860, Mr. Wilson laid before the Council a series of financial reforms, the salient features of which can be summed up as follows:—A reduction to 10 per cent. *ad valorem* of the import duties on all merchandise except tobacco, wines, beer, and spirits, which continued to be taxed very heavily; the complete removal of all export duties on the products of the country, except saltpetre, which was a monopoly, and the increased value of which exclusively fell on the consumer; a tax of 2 per cent. on incomes between 20*l.* to 50*l.*, and of 4 per cent. on all above this amount. The stamp duty, which had hitherto been obligatory only in legal proceedings, was now made equally so for every species of documents, receipts, bills of exchange, bills of lading, powers of attorney, &c.

Mr. Wilson was not able to complete his task; worn out by overwork and the climate, he died at the end of 1860. His successor, Mr. Laing, a well-known economist, only entered upon the scene in 1862, when by a decided return to the former state of things, he brought back the duties on piece-goods and yarns, so opposed to the manufacturing interests of Great Britain, to the old tariff of 5 and 3½ per cent. The duty on tobacco, which for ordinary qualities was actually 100 per cent., and therefore almost put a stop to trade, was reduced to 20 per cent. The same reduction was made on the tariff of wines, beer, and spirits, which had hitherto been taxed at 50 per cent. *ad valorem*. As to the tax of 2 per cent. on incomes below 50*l.*, the expenses for perception of which exceeded 30 per cent., it was definitively abolished. Mr. Laing's successors followed the fiscal system he inaugurated, and little by little all traces of the recent innovations disappeared from Indian finances. The tax on incomes above 50*l.* produced but 8,000,000*l.* in five years, and was not renewed at the expiration of its legal term in 1865. In 1867, it was replaced by a licence-tax, varying from a minimum of eight shillings to a maximum of 20*l.*, from which incomes under 50*l.* were exempt. This latter imitation of European taxation has been effaced from the Indian budget since April 1, 1873.

This rapid summary of the financial history of India

during the last fifteen years sufficiently indicates the secret resistance of all kinds which has nullified all endeavours to improve the machinery of taxation. We may suppose, however, that the refractoriness shown by India towards improved methods of political economy must not be exclusively attributed to her inability to support fresh burdens. The causes of this failure are of another kind, and far more complicated. How is it possible to apply fresh taxation to a country as vast as Europe, with a population of nearly two hundred million souls, without meeting, at least in some provinces, with insurmountable obstacles? Let the attempt be made to apply the budget of France to Russia, and the problem will prove no less arduous and complicated than that of forcing a uniform system of taxation on the inhabitants of Oude, the Punjab, or those of the great commercial cities of the Indian Ocean. Latent and natural difficulties such as these explain the failure of fiscal innovations, in spite of a steady increase in the public revenue, which it still remains for us to consider.

During the last thirty years, the receipts have increased by a million sterling yearly, notwithstanding constant wars and the unfinished state of the roads of the country.[1]

Annexation of territory must undoubtedly be taken into account in this increase of revenue, which is, however, principally due to the indisputable development of public wealth. On the other hand, figures like the above-mentioned are reassuring as to the future, though State expenditure

[1]

Years.	Revenues.	Years.	Revenues.
1840	£20,124,038	1864	£44,613,032
1845	23,666,246	1865	45,652,897
1850	27,522,344	1866	48,935,220
1855	29,133,050	1867	42,122,433*
1857	31,691,015	1868	48,534,412
1859	36,060,788	1869	49,262,691
1860	39,705,822	1870	50,901,081
1861	42,903,234	1871	51,413,686†
1862	43,829,472	1872	50,110,215
1863	45,143,752	—	—

* In consequence of a change in the official year, the accounts were only made up for eleven months.

† See Documents No. XVI.

has followed an upward progression which is fully justified by the extension given to public works, such as roads, irrigation, and railways. Moreover, we must remember that certain articles in the budget of receipts have not attained their presumable expansion, whilst corresponding ones in that of the expenditure will ultimately be diminished, if not altogether suppressed. In the first place, the State has for ten years paid large subsidies to the various railways, the amount of which cannot possibly remain the same when the network of railways is finished in the whole extent of the empire. The actual returns of the Customs, 2,500,000*l.*, are quite out of proportion with the population of India, which numbers more than 150,000,000 inhabitants. There is reason to believe that owing to the greater facility of communication, the products of Europe will, within a calculable period, come into more common use among the natives, and that the Customs of the empire will emerge from the stagnation in which they have remained for years. But without going beyond the bounds of actual facts, it can be prophesied that in another twenty years the revenue of India will be quite equal to that of Great Britain, and will amount to 70,000,000*l.*

As to the debt of India, it was in 1857 some 59,500,000*l.*, and in 1861, 107,500,000*l.*, that is to say, in less than five years it was increased by 48,000,000*l.* Yet if the enormous expenses entailed by modern warfare be taken into consideration, this sum is not an exorbitant one. If the colonial government had been acquainted with modern financial methods in 1857, it is probable that by negotiating a loan to cover the expenses of the war, its financial reputation would have come out of the crisis intact. Their measures were not equal to the occasion. The expenses of the war were charged on the ordinary budget, and an open loan, at a fixed interest, the success of which remained uncertain, was resorted to. This uncertainty, and the deficit[1] which marked

[1] Deficit:

Deficit	1857–58	£7,864,322
	1858–59	13,393,137
	1859–60	9,290,129
	1860–61	4,026,225
	Total	£34,573,713

the year of the Mutiny and the following one, cast serious discredit for some time on the solvency of India. The equilibrium of the budget was soon re-established, and the debt was even reduced in 1867 to 98,500,000*l.* Since then, the development given to public works has weighed heavily on the resources of the country. The debt, however, has only increased in extremely small proportions. Thus, the interests paid by Government, which were 5,732,757*l.* in 1867–68, amounted merely to 5,966,299*l.* in 1871–72.

The receipts of 1871–72, according to official documents, amounted to 51,413,686*l.*, and show an increase of 512,605*l.* on those of the preceding year. The expenditure, on the contrary, amounted to 49,930,696*l.*, showing a diminution of 611,870*l.* The excess of receipts over expenditure amounted to 1,483,990*l.* As we have already stated, the Viceroy had announced that the income-tax would not be renewed on the expiration of its legal term, March 31, 1873. Indian finances emerged triumphant from the disasters of 1857, and, if the specialists to whom the home authorities added to the Indian Council did not succeed in creating new sources of revenue, their special knowledge at least exercised a beneficial influence over India. London financiers bore in mind that though accurate book-keeping is not enough to ensure that the finances will be in a flourishing state, yet the prosperity of the latter is not compatible with ill-kept accounts. This branch of Indian administration, which was reorganised and improved by Mr. Wilson and his successors, leaves little to be desired, and its results rarely differ from the estimates. The budget of India is in a state of perfect equilibrium, and stands fourth on the list among those of the great nations of the world; before long it will have outstripped that of Russia. We may therefore wind up by asserting that the condition of public finance in the Asiatic dominions of Queen Victoria is eminently satisfactory for the present, and gives good promise for the future. This state of things cannot fail to attract the attention of bankers and persons in search of safe investments, and the day will surely come in which Indian Stocks will be in high favour on the markets of Europe.[1]

After fifteen years' trial, it can safely be asserted that the crisis of 1857 left the English stronger than it found them, and that the result has justified the transfer of the Company's dominions to the Crown. Yet the great Indian problems remain still to be solved. The system of castes, considered superficially, seems to touch but remotely on great political questions, and, *à priori*, it is allowable to ask what would be the advantage to England if all her subjects were miraculously to be united by a feeling of fraternity, and became free to sit at the same table, to intermarry, and to have full liberty to choose their own profession. Fraternity! though the word still adorns the smoking ruins of the finest monuments of one of the most beautiful cities in Europe, it will always be without meaning for the vast majority of men. The frugal races of Asia take their meals in the family circle, and the names of host and guest are unknown to them. How could such determined water-drinkers, such obstinate rice-eaters, such rejectors of the use of the fork as they are, find any pleasure in sharing the banquets of modern civilisation, in which the richest plate, the most delicate dishes, and the most exquisite wines gratify alike the palate and the eye? The prohibition of marriage between the different castes is

[1] The financial results of the last few years bear out these favourable prognostics, in spite of the burdens which the Bengal famine laid on the Government. The year 1872–73 surpassed all former ones in financial prosperity. Thus the revenue, estimated at £48,286,000, reached £49,476,000, while the expenditure, calculated at £48,066,000, was diminished to £47,657,300. The surplus, which in the budget estimates was valued at £210,000, actually reached £1,818,700.

The current year 1873–74 gives the following figures:—Receipts, £48,984,000; ordinary expenditure, £47,720,000; that is to say, a surplus of £1,264,000. But the estimated expenditure for the famine amounted to £6,500,000, of which £3,920,000 had already been spent and carried to account, thus converting the expected surplus into a deficit of £2 101,300. The balance of the expenses of the famine, £2,580,000, placed to the debt of 1874–75, converted the surplus for this period, estimated at £1,192.000, into a deficit of £1,138,000. The expenditure caused by the famine may be said to have been more than half covered by the surplus of the receipts over the expenditures of the budgets of 1872–73 and 1873 74.

little felt in a country where social relations do not exist, and where the precocity of the race causes unions to be contracted in very early youth. Moreover, there never has been, and there never will be, a social condition in which distinctions of birth, of education, and of fortune have no value, and where marriage between noble and plebeian, between the rich and the poor, even if not forbidden by law, will be encouraged by public opinion. In countries where public education is widely extended, an adult may naturally choose his profession, but in India, where the father is the best and almost the only teacher of his son, the hereditary nature of professions is almost an indispensable necessity.

The three fundamental laws of the native community, when expressed in these simple terms, would scarcely seem to deserve the attention of statesmen. Unfortunately, these details of private life, of domestic etiquette, under their inoffensive exterior, go to form the intricate meshes of the ast and heavy net under which Brahminical influence still holds down modern India. How could a civilised government pass over the strange tyranny, and the extraordinary crimes which naturally flow from the system of castes? Ought Pariahs to be forced to wear a bell round their necks, according to the prescriptions of the laws of Manou? Shall the Brahmin who strikes down a Nazyadi by an arrow, or a shot from a gun at the distance of seventy-four paces, in order to avoid pollution from the shadow of the unclean being—shall he, in accordance with the laws of Manou, escape the vengeance of the law?

The lessons of the Mutiny, which have but too fully shown the danger of concessions to the prejudices of the sepoys, forbid the continuance of the same perilous system. The native soldiers must not only fight but eat together, perform every kind of military duty, and accept the order to march to any destination without a murmur. Neither in the public administrations must the spirit of caste, so opposed to the good of the service, be considered. Caste must also disappear from railway stations, hospitals, and prisons, where it is impossible to separate, according to their orthodoxy, the different castes whom the chances of travel, of illness, or of crime may bring together.

These reforms, which have been carried out with steady perseverance, have not as yet met with any insurmountable obstacles, for if the Brahmins still persist in asserting the infallibility and immutability of the laws of Manou, the decrease of their influence is daily proved by a thousand different facts. In the various branches of the public service men of the highest castes recognise as their superiors men belonging to the most degraded. Brahmins themselves trade in spirituous liquors and butchers' meat, and wear sandals of cowhide. The intercourse between Europeans and natives in large towns is incessantly wearing away the system of caste. The time seems to have arrived for the downfall of the political and religious institutions which have been India's weakness and misfortune for thousands of years. The equality of castes before the law, which is no violation of the solemn engagement entered into by the English Government to respect scrupulously the religions of its Asiatic subjects, is the real and desirable solution of the problem, the object which all Indian statesmen ought to keep in view. But no intervention ought to go further, and any interference with the intimate details of native life and hierarchy would be as useless as dangerous.

Catholic and evangelical missions are not obliged to act in the same spirit. The relations between the missionaries and the natives are of a strictly private character, and in the school or the church it would neither be politic nor liberal to force men of high birth to associate with the lower classes of the population. The native who embraces Christianity is, by the very fact of his conversion, cut off for ever from his relations and friends without thereby acquiring a position in English society, and the life of isolation to which neophytes are condemned, is one of the greatest hindrances to the success of proselytism. Such is not the case with Hindoo converts to Islamism, who are at once received as brothers by their new co-religionists. Therefore, it is but just to leave the advantages of his birth to the high-class convert in compensation for his sacrifices. We cannot conclude these sketches without pointing out once more that the English Government must take no share whatever in the work of Christian missions, and that any attempt at, or suspicion of, official propagandism would suffice to let loose on India a more terrible storm than that of 1857, which would assuredly shipwreck the fortunes of England.

CHAPTER XII.

PUBLIC WORKS, EXPORTATIONS, AND IMPORTATIONS—THE ISTHMUS OF SUEZ—RUSSIAN PROPAGANDA AND INDIAN RAILWAYS.

Reforms in the legislation on landed property—The Anglo-Indian telegraph system—Postal reforms—New military works—Canals—Roads—Railways—Basis of the contracts with the railway companies—Government supervision—The great Anglo-Indian companies—Exportations and importations—Shipping—Rice—Jute—Tea—Coffee—Cotton—Progress of local manufactures—Importations, merchandise, and precious metals—Trade by land—The Suez Canal and the Eastern question—Anglo-Indian policy considered as such—The Duke of Edinburgh's excursion in India.

INDIA has never been and never will be a colony of England in the strict sense of the word; the Anglo-Saxon race will never be able to people the deltas of the Ganges and of the Indus. Nature, with her own powerful hands, has placed impassable obstacles in the way of such an occupation. If grown men lose their strength in the deleterious climate of India, its action is still more pernicious to children and adults. Every well-to-do family of the European community sends its children home at three or four years of age at the latest. The statistics of mortality among the children of common soldiers, the only offshoots of the Caucasian race who are brought up in India, explain more than sufficiently these early but necessary separations. The Asiatic dependency of Great Britain will never be aught for its masters but a conquered territory, where they can only maintain their power by preserving their physical and moral superiority over the indigenous population. It is no less indispensable for England to develop the immense resources of her empire, and we cannot conclude without saying a few words of the progress made in India during the last fifteen years.

It is only recently that the Government of India has shown any concern for material interests. From the beginning of the century to the annexation of the Punjab (1849), the representatives of the Company, either from necessity or from ambition, gave themselves up entirely to questions of external policy, and did little for the development of the riches of the country. The energetic and enlightened administration of Lord Dalhousie inaugurated the era of great public works. The Great Trunk road, which connects Calcutta with Delhi, was opened to the public in 1851. In 1854, India was endowed with a complete network of electric telegraphs, and nearly at the same time a thorough and much needed reform in postal matters was carried out. A system of railways, connecting the centres of commerce and production in the three Presidencies, was projected, and before Lord Dalhousie's departure (1856), important sections of the lines were ready for traffic in Bengal and Bombay. The Mutiny attracted attention to India, led to the reform of the whole administrative machinery, and did more in a few months for the material development of the country than would have been done by fifty years of monotonous and peaceful prosperity. The terrible storm cleared the atmosphere, and paved the way for the peaceful victories which, to be thoroughly successful, only require the assistance of European capital and energy, and the protection of an honest and enlightened government.

A radical reform was to precede all others. In its suspicious dread of foreign interference, the Company had never allowed even Englishmen to possess or acquire land in its dominions. This state of things naturally called forth protests on all sides, and under the pressure of public opinion, the new authorities from the outset boldly attacked the fundamental principles of Anglo-Indian legislation. For many years now the enterprising European, of whatever nationality, has the right to become a landed proprietor in India on the same conditions as the natives themselves. Waste land, or land recently brought into cultivation, may be bought of the Government in fee simple; as for land on the regular rent roll, a legal artifice baffles the strictness of the fundamental law, which recognises the Government as the sole legitimate owner of the soil. By depositing in the hands of the district collector a capital in Government bonds yielding interest equal to the assessment, the buyer frees himself for ever from the land-tax, and his position is exactly what it would be if he had sold his Indian stock to invest it in real estate. This desirable change in Indian legislation was preceded by the establishment of a telegraphic system and the reform of the post, both which ameliorations belong to Lord Dalhousie's administration (1849-56). We shall now briefly consider them.

The first works on the line from Calcutta to Agra were begun in November, 1853, and finished in five months. On March 24, 1854, the two great centres were connected by telegraph. On February 15 following, the wires were extended to Madras *viâ* Bombay, and on the north to Attock, on the Indus. In 1855, the system was completed by the lines of Rangoon on the east, and Peshawur on the north, and gave a magnificent total of four thousand miles of telegraphic wires. The learned Sir W. O'Shaughnessy, to whom is due this fine monument of modern science and civilisation, had to contend against all the obstacles which nature can oppose to the efforts of men: pestiferous jungles, which for months together exhaled pestilential fevers, and were moreover inhabited by wild beasts,[1] moun-

[1] The following lines give some idea of the difficulties and dangers which beset the pioneers of science and progress in India:—

'One extraordinary feature of Indian life is the number of human beings destroyed by wild beasts. Rewards are offered by the Government for the killing of these animals; but in some districts the loss of life is very great, and in others, where it is less excessive, the reason given is that the goats are very abundant, and that wolves prefer kids when they can get them. Deaths from snake bites are very frequent, no fewer than 14,529 persons having lost their lives in that way in 1869, while in 1871 the total deaths caused by dangerous animals of all classes amounted to 18,078. Dr. Fayrer is of opinion that if systematic returns were kept, the annual number of deaths from snake-bites would be found to exceed 20,000. The inhabitants of the border-lands between jungle and cultivation are killed and eaten by tigers in such numbers as to require the immediate and serious attention of Government both in India and England. The following are a few out of many instances. A single

tains, rocks, precipices, impenetrable forests, swamps, and rivers. The cable which carries the electric wire through the river Soane is fifteen thousand eight hundred and forty feet long. The expense of laying down the original four thousand miles of wires amounted to twenty-one lacs of rupees, or about five hundred rupees a mile. The system has since been increased by new local lines, with a special view to opening telegraphic communications with Europe. There is now, and marvellous indeed is the fact, no European, living in the remotest parts of the empire of Tamerlane and Aureng-Zeb who is not able to communicate in a few days, nay, in a few hours, with the mother-country. It is useless to dwell on the political advantages which England derives from telegraphic communication with India. We have already pointed out the important part played by the wires in the beginning of the Mutiny before they were destroyed. The enormous extent of India forbids any comparison with a European state,[1] and one must turn to the United States in order to find points of comparison in the tariff used. The latter are very advantageous to the Anglo-Indian public, who, whatever the distance, merely pay a rupee for a telegram of six words, address free.

At the present moment India is connected with Europe by three separate telegraphic lines. The first passes by Constantinople, Mossoul, Bagdad, and Fao, on the Persian Gulf, from whence starts the submarine cable connecting the

tigress caused the destruction of thirteen villages, and 256 square miles of country were thrown out of cultivation. In January 1868 a panther broke into the town of Chicacole and wounded four persons, and one died. It appears that there are difficulties in the way of killing down these tigers. First, the superstition of the natives, who regard the "man-eating" tiger as a kind of incarnate and spiteful divinity, whom it is dangerous to offend; secondly, the failure of Government rewards; thirdly, the desire of a few in India actually to preserve tigers as game, to be shot with the rifle as a matter of sport.'—*Moral and Material Progress and Condition of India*, 1871–72.

[1] From Calcutta to Peshawur . . . . . . 1,550 miles
" " Bombay . . . . 1,548 "
" " Palamcottah . . . . . . 1,665 "

The distance from Peshawur on the extreme north-west frontier to Palamcottah to the far south of the Madras Presidency is 2,631 miles. The line from Peshawur to Moulmein, British Burmah, comprises 2,863 miles of wire.

latter town with Kurrachee; the second (the Indo-European Telegraphic Company) passes through Berlin, Warsaw, Kertch, Tiflis, Tabriz, Teheran, Bushire, Cape Yask and Gwadur; the third, inaugurated in 1870, connects Suez with Bombay by submarine cable. Another line, opened in 1871, completes communication between Europe and the far East, *viâ* Madras, Penang, Singapore, and Hong Kong. In spite of the advantages they offer, the Indian telegraphs are far from giving satisfactory financial results. The net profits of the Suez Company, with a capital of 1,200,000*l.*, amount to 8 per cent., which just about pays the annual wear and tear of the cable. The Indo-European Telegraphic Company, with a capital of 450,000*l.*, is unable to meet its working expenses after paying the charges made by the different Governments whose wires it uses. The revisions of the tariff have not proved an efficacious remedy. Telegrams of twenty words, which originally cost 5*l.*, and subsequently 2*l.* 18*s.*, were raised again to 4*l.*, without producing any considerable effect on the receipts.

As soon as Lord Dalhousie arrived in India he was struck by the insufficiency of the postal administration, and in 1850 he named a commission to report upon the necessary reforms to be made. The labours of this commission brought about the following changes for the better: The post became a special administration, with a director-general under the control of the Supreme Government; a uniform rate of one anna (1½*d.*) for letters weighing half-an-ounce, and of half an anna for papers and printed matter, whatever the distance; the system of stamps was also introduced. These innovations were completed by the fixed rate of sixpence on letters to Europe weighing half-an-ounce. India, it may be said, is the country where the public profits by postal arrangements at the least cost to themselves. For the modest sum of less than three half-pence a letter may be sent from Cape Comorin to Peshawur, a distance of three thousand miles; under the former system, the rate, though very moderate when the distance is taken into account, would have amounted to one shilling. This great reform, be it added, is not burdensome. According to the budget of 1870-71, the receipts were 805,235*l.*, and the expenditure 613,041*l.*, showing a surplus of 192,194*l.*[1]

Thirty years ago, public works in India were limited to keeping up military and civil buildings, such as barracks, arsenals, hospitals, public banks, and prisons. Besides this, the action of the Government only extended to works of irrigation. A committee, composed of the principal functionaries belonging to the civil departments of the army, was amply sufficient for the modest requirements of a *statu quo* policy, which, if not hostile, was utterly indifferent to the development of the wealth of the country. Lord Dalhousie, on taking office, broke with these traditions of the past, and separating public works from the army, made the former branch of the service a separate department of the Supreme Government. The new department soon enlarged its sphere of activity. The budget of public works, which in 1852-53 amounted to 600,000*l.*, a fifth of which was set apart for the maintenance and construction of roads, exceeded seven millions in 1867-68, viz :—

	£
Military works (new barracks, &c.)	2,856,000
Civil buildings	1,144,240
Public Works—Roads	1,358,640
Irrigation	1,136,280
Various works	218,640
Grants to railways	502,500
Total	7,116,300

These figures show that by an odd freak of fortune the new administration was called upon to reconstruct the military buildings of the Company. The Mutiny led to a great increase in the number of European troops in India. Barracks were wanting in which to lodge the new-comers,

[1] The number of letters which passed through the Indian Post Office in 1873 amounted to 83,127,098, showing an increase of nearly three millions over the preceding year, 80,636,643. Papers, reviews, &c., were 7,928,090 and 6,840,130. The Anglo-Indian Press comprises 255 papers printed in Indian dialects, 67 half in English, half in native languages, 156 in English alone, total, 478; 48 new papers appeared in 1873.—*The Englishman*, February 13, 1874.

and the old ones, built in the time of the Company, were sadly notorious for their unhealthiness. Moreover, the English, in their blind infatuation, had been satisfied to keep up in a sort of fashion the fortifications raised by the native princes, without constructing any additional works of defence. This state of things attracted at the very beginning the attention of the new authorities, and a credit of eleven millions, charged on the budgets of several years, was assigned to the construction of new military buildings, the improvement of those already existing, and the erection of works required to ensure the defence of the great centres and principal ports. At this moment most Indian barracks possess the conditions of space and ventilation necessary for the health of Europeans in that deleterious climate, and if epidemics still sweep off whole regiments, the fault can no longer be attributed to the negligence or parsimony of the Government. Moreover, Allahabad, Lucknow, and Delhi are now surrounded by formidable fortifications, which would enable even weak garrisons to defy the utmost efforts of the native population for a considerable period. The plans for the defence of the great seaports have been pushed forward with less activity, and are still buried in the portfolios of the commissions of inquiry.

The other portion of the former budgets of public works in India has not been treated less liberally, and we willingly acknowledge that since the transfer of the Company's possessions to the Crown, the European authorities have endeavoured, with an ardour which does them credit, to make their mission a providential one. The plague of famine, which civilisation has almost banished from modern Europe, still exists in India, and in years of drought whole populations succumb to the attacks of the fell enemy and its accompanying diseases.

Great calamities of this description paralyse commerce and trade, and make themselves felt by formidable deficits in the public revenue. For their own interests, no less than from a humanitarian point of view, one of the first duties of an Indian administration is to combat these disastrous eventualities by extending the means of artificial irrigation. The creation of such works in the North-West Provinces is due to the Mogul Emperors; Firoz Shah had the first canal dug in the plains, in order to water a favourite hunting-ground of his. The reign of Shah Yekan was marked by the opening of the Delhi Canal, executed under the direction and on the plans of the eminent architect Ali Murdan Khan, which for the space of a century fertilised the districts in the neighbourhood of the capital. Other canals, which it would be too long to enumerate, testified to the far-seeing philanthropy of Akbar's successors; but in the midst of the disorders which preceded and followed the fall of the Mogul Empire, the land became covered with ruins, and the great arteries ceased to provide it with their fertilising streams.

On becoming the heirs of the great Moguls, the English, who studiously followed the tradition of their predecessors, lost no time in repairing the canals damaged by time. Between 1803 and 1822, the Eastern Jumna Canal, which is one hundred and fifty miles long, and waters a hundred and fifty thousand acres, and the Western Jumna Canal, which has a length of four hundred and forty-five miles, were opened. These restorations were the mere prelude of the greatest and most useful work which honoured the long reign of the East India Company. The great canal of the Ganges is eight hundred and ninety-eight miles long, irrigates one million four hundred and seventy-one thousand five hundred acres, and protects a population of six million persons from the horrors of famine. The principal branch, opened on April 8, 1854, which is prolonged for a distance of one hundred and twenty-five miles, and is ten feet at its greatest depth, and one hundred and seventy at its greatest width, is almost unequalled in the world, and is larger by a third than the largest navigable canals in the United States. The efforts made in the Company's time to create new irrigation works never extended beyond the North-West Provinces. In Bengal nothing more was done than to keep up the dykes and embankments which defend the coast from inundations, and to cut several navigable canals in the neighbourhood of Calcutta. The configuration of the ground in the Madras and Bombay Presidencies generally allows of irrigation by means of reservoirs formed by banking up the waters of the valleys. These reservoirs were almost all established before the European conquest, and did not involve the Government in very considerable works, as they entailed little expense to keep in repair. The occurrence of the Mutiny called away for some time attention from the question of irrigation, but this vital matter was again brought into prominence by the famine which, in 1861, prevailed in a large portion of the North-West Provinces, and in 1866 in the provinces of Orissa and Lower Bengal.[1]

[1] A few words will suffice to give the reader some idea of the horrors of a famine in India. We borrow the terrible details from the declarations made by Mr. Justice Wauchope and the Rev. A. Miller, before the court of inquiry on the famine in Bengal and the province of Orissa in 1866.

Mr. Wauchope's deposition before the Committee at Cuttack, on January 12, 1867, is as follows:—'I went to Midnapore from Hooghly on March 26, 1866, and noticed that there were many starved and emaciated people about the station, picking up berries and living on what they could get. This was the state of things immediately on my arrival, and people said that they had never seen such a thing before. I was only at the station three weeks, and knew little of what was going on there. I had before me at that time a number of dacoity cases in which the crime had been evidently committed by starving people. That was also the opinion of the Commissioner. Many of the prisoners admitted the robbery, pleading want of food. The persons tried principally belonged to the jungle tribes. On April 17 I went back to Hooghly. I did not there notice any particular appearance of famine. I left Hooghly again for Balasore on May 19, and went back to Balasore, arriving on May 22. There was nothing, so far as I recollect, that particularly attracted my attention between Calcutta and Midnapore, and at Midnapore I was only a few hours in the house. On the road from Midnapore to Balasore, from about twenty miles out of Midnapore, I saw real signs of famine. The villages seemed to be nearly deserted, the men, women, and children seen on the road were literal skeletons, and wherever I stopped I was surrounded by hundreds of the skeleton beggars. This increased in intensity from beyond Dantoon all the way to Balasore. I never had seen such scenes in my life. I cannot say where I first saw dead bodies. At Balasore there were several thousand starving people, and they were fed daily at the "dhurmsala." But the state of things about Balasore was literally horrible. Every road and every part of Balasore was covered with living skeletons, picking up bits of sticks to cook the rice given to them; hundreds of them were lying on every side of the road; they seemed as if black parchment were stretched over bones. As time passed, starving people kept pouring in from the interior, nearly all skeletons, and things got worse; deaths became numerous. On July 2, I left Balasore and returned to Calcutta.

Another famine laid waste Bengal in 1874, but the generous and vigorous efforts of the Government succeeded in averting the evil, which, anyhow, was greatly exaggerated by articles in the English papers.

From 1860 the Home Government gave *carte blanche* to Indian authorities to undertake irrigation works on a hitherto unprecedented scale. A first credit of a million sterling, assigned for this purpose in 1867, could not be employed on account of the insufficiency of the preliminary calculations. Since then these works have been pushed on with steady activity, and it may be hoped that India in twenty-five years will be provided with a complete system of irrigation. By indefatigably promoting this great undertaking, England shows herself truly worthy of the civilising mission which Providence has entrusted to her. The duty of European rulers towards their Asiatic subjects does not merely consist in giving them order and peace, but in protecting them, as much as lies in the power of modern art and science, from the terrible eventuality, the very name of which causes the bravest to grow pale—against famine. India must not only be benefited by irrigation in places where it is profitable, but wherever it is possible, and when this

The roads were almost impassable from the rains, and horrible as were the scenes I had seen on my previous journey, they were ten times more horrible on my return.'

The Rev. A. Miller says:—'Towards the end of May, people were dying very rapidly about the station, and I think that June, July, and August were the worst months. Hundreds died in fields and out-of-the-way places, where no one saw them. If one chanced to cross the country, one saw the bodies lying about and the jackals eating them. I should say, to be within bounds, that about one-fourth of the population of Orissa has died. In this neighbourhood, I think the mortality has been one-third; but I believe that in other parts of the province it has not been so severe. As to the number of deaths in a certain day, I have seen some exaggeration in the papers; it was said that 1,000 had died in one day in the streets of Balasore—that was an exaggeration. I think the worst day we ever had about 290 or 300 were carted off dead from the station, and thrown into the river. But, as respects the general misery and suffering, I do not think that it has ever been fully described; it would have been almost impossible to exaggerate it. I heard a well-authenticated instance in which a mother and son were found eating a dead child.'—*Report of the Commissioners appointed to Inquire into the Famine in Bengal and Orissa in* 1866, vol. i. Nos. 73 and 86.

immense task is accomplished, England will have acquired imperishable claims to India's gratitude.

Twenty-five years ago India was without roads, and the traveller could only depend on his own legs, a palanquin, the backs of native bearers, a donkey, a horse, a dromedary, or an elephant; but means of communication are not as indispensable in Asia as in Europe; nature sometimes greatly favours, sometimes completely arrests all transit. The dryness, which lasts nine months in the year, makes every path practicable both to those on foot and those on horseback, and facilitates, moreover, the crossing of rivers and torrents. In the rainy season all locomotion is suspended, and the most perfect road ever made will never allow, otherwise than exceptionally, the passage of goods or travellers under the deluges which inundate the country between June and September. The old servants of the Company, who were generally opposed to progress of any kind, whether material or not, easily accustomed themselves to the expenses and length of the journey, which for them were the only drawbacks of this state of things, and were even heard to praise its advantages. Thus, stress was laid on the fact that the want of roads necessitated holding in readiness on every point stores of provisions and means of transport for the troops, which, with very slight preparation, could pass from a peace to a war footing. Hence the extraordinary promptness with which Anglo-Indian armies took the field in certain wars; hence, also, the skill and marvellous resources of the commissariat, which was always kept in activity; and thus to the troops who, in their changes of garrison, experienced for months together real camp life, a military school of the most useful character was afforded. Experience has, however, shown the fallacy of these paradoxes, and the construction of roads is at present one of the questions which most preoccupies the Queen's representatives in India.

The first roads were made in the North-West Provinces, where the configuration of the country was favourable to the works, and where, moreover, the necessary materials abounded. Towards 1851 the road from Calcutta to Delhi was opened for traffic. The impulse had been given, and was especially followed in the Punjab, then recently annexed, whose progress Lord Dalhousie was following with paternal care as Governor-General. The movement, however, only reached its full development when a parliamentary vote transferred the sceptre of India to the Crown. The progress made under the new rule is sufficiently shown by the following figures. In 1851–52, the credit granted for the construction and maintenance of roads in the three Presidencies amounted to 120,000*l.* Fifteen years later, the same credit was ten times as high, and in 1867–68 it reached the sum of 1,358,640*l.*, viz., 531,840*l.* assigned to the maintenance of roads already existing, and 826,800*l.* for the extension of the system. A good macadamised road averages about 1,000*l.* a mile in India. The cost, it is true, varies very greatly in different localities, and is much higher in Lower Bengal, where materials are totally wanting, and where stones have to be brought at a great expense from a distance, or else broken bricks have to be used, which makes the keeping up of the roads a costly matter.

A characteristic feature of Indian roads is their incompleteness; bridges over rivers are invariably wanting. In reality, the latter, which are very expensive constructions, are of little use. In summer, the rivers can be easily forded or crossed in boats, whilst only the strongest structures could resist the violence of the currents in winter, and would in any case be very little used. The actual budget would enable about eight hundred miles of roads to be opened yearly, at the average cost of 1,000*l.* per mile; but the maintenance of new thoroughfares is incumbent on the State, and in India there are no public revenues, subsidies, forced labour, or local taxes which can be assigned to this object, as in Europe. Turnpikes were established at first, but the proceeds scarcely covered the expenses of collecting the tolls; they were destroyed in the Mutiny, and have not been set up again. The problem of the maintenance of roads still remains to be solved, and is one of great importance; for if we estimate the average cost at 75*l.* per mile, and the annual construction at eight hundred miles, we see that the budget of public works is yearly charged with an increase of 60,000*l.*, owing to new and indispensable expenses of maintenance. At this moment the length of the macadamised roads in India is ten thousand miles; and though this shows great and remarkable progress as compared with twenty years ago, the work of opening up the empire has, we may say, scarcely begun. The laying down of railways makes it still the more indispensable to speedily finish the work of road making. Many stations are hundreds of miles away from any road fit for vehicles, and the railways will not produce their full results until a system of improved roads enables the produce of the districts they traverse to reach the trucks without exorbitant cost of carriage.

Lord Dalhousie, to whom belongs the honour of having conceived and inaugurated the great work of Indian railways, felt that the Government's aim ought not merely to be the protection of the military and political interests of the conquest. Above all, he intended that a network of railways should serve to develop the wealth and the resources of the country, by connecting the centres of production with the large seaports. The eminent statesman felt, moreover, that to carry out the undertaking successfully, it was necessary to combine the action of both private and public enterprise, and that European capitalists, from whom alone assistance could be expected, would not venture on a task full of unknown difficulties, if left solely dependent on their own resources. The fundamental basis of the contracts made with the various companies was generally as follows:—The Government engaged to provide gratis the ground necessary for the lines, and to guarantee a minimum interest of 5 per cent. on the capital invested since the beginning of the work. As reimbursement for these advances, it was agreed that the net profits of the works should be paid into the public treasury. As long as the amount of these payments did not exceed

5 per cent. of the capital expended, the whole sum was kept by the State; above 5 per cent. the surplus was divided into equal portions, one for the shareholders, the other for the treasury. The sums thus received by the latter were to be applied to liquidate the interest previously paid to the shareholders, and when the total reimbursement thus effected should balance the total of the advances made by the State, at simple interest of 5 per cent., the profits should belong definitively and entirely to the shareholders.

Another important question still remained to be solved. As all the capital had to come from England, it was indispensable to guard against the fluctuations of the exchange, and it was determined that the latter should be fixed at 1*s.* 10*d.*, a rate less by 9 per cent. than the legal value of the rupee. The Government, in short, sold its bills at a fixed rate, but much lower than the market price. The wisdom of this proceeding has been clearly shown since 1869, and in the last budget, 1872–73, the profits accruing to the public treasury amounted to 2,800,000*l.*

On December 30, 1871, the advances made by the State as guarantees to the various companies reached the sum of 20,000,000*l.* Though these figures are very high, it can be safely asserted that the Indian budget has never been charged with a more honourable and more useful debt.[1]

In return for the help given to the various companies, the Government reserved to itself the right of interference in their proceedings; its sanction was necessary for all expenses of laying down lines or working them. The general accounts are revised by its comptrollers, and the various companies have absolute power only over their own clerks, whom they can appoint or dismiss at will, but whose salaries and functions are determined by the Government.

The various companies are represented in England by administrative councils, subject to the control of a Government director, who sits on all the committees, and has a right of veto on their decisions. In India, an agent delegated by each company presides over the staff of clerks, and the

[1] See Documents No. XVII.

carrying out of the works under the supervision of a consulting engineer, an official who acts as intermediary between the companies and the State. In theory, the Government exercises an absolute authority over Indian railways, but in practice this control is non-existent. In England, a single agent would not suffice for the business of eight great companies; in India, the consulting engineer only attends to the works of the line entrusted to him, and to this his powers are limited. Hence it has happened that the costs of certain companies have much exceeded the estimates, and that in others the work has been carried out with lamentable parsimony. Moreover, the stimulus which in general calls forth the energetic supervision of the directors of companies and their agents, the desire to establish an excess of receipts over expenditure, which may allow the payment of a dividend to the shareholders, is not to be found among the officials of the Anglo-Indian lines. As they have no anxiety on this score, whatever be the result of the working, they show neither zeal nor economy in their management of affairs. Government intervention has also encountered serious difficulties in the management of the railways whenever the interests of the public, which it represents, are in direct opposition to those of the companies. The latter try to combine a maximum of profit with a minimum of traffic, whilst the public, on the contrary, wish to obtain the same result by means of the lowest possible tariffs. At this point Government action stops, and it can neither force the companies to reduce their fares to the minimum, nor to multiply the number of trains. So that railway freight is exorbitant and almost prohibitive for certain articles—coal, for instance.

The original system of Indian railways[1] comprises nine principal lines, worked by as many companies, with a guarantee of interest. The first, the 'East Indian,' connects Calcutta with the Punjab, passing through the large towns of Bengal and the North-West Provinces. The second, the 'Great Indian Peninsular,' connects Bombay with Calcutta by

[1] See Documents No. XVIII.

its junction with the 'East Indian' at Allahabad and Bombay, with Madras, by its junction with the Madras line at Koulburga. The third is the 'Madras Railway,' whose various branch lines connect the Arabian Gulf with that of Bengal, Madras with the fine plateau of the Neilgherries and with the 'Great Indian Peninsular.' The fourth, the 'Scinde, Punjab, and Delhi,' offers a substitute for the difficult navigation of the Lower Indus. Besides these, there are the 'Bombay, Baroda, and Central India,' the 'Great Southern of India,' the 'Eastern Bengal,' the 'Oude and Rohilkund,' and lastly, the 'Carnatic,' which is intended to supply the wants of Madras and Pondicherry. Experience has since then revealed new wants, but any supplementary lines which have been grafted on to the original system are now constructed by the State, and are entirely under its control. Such, for instance, are the 'Calcutta and South-Eastern,' the 'Northern Punjab,' and the 'Rajpootana.' In the official year 1871–72 (April 1 to March 31) 408 miles of railway were opened for traffic, and there are now in full activity 5,204 miles, of which 5,136 belong to companies, and 68 to the State. The completion of the projected lines will necessitate laying down another 2,440 miles, of which 940 by the companies and 1,500 by the State.

The expenses of the various companies, from the first works (1849) to March 31, 1872, amount to 90,623,793*l.*, that is to say: Sums expended in India for materials and labour, 53,688,044*l.*; cost of material, freight, insurance in England, 36,935,549*l.*[1] The cost of construction and materials may be computed approximately thus: Bridges, 28,000,000*l.*; permanent ways and stations, 27,000,000*l.*; rolling stock and engines, 13,000,000*l.* The supplement of 90 millions having defrayed various expenses—such as the salary of the officials, freight, and insurance, electric telegraphs,[2] according to the specification, the land was given gratis by the Government to the companies.

The receipts of Anglo-Indian railways during the year 1871–72 amounted to 6,146,130*l.*, and the expenditure to

[1] See Documents No. XIX. [2] See Documents No. XX.

3,302,050*l.*; that is to say, the net profit was 2,844,080*l.*, with a proportion of 54 per cent. between receipts and expenditure. These figures differed little from those of the preceding year, but it must not be forgotten that 408 fresh miles of permanent way were opened for traffic in 1871–72, and by this very fact the original cost of the construction was increased by 2,300,000*l.* The diminution of receipts fell exclusively on the 'East Indian' and the 'Scinde, Punjab, and Delhi.' The other lines have fared better; thus the 'Great Indian Peninsular' showed an increase of 200,000*l.* The receipts for 1871–72 may be divided as follows: 18,940,585 passengers gave 1,940,549*l.*, and 3,289,561 tons of merchandise, 4,025,309*l.*, the remainder being supplied from various sources, such as telegraphs and transports. The total of train miles run reached 14,080,064, 4,789,184 of which was by passenger train, 4,921,434 by luggage trains, and 4,309,446 by mixed or exclusively mineral trains.

Train mileage receipts and expenses vary considerably. On the 'Bombay, Baroda, and Central India' the receipts are 12·46, on the 'Carnatic' 2·52. The expenditure amounted to 7·43 on the former, 1·64 on the 'Carnatic,' and 4·03 on the 'East Indian.' The average for the whole system is 8·74 and 4·50. In England, the same year, the average was 5·13 and 2·54. The great diversity of expenses on the various Indian lines is due to the different sorts of fuel in use. Some of them bring their fuel at great expense from England, while others use only wood. The 'East Indian' passes through the fine coal districts of Lower Bengal, and gets its fuel at a lower price than the most favoured European lines. Recent investigations have revealed the presence of coal in large quantities in certain parts of Central India, and these mines will shortly supply the 'Great Indian Peninsular.' The geological researches made during these last years in the Presidency of Madras have proved fruitless, and no beds of coal have been discovered.

On September 30, 1871, 68,517 officials were employed

by the Anglo-Indian railways, of whom 4,852 were European. The latter figures give an idea of the magnificent opening which the working of railways in India offers to the English middle and lower classes. We will conclude these dry details by stating that passengers on the more important Indian lines travel with far greater security than is the case, unfortunately, anywhere in Europe. Only one accident of any consequence, in which eight passengers were hurt, occurred in 1871-72. Less serious accidents, to the number of 548, may be classed thus: 76 from fire, 70 from trains getting off their proper lines, 35 from collisions, 53 from various causes, and 314 from cattle straying on the line. Let it be noted here that under the name of cattle, hyenas, deer, buffaloes, tigers, and other dispossessed inhabitants of the jungle are included. Death has none the less stricken down its victims among the crowd of passengers: 110 natives, with but two or three exceptions, died in railway carriages from fever, dysentery, or cholera.

A few pages back we showed that the net profits of Anglo-Indian railways in the year 1871–72 rose to 2,844,000*l.*, or about 3½ per cent. of the capital invested by the companies (85,000,000*l.* approximately). In order to fulfil its engagements towards the shareholders and to make up the interest of 5 per cent. promised, the Indian Government was obliged to supply a sum of about 1,200,000*l.* This, it must be confessed, was a heavy burden for the colonial budget, and hitherto the extensive works undertaken for the public good have not justified the hopes indulged in at the first. Exceptional circumstances were at fault in 1871–72 in diminishing traffic on the 'East Indian,' which is the most active and extensive line in India. Moreover, on these recently constructed lines passenger and merchandise traffic is far from having reached the development it is capable of. On the lines first opened the average of receipts increases considerably every five years.[1] These statistics give grounds for anticipating a better future for Indian railways.

As to the system of companies guaranteed by the State,

[1] See Documents No. XXI.

the results have been such as to furnish its adversaries with powerful arguments. On several lines the cost of construction has largely exceeded the estimates. The officials, who are not interested in procuring a dividend, show neither economy nor activity in their management, without which no great enterprises can be profitable. Finally, the interests of the public are constantly sacrificed to those of the companies, without the Government having the power to take vigorous action in the cause of justice. These unquestionable facts have long made the system unpopular, and as early as 1862 Lord Elgin, the Governor-General, objected to applying it to the new lines which have since been exclusively made and worked by the State. Many people have even been found favourable to the idea of ousting the companies for the advantage of the Government, and they take their stand on a clause in the contract by which the latter reserved to itself the right of buying up the lines at the end of twenty-five years. There would be little difficulty in doing this, and the Indian Government would find it all the more easy to negotiate a loan of two milliards, that after all it would only be a question of a simple conversion.[1]

Without prejudging the future of Indian railways, we

[1] The rate of interest paid to the companies is actually 1 per cent. higher than if the Government borrowed directly. Moreover, while the State only detains half of the profits above 5 per cent., it is responsible not only for the guaranteed interest, but also for all the working expenses beyond those that are covered by the receipts. Finally, any company when in great straits may call upon the State to take its place and to repay its capital and its debts. These considerations militate undeniably in favour of buying up all railways without distinction, whether remunerative or not. With regard to the time at which this purchase should be made, Mr. Hector Malot, the Director of the Bank of Bengal, in a recent pamphlet, gives in favour of immediate action figures which seem decisive. In 1868, the 100*l*. shares of the good Indian companies varied from 103⅜ to 107⅝, whilst in 1873 they were quoted at from 113 to 120. The rise in 1869 giving a premium of 10 per cent. to the shares, the expenses of the budget in 1878 would have only been 56,000*l*.; and ten years later, in 1888, the State would benefit to the extent of 1,500,000*l*. Buying up of the lines at this present moment would not cost the budget much more than what its actual engagements oblige it to pay, whilst the uniformity of the lines, reductions in the number of officials both at home and in India, would result in immediate and considerable economy in the working.

will confine ourselves to impartially examining the great work initiated by Lord Dalhousie. Questions of finance, of systems of construction and working disappear before considerations of a far higher order. By giving to the India of the Brahmins a complete system of railways in less than twenty years, England has finally taken root in this land, where change is unknown. The lines of rail which are now laid down on the banks of the Ganges and the Indus will certainly bring in their train the seeds of moral and material progress and of true civilisation, as they have done everywhere else. The conquerors, who have gifted their subjects with 5,000 miles of permanent way, have successfully achieved a task without precedent in history, and we must acknowledge that the English in the last twenty years have shown themselves worthy of the favours which fortune has showered on them for a century in Asia.

The statistics of the Anglo-Indian empire for 1871–72 place the exports from the great seaports of Kurrachee, Bombay, Madras, Calcutta, Moulmein, and Rangoon at the high figure of 64,661,940*l.* Imports, too, for the same places during the same time amounted to 42,657,560*l.* The returns of the previous nine years show clear proof of the extent to which external politics are felt in commercial transactions in India. During the American civil war, which gave an enormous impulse to cotton growing, the exports reached the maximum. The European wars of 1866 and 1870 disturbed all the markets of the world; when peace returned trade revived, and the statistics of maritime trade in 1871–72 differ very slightly from those of the period of the American crisis.

The port of Calcutta stands at the head of Indian mercantile traffic, and in 1871–72 the imports amounted to 19,741,420*l.*, the exports to 27,849,329*l.* Trade on the banks of the Hooghly follows a progressive course, and the year 1872 showed over the first of the last decennial period an increase of 5,497,954*l.* in the imports and of 12,458,606*l.* in the exports. It was not so with Bombay, where the exports rose to almost a milliard during the cotton fever (1864–65), to fall in the last return lower than in 1863. The statistics for the ten years previous to 1872 places imports to Bombay at 10,432,058*l*. and exports at 25,899,239*l*. These figures are much the same as in 1863—viz., imports 9,905,637*l*., exports 25,849,848*l*.

Indian maritime trade in 1872 was represented by 45,885 ships of 8,333,638 tons, comprising inward and outward entries.[1] If these figures be compared with those of the first budget of the decennial period—41,501 ships of 5,612,205 tons—it is clear that the number of ships has remained nearly stationary, while the tonnage is nearly double. During the last few years a twofold change has taken place in English merchant shipping. Vessels of small tonnage have given way to large clippers, and since the opening of the isthmus of Suez steamers have competed with sailing vessels for freight in the Indian Seas. Though modern discoveries have not yet solved the question of superiority between the two great Indian metropoli, they have nevertheless developed fresh sources of wealth in and around them. If, since the opening of the Suez Canal, Bombay is ten days nearer Europe than Calcutta, the latter has much the advantage in point of railway communication. There are but 560 miles between Calcutta and Allahabad, which latter place is the point of junction of the 'East Indian Railway,' running through the North-West Provinces and the Punjab and the 'Indian Peninsular,' whilst the distance from Bombay to Allahabad is some 850 miles. The Calcutta line is supplied with fuel from the mines of Raniganje at a much lower rate than that paid by the Peninsular Company, which draws all its fuel from Europe. The influence of the Suez Canal is felt at Bombay by the increase in steam navigation, which in 1872 numbered 88 inward and 90 outward-bound steamers, as against 75 and 76 in the previous year. The completion of M. de Lesseps' work also induced the ports of Genoa, Trieste, Constantinople, and Odessa to enter into direct communication with India. The efforts of the Trieste ship-owners were crowned with

[1] See Documents No. XXII.

success, and in 1872 the exports from Bombay to the Adriatic rose to 500,000*l*. Attempts made with the same object by the Russian Government proved less successful: the line of steamers under its protection lasted but a short time, with most unsatisfactory results.

Were we to examine item by item the commercial statistics of India, we should outstep the limits of these sketches. We shall therefore confine ourselves to the mention of the new products which, while already of considerable importance, have not yet reached the full development which the future holds in reserve for them. Foremost on the bill come rice from British Burmah, jute, coffee, tea, and cotton.

Rice is the great article of export of India, if not in value, at least in quantity. Its total yearly amount is about 16,990,890 cwt. In 1871–72, more than half this amount was furnished by British Burmah, a territory annexed to the Anglo-Indian possessions after the second Burmese war twenty years ago. Rice from Rangoon and Moulmein not only competes with that from Saigon and Bangk in the European market, but also in those of China, the Mauritius, and the Island of Bourbon. English speculation has neglected nothing in order to give the Burmese rice trade the fullest development it is capable of, and at the present moment there are sixteen recently built rice mills, provided with all the latest improvements in working order, in the neighbourhood of the two European centres of that country.

Jute, the hemp of Bengal, which grows wild in the delta of Eastern Bengal, between the Ganges and the Brahmapootra, only began to play its present important part in the Calcutta trade about the time of the War of Secession. Jute is brought by the native cultivators to the markets of Seraoganje, Naraganje, and Dacca, from whence it is forwarded to Calcutta, and eventually to Europe. Dundee, in the United Kingdom, is the centre of the manufacture of articles in jute, such as ropes and cordage, cloths, and coarse carpets. The factories of Messrs. Cox Brothers, who employ 3,000 horse-power and more than 2,000 workmen, and transport the jute on their own steamers, are fully equal in importance to the gigantic cotton spinning establishments of Manchester. Jute is also used in India to make gunny bags for packing rice, and is sent in enormous quantities to Burmah, China, and America (5,112,421 sacks). The following table shows, without need of commentary, the progress made in the culture of jute during the last thirty years, and the importance which this article, unknown fifty years ago, has already acquired in European trade:—

Exportation of Jute.

	£		£
1842 . . .	24,941	1862 . . .	537,610
1852 . . .	180,976	1872 . . .	4,299,767

Like everything in India, tea has a legend of its own. An Indian devotee, called Durmah, who lived some five hundred years before the Christian era, touched by the religious ignorance of the Chinese, undertook to make known the divine revelation to them. Indifferent to comfort, the holy man started on his journey without provisions. One day, worn out by hunger and fatigue, he lay down and fell asleep. On awaking, Durmah, ashamed of having given way for a moment to the wants of nature, tore out his eyebrows by way of self-chastisement, and threw them away. They were immediately changed into graceful leafy shrubs; the astonished traveller plucked and tasted the leaves, and perceived that they restored vigour both to his body and to his mind. The renown of Durmah's sanctity soon spread; he advised his numerous followers to make use of the new plant, and soon the taste for the beverage, which cheers without inebriating, became universal in China.

The culture of the tea-plant, with a view to trade, is of recent origin in India, and goes back only fifty years. The first Burmese war made the English masters of the Assam territory in 1816, and soon after tea-plants were discovered in the conquered territory. Were these shrubs indigenous, or did they date from an epoch of former civilisation whose undeniable traces are visible in the Brahmapootra valley?

Whatever their origin, their discovery did not pass unnoticed, and a mission sent by the Governor-General, Lord Bentinck, in 1834, reported that the tea-plant was indigenous in Upper Assam, and its leaves available for purposes of trade. The Government at once brought labourers and seed from China, and in 1839, eight chests of Assam tea were sold in the London market. This first success attracted the attention of speculators; a company was formed under the auspices of the Babou Dwarkanaught Tagore, whose name is honourably connected with all progress in commerce and agriculture made in India during the first half of the century, and bought up all the Government tea plantations. The beginnings of the Assam Tea Company were not successful, but a change of administration re-established order and economy in its affairs, and its property caused a regular tea mania, both in the markets of London and Calcutta. Demands for grants of land increased, and companies sprang into existence on all sides. Unsafe or dishonest speculations led to catastrophes, and to a temporary check to production, until badly managed undertakings collapsed and gave way to companies worthier of the confidence of the shareholders. Assam is not the only part of India fit for tea-planting, and the shrub is found wild in the neighbouring province of Cachar, as well as in the lower slopes of the Himalaya, in the North-West Provinces, and in the Punjab. Lord Dalhousie's government, wishing to extend tea-planting in the north as well as in the west, organised plantations at Kumaon, and at Dehra Doun, and sixteen years ago we visited these interesting gardens, then in their first novelty. In 1864, they were sold to companies, and, if properly managed, they ought one day to rival those of Assam and Cachar. The following figures give a correct notion of the progress made by tea planting:—

Exports of Tea.

Year	£	Year	£
1842	17,244	1862	192,242
1852	59,220	1872	1,482,186

The latter figures representing 17,460,138 pounds of tea,

and the whole amount being far from conveying a true idea of the total production of India. The tea from the Himalaya districts finds an advantageous market on the spot, in Thibet and Afghanistan, and is not included in the total of the exports by sea. Assam tea is largely consumed in India, and is furnished in great quantities to the European army. We shall not go further into the matter, as what we have said shows clearly enough the important place which tea will certainly occupy in the commerce between India and England.

Coffee-planting, which is peculiar to the Madras Presidency, has long been carried on there; and local tradition asserts that the shrub was introduced into the table-land of Mysore by a pilgrim, who brought back seven grains of coffee from Mecca. But it has only become of importance as an article of exportation within the last twenty years, in consequence of the abolition of a heavy duty which formerly hampered the trade. Coffee plantations exist only in Mysore, the Neilgherries, and in the Courg and Wyniad districts on slopes 3,000 or 4,000 feet above the level of the sea. This agricultural industry, which is pursued in a climate favourable to European constitutions, where, during the south-west monsoon, a planter may oversee his labourers during the entire day without fear of sunstroke, was the very thing for retired officers, who were desirous of occupying their leisure time. There are numbers of veterans formerly in the Company's service to be found among the planters. The progress and the importance of coffee-planting are shown by the following table:—

	£		£
1842	74,957	1862	462,380
1852	84,306	1872	1,380,410

The figures of 1872 represent a weight of 56,889,888 pounds.

The use of cotton in India, where the sun, the climate, and labour are exceptionally favourable to it, goes back to the earliest ages. It was, however, only under the influence of an external and unforeseen event, the American War of Secession, that cotton-planting made a great stride. It is noticeable that the East India Company, though generally not inclined to favour material progress, yet took great interest in the question of cotton from the outset. Already in the last century official efforts were made to improve the indigenous plant. In 1829, for the first time, seeds of upland Georgia, Sea Island, Demerara, were imported by the Royal Agricultural Society, and the Government of India granted the sums necessary for the expenses of the first trial. The climate of the country round Calcutta, where the first attempts were made, was both too hot and too damp, and the result was a total failure. Ten years later, an agent sent out by the Court of Directors brought back from America ten experienced planters, and many kinds of seeds, and the experiment was resumed on a vast scale in the three Presidencies. In Bengal, the American seeds did not succeed even in the soil most adapted to the indigenous species. In the Madras Presidency, on the contrary, the official report stated that they gave a superior yield both as to quantity and quality. In that of Bombay, where cotton-planting is most widely diffused, the results varied greatly, and were not equally favourable; in the Dharwar they were negative, in Guzerati they were everything that could be desired. It was even observed that in certain seasons, when the native plant perished from cold or heat, American cotton resisted vigorously these deleterious influences. These differences must be ascribed, as was recognised afterwards, to the unfortunate choice of locality and the exclusive employment of the American system of planting. In so vast a country as India, experience and time alone can determine the soil and the climate specially favourable to certain products. As to the method of cultivation, in the very places where the American system had failed, the foreign seeds yielded later on an abundant crop, when managed according to the old Indian tradition—as, for example, in the districts of Khandeish and Dharwar, in Central India, and in the Presidency of Bombay.[1]

The question of introducing American seeds into Indian

[1] See Documents No. XXIII.

agriculture was now settled, but there were other elements to be taken into account with regard to the greater development of production. Up to the moment when the American War threatened the great European manufactures for spinning and weaving cotton with an immediate stoppage—with a famine, according to the forcible expression of the day —the market for the Indian article was always uncertain, and the price so low as scarcely to be remunerative. The demand for China, one of the two great cotton markets for India, never goes beyond certain limits. That for England, on the contrary, varies according to the crop in the United States. If the crop is a poor one beyond the Atlantic, Indian cotton is much sought after, and bought up immediately; but the following year, a good crop at New Orleans is enough to throw back Indian cotton into a state of stagnation, to the great loss of the planters, who had increased their production in the hope that their cottons will always be in demand for the English market. We may add that the bad condition of the Indian cotton, which is damp, and full of dry leaves and sand, fully explains this variation in the export to Europe. The Asiatic article is accepted there as a last resource when the finer products of the Southern States of America are not to be had. Owing to the many hands through which the cotton has to pass, and to the insufficiency of means of transport, it only reaches the port of shipment after long delays, burdened with the costs of numerous commissions and heavy expenses of transport, and often after having been repeatedly adulterated.

This state of things has been much improved by the completion of the Indian railway system, which enables European merchants to deal directly by means of agents with the native producer, to the immense gain of the latter. The planter had hitherto been a prey to the village usurer, and however diligent his labour or abundant his crop, it was a matter of difficulty for him to pay the rent of his land and advances, the interest on which was generally 36 per cent. As he now comes into contact with the representatives of the Bombay and Calcutta merchants, he sells his cotton for ready money only, and at a remunerative price, so that in certain districts, after the sale of the crop, there are not jewellers enough to be found to convert into ornaments the gold and silver which abound. Railways have done quite as much towards improving the quality of the produce. Formerly the bales were exposed to all the changes of the weather in long journeys, which kept them weeks on the road; now they reach the port of shipment in fewer days than it would have taken months to convey them to their destination some years ago, and at a far lower cost of transport. In 1867, there were 8,000,000 acres of land given up to cotton planting, of which 552,520 were in the Central Provinces, and 1,254,552 in Berar. In 1871–72, in the Bombay Presidency alone, the number rose to almost three millions. The total value of cotton exports reached 21,272,430*l.*, with a gross weight of 809,246,087 lbs. The port of Bombay stands at the head of the list, and contributes to the above total 540,404,613 lbs., worth 14,820,637*l.* For the port of Calcutta the figures were only 164,476,962 lbs., worth 4,036,956*l.* A proof that the development of the cotton culture has not attained its full extent is that the exports of 1871–72 were almost twice what they were in the first year of the preceding decennial period, and surpassed the maximum reached in the height of the American crisis. But if one wants to get a thorough notion of the progress made in this branch of Indian agriculture, one must go back still further; in 1852–53 the exports amounted to 217,433,911 lbs., and have thus increased nearly fourfold in twenty years.[1]

The Universal Exhibitions in London and Paris, and more recently in Vienna, have made known to the public the variety and number of Indian fabrics. The shawls, the many woollen stuffs, the carpets from the Punjab, the

[1] *Exportation of Cotton.*

	£		£
1863 . . .	473,678,421	1868 . . .	614,056,149
1864 . . .	550,126,402	1869 . . .	697,630,796
1865 . . .	525,052,876	1870 . . .	554,834,522
1866 . . .	803,150,124	1871 . . .	577,600,764
1867 . . .	427,563,892	1872 . . .	809,246,087

embroidered silks from Delhi, the cottons from Nagpore, the specimens of cabinet work from Bombay, the fine muslins of Dacca, occupied a high place even among the marvellous products of European industry. Native trade, far from being ruined by English imports, fully holds its superiority for articles of high quality, such as woollen or cotton tissues, hand-embroidery, &c. This persistent existence of local industry shows clearly enough that the raw products are consumed in the country; so that statistics of the commercial relations between province and province would form an interesting chapter in the economical history of India. Unfortunately, these are yet in their infancy, and exist only in exceptional cases. For instance, it is well known that in the Punjab the value of imports and exports is almost equal: 2,350,000*l.*, as against 2,780,000*l.* The trade on the Indus is registered at Sakkar in Scinde, and shows a value of 105,000*l.* going up, and 630,000*l.* going down. Approximate calculations estimate the foreign trade of the Central Provinces at 14,003,917*l.* Native production has been considerably increased of late years by the establishment of factories on a vast scale, provided with the latest improvements of modern industry. There are nineteen such for spinning and weaving cotton in the Bombay Presidency, of which Bombay itself contains eleven. They employ 404,000 spindles, 4,294 looms, and nineteen steam-engines. Among other great establishments of Anglo-Indian industry, the Elgin Cotton-Spinning and Weaving Company at Cawnpore, and the Goosey Cotton Mills Company, in the neighbourhood of Calcutta, must be mentioned. Let us also note in the same Presidency, 153 licensed steam presses and 287 hand presses for pressing bales of cotton. We have already mentioned the mills for cleaning rice, established some years ago at Calcutta and in the two ports of British Burmah, Moulmein and Rangoon.

The value of the imports to the great Indian seaports in 1871–72 amounted, without including precious metals, to 31,084,347*l.*, that is to say, to an increase of nearly 10,000,000*l.* over the year 1862–63. The great economical changes which have occurred in India have left their mark on the returns of the last ten years. The progress of local industry, and the consequences of the completion of the railway system, are visible in the increase in the importation of machinery, worked iron, and iron in bars. A considerable augmentation in the quantity of wines corresponds to the increase of the European army and of the white population. The growing expansion of imports in woven and spun cottons deserves notice; in the last budget they rose to 17,484,837*l.*, or almost twice the value of the same articles imported in the first year of the decennial period, 9,630,530*l.* Considerable as is the amount of the imports from home taken by India, its full importance can only be understood if we go back some sixty years, to the first importation of English cotton. The same articles which in the last returns are quoted at 16,000,000*l.*, in 1814 only amounted to a single lac of rupees, 10,000*l.*

Of all the articles of consumption furnished by Europe to India, the precious metals most deserve to attract the attention of economists and financiers. From time immemorial India has drawn immense sums from Europe, which are there converted into personal ornaments. Before the Mutiny the annual average consumption was estimated at 3,000,000*l.* Public works and the cotton crisis caused precious metals, and amongst them, gold for the first time, to abound in the Indian market. In the ten years between 1862–63 and 1871–72, India drew from Europe in round numbers 103,000,000*l.* in silver and 59,000,000*l.* in gold.[1] The exports rose to 13,000,000*l.* in silver and 2,500,000*l.* in gold, that is to say, to an absorption of 146,500,000*l.*, or an annual average of 14,500,000*l.* It is true that the period which we have just considered offers certain special circumstances which can never recur: the great work of the Anglo-Indian railways now finished and the American War created an exceptional demand for the precious metals. It is none the less certain that if, by a special decree of Providence, the era of wars and revolutions were to end in Europe, Australia and

[1] See Documents No. XXIV.

California would still for many years find a sure and vast market for their gold and silver in England's Asiatic dependency.

Let us conclude by giving the figures of the general trade of India in 1871–72, including precious metals. It reached two milliards and a half of francs, a total which needs no commentary to give a true idea of the important part played by the three Presidencies in the commercial transactions of the world.[1]

Besides her maritime commerce India possesses a trade by land through the passes of the Himalaya leading to Afghanistan, Turkestan, and Thibet. The nomadic tribes by whom it is carried on start on their journey about the month of October, and move towards the Punjab, from whence their merchandise reaches the great markets of India, Amritsur, Benares, Calcutta, &c. These importations comprise wool for Cashmere shawls of inferior quality, which are manufactured in the Punjab, raw silks, ingots of gold and silver, borax and fruit both fresh and dry. On their return the caravans take back cotton and woollen stuffs, embroidered Delhi scarves, indigo, and Benares brocades. This traffic has existed from time immemorial, in spite of the high duties and the vexations it is subjected to by the petty rulers of the Indian Caucasus and their agents. In the last few years the English Government has attempted on several occasions to diminish the difficulties of the road, and to open up new routes for traffic on the land frontiers of its dominions. In 1867 the initiative of the political agent at Ladakh developed commercial relations through the passes of the Himalaya between India and Eastern Turkestan. Three years later, in 1870, the Maharajah of Cashmere, under pressure from the English agent, granted, on condition of reciprocity, a free transit through his possessions to the expedition sent to Central Asia. These new routes cannot fail to attract the attention of the Manchester and Bradford manufacturers, for they open up the markets of Central Asia, where their cotton goods can be sent at less

[1] See Documents No. XXV.

cost than similar articles from Moscow.[1] On the other hand, the articles brought back by the returning caravans, such as raw silks and precious metals, are eminently fitted by their small volume for transport over difficult roads. Those which lead from India to the table-lands of Thibet do not exclusively pass through the Northern Himalaya; there are others which lead through the passes of the eastern chain by way of Nepaul and Assam. In the latter province we must take note of the fair at Sudya, to which the neighbouring tribes bring skins and indiarubber, and which is destined to be one day the great point of junction of trade between India and Eastern China.

The fairs which are held after a pilgrimage to some holy place play a most important part in the internal trade of India. Among these solemnities, which partake at once of a commercial and religious character, we must note the fair which is held every year in the beginning of April at Hardwar,[2] at the mouth of the Ganges, in the plains where,

[1] The cost of transport from England to Kashgar, one of the principal markets of Eastern Turkestan, amount to 3*l.* 17*s.* 10*d.* on every 100 lbs. of manufactured cotton. The same amount of goods sent from Moscow would cost 4*l.* 7*s.* 8*d.*

[2] Though more than a week had yet to elapse before the great day, the Twelfth of April, the roads from Mirut to Hardwar, for ninety miles round, were literally covered with people. There was a continuous stream of foot passengers, of camels, of ox-carts—a regular immigration, so to speak. Looking from my palanquin, I might have thought myself in the midst of an entire nation on its travels, more numerous than the Jews when they left Egypt for the promised land. There the resemblance ends, for no Pharaoh was in pursuit of this multitude. Nothing could give a truer notion of the enormous population of India, and of the influence still exercised in spite of a century of foreign and Christian rule, by the prejudices of an imbecile religion, than the aspect of this throng crowding on one long road. Every race of India was represented in the medley: here a valiant Rajpoot with a herculean frame, there a timid Bengalee, here Punjabis, there Arabs from Scinde. The customs of all these pilgrims were of the strangest! Some had come from the most distant part of the Madras Presidency, with a stick and a copper pot as their only baggage. In that ox-cart, packed closer together than herrings in a barrel, were some twenty individuals—men, women, and children—who had travelled in this fashion for months. Here a long file of camels carried pilgrims from the deserts of Upper India. There a troop of women of doubtful character, dressed in sombre colours, marched along the road, uttering wild cries, whose discordant sounds rose above the roll of the drum, with which travellers seek to relieve the tedium of a halt. Finally, in yonder gilt

according to tradition, Vishnu took his celebrated stride to Ceylon.

More than fifteen years ago our good star led us to this

palanquin there must surely be some rich Baboa, who has abandoned the care of temporal concerns to give himself up to spiritual matters and do homage to the god Ganges.

Strange scenes, strongly coloured by local peculiarities, announced the approach to the camp. On the sides of the road hideous beggars complacently displayed to the eyes of the passers-by repulsive leprosies, shocking sores, marvellously contorted limbs! Naked devotees, with filthy matted hair, were seen loudly demanding charity; phenomenal sacred bulls, covered with trappings adorned with shells, and with a fifth leg attached to the shoulder or the rump; which deception, though of the grossest kind, was yet accepted without a doubt by the credulous spectators. The greatest amount of alms was collected on the carpet of a 'Sannyassi,' who had hit upon the curious plan of lying down in the middle of the road with several inches of dust on his face and chest—a pneumatic exhibition which had ruined the business of a poor sacred bull a few steps off, who vainly strove to attract the faithful by the sight of an extra leg artistically attached to its neck!

As far as one could see, in the plain and on the precipitous sides of the mountain, the pilgrims had pitched their temporary abodes, the result being the most varied assemblage of every species of shelter which man's industry or ingenuity can devise against the elements. Elegant and strangely-coloured tents, huts made of branches, a rug or a few rags hung on bamboos, often merely the forepart of a cart served to shelter some twenty people. The English authorities, with their usual prudence, had taken care to trace out the plan of the camp beforehand. The different streets intersecting it radiated from the centre, where the tents of the sepoy regiment entrusted with the maintenance of order were pitched. Night and day every available space was thronged with a crowd denser than the throng which flocks to see fireworks on the Place de la Concorde. The strange power of primitive superstition had brought together more than a million of people on this plain, which yesterday was an absolute desert. So serried were the ranks of the multitude that only on the back of an elephant could a visit to the camp be made without running the risk of suffocation. There was really something marvellous in the sagacity with which these noble beasts picked their way through the human sea around them, and the natives have such trust in their sagacity and kindly disposition, that when comfortably resting on the ground they did not disturb themselves, but let the enormous creatures walk over them without stirring.

The camp of the Baïgaris, situated close to the canal, offered several characteristic episodes illustrative of their senseless customs. There they were like so many dozens of hideous animals. I crave pardon of you, sagacious elephant; of you, O dog, the friend of man; of you, O horse, the companion of his pleasures and labours, for being obliged by the poverty of language to apply to this species of the human race the generic name under which you are generally known. In the animal kingdom I see but quadrumans, and even amongst them only monkeys, which bite their tails, fit to be compared to these repulsive and idiotic mammifers. There they were, I repeat, squatting by dozens on the

wonderful festival, and we witnessed strangely picturesque scenes which we can never forget, in the midst of a million

sides of the road at the doors of the huts, in every sort of fantastic and ridiculous posture, all as little clothed as Adam before the fall; their bodies plastered with ashes or painted with all the colours of the rainbow. One individual, in sign of homage to the Deity, had for years held his right arm pointing to the sky, so that the poor decrepit, dried-up limb had become rigid and motionless. This other one had held his two hands closed for so long, that the nails had grown through the flesh in the midst of nauseous suppuration. That holy man, or more correctly, that hoary goose, had from his youth remained standing on one leg at the same spot, his chest supported by a sort of see-saw. The head-quarters of these fanatics was worthy of their private habits; a sort of altar on which were some copper-plates covered by rice and flowers, rose in the shade of a *Zeus indica*. Four fakirs in a state of nature, more hideous far than the most hideous Chinese figures, crouched at the four corners: a choir of the faithful were praising the Deity by howlings, drummings, and the clang of brass instruments. At night, this truly diabolical scene, which the wildest efforts of an artist could not reproduce, was lit up by torches of resin.

On April 12, at six in the morning, the Baigaris were to leave the head-quarters of the sect for the sacred ghaut. The camp, which, as I have said, was pitched on the embankment along the Ganges, was guarded by a company of Goorkhas. The martial bearing of these men, who were all mountaineers and well proportioned, notwithstanding their low stature, reminded me of that of our Basque Voltigeurs. They wore the dark green uniform of the Rifle Brigade, and by way of a sabre, a cutlass, which, in their hands, proved, I was told, a very formidable weapon. The authorities and their guests, all of them on elephants, took their places close to the soldiers in a vast open space, which the procession had to cross. An immense multitude was assembled on this point, and the green-turbaned irregulars could only keep out the throng from the space reserved for the Baigaris by the most energetic efforts. Exactly at six o'clock, tumultuous shouts were heard in the direction of the latter's encampment. The Goorkhas abandoned the position across the quay, which they had hitherto occupied; the procession had just started! At its head came twelve elephants richly caparisoned, carrying fakirs almost devoid of clothing, who bore gigantic standards with hamps more than twenty feet high, and silk flags of the most glaring colours as large as the sails of a ship. Twenty yards in advance marched a splendid elephant, bearing on its back in a silver basket one of the heads of the sect—a middle-aged man of austere countenance—wrapped in the folds of a magnificent crimson Cashmere shawl. Immediately behind this dignitary came several led horses with rich trappings, destined as presents for the Brahmins, who guarded the sacred spot. A band of musicians, armed with monstrous trumpets, frightful tam-tams, and discordant cymbals, advanced proudly at the head of the mass of Baigaris, who formed a battalion of more than 3,000 men, while shouts formed a fit accompaniment to this infernal symphony.

As soon as the march-past was over, our object was to reach the sacred ghaut at the same time as the procession, and we turned the heads of our intelligent beasts in that direction.

of human beings, whom half a dozen European magistrates and half a sepoy battalion sufficed to keep in absolute order. The India of former days, with its princes, its rajahs, its Brahmins, fakirs and sorcerers, its luxury and its misery, its ardent faith, its peaceful manners, its elementary or refined industry, was there as a whole, an unchanged and grandiose picture forgotten in the gallery of time! Nowadays, pilgrims and merchants reach the foot of the Himalaya, and almost the very place of purification, in a fourth-class

The aspect of the place had really something wild and grand about it. A countless multitude covered the surface of the waters, the roofs of the houses and temples. Everywhere, as far as the eye could reach, there was no clear space but the holy staircase, which was guarded by a triple line of sentinels. From the middle of the stream rich natives and European visitors on elephants looked down upon the vast panorama, where the diligent observer might catch sight here and there of some scenes full of national characteristics. A fat Brahmin, with a double chin and protruding abdomen, a regular Triton except for the shell, was playing about in the water, shouting for joy like a child. A more graceful sight was the meeting of two young girls, the only pretty creatures I saw among this assembled million, who kissed one another tenderly, and offered each other reciprocally the sacred liquid. Children led their blind and feeble parents into the purifying bath. Here a pious Æneas on the most herculean scale carried astride on his hip a little old woman who could not be less than a hundred years old, judging by her decrepit, shaking body, her red eyes, and the cracked voice with which she joined in the acclamation of the populace. On a sort of platform, almost on a level with the river, stood children dressed in scarlet with a gilt paper helmet, adorned with peacock feathers, who received considerable alms. Finally, sentinels in red uniforms, their loins girt with a cloth, kept the crowd away from dangerous places in the river, and strange to say, did not compel obedience by means of the cudgel they carried, but by threatening to throw water in the face of adventurous bathers—a threat before which the latter quailed with the utmost terror.

I was looking on with great curiosity at these scenes, typical of another age, when the first part of the procession of the Baigaris appeared on the summit of the ghaut. In a second, the human flood covered every step of the sacred staircase. It was a human anthill, an avalanche of black heads and brown bodies, in the midst of which the scarlet uniform of the sepoys stood out prominently. Now at last the latter used their sticks, which they brandished right and left. The elephants of the procession entered the river by a bye-path, and the fakirs threw themselves off their backs into the water with the wildest fervour. An immense saturnalia, with a million actors in it, was before me, the minute reproduction of which could only be attempted by the brush of Decamps. In conclusion, let me point out the inoffensive, good-natured behaviour of the crowd; the European traveller could freely circulate in its midst without once hearing a rude remark or meeting with looks of hatred and anger.

waggon or in a sleeping car; but the increased rapidity and facility of communication can only increase the commercial transactions which follow on the fair of Hardwar. The Delhi fair also brings together vast multitudes every year. In the Punjab alone a hundred and twenty-seven fairs take place annually. In Scinde and in the Bombay Presidency the number is no less considerable, but in the former pilgrimages have only for objects the places venerated by Mohammedans.

The Suez Canal and Indian railways have introduced into the great questions which may one day convulse the world new factors which still require consideration. We have already stated that the work done by M. de Lesseps must exercise paramount influence on events occurring in the Indian seas, but its action begins in the Mediterranean. It would be unjust, however, to attribute the change in the principal stations of the Peninsular and Oriental Company to the opening of the isthmus. It was evident that as soon as the system of Italian railroads was finished, the English steamers, in order to accelerate communications, would abandon Marseilles, and transfer their head-quarters to the port of the peninsula nearest to Egypt. The choice of Brindisi as the Company's principal station has not only seriously compromised the prosperity of Marseilles, but has also brought about constant relations between England and Italy, which will have a great influence on European politics. The fate of the Indian mail, and of the passengers who travel by it, is intimately connected with the tranquillity and unity of Italy. In default of a public or private treaty, a common interest insures to the latter the protection of England and the British fleet; even a Gladstone Ministry would certainly oppose any attempt to interfere with the results of the fatal day of Sedan, from whatever quarter it might come. The reader must be good enough to excuse this digression. We will now return to the Suez Canal, and to the important part it will be called upon to fill when the Eastern question, now dormant but not settled, is again brought forward.

The Crimean war proved clearly that had it not been for

the French alliance, England, left to herself, could not have prevented Russia from entering Constantinople. To-day the situation has completely changed, and one wonders rightly enough that Lord Palmerston should have thrown obstacle upon obstacle in the way of an undertaking the accomplishment of which would open the gates of Europe to an Anglo-Indian force. To-day, and as long as the British fleet retains its superiority in the Mediterranean, whatever question arises—whether Eastern, Italian, or Spanish—England can always throw the weight of her Indian army into the balance. Her army is no longer limited, as at the siege of Sebastopol, to seek for recruits to its ranks from the population of the United Kingdom alone. Her two hundred millions of Asiatic subjects furnish an inexhaustible supply of auxiliaries whom it is easy to despatch to the theatre of war. From Bombay sepoy regiments can be conveyed by steam, and landed on any given point of Syria or European Turkey in a period of time only a few hours longer than would be required by an expedition despatched from Plymouth. At the call of the Viceroy, we repeat, these warlike races, these low caste natives who have shown their courage and loyalty on every Indian battlefield, would hasten to join the royal standard, and regiments would appear as by magic as long as they were certain of a regular pay. The credit of England is sufficiently good to bear the strain of an armament on the vastest scale, so that without giving the reins to the imagination, we may well look forward to a time when the Anglo-Indian forces could muster round Constantinople in sufficient numbers to withstand the Russians.

Here we have a new and important element in England's means of military action which we must needs point out; and perhaps of all the astonishing surprises which the future reserves for coming generations, the strangest may be the intervention of a Sikh army sent into Europe under the flag of Great Britain for the defence of the Prophet's legitimate successor. Let us hasten to add, thanks be to Providence, the Eastern question seems at rest for many years. The eminent statesman who directs affairs in Russia appears satisfied with having, at little cost to his country, regained supremacy in the Black Sea, and only leaves his retirement to take part in the politics of the far East, and to turn the active forces of Russia towards Central Asia and the river Amoor. However distant the first appearance of the Anglo-Indian forces on the shores of the Mediterranean may be, the possibility of such a fact is worthy of attracting the attention of statesmen and thinkers.

It is now time to return to exclusively Indian questions, and examine the difficulties and dangers which may arise on the frontiers of the empire. The first glance falls on the defiles of the Himalaya and the table-lands of Central Asia, where even people of common sense persist in seeing the two-headed eagle ready to swoop down upon the valleys of the Indus and the Ganges. The results of an untimely interference, the recollection of the terrible Cabul disaster, have borne fruit; and though the phantom of Russian invasion still alarms public opinion in England, it has no longer any weight with the men who rule India. Anglo-Indian policy wisely rejects all thought of territorial aggrandisement, or even of intervention in the internal affairs of the countries north of Peshawur. It has been finally acknowledged that the advance of a Russian army on India threatens above all the independence of Afghanistan, and that at its first approach the native chieftains, who are devotedly attached to their mountains, would at once ask assistance from their European neighbours and place the principal strategic points of the country, such as Guznee, Quettah, Candahar, in their hands. Why compromise this position by useless diplomatic manœuvres, and not rather wait for the day when the British flag may appear beyond the Khyber Pass as the herald not of enemies but of allies and liberators! But after the results of the Crimean war and the disasters of the Russian columns in their marches between Moscow and Odessa, how can the invasion of India from the north, through mountainous regions inhabited by the most intractable races of the globe, be admitted as a serious eventuality? To procure food the invaders must subdue the wandering, marauding tribes who are to be found everywhere between the Russian frontiers and the Indus, and, if successful, they would still encounter fevers and epidemics resulting from hardships, privation, and climate. Even allowing for one moment that all these difficulties were overcome by the admirable military qualities of the Russian soldier, the invasion, on debouching into the plains, would find, thanks to the completion of the Indian railway system, 40,000 at least of excellent European troops, besides innumerable native soldiers drawn up to bar its passage, provided with arms and artillery of the most improved description.

Anglo-Indian diplomacy has so entirely disposed of Russophobia that when civil war broke out in 1862 in Afghanistan on the death of Dost Mohammed, the then Viceroy, Sir Henry Lawrence, refused to interfere in favour of either prétender to the throne. He remained four years an impartial and impassible spectator, without compromising the neutrality of his government by the slightest demonstration. He only emerged from his apparent indifference to lend his moral influence and a few subsidies to the new government, the day after Shere Ali, unaided, reconquered the capital and the throne of his ancestors (1868), when not even the most determined opponent of the new state of things could pretend to attribute the victory to help sent from beyond the Indus. Afghanistan, according to the answer of one of its chieftains, only produces men and rocks, and is not likely to arouse the cupidity of any conqueror. A wise policy, like that inaugurated by the eminent dictator of the Punjab, during his viceroyalty, and since followed by his successors—a wise policy, we repeat—ought to limit itself to favouring the establishment in the Indian Caucasus of a strong military power capable of holding in check its barbarous subjects, and of efficaciously protecting the passage of caravans, whilst leaving to the future the care of solving the mystery of Russian designs in that part of Asia. A few years were sufficient to prove the wisdom of non-intervention.

At the very time of our writing these lines the last news from India points to fresh and bloody quarrels in Afghanistan, even before nature has opened the succession of Shere Ali. This prince, influenced by intrigues of the harem, or by some motive of the kind, in choosing his second son, Abdallah Jan, as his successor, to the detriment of his elder son, Yakoub Khan, has made a formidable enemy, and has fanned into a blaze, doubtless for many years, the still smouldering embers of civil war.[1]

On all the other frontiers are the dominions of princes who in the most critical days of the mutiny gave undeniable proofs of loyalty to England, and on whom she may apparently rely: such as the Maharajah of Nepaul, the King of Cashmere, the Rajah of Khelat, and the petty chiefs of Beloochistan. A most serious danger arising from

[1] The contest which placed Dost Mohammed on the throne was scarcely over when serious dissensions broke out in the family of the new Emir. Yakoub Khan, the Dost's eldest son, who had proved his father's ablest and most active general, was excluded from the succession, and his younger brother Abdallah Jan declared heir presumptive. Whatever were Dost Mohammed's motives for this determination, he could not but know that Yakoub Khan would be a dangerous enemy for his successor. So that in an interview which took place at Amballah (1869), between the Governor-General and the Emir, the latter attempted to have the rights of his favourite son to the throne openly recognised; but Lord Mayo refused to bind himself by any promises. The Dost's fears were soon justified, and since his disgrace, Yakoub Khan has lived in a state of intermittent revolt. One of the many reconciliations between father and son was of so solemn a nature that it might have been expected to last. Yakoub Khan was made Governor of Candahar and Herat, which two provinces are so distant from the centre of the empire, that it was hoped the prince would no longer be able to carry on the court intrigues of which he was the soul. Placed as he was on the frontier of Persia, he made a point of following a policy diametrically opposed to that of his father, towards the Russians, English, Persians, and the Khans of Khiva and Bokhara. Any exile, any discontented person from Cabul, was sure to find shelter and protection at Herat. The last news (August 1874) announces that Yakoub Khan has at last thrown off the mask, and is marching at the head of considerable forces into the districts of the interior. On his side, the Emir of Cabul seems determined to push matters to extremity. Yakoub Khan's spies have been executed at Cabul, and it is well known that the name of spy, a most elastic one in Asia, includes all the partisans of a political adversary. In short, the two parties are about to come to an open quarrel, and unless one of those sudden reconciliations, so characteristic of political conflicts in Afghanistan, takes place, the country will soon be a prey to a fresh civil war.

external causes might, however, lead to a catastrophe as sudden as terrible, in which the very foundations of British power in India would be shaken. If one day the influence of Exeter Hall prevails in Parliament and the Viceroy, together with the President of the Board of Control, become the blind instruments of Protestant propaganda, railways, telegraphs, administration, police, European army, all the active forces of the conquest will disappear before the violent or passive resistance of the two hundred million subjects. The sound doctrines of toleration which are in force in England will never allow of official intervention in the religious concerns of India, and the safety of the country must be left to Him who makes and unmakes empires.

We have reached the limits of these sketches, and shall not even attempt to sum up the principal events which marked the administration of Lord Canning's successors, Lord Elgin, Sir H. Lawrence, Lord Mayo, and Lord Northbrook. There is, however, one episode of the years just passed which we intend bringing under the reader's notice. On December 26, 1869, the Duke of Edinburgh, then a captain in the Navy, landed at Calcutta. For the first time a prince of the House of Hanover set foot on the soil of India. The reception was worthy of the visitor, and the young sailor found the most illustrious feudatories of his august mother assembled on the banks of the Hooghly to do him honour. There were the Maharajah of Jeypore, Scindiah, the princes of Bartpore, of Kapoortala, and the Ranee of Bhopal, all of them illustrious by their wealth and the antiquity of their race. Never was a more striking testimony to the power and equity of the Europe of the nineteenth century.[1] In presence of this illustrious assemblage, the mind involuntarily travels back through the cycle of past ages; and the incomprehensible decrees which determine the fate of empires, appear to it in all their marvellous incon-

[1] Here is a curious detail of these festivities. At one of the banquets offered to his guests by the Viceroy, a small elephant made its appearance, the offspring of the favourite elephant of the Ranee of Bhopal during the latter's journey. The huge four-legged baby walked round the table, and was rewarded for its gambols by gifts of fruits and sweetmeats.

sistency. In the far-off centuries, when kingdoms which had already reached the height of civilisation and prosperity were flourishing on the banks of the Ganges and the Jumna, what was a small island in the North Sea, apparently so little favoured by nature, but now the undisputed mistress of the whole country between Cape Comorin and the Himalaya? Scarcely a hundred years ago, a few insignificant clerks, exclusively concerned in commercial matters, represented the vanguard of the conquerors on the scene of their future victories! Force of arms, diplomacy, and even duplicity have raised the fabric of English rule in India.

The sceptre of the Great Mogul has passed into the hands of Queen Victoria; but statesmen formed in the school of modern liberty have completed the work of force and chance. The inviolability of property and person, universal equality before the law, and absolute religious toleration exists to-day in India as in England, and this it is which pre-eminently distinguishes the present state of things from the past, the rule of Queen Victoria from that of the Mogul conquerors. So that the successors of the great vassals of Timour and Aureng-Zeb, who, in their distrust of their suzerains, would rather have taken up arms than ventured within the walls of Delhi, hastened to the capital of modern India at the first summons, in order to do homage to their sovereign's son. They were well aware that, even in the midst of European bayonets, they were under the protection of the law, and that neither a jewel of their crowns nor a hair of their heads would be touched. This is, indeed, a great and noble homage paid by these Oriental potentates to the spirit of justice of their European masters. This is indeed an unanswerable argument against those partisans of brute force who assert the impotence and the sterility of free government. Despotism cannot alone boast of great military prowesses which have altered the face of the world. The names of the two Lawrences, of Outram, of Nicholson, the glorious deeds of the armies of Delhi and Lucknow, one hundred and sixty millions of pounds spent in less than twenty years on works of every kind—roads, railways, canals, telegraphs—are sufficient proof that great men and great actions are not wanting among the favoured nations who have found a safe anchorage in hereditary and constitutional monarchy.

H. L.

MIMWOOD, HERTS: *October* 1, 1881.

APPENDIX.

DOCUMENTS.

I.

Provinces	Square miles	Population	Value
			£
Bengal	245,000	38,500,000	3,838,000
North-West	83,000	30,000,000	3,994,000
Madras	124,000	26,500,000	4,376,000
(Sq. miles)			
Bombay . . . 63,000	117,000	12,500,000	2,944,000
Scinde 15,000			
Desert 39,000			
Punjab	95,000	15,000,000	1,877,000
Oude	23,000	8,000,000	1,033,000
Central Provinces	84,000	6,500,000	571,000
Burmah	90,000	2,300,000	283,000
Berar	17,000	1,000,000	493,000
Courg	2,000	100,000	21,000
Total . .	880,000	140,900,000	19,452,000
Native States under the protection of England:—			
(Sq. miles)			
Mysore 31,000	326,000	3,500,000	—
Hyderabad 95,000		10,500,000	—
Rajpootana 123,000		8,500,000	—
Central India . . . 77,000		7,900,000	—
Native States under the protection of the Government of—			
(Sq. miles)			
Madras 21,000	271,000	1,750,000	—
Bombay 60,000		4,500,000	—
Bengal 46,000		1,500,000	—
North-West Provinces . . 6,000		400,000	—
Punjab 103,000		3,000,000	—
Central Provinces . 35,000		300,000	—
Total	597,000	45,400,000	—
General Total . .	1,477,600	186,300,000	—

II.

Caste and Race in the Sepoy Army.

Extracts from the official return showing the number, caste, and country of the native officers and soldiers of each regiment, regular and irregular, of each Presidency, confined to regiments borne on the returns of each Army respectively; so far as can be stated from the record in this House.—East India House, September 1858.

Bengal.

Native Infantry, 7 *Regiments—viz.*, 21*st*, 31*st*, 47*th*, 65*th*, 66*th*, 70*th*, 73*rd*:—

Native Officers. Caste.		Non-Commissioned, Rank and File. Caste.	
Mohammedans	25	Mohammedans	1,170
Brahmins	52	Brahmins	1,878
Rajpoots	39	Rajpoots	2,637
Hindoos of inferior description	23	Hindoos of inferior description	2,057
		Sikhs and Punjabees	54
	139		7,796

Irregular and Local Infantry, 12 *Regiments—viz.*, *Regiment of Khelat-i-Ghilzi, Regiment of Ferozepore, Regiment of Loodianah, Timour Battalion, Kumaon Battalion, Nusseree Battalion, Hill Rangers, Assam Light Infantry Battalion, Mhairwarrah Battalion, Sylhet Light Infantry Battalion, Arracan Battalion, and Shekhawattee Battalion*:—

Native Officers Caste.		Non-Commissioned, Rank and File. Caste.	
Mohammedans	38	Mohammedans	1,185
Brahmins	23	Brahmins	849
Rajpoots	59	Rajpoots	2,711
Hindoos of inferior description	43	Hindoos of inferior description	2,247
Sikhs	17	Sikhs	1,309
Hill men	16	Hill men	1,112
Mughs	6	Mughs	705
Burmese	1	Burmese	6
Munniporees	1	Munniporees	167
		Thats	48
	204		10,339

MADRAS.

Native Cavalry, 7 *Regiments* :—

Native Officers.

Caste.

Mohammedans	68
Mahrattas	6
Rajpoots	3
	77

Country.

Central Carnatic, Madras, Vellore, &c	64
Southern Carnatic, Trichinopoly	7
Mysore	3
Tanjore, Madura, and Tinnevelly	1
Ceded districts	2
	77

Non-Commissioned, Rank and File.

Caste.

Christians	32
Mohammedans	1,956
Rajpoots	90
Mahrattas	300
Other castes	2
Indo-Britons	159
	2,539

Country.

Hindustan	22
Northern Circars	67
Central Carnatic, Madras, Vellore, &c.	1,841
Southern Carnatic, Trichinopoly	205
Baramahal	48
Ceded districts	54
Mysore	212
Tanjore, Madura, and Tinnevelly	90
	2,539

Native Infantry, 52 *Regiments* :—

Native Officers.

Caste.

Christians	4
Mohammedans	584
Brahmins and Rajpoots	83
Mahrattas	12
Telingas (Gentoo)	242
Tamil	97
Other castes	8
Indo-Britons	0
	1,030

Country.

Hindustan	51
Northern Circars	317
Central Carnatic, Madras, Vellore, &c.	239
Southern Carnatic, Trichinopoly	177
Baramahal	29
Ceded districts	32
Carried forward	845

Non-Commissioned, Rank and File.

Caste.

Christians	1,853
Mohammedans	15,272
Brahmins and Rajpoots	1,922
Mahrattas	385
Telingas (Gentoo)	15,371
Tamil	4,275
Other castes	1,616
Indo-Britons	1,011
	41,705

Country.

Hindustan	1,938
Northern Circars	16,938
Central Carnatic, Madras, Vellore, &c.	8,841
Southern Carnatic, Trichinopoly	4,760
Baramahal	1,022
Ceded districts	1,705
Carried forward	35,204

Country.	
Brought forward	845
Mysore	59
Tanjore, Madura, and Tinnevelly	119
Deccan and Mahratta	7
	1,030

Country.	
Brought forward	35,204
Mysore	2,698
Tanjore, Madura, and Tinnevelly	3,617
Canara, Moulmein, Taullah, and Belgaum	73
Deccan and Mahratta	99
Portugal	1
Other parts	58
	41,705

Bombay.

Native Cavalry, 3 *Regiments*:—

Native Officers.

Caste.	
Christians	1
Mohammedans	12
Brahmins and Rajpoots	9
Mahrattas	1
Telingas (Gentoo)	0
Tamil	0
Other castes	12
Indo-Britons	1
	36

Country.	
Hindustan	29
Northern Circars	1
Central Carnatic, Madras, Vellore	2
Southern Carnatic, Trichinopoly	0
Deccan	2
Concan	1
Mysore	0
Tanjore, Madras, and Tinnevelly	0
Bombay	1
	36

Non-Commissioned, Rank and File.

Caste.	
Christians	66
Mohammedans	459
Brahmins and Rajpoots	282
Mahrattas	118
Telingas	0
Tamil	5
Other castes	508
Indo-Britons	22
	1,425

Country.	
Hindustan	1,073
Northern Circars	21
Central Carnatic, Madras, Vellore	30
Southern Carnatic, Trichinopoly	0
Deccan	125
Concan	114
Mysore	0
Tanjore, Madura, and Tinnevelly	0
Guzerat	14
Persia	1
Lisbon	4
Africa	2
Bombay	4
Punjab and Scinde	21
Cabul and Afghanistan	15
Europe	1
	1,425

Native Infantry, 29 *Regiments* :—

Native Officers.

Caste.

Caste	
Christians	5
Mohammedans	111
Brahmins and Rajpoots	188
Mahrattas	116
Telingas	6
Tamil	1
Jews	3
Other castes	130
Purwarrees	3
	563

Country.

Country	
Hindustan	268
Northern Circars	7
Central Carnatic, Madras, Vellore	37
Southern Carnatic, Trichinopoly	13
Deccan	57
Concan	173
Mysore	4
Tanjore, Madura, and Tinnevelly	0
Guzerat	4
	563

Non-Commissioned, Rank and File.

Caste.

Caste	
Christians	270
Mohammedans	2,048
Brahmins and Rajpoots	6,421
Mahrattas	7,980
Telingas	107
Tamil	55
Jews	12
Other castes	7,728
Indo-Britons	22
Purwarrees	170
Mochees	29
Sikhs	28
	24,870

Country.

Country	
Hindustan	11,089
Northern Circars	135
Central Carnatic, Madras, Vellore, &c.	412
Southern Carnatic, Trichinopoly	203
Deccan	1,820
Concan	10,878
Mysore	36
Tanjore, Madura, and Tinnevelly	33
Mysore and Punjab	28
Guzerat	80
Scinde, Punjab, and Rajpootana	155
Europe	1
	24,870

III.

COMPOSITION OF THE INDIAN ARMY.

Return showing the Number of Troops, Regular and Irregular, which were serving in the three Presidencies immediately before the Mutiny.

	Royal Troops		East India Company's Troops.												
				Artillery			Native Cavalry		Infantry						
	Cavalry, 4 Regiments	Infantry, 22 Regiments	Engineers and Sappers	Horse, 5 Brigades	European Foot, 12 Battalions	Native Foot, 6 Battalions	Regular, 21 Regiments	Irregular, 33 Regiments	European, 9 Regiments	Native Regular, 155 Regiments	Native Irregular, 45 Regiments	Veterans	Medical Establishment	Warrant Officers	Total
Officers	115	693	251	119	231	138	284	106	335	2,769	152	163	814	—	6,170
European non-commissioned officers, rank and file	2,571	20,884	110	2,029	4,390	37	60	—	8,103	259	59	—	—	—	38,502
European veterans	—	—	—	—	—	—	—	—	—	—	—	465	—	—	465
Native commissioned, non-commissioned, rank and file	—	—	3,043	659	—	3,517	9,532	20,941	—	149,832	35,215	3,613	—	—	226,352
Gun lascars	—	—	—	449	1,658	343	—	—	—	—	—	—	—	—	2,450
Ordnance drivers	—	—	—	—	1,489	848	—	—	—	—	—	—	—	—	[illegible]37
Apothecaries and stewards	—	—	—	—	—	—	—	—	—	—	—	—	434	—	434
Native doctors	—	—	—	—	—	—	—	—	—	—	—	—	651	—	651
Warrant officers (ordnance)	—	—	—	—	—	—	—	—	—	—	—	—	—	385	385
	2,686	21,577	3,404	3,256	7,768	4,883	9,876	21,047	8,438	152,860	35,426	4,241	1,899	385	277,746
	24,263		3,404	15,907			30,923		196,724			4,241	1,899	385	277,746

Indian Army Commission—Total Europeans.—Officers, 6,170
Men, 33,967
Natives, 232,609

277,746

R. B. WOOD, Colonel and Secretary.

IV.

The Chuppaties.

In the course of the trial of the King of Delhi great pains were taken to extract from the witnesses, both European and native, some explanation of the 'Chuppati mystery,' but nothing satisfactory was elicited. The following opinions, however, were recorded:—

From the Evidence of Tat Mall, News-writer to the Lieutonant-Governor.

Q. Did you ever hear of the circulation of chuppaties about the country some months before the outbreak; and if so, what was supposed to be the meaning of this?

A. Yes, I did hear of the circumstance. Some people said that it was a propitiatory observance to avert some impending calamity; others, that they were circulated by the Government to signify that the population throughout the country would be compelled to use the same food as the Christians, and thus be deprived of their religion; while others, again, said that the chuppaties were circulated to make it known that Government was determined to force Christianity on the country by interfering with their food, and intimation of it was thus given that they might be prepared to resist the attempt.

Q. Is sending such articles about the country a custom among the Hindoos or Mussulmans; and would the meaning be at once understood without any accompanying explanation?

A. No, it is not by any means a custom; I am fifty years old, and never heard of such a thing before.

Q. Did you ever hear that any message was sent with the chuppaties?

A. No; I never heard of any.

Q. Were these chuppaties chiefly circulated by Mohammedans or Hindoos?

A. They were circulated indiscriminately, without reference to either religion, among the peasantry of the country.

From the Evidence of Sir Theophilus Metcalfe.

Q. Can you give the Court any information about the chuppaties which were circulated from village to village some months before the outbreak; and has it been ascertained how they originated, or what was the purport of their being circulated?

A. There is nothing but conjecture regarding them, but the first suggestion made by the natives in reference to them was, that they were thus sent about in connection with some sickness that prevailed; but this was clearly an error, as I took the trouble of ascertaining that the chuppaties were never sent into any native states, but were confined always to Government villages; they were spread through only five villages of the Delhi territory, when they were immediately stopped by authority, and they never proceeded far upcountry. I sent for the men who had brought them from the district of Bolundshuhr, and their apology for circulating them was that they believed it to be done by order of the English Government, that they had received them elsewhere, and had but forwarded them on. I believe that the meaning of the chuppaties was not understood in the Delhi district; but originally they were to be taken to all those who partook of one kind of food, connecting a body of men together in contradistinction to those who lived differently and had different customs. I think these chuppaties originated at Lucknow, and were, no doubt, meant to sound a note of alarm and preparation, giving warning to the people to stand by one another on any danger menacing them.

From the Evidence of Captain Martineau.

Q. Had you any conversation with these men—*i.e.* with the men assembled at Umballa for musketry instruction—relative to some chuppaties that were circulated to different villages in these districts before the outbreak?

A. Yes, I had frequent conversations with various sepoys on the subject. I asked them what they understood in reference to them, and by whom they supposed that they were circulated; they described them to me as being in size and shape like ship biscuits, and believed them to have been distributed by order of Government through the medium of their servants for the purpose of intimating to the people of Hindustan that they should all be compelled to eat the same food, and that was considered as a token that they should likewise be compelled to embrace one faith, or, as they termed it, 'one food and one faith.'

Q. As far as you could understand, was this idea generally prevalent among all the sepoys of the various detachments at the depôt?

A. It was prevalent, as far as I could judge, among all the sepoys of every regiment that furnished a detachment to the depôt at Umballa.

Q. Was there any report of the Government having mixed ground bones with flour for the purpose of having it distributed to the sepoys, and so destroying their caste?

A. Yes, I heard of this in the month of March. It was told me that all the flour retailed from the Government depôts for the supply of troops on the march was so adulterated.

Q. Do you think the sepoys generally firmly believed this?

A. I have seen correspondence from various men, which the sepoys of the depôt voluntarily placed in my hands, the writers of which, themselves sepoys, evidently believed that such was the case.

Q. Did the sepoys ever speak to you about any other cause of complaint, or points on which they sought information?

A. Their complaint, or rather fear, was this: they apprehended that Government was going forcibly to deprive them of their caste.

Q. Did any of them ever speak about Government interference regarding the re-marriage of Hindoo widows?

A. Yes, they alluded to that as an invasion of their social rights.

[The following translation from a native letter shows how general was the belief among the sepoys in all parts of the country that the Government had mixed ground bones with the flour, and purposed to compel or to delude them to eat it.]

Translation of an anonymous Petition sent, in March 1857, *to Major Matthews, commanding the* 43*rd Regiment at Barrackpore.*

The representation of the whole station is this, that we will not give up our religion. We serve for honour and religion; if we lose our religion, the Hindoo and Mohammedan religions will be destroyed. If we live, what shall we do? You are the masters of the country. The Lord Sahib has given orders which he has received from the Company to all commanding officers to destroy the religion of the country. We know this, as all things are being brought up by Government. The officers in the salt department mix up bones with the salt. The officer in charge of the ghee mixes up fat with it; this is well known. These are two matters. The third is this: that the Sahib in charge of the sugar burns up bones, and mixes them in the syrup the sugar is made of; this is well known: all know it. The fourth is this: that in the country the Burra Sahibs have ordered the Rajahs, Thakurs, Zemindars, Mahajans, and Ryots all to eat together, and English bread has been sent to them; this is well known. And this is another affair, that throughout the country the wives of respectable men, in fact, all classes of Hindoos, on becoming widows, are to be married again; this is known. Therefore we consider ourselves as killed. You all obey the orders of the Company, which we all know. But a king, or any other one who acts unjustly, does not remain.

With reference to the sepoys, they are your servants, but, to destroy their caste, a council assembled and decided to give them muskets and cartridges made up with greased paper to bite; this is also evident. We wish to represent this to the General, that we do not approve of the new musket and cartridge; the sepoys cannot use them. You are the masters of the country; if you will give us all our discharge we will go away. The native officers, subahdars, jemadars, are all good in the whole brigade, except two, whose faces are like pigs: the subhadar major of the 70th Regiment, who is a Christian, and Thakur Misser, jemadar of the 43rd Regiment Light Infantry.

Whoever gets this letter must read it to the major as it is written. If he is a Hindoo and does not, his crime will be equal to the slaughter of a lac of cows; and if a Mussulman, as though he had eaten pig; and if an European, must read it to the native officers, and if he does not, his going to church will be of no use, and be a crime. Thakur Misser has lost his religion. Kchratrizas are not to respect him. Brahmins are not to salute or bless him. If they do, their crime will be equal to the slaughter of a lac of cows. He is the son of a Chumar. The Brahmin who hears this is not to feed him; if he does his crime will be equal to the murdering of a lac of Brahmins or cows.

May this letter be given to Major Matthews. Anyone who gets it is to give it; if he does not, and is a Hindoo, his crime will be as the slaughter of a lac of cows; and if a Mussulman, as if he had eaten pig; and if he is an officer, he must give it.

V.

Mutiny at Barrackpore.

About the middle of the year 1824, the 47th Bengal Native Infantry had been marched to Barrackpore, from which, at a later period of the year, they were to proceed to share in the operations of the Burmese war. To European readers it will be unnecessary to explain that no military force can move in India without a large number of bullocks and other beasts of burden, which are requisite not only for carrying provisions and stores, but also for transporting a considerable portion of the personal baggage of the men, such as their knapsacks, cooking utensils, &c.: the expense of these animals and their drivers so far as employed for the use of the sepoys, being defrayed by the sepoys themselves. Unfortunately, on the present occasion, no bullocks could be provided for hire, and they could only be purchased at an extravagant price; and when application was made for assistance from the Commissariat, the men were curtly told that they must provide the required accommodation for themselves.

The great inconvenience and hardship occasioned by this circumstance on the march rankled in the minds of the men, and made them brood so bitterly upon other real or supposed grievances, that by the time they arrived at Barrackpore they were, unfortunately, too well prepared for the unhappy scenes that occurred soon after their arrival. On October 30, at a heavy marching order parade, the greater part appeared without their knapsacks, and the cause of the neglect being demanded, they replied that their knapsacks were unfit to produce. They were informed that the new ones were on their way, and that till their arrival they must use the old ones. They refused, however, to produce them; and part of the regiment, moreover, declared that they would not proceed to Rangoon or elsewhere by sea, as it involved the forfeiture of caste. After some vain attempts to subdue the prevailing discontent by reasoning, Colonel Cartwright, the commanding officer, being unable, from the number of the mutineers, to take any more vigorous measures, dismissed the regiment, and sought the advice of General Dalzell. The latter officer proceeded to Calcutta to consult the Commander-in-Chief, Sir Edward Paget, and on his return ordered a parade to take place at daybreak on the morning of November 1.

At this parade all semblance of duty was cast aside, and the regiment, with the exception of the officers, commissioned and non-commissioned, burst into acts of open violence. During the night the mutineers had slept on their arms, maintaining regular guards and pickets, and a strong chain of sentries and patrols. In this state of affairs, Sir Edward Paget arrived. Two native regiments, beside the 47th, were stationed at Barrackpore, preparatory to their proceeding on service; but both of them were infected in some degree with the mutinous spirit which had taken entire possession of the regiment last mentioned. It was necessary, therefore, to seek the means of overawing the mutineers elsewhere; and His Majesty's Royals and 47th Regiments, with a battery of light artillery, and the Governor-General's body-guard, promptly arrived from Calcutta. The force intended to act against the mutineers having taken position, the Commander-in-Chief deputed the Quartermaster-General and the Adjutant-General, accompanied by Captain Macan, of the 16th Lancers, as interpreter, and by the commanding officer of the regiment in rebellion, to give, on his part, an answer to a paper which had been forwarded by the malcontents, as well as to explain to them their situation, and the consequences that must result from their adhering to the course which they had adopted. Their fate, they were informed, would depend on their obedience to the command which they were about to receive from the Adjutant-General.

The word to order arms being given, was instantly obeyed. The next order was to ground arms; with this only one man complied, while the silence which had hitherto been maintained was now broken by loud and continued murmurings. These were silenced by a few discharges of grapeshot from a battery in their rear, when the rebel troops speedily broke and fled in every direction, throwing away their arms and accoutrements, and, wherever practicable, divesting themselves of the military dress altogether.

A few of the mutineers were killed by this painfully necessary proceeding; and the fugitives being hotly pursued, many were taken prisoners. These were forthwith brought to trial before a court-martial. A considerable number were found guilty and sentenced to death, but a few only of the more active were executed. The regiment was disbanded, and its number most properly erased from the list of the Army, the European officers being transferred to another raised in its place.

'Our Indian Army,' by Captain Rafter.

VI.

Final Orders to the Musketry Schools.

The Adjutant-General of the Army to Major-General Hearsey.

Sir,—Referring to the telegraph message from this office dated the 23rd ultimo (and your acknowledgments of the 25th idem), communicating the Commander-in-Chief's orders to postpone the target practice of the native soldiers at the rifle depôt at Dum-Dum pending further instructions from this department, I am now desired to request you will be good enough to inform the officer commanding at Dum-Dum, and through him the depôt authorities concerned, that the course of instruction is to be completed by the native details, and that their target practice is to be commenced as soon as practicable after the Government general order disbanding the 19th Regiment of Native Infantry has been read to the troops at the station, including the detachments of native regiments at the depôt.

2. The grease for the cartridge is to be any unobjectionable mixture which may be suited for the purpose, to be provided by selected parties comprising all castes concerned, and is to be applied by the men themselves.

3. The paper of which the cartridges are constructed having been

proved by chemical test, or otherwise, to be perfectly free from grease, and in all respects unobjectionable; and all possible grounds for objection in regard to the biting of the cartridge and the nature of the grease to be used having been removed, it is not anticipated that the men will hesitate to perform the target practice; but in the event of such unexpected result the Commander-in-Chief desires that their officers may be instructed to reason calmly with them, pointing out the utter groundlessness for any objection to the use of the cartridges now that biting the end has been dispensed with, and the provision and application of the necessary greasing material has been left to themselves; and, further, to assure them that anyone who shall molest or taunt them on return to their corps shall be visited with severe punishment.

4. The officer commanding the depôt will be held responsible that the above directions respecting the greasing mixture and those recently issued in regard to the new mode of loading are strictly observed.

5. If, notwithstanding all these precautions and considerate measures, any disinclination to use the cartridges shall be manifested, the parties demurring are to be warned calmly and patiently, but firmly that a persistence in such unjustifiable conduct will be viewed as disobedience of orders and insubordination, and treated accordingly, and in the event of any individuals after such warning obstinately refusing to fire, the officer commanding at Dum-Dum will at once place such parties in arrest or confinement, according to the rank of the offenders, and cause them to be tried by court-martial.

6. If, however, the entire depôt shall combinedly refuse to fire, which is very improbable, the Commander-in-Chief, under such circumstances, empowers you to place all the native officers in arrest pending his Excellency's further orders, which you will immediately apply for; to deprive the non-commissioned officers and sepoys of their arms and accoutrements, and to pay them up and summarily discharge them on the spot, excepting, of course, any ringleaders in these latter grades or parties whose refusal may be accompanied by insolence or insubordination, who are to be placed under arrest or confinement, in view of their being arraigned before a district or general court-martial, as the case may require.

7. This communication is to be considered purely confidential, and his Excellency relies implicitly on your carrying out the instructions it contains with the utmost caution and discretion.

I am, &c.,

C. Chester, Colonel,

Adjutant-General of the Army.

VII.

Danger of the Position of the English at Delhi.

It does not appear that Lord Dalhousie laid any stress upon the fact that no European troops were posted in Delhi, nor, indeed, did Sir Charles Napier, who at this time was Commander-in-Chief of the British Army in India. He saw clearly that the military situation was a false one, and he wrote much about the defence of the city, but without drawing any distinction between European and native troops. In both cases the anticipated danger was from a rising of the people, not of the soldiery. With respect to the situation of the magazine, Sir Charles Napier wrote to the Governor-General (Lahore, December 15, 1849), saying:—'As regards the magazine, the objections to it are as follows: 1st. It is placed in a very populous part of the city, and its explosion would be very horrible in its effects as regards the destruction of life. 2nd. It would destroy the magnificent palace of Delhi. 3rd. The loss of Government property would also be very great, especially if my views of the importance of Delhi, given in my report, be acted upon—namely, that it and Dinapore should be two great magazines for the Bengal Presidency. 4th. It is without defence beyond what the guard of fifty men offer, and its gates are so weak that a mob could push them in.'

At the same time the Governor-General, Lord Dalhousie, wrote to the Board of Directors:—

'Here we have a strong fortress in the heart of one of the principal cities of our empire, and in entire command of the chief magazine of the Upper Provinces, which lies so exposed both to assault and to the dangers arising from the carelessness of the people dwelling around it, that it is a matter of surprise that no accident has yet occurred to it. Its dangerous position has been frequently remarked upon, and many schemes have been prepared for its improvement and defence; but the only eligible one is the transfer of the stores into the palace, which would then be kept by us as a British post, capable of maintaining itself against any hostile manœuvre, instead of being, as it now is, the source of positive danger, and perhaps not unfrequently the focus of intrigues against our power.'

VIII.

Letters of General Anson and Sir John Lawrence.

General Anson to Sir J. Lawrence.

Amballah, May 17, 1857.

It becomes now a matter for your consideration whether it would be prudent to risk the small European force we have here in an enterprise on Delhi. I think not. It is wholly, in my opinion, insufficient for the purpose. The walls could, of course, be battered down with heavy guns. The entrance might be opened and little resistance offered, but so few men in a great city, with such narrow streets, and an immense armed population, who know every turn and corner of them, would, it appears to me, be in a very dangerous position, and, if six or seven hundred were disabled, what would remain? Could we hold it with the whole country around against us? Could we either stay in or out of it? My own view of the state of things now is that by carefully collecting our resources, having got rid of the bad material which we cannot trust, and having supplied their places with others of a better sort, it would not be very long before we could proceed without a chance of failure in whatever direction we might please. Your telegraphic message informing me of the measures which you have taken to raise fresh troops confirms me in this opinion. I must add also that this is now the opinion of all here whom I have consulted upon it—the major-general and brigadier, the adjutant-general, quartermaster-general, and commissary-general. The latter has, however, offered a positive impediment to it in the impossibility of providing what would be necessary for such an advance under from sixteen to twenty days. I thought it could have been done in less, but that was before I had seen Colonel Thompson. Indeed, it is very little more than forty-eight hours since I came here, and every turn produces something which may alter a previous opinion.

Anson.

Sir John Lawrence to General Anson.

Rawal Pindee, May 17.

I do not myself think that the country anywhere is against us, certainly not from here to within a few miles of Delhi. I served for nearly thirteen years in Delhi and know the people well. My belief is, that with good management on the part of the civil officers it would open its gates on the approach of our troops. It seems incredible to conceive that the mutineers can hold and defend it. Still, I admit that on military principles, in the present state of affairs, it may not be expedient to advance on Delhi; certainly not until the Meerut force is prepared to act, which it can only be when set free. Once relieve Meerut and give confidence to the country, no difficulty regarding carriage can occur. By good arrangements the owners will come forward, but in any case it can be collected. From Meerut you will be able to form a sound judgment on the course to be followed. If the country lower down be disturbed and the sepoys have mutinied, I conceive it would be a paramount duty to march that way, relieve each place, and disarm or destroy the mutineers. If, on the other hand, all were safe, it would be a question whether you should consolidate your resources there or march on Delhi. I think it must be allowed that our European troops are not placed at this or that station simply to hold it, but to be ready to move wherever they may be required. Salubrious and central points for their location were selected; but so long as we maintain our prestige and keep the country quiet, it cannot signify how many cantonments we abandon. But this we cannot do if we allow two or three native corps to checkmate large bodies of Europeans. It will then be a mere question of time, by slow degrees; but of a certainty, the native troops must destroy us. We are doing all we can to strengthen ourselves and to reinforce you, either by direct or indirect means. But can your Excellency suppose for one moment that the irregular troops will remain staunch if they see our European soldiers cooped up in their cantonments tamely awaiting the progress of events. Your Excellency remarks that we must carefully collect our resources; but what are these resources but our European soldiers, our guns, and our material: these are all ready at hand, and only require to be handled wisely and vigorously to produce great results. We have money also, and the control of the country. But if disaffection spread, insurrection will follow, and we shall then neither be able to collect the revenues nor procure supplies. Pray only reflect on the whole history of India. Where have we failed when we acted vigorously? Where have we succeeded when guided by timid counsels? Clive, with 1,200, fought at Plassey in opposition to the advice of his leading officers, beat 40,000 men, and conquered Bengal; Monson retreated from the Chambal, and before he gained Agra his army was disorganised and partially annihilated. Look at the Cabul catastrophe. It might have been averted by resolute and bold action. The irregulars of the army, the Kazilbashis—in short, our friends, of whom we had many, only left us when they found we were not true to ourselves.

How can it be supposed that strangers and mercenaries will sacrifice everything for us? There is a point up to which they will stand by us, for they know that we have always been eventually successful, and that we are good masters; but go beyond this point, and every man will look to his immediate benefit, his present safety. The irregulars of the Punjab are marching down in the highest spirits, proud to be trusted, and eager to show their superiority over the regular troops—ready to fight, shoulder to shoulder, with the Europeans. But if, on their arrival, they find the Europeans behind breastworks, they will begin to think that the game is up. Recollect that all this time, while we are halting, the emissaries of the mutineers are writing to and visiting every cantonment. . . . I cannot comprehend what the Commissariat can mean by requiring from sixteen to twenty days to procure provisions. I am persuaded that all you can require to take with you must be procurable in two or three. We have had an extraordinarily good harvest, and supplies must be abundant between Amballah and Meerut. The greater portion of the country is well cultivated. We are sending our troops in every direction without difficulty, through tracts which are comparatively desert. Our true policy is to trust the Maharajah of Puttyalah and the Rajah of Jheend and the country generally, for they have shown evidence of being on our side, but utterly to distrust the regular sepoys. I would spare no expenses to carry every European soldier—at any rate, to carry every other one. By alternately marching and riding, their strength and spirits will be maintained. We are pushing on the Guides, the 4th Sikhs, the 1st and 4th Punjab Regiments of infantry, from different parts of the Punjab, in this way. If there is any officer in the Punjab whom your Excellency would wish to have at your side, pray do not hesitate to apply for him.

LAWRENCE.

(Sir John Kaye's 'History of the Sepoy War.')

IX.

THE FIRST SIKH WAR (1844–1845.)

Like the news of Napoleon's movements received at Brussels, the intelligence of the passage of the Sutlej by the Sikhs arrived at Amballah on the day (December 11) on which a great ball was to be given by the Commander-in-Chief, and he moved the next day at the head of all the available troops. In six days the force marched 150 miles, getting little food and less rest, and on December 28, after a long march of twenty-one miles, at four o'clock in the afternoon, the cavalry of Lall Singh's division of the Sikh army attacked the leading divisions of the British forces at Moodkee. On the confirmation of Major Broadfoot's news, the Governor-General had published a manifesto by which, in consideration of an unprovoked attack of a friendly Power, all the Sikh possessions east of the Sutlej were declared forfeit. He then threw 5,000 men from Loodianah into Busseau, where Major Broadfoot had collected provisions and stores: Meanwhile, Lall Singh, passing Sir John Littler, had pushed on to Feroze-Shuhr, where he formed a vast entrenched camp; and hearing that the British force advancing was a slight one, had moved on the 18th with 20,000 men and twenty-two guns to oppose it.

While it lasted, the battle of Moodkee was sharp and bloody; and at first, sepoys and even English soldiers, exhausted as they were, reeled under the excellent fire and energetic attack of the Sikh infantry; but before night finally closed seventeen guns had been taken and the Sikh army retreated with heavy losses; that on the side of the British—872 (215 killed and 657 wounded)—included Sir Robert Sale and General MacCaskill, both deeply regretted. On the 19th and 20th the army halted, and two European and two native regiments joined the Commander-in-Chief.

It was now determined to assault the great Sikh entrenchments at Feroze-Shuhr on the 21st, and Sir John Littler was directed to join on that day with as many troops as he could spare from Ferozepore. He therefore marched with 5,000 infantry, two regiments of cavalry, and twenty-one guns, and took up his place in the general disposition of the troops about noon. Had the army—17,000 strong, with sixty-nine guns—advanced at once, much precious time would have been saved, the action would have been more decisive, and the loss and confusion of the night averted; but the Commander-in-Chief had formed no definite plan beyond, as were his only tactics, storming batteries and carrying them by the bayonet; and in moving troops from place to place, and making such hasty and imperfect arrangements as ensued, four precious hours were wasted. At about four in the afternoon of the shortest day in the year, when but little daylight remained, the British forces were led, in three divisions—the right by Sir Hugh Gough, the left by Sir John Littler, and the centre by the Governor-General—to the attack of a strong entrenchment, a mile and a half long by half a mile wide, defended by 35,000 of the flower of the Sikh army, with 100 guns. There were weak points in the Sikh works which might have been discovered by previous reconnaissance, but they were overlooked or neglected, and the very strongest positions assaulted. Her Majesty's 50th Regiment, directed by Captain Pringle O'Hanlon, of the Staff, was the first to gain a footing in the Sikh camp, and the combat everywhere became general; but the enemy was as resolute in defence as the British troops were persevering in assault. Regiment after regiment of Sir John Littler's division staggered under the tremendous fire of grape and musketry by which they were met. Her Majesty's 62nd Regiment was much shattered, and at nightfall this division was obliged to retire. Sir Harry Smith, whose brigade had carried and occupied the village of Feroze-Shuhr, was unable to hold it during the night, and also drew off; but General Gilbert's division held what it had won. During the hottest part of this furious combat the 3rd Dragoons rode through the Sikh camp from end to end, with a desperate valour only equalled by the charge of the Light Brigade at Balaclava.

Before the camp was carried darkness fell upon the scene, and the night that ensued was truly designated as the 'night of horrors.' Portions of the camp were held by the English troops, others by the still unconquered Sikhs. A hard frost set in: the English forces had had neither food nor water for many hours, and the intense cold aggravated their sufferings. Men of different regiments, European and natives, separated in the darkness and confusion, huddled together; and the noble 'Husseinee Pultun,' the 16th Bengal Native Infantry, under Colonel Hall, victorious and unbroken, was a rallying point for many a weary soldier during the night. By the bright starlight the Sikh artillery from time to time fired upon the exhausted troops, and one large gun in particular did so much execution, that about two in the morning Sir Henry Hardinge, calling upon Her Majesty's 80th and the 1st European Regiment, among whom he was lying, led them to attack and spike it, driving away the Sikh infantry by whom it was guarded. When daylight broke order was restored; the various regiments on the field took up their positions in line with alacrity, and leading their respective divisions Sir Hugh Gough and the Governor-General advanced steadily, swept through the camp with cheers, and changing front to the centre, completed the victory.

But at this juncture, Tej Singh brought up from the Sutlej a fresh force of 20,000 regular and irregular infantry, 5,000 superb cavalry, and seventy guns, and the action was partially renewed. It was at this crisis that the greatest peril existed; for the ammunition of all arms was nearly expended; the formation of regiments was by no means complete, and the troops were thoroughly exhausted alike by fatigue, thirst, and want of food. The advance of the Sikh cavalry, accompanied by horse artillery, is described as the most splendid sight of the campain. Their horses caracolling and bounding, and the bright sunlight flashing from steel armour, sabres, and spears, they came on at a rapid pace to within 400 yards of the British line, which, availing itself of such cover as could be found, awaited the charge with little hope of repelling it. Suddenly, however, after firing a few shots from their guns, the whole, as if stricken by a sudden panic, upon a movement of English cavalry on their flank, wheeled about and retired as they had come. It was rumoured that Tej Sing had been bribed by English gold, but this has never been substantiated, and his retreat is accounted for by the fact that what he had come to save was already lost, and subordinate as he was to Lall Singh, who had fled to the Sutlej, he was bound to follow his commander. What he did was, as he said, to save his honour as a soldier.

The British losses had been very severe, 694 killed and 1,721 wounded, with a large proportion—103—of officers, among whom were many very distinguished men; Broadfoot, who had won a high reputation in Afghanistan, and who had proved invaluable as a political officer; Somerset d'Arcy Todd, of Herat fame, and many others. On the part of the Sikhs, the loss was estimated at 8,000 men, and seventy-three noble guns and many standards remained in the hands of the victors.

In the Sikh camp during the night dissensions had run high, and the military chest of Lall Singh, who had fled at an early period, was plundered by an exasperated soldiery. Under a better and braver leader the result might indeed have been very different, for never before had so hardly contested a battle been fought in India, nor, with eventual victory, had ever such great peril of defeat been encountered.

The British forces could not immediately follow up the success they had achieved; heavy guns, stores, and ammunition were all wanting, and till their arrival from Delhi no forward movement could be made. The Sikhs, attributing this delay to fear, took heart, and towards the middle of January, Sirdar Ranjoor Singh recrossed the Sutlej and threatened the station of Loodianah, then weakly garrisoned. Sir Harry Smith was therefore despatched with four regiments of infantry, three of cavalry, and eighteen guns to relieve it. He had been cautioned against approaching the fort of Buddewal, which lay on his route; but nevertheless, moving under its walls, suffered sharply from its fire and from the splendid artillery of Ranjoor Singh, lost some of his baggage, and was only saved from further disaster by the dashing charges of the cavalry under Colonel Cureton. Being reinforced, however, by his junction with the

Loodianah troops and Brigadier Wheeler's brigade, Sir Harry Smith now advanced in turn to attack the enemy, who had taken up an entrenched position at Aliwal, and had been reinforced by 4,000 men of the best disciplined Sikh infantry. Their army amounted by estimate to 15,000 men, with seventy-six guns; that of the British was about 10,000 men, with thirty-two guns. On January 28, the Sikhs had advanced from their entrenched camp to meet Sir Harry Smith, and a brilliant action ensued. The Sikh squares were penetrated and overthrown by charges of cavalry, in which Her Majesty's 16th Lancers, under Colonel Cureton, in particular, were nobly distinguished. Position after position, battery after battery, were stormed, sixty-seven guns were taken, and the enemy, driven to the bridge of boats they had constructed, fled precipitately across the Sutlej, many of them perishing in the stream, and under the fire of the artillery, which played with great effect upon the boats.

Although the Sikh army had suffered three notable defeats, they still continued to retain their mischievous and turbulent predominance in the State. Golab Singh, who had undertaken the office of minister, from which Lall Singh had been deposed, although he entered into negotiations with the Governor-General, who demanded the dismissal of the Sikh army, declared that he was helpless to effect it. No act of submission or peaceful overtures from the army having been offered, hostilities were resumed on the arrival of the siege-train from Delhi, which reached camp on February 8. For some weeks, the Sikhs, under the direction of a Spanish officer, named Huerba, had been employed in constructing a remarkably powerful *tête de pont*, at the village of Sobraon, to cover a bridge of boats which they had thrown across the river Sutlej, below the ford of Hurrekee, and it was now completed in a series of half-moon bastions, connected by curtains, and covered by a ditch in front, both flanks resting on the river. This great work, two-and-a-half miles in length, was protected by batteries on the right bank of the river, so as to command the passage, and manned by 35,000 of the best of the Sikh troops, with sixty-seven heavy guns. It had been difficult to restrain the British army during its inaction in the presence of the daily progress of this entrenchment; but one day only intervened between the arrival of the heavy guns, stores, and ammunition, and the assault. The British army consisted of 15,000 men, of whom 5,000 were Europeans; and under the cover of a fog, on the morning of February 10, all the dispositions for attack were made without being noticed by the enemy.

When they were complete, about seven in the morning, the fog suddenly rolled away, displaying the British forces in order of battle;

and the heavy guns opened on the Sikhs; but they made no impression on the earthworks; the enemy's fire was not checked, and the only resource that remained was a general assault, which was forthwith carried out amidst the thunder of 120 pieces of artillery on both sides. About nine o'clock the whole of the infantry divisions advanced. Of Sir Robert Dick's division on the left, the horse artillery, under Colonel Lane, galloped up to within 300 yards of the Sikh batteries, and delivered their fire, while the brigade under Colonel Storey, Her Majesty's 10th and 53rd Regiments, with the 43rd and 59th Native Infantry, advancing in line with the regularity of a parade movement, were the first to reach the entrenchments; and the Sikhs gathered to defend it, which they did by a withering fire that checked the leading troops, but did not repulse them. The divisions of Sir Harry Smith on the right, and General Gilbert in the centre, were led on in turn, and after a severe carnage, the entrenchment was won. The Sikh troops, fighting desperately to the last, retired to the bridge, where their retreat became a flight; and the British horse artillery coming up at a gallop, poured grape and shrapnel on the flying masses, till the stream, now barely fordable, was choked with corpses, and the water dyed with blood. Nearly 10,000 Sikhs perished in two hours, and the whole of their guns, sixty-seven in number, with standards, and immense military stores, remained as trophies to the victors. The battle had begun in earnest at nine o'clock, and by eleven there was not a single Sikh soldier, except the dead and wounded, on the left bank of the river. The British loss was also severe, amounting to 2,383 in killed and wounded, and General Sir Robert Dick, who fell in the assault.

No time was lost in throwing the British army across the river by a bridge of boats, which was constructed by Major Abbott, with the boats that Lord Ellenborough had procured from Scinde; they crossed on the night of the action, and on the 11th envoys arrived from Lahore, followed by Rajah Golab Singh on the 15th, and the boy, Maharajah Dhuleep Singh, on the 17th. On the 20th, having advanced by easy marches, the army encamped on the plain of Meean Meer, without Lahore, and the citadel was partly occupied by British troops. Sir Henry Hardinge, on February 22, issued a public notification, reviewing the events that had occurred, and dwelling with a proud satisfaction on the fact, that in sixty days he had defeated the flower of the Khulsa army, in four general actions, and taken from them 220 pieces of artillery; that only 14,000 of the great army remained, and that he was now dictating a treaty, the conditions of which will tend to secure the British provinces from the repetition of a similar outrage. On the 23rd, at a public durbar, the treaty itself was executed. All the Sikh territories on the left bank of the Sutlej, with the Jullundur Doab, a fertile tract lying between the Sutlej and the Beyas, were to become British; 1,500,000*l.* to be provided, partly by cash, and partly by the sale of the mountain territory, which includes Cashmere; all the mutinous troops to be disbanded, and the army for the future to consist of twenty-five battalions of 800 each, or 20,000 men with 12,000 cavalry. Golab Singh became the purchaser of Cashmere for a million sterling, and a separate treaty was made with him on March 16, at Umritsur, which secured to him and his heirs the sovereignty of the districts he had purchased. The sale of Cashmere was sharply criticised at the time; but its inaccessible character, and the still uncertain relations with the Punjab, are conclusive reasons as to the reason of their abandoning it.

('Manual of Indian History,' by Meadows Taylor.)

X.

The Second Sikh War and Annexation of the Punjab, 1848–1849.

'Unwarned by precedent, uninfluenced by example, the Sikh nation has called for war; and, on my word, Sir, they shall have it with vengeance.' Such was Lord Dalhousie's memorable expression at a farewell banquet before he left Calcutta, on October 10, 1848, on his way to the upper provinces. Although the whole of the Punjab was seething with disaffection, Chutter Singh was the only chieftain to begin war openly in the field. He applied for aid to Dost Mohammed, agreed to deliver Peshawur to him if he would join the Sikhs against the English; and this strange compact between people who hated each other mortally was actually made. Major, afterwards Sir George, Lawrence, was then in charge of Peshawur, with 8,000 Sikh troops, whose fidelity was in the last degree questionable; but he contrived to keep them to their duty, until Sultan Mohammed, the brother of Dost Mohammed, a person to whom he had shown the utmost kindness, treacherously seduced them, and, on October 24, led them to attack him in the Residency. Major Lawrence and his companions were conducted to Kohat, but afterwards delivered or sold to Chutter Singh, who confined them at Peshawur. Meanwhile, Shere Singh, who had marched from Mooltan, had joined his father, and round their standards collected most of the old soldiers of the Sikh army.

The forces assembled at Ferozepore for operations in the Punjab, were completed in equipment during October 1848, and under the personal command of Lord Gough crossed the Ravee (Beyas) on November 16. They consisted of fifteen regiments of infantry—four European and eleven native, three regiments of English and ten of native regular and irregular cavalry, with sixty field guns and eighteen heavy guns, the latter now, for the first time, drawn by elephants instead of bullocks. On November 22, Lord Gough found Shere Singh encamped at Ramnuggur, on the right bank of the Chenab, with 15,000 men, and a powerful artillery, with an advanced force on the left bank covered by his batteries. It was too strong a position to assail in front; but the advanced Sikh force was attacked and driven back without material result, and in a charge of the British cavalry to clear the left bank of the river, it was rendered helpless in the sands, and suffered heavily from the Sikh guns on the right bank. In this desultory and ineffective skirmish, Colonel Cureton of the Lancers, who commanded the cavalry division, and Colonel William Havelock, the 'el chico bianco' of many a Peninsular fight, lost their lives, to the universal regret of the army. A flank movement, which might have been made at first, was now arranged, and on December 2, Sir Joseph Thackwell, with 8,000 men, crossed the river at Vizarabad, twenty-four miles above Ramnuggur. It was proposed that he should advance upon Shere Singh's camp from the right flank, while the main army crossed the river in front. Shere Singh, however, did not await this issue. Abandoning his entrenchments, he marched to attack General Thackwell, whom, with a diminished force, he met at Sadoollapore, but did not close with him, and after sustaining a heavy, but ill-directed cannonade, which lasted till evening, General Thackwell discovered during the night that the Sikhs, now 30,000 strong, with forty guns, had retired towards the Jhelum. Lord Gough, in his despatch, claimed the movement as a victory over the Sikh army, and even asserted its dispersion; but the fact was soon evident that Shere Singh had only retired to a better position, and had carried with him all his guns and equipment unmolested.

The position chosen by Shere Singh was one of singular strength, and its selection displayed his skill as a general in no mean degree. To have followed him up, and forced him to fight at a disadvantage, would probably have been effected by Lord Gough after the affair at Ramnuggur, but he was restrained by the Governor-General for upwards of three weeks, and unable to interfere with Shere Singh, who was thus able to carry out his plans leisurely, and without interruption. On January 11, however, Lord Gough reviewed his troops, and on the 12th they advanced twelve miles to Drujee, and on the

13th were near the Sikh entrenchments at Chillianwallah, which were held by them with 30,000 men and sixty guns. Of this place no reconnaissance had been made, nor were the enemy's dispositions understood, as they were covered by a thick jungle; and Lord Gough was about to encamp for the night, when the Sikhs fired upon him from some advanced guns, and he rashly gave orders for an immediate action. The whole of the Sikh guns now opened fire, after enduring which for upwards of an hour, the British troops advanced on the position. The first regiment which reached the Sikh batteries was Her Majesty's 24th, which was overwhelmed by a fearful fire of grape and musketry; 459 men, with twenty-three officers, were at once killed or wounded. General Colin Campbell, afterwards Lord Clyde, had carried the position before him, spiking the guns; and other divisions, under Sir Walter Gilbert, with brigades under Penny, Mountain, and others, though suffering heavily, finally conquered, and the Sikhs retired into the forest behind them. The cavalry had been less successful. Charged by a comparatively small body of Sikh horse, the 14th Dragoons, under a false order, uttered it was supposed by some coward in its ranks, went about, and galloped to the rear, pursued by the Sikhs; and the misadventure was only redeemed by a desperate charge made by Captain Unett. It was found impossible to hold the field during the night, now closing in, and Lord Gough unwillingly withdrew the army to Chillianwallah for water and rest. During the night the Sikh troops returned, carried off all the captured guns except twelve, and barbarously murdered all the wounded who could not be recovered before the close of the action. The loss in this consequent battle, which had nearly been a disastrous defeat, was 2,357 men and eighty-nine officers in killed and wounded; three regiments had lost their colours, and four horse-artillery guns had been taken.

After the conclusion of the siege of Mooltan, General Whish moved up to reinforce the Commander-in-Chief. Shere Singh, perceiving this movement, and probably desiring to destroy General Whish's force before it could cover Lahore or form a junction with the main army, left his camp at Russool on February 6, and marched in the direction of Lahore; but if the conception had been that of a clever tactician, its execution was extremely indifferent. He allowed British detachments to occupy the fords of the Chenab, and, thus foiled, took up a position at Goojerat. He had been joined by his father, Chutter Singh, and a considerable force, and by Akram Khan, a son of Dost Mohammed, with a division of Afghans; and the whole Sikh army, now collected in one place, amounted to upwards of 50,000 men, with sixty guns. On the other hand, Lord Gough, reinforced by General Whish on February 20, had under him 20,000 men and 100 guns. It will have been remarked in all Lord Gough's battles that artillery had been an arm of only very secondary consideration; and its disuse was even freely commented upon by the Sikh generals to Major George Lawrence, and so became the subject of open conversation. Lord Gough was urged by all the best officers of the army, and even by the Governor-General, to employ it in the next engagement, and he happily consented to do so, though, it was said, against conviction.

On February 27, 1849, the British army advanced in line in parade order upon the Sikh position at Goojerat. The centre was composed of eighty-four guns, many of heavy calibre, drawn by elephants, and when within easy range of the Sikh batteries the whole opened fire, forming a magnificent spectacle. The effect was just what had been anticipated. The Sikh fire in two hours and a half was nearly silenced, and the British infantry, advancing from both flanks, carried the entrenched villages one by one, and drove out the Sikh infantry, without a check. One brilliant charge was made by the Sikh and Afghan horse, but it was gallantly met and defeated by the 9th Lancers and the famous Scinde horse, under Captain Malcolm, and hurled back. Finally, the British cavalry charged the now broken Sikh infantry, and pursued it for fifteen miles beyond the field of battle, doing immense execution. The whole of the British loss in this brilliant and scientifically fought battle was only ninety-two killed and 682 wounded, and fifty-three guns were taken, with many standards. It was impossible to estimate fully the loss of the Sikhs, but it amounted to several thousands, and the whole army had become totally broken and disorganised.

The pursuit of Shere Singh was taken up by General Gilbert with 12,000 men and forty guns; but the Sikh general was in no condition to renew the struggle. Having been joined by Major George Lawrence, who had been allowed absence to Lahore on parole, and whose good faith in returning was welcomed with enthusiastic shouts by the Sikh soldiers, negotiations were entered into with General Gilbert, who consented to receive the submission of the Sikhs if they laid down their arms unconditionally. On March 12, at the great Buddhist monument of Mamkyalah, Shere Singh and the wreck of his army, about 8,000 men, met General Gilbert, and Shere Singh set the example by delivering up his sword. Then followed an astonishing and affecting spectacle. Chief after chief laid his sword at the general's feet, and after them the brave Sikh soldiers, one by one, passed by, casting their arms, sometimes in silent grief and tears, sometimes with passionate exclamations, upon the heaps which received them. Forty-one more guns were surrendered, the last of the parks of the whole army, which had been buried 'till they should be needed.' This finished, General Gilbert, with the cavalry, hunted the Afghans back to the passes, into which they fled ignominiously, and, as the Sikhs said, 'like dogs.' The Sikhs had submitted honestly and without shame to a Power which they now respected, and to which, since then, they have been admirably faithful in many trying scenes.

During the progress of the war the British civil officers, with a wonderful skill and perseverance, held their posts; and many brilliant affairs, into which it is impossible to enter, occurred in different localities. Of these the most remarkable was the retention of the Jullundur Doab, the province lately ceded by Mr., the present Lord Lawrence, who, without regular troops, and with a few hastily collected levies of Sikhs and hill-men, routed the rebels, and overawed all attempts of local disaffection. Major Herbert, too, had defended the fort of Attock against many attacks, and received the emphatic thanks of the Governor-General.

The fate of the Punjab was not long in suspense; and by a proclamation of March 29, 1849, the Governor-General, reviewing past events and the fact of the Lahore territories having been already once spared after a treacherous attack upon its allies, coupled with the uncertainty which would remain in future, boldly annexed the whole territory—a measure which no one then ventured to impugn, or which has since been questioned. On the young Maharajah Dhuleep Singh a pension of five lacs of rupees (50,000*l.*) a year was conferred. He is now a Christian and an English country gentleman, owning large estates in Suffolk, one of the best shots in England, and respected by all who know him. The chiefs were settled in their hereditary villages on pensions according to their rank, and the whole of the population submitted with extraordinary unanimity to the new rulers. Lord Dalhousie was created a marquis, Lord Gough a baron, and the honours of the Bath were conferred upon several of the most distinguished officers; but there were some, nevertheless, who, deserving as much or more than others, were unaccountably passed over. Thus ended the second and final Sikh war. With it the conquest of India, within its natural boundaries, the Indus, the Himalayas, and the ocean—more universal and more complete than any by which it had been preceded—had, after many vicissitudes, been effected in less than a hundred years by the English nation.

('A Student's Manual of the History of India,' by Meadows Taylor.)

XI.

Letter of Sir John Lawrence relating to the Executions at Peshawur.

In respect of the mutineers of the 55th, they were taken fighting against us, and so far deserve little mercy. But on full reflection, I would not put them all to death. I do not think that we should be justified in the eyes of the Almighty in doing so. A hundred and twenty men are a large number to put to death. Our object is to make an example to terrify others. I think this object would be effectually gained by destroying from a quarter to a third of them. I would select all those against whom anything bad can be shown—such as general bad character, turbulence, prominence in disaffection or in the fight, disrespectful demeanour to their officers during the few days before the 26th, and the like. If these did not make up the required number, I would then add to them the oldest soldiers. All these should be shot or blown away from guns, as may be most expedient. The rest I would divide into batches; some to be imprisoned ten years, some seven, some five, some three. I think that a sufficient example will then be made, and that these distinctions will do good, and not harm. The sepoys will see that we punish to deter, and not for vengeance. Public sympathy will not be on the side of the sufferers. Otherwise, they will fight desperately to the last, as feeling certain that they must die.

Lawrence.

(Sir John Kaye's 'History of the Sepoy War.')

XII.

Correspondence relating to the Abandonment of Peshawur.

Sir John Lawrence to Colonel Herbert Edwardes.

Rawal Pindee, June 21.

Here we are, with three European regiments, a large artillery, and some of our best native troops locked up across the Indus—troops who, if at Delhi, would decide the contest in a week. What have we got for all the rest of the Punjab? We have barely two thousand Europeans. I doubt if we have so many holding the port of Philour, Govindourgh, Ferozepore, Lahore, and Mooltan. We have not a man more with a white face whom we can spare. We cannot concentrate more than we have now done, except by giving up Rawal

Pindee and eventually Peshawur. Should the Sikhs rise, our condition on this side of the Indus will be well-nigh desperate. With the Peshawur force on this side we should be irresistibly strong. There was no one thing which tended so much to the ruin of Napoleon in 1814 as the tenacity with which, after the disasters at Leipsig, he clung to the line of the Elbe, instead of falling back at once to that of the Rhine. He thus compromised all his garrisons beyond the Elbe, and when he was beaten in the field, these gradually had to surrender. But these troops would have given him the victory had they been at his side at Bautzen, and the other conflicts which followed Leipsig.

Sir John Lawrence to Colonel Herbert Edwardes.

Rawal Pindee, June 25.

A severe action at Delhi apparently with little results; on the 25th Bareilly mutineers *en route* to Delhi. Gwalior contingent have mutinied. Agent has left. If matters get worse, it is my decided opinion that the Peshawur arrangements should take effect. Our troops before Delhi must be reinforced, and that largely—they must hold their ground.

General Sidney Cotton to Sir John Lawrence.

Peshawur, June 25.

We have pushed our conquests up to the very mouth of the Afghanistan passes, and at this very moment, by God's blessing, our strongest position in India is at the mouth of the Khyber. By our good rule, we have engaged the affections (I may say) to a considerable extent of the border tribes, and in the hour of need they (who, not many years since, were our most bitter enemies), relying on our great name and power, have come forward to help us against the disaffection of the very troops with whom we have conquered the Sikhs, Punjabis, and others. A retrograde movement from Peshawur, believe me, would turn all these parties, now our friends, against us. The Punjab irregular force, Pathans, Sikhs, Punjabis, and such like, no longer respecting our power, will, in all likelihood, turn against us, and their most valuable services be lost to us for ever. My dear Sir John, our removal from Peshawur cannot fail to be disastrous, and cannot be effected without immediate confusion throughout the whole of this part of this country, and throughout the length and breadth of British India. Hence the measure will seriously injure the interests of our forces in all quarters, whilst the additional strength to be gained would be small, and, indeed, we could afford no timely aid. In handing over the Peshawur district to the Dost (a measure which we may pretend to be a mere matter of expediency, and not of necessity), the Afghans will at once see our weakness, and will duly profit by the same against the common enemy. To this frontier, and to the present strength of our position on it, as well as to Calcutta at the opposite end of our territory, we must look for the recovery of our power throughout the intermediate kingdoms of the Bengal Presidency. Our great name is upheld on our frontiers, whilst Calcutta and this seaboard, in the plenitude of power, with European reinforcements continually arriving, will afford eventually and more surely the necessary succour. At this very moment six or eight regiments of Europeans must be between Calcutta and Delhi, *en route* to the seat of war, and triple that amount will be eventually thrown in from home and elsewhere, and by such means must our supremacy be recovered. When could our troops reach the seat of war, and in what numbers and conditions? These questions must be duly considered, and by them the loss and gain of our removal from hence be balanced and determined on. I earnestly implore of you, my dear Sir John, to hold to our position on this frontier. The required succour must indeed be thrown in from Calcutta, not from this. When the reinforcements from above and below, at present in progress towards Delhi, have reached their destination, I feel confident that that city will again fall into our hands, and I am very much mistaken if disaffection does not then cease in all quarters, and, our power being thus established, mutiny will gradually disappear throughout the land.

Colonel H. Edwardes, Commissioner at Peshawur, to Sir John Lawrence.

Peshawur, June 26, 1857.

General Cotton, James, and myself are all of opinion that you should not go on throwing away your means in detail, by meeting General Reid's demands for reinforcements. Delhi is not India, and if General Reid cannot take it with 8,000 men, he will not take it with 9,000 or 10,000. However important a point, it is only a point, and enough has been done for it. You will serve the empire better by holding the Punjab, than by sacrificing the Punjab and recovering Delhi. You will sacrifice the Punjab, if you either withdraw General Collins's force from Peshawur, or fritter away Nicholson's moveable column, already too weak. 'Make a stand! anchor, Hardy, anchor!' Tell General Reid he can have no more men from here, and must either get into Delhi with the men he has, or get reinforcements from below, or abandon the siege and fall back on the

Sutlej, leaving Delhi and its dependencies to be reorganised in the cold weather. There are two policies open to you—to treat the Punjab as secondary to the North-West Provinces, and go on giving and giving troops to General Reid till you break down in the Punjab, or to maintain the Punjab as your first duty, and the most important point of the two, and to refuse to give General Reid any more troops than you can spare. We are decidedly and distinctly of the latter opinion. . . . We consider that if you leave the Peshawur frontier, we shall not hold together for a month, but be demoralised and despised, and reduced to the condition of a flock of sheep. . . . If you hold the Punjab, you will facilitate the reconquest of India from the seaboard. We have only got to hold on three months. Do not try too much. We are outnumbered. Stick to what you can do. Let us hold the Punjab, *coûte que coûte*, and not give up one European necessary to that duty. Whatever takes place in Central India, we shall stand on a firm and honourable attitude if we maintain the capitals on the sea and the frontiers here. Between the two it is all a family quarrel—an insurrection in our own house. If we let foreigners in from the frontier, the Empire is invaded. We may pretend to make friendly presents of provinces, but we cannot disguise that we have lost them by weakness. India has not yet recovered from our expulsion from Afghanistan. The world ignores our voluntary cession of it after Pollock's expedition, and knows well that we could not hold it. Do not repeat the policy and give up the trans-Indus. No words of mine can express my sense of the disgrace and ruin that it will bring upon us. It is abandoning the cause of England in the East. Don't yield an inch of frontier; gather up your resources and restrict yourself to the defence of the Punjab. It is a practicable and a definite policy, and we will support you to the last. If General Reid, with all the men you have sent him, cannot get into Delhi, let Delhi go. Decide on it at once. . . . Don't let yourself be sucked to death as General Reid is doing. He has his difficulties, and we have ours. You have made vast efforts for him, and no one can blame you for now securing your own promise. . . . . . . The Empire's reconquest hangs on the Punjab.

Sir John Lawrence to Lord Canning.

July 24, 1857.

All these reinforcements ought to enable our army to maintain itself in its present condition and allow the mutineers to expend their power against our entrenchments. But should further aid be required from this quarter, our only resource would be to abandon Peshawur and Kohat, and to send the troops thus relieved to Delhi.

It seems to me vain to attempt to hold Lahore, and insanity to try to retain Peshawur, &c., if we are driven from Delhi. The Punjab will prove short work to the mutineers, when the Delhi army is destroyed. . . . My policy would then be to bring the troops from across the Indus and send them to Delhi; in the meantime to send all our women and children down the river to Kurrachee, and then, accumulating every fighting man we have, to join the army before Delhi, or hold Lahore, as might appear expedient. Colonel Edwardes, Generals Cotton and Nicholson, are for maintaining our hold on Peshawur to the last. They argue that we could not retire in safety, and that the instant we attempt to make a retrograde movement all would be up against us. This I do not believe; but granting that insurrection would immediately ensue, I maintain that the force at Peshawur would make good its retreat. It contains more soldiers, more guns, more power than that with which Pollock recovered Cabul after forcing the passage of the Khyber. Between Peshawur and the Indus are no defiles, but an open country; the only difficulty is the passage of the Indus, which, with Attock in our hands, ought not to be a work of danger. It is for your lordship to decide what course we are to pursue. In the event of misfortune at Delhi, are we to leave that army to its fate and endeavour to hold its own, or shall we, by timely retirement from beyond the Indus, consolidate our resources in the Punjab, and maintain the struggle under the walls of Delhi? I pray that your lordship will decide one way or the other. If we are left to decide the matter ourselves, time will be lost in vain discussions, and by the time we decide on the proper course to follow, it will prove too late to act effectually.

The question of the abandonment of Peshawur was decided by the following despatch of Lord Canning :—

Calcutta, July 15, 1857.

The outbreak at Indore on the 1st will no doubt have interrupted the dâk as well as the telegraph to Bombay. I therefore send a steamer to Madras with this letter and the despatches which accompany it; and I shall request Lord Harris to telegraph to Lord Elphinstone my answer to your question regarding Peshawur. It will be, 'Hold on Peshawur to the last.' I should look with great alarm to the effect in Southern India of an abandonment of Peshawur at the present time, or at any time until our condition becomes more desperate or more secure.

(Sir John Kaye's 'History of the Sepoy War.')

XIII.

Difficulties of the English Agents for the Communications between the Punjab and Calcutta during the Mutiny.

In consequence of the disturbed state of the country great difficulty was experienced in securing the safe transit of the mails; indeed it was often impossible, though the accidents and delays which occurred in this department of the public service were much fewer than might have been expected. By degrees, however, one road after another became stopped. The road between Calcutta and the Punjab was interrupted by the state of the districts about Mirzapore, Mynpooree, Meerut, and Delhi. The mail road between the Punjab and Bombay ran through Agra, Indore, and Mhow; this, too, after a time became unsafe, in consequence of the bands of rebels hovering about the country between Mhow and Agra. Another line of road from Ajmere and Nusseerabad to Bombay took the direction of Pallee, Erinpoora and Deesar; from thence a branch led up to Mount Abou. Communication was kept up between Ajmere and Agra pretty regularly, as the road lay through the States of independent chiefs in alliance with the British Government; and as this was the most direct and the nearest route by which communication could be kept up with Kurrachee—a place that was daily growing in importance, in consequence of its being a harbour and a landing place for European troops, and the seat of government of the North-West Provinces—Mr. Frere, the Commissioner of Scinde, conceived the idea of establishing a post line across the desert between Hyderabad in Scinde and Jodhpore, from whence communication was easily extended to Ajmere and so on to Agra. Mr. Frere's views and instructions were ably carried out by an officer named Lieutenant Tyrwhitt, who held the office of Deputy-Collector of Meerpore. This appointment placed him in charge of the whole desert between Hyderabad and the frontier of Marwar, though Meerpore, where his head-quarters were, was only about two or three marches from Hyderabad. During the summer months the heat in the desert is such as to render travelling not only inconvenient but dangerous, but Lieutenant Tyrwhitt was not to be daunted, and he set out in the burning month of May and rode up, attended by a few followers, all the way to Jodhpore. Resting at certain distances and calling around him the chiefs of the surrounding tribes, he struck a bargain with them, by which they engaged themselves to keep three camels at each station, about ten miles apart, for the conveyance of the mails. A considerable expense was incurred by this means, but Mr Frere was one of those men who do not shrink from responsibility, and who recognise the importance of individual energy and the necessity of departing from the routine of established regulation in times of great emergency. Sir John Lawrence was another, and it was to men of their stamp that, we may say, humanly speaking, we owe the retention of our Indian Empire. Captain Mason, the political agent at Jodhpore, eagerly co-operated with Mr. Frere and his active subordinate Lieutenant Tyrwhitt, and the plan was extended beyond the limit originally designed by a line of camel dâks, as they are called, being established between Jodhpore and Bhawulpore on the Sutlej, by which means communication was easily kept up with the Punjab, and a line of road open that was not likely to be affected by the movements of the rebels, who would hardly penetrate so far into the desert. Another mounted post was established between Jodhpore and Ajmere. The former place thus suddenly became the centre of communication between some of the most important parts of our Eastern Empire. A deputy-superintendent of the line, Mr. C. Hewitt, who is now dead, took up his residence near the Agency, and made it his head-quarters, from whence he set out on a periodical inspection of the line, and was ready to go to any point where the presence of a supervising officer was requisite. These lines were begun in the latter end of May, but the several branches were not completed till the end of June or beginning of July, and it was some little time before the various streams of communication, so often thwarted in their progress, began to find out there was an open channel for them, and turned their course accordingly. Now, however, the influx of work upon the poor little post-office established at Jodhpore, presided over by a native writer on a salary of seventy-five rupees a month, was so great as utterly to bewilder the methodical old gentleman, who had never before had anything more to do than start off a bag of letters once or twice a day by the regular runners, and receive and distribute a few English Letters to the Political Agent, his family, and the few European residents attached to the Agency and the Maharajah's court, and a small quantity of native correspondence in the city. The Jodhpore lines, as they may be called, as they all centred there, were enormously expensive. Three camels were maintained at each post, two for work, and one spare in case of accident and for expresses, and for each the sum paid by contract was sixteen rupees per mensem; but the money was usefully spent. It was of the last importance to keep up communication, and whatever roads throughout North and Central India were stopped, the Jodhpore lines were always open l in working order. But supervision was required, and as there was no immediate prospect of the unattached Bengal officers going to Agra, and I was therefore unemployed in any capacity, Captain Monck Mason easily procured the sanction of the Governor-General's agent to my being placed in charge of the Jodhpore post-office. I gladly accepted the task, and was soon deep in the postal department's rules and regulations. At times, as many as eight mails arrived during the day, not small letter-bags, such as are usually seen on the backs of runners in India, but regular camel-loads; and often as many as two camels were required at once to bring on the bags, or rather sacks of letters. The packets were deposited in a part of the verandah of the Agency that was enclosed to serve for a post-office, distributed and started off again on their route, either to Scinde across the desert, or to Ajmere, Nusseerabad and Agra, or to Bhawulpore and the Punjab, or to Bombay *viâ* Pallu and Erinpoora.

At one time letters and despatches from Calcutta to Meerut had to be sent across the country to Bombay, thence to Jodhpore, thence to Lahore *viâ* Bhawulpore, and from Lahore down to Meerut, and for a very long time the only communication with the army before Delhi was by this roundabout route.

('The Mutinies in Rajpootana,' by T. T. Prichard.)

XIV.

The last Nazzar given to the King of Delhi by English Officers.

As soon as the camp arrived at Delhi, the Government records were produced, in order that reference should be made to the etiquette followed as regarded the Emperor on those previous rare occasions in which Governor-Generals had visited the Imperial city. It was found that although the relative position of the Governor-General and the Emperor did not admit of their exchanging visits, yet that a deputation had been sent on the part of the Governor-General to ask after the health of his Majesty, and tender him a 'nazzar' of a certain amount of gold mohurs, which in reality amounted to an expression of submission and fealty on the part of the British Government to the Great Mogul, and an acknowledgment of holding our Indian possessions as his feudatory. As, however, this had been the usual practice, no question was raised as to its propriety; and, therefore, without any previous intimation to the Governor-General of what was about to be done, Mr. Thomason and myself, accompanied by Colonel Broadfoot, proceeded to the pal» on elephants, each being provided with a silk bag full of gold mohurs for presentation to the King. We were required to proceed without any shoes into the immediate presence—such having been in all ages in India the usual mark of respect on the part of an inferior on approaching a superior. On this occasion, we compromised the matter by putting short worsted Cashmere socks over our boots, and thus entered the hall of audience. On a curtain being drawn aside, we saw the old King, then apparently a very feeble old man, about seventy years of age, seated on his throne, which was elevated so as to have the royal person, as he sat cross-legged, on a level with our faces. We made a low obeisance to the Emperor, and on approaching the throne, each in succession presented his bag of gold mohurs, and inquired after his Majesty's health and prosperity. I confess to a feeling of awe and solemnity passing over me as I stepped up and addressed this representative of a long line of kings and of a once powerful empire, and presented my 'nazzar' for his Majesty's acceptance, which was remarkable as being the last that was ever offered on the part of a British subject to the Imperial house of Timour. The King simply accepted it, and ordered us to be robed in dresses of honour, and to have turbans bound round our heads. This was done in due form; we made our obeisance to the King, and departed. We remounted our elephants, and were paraded through the chief streets of Delhi as 'those whom the King delighted to honour.' The ridiculous transformation we had all three undergone, clad in these robes of tinsel tissue, drove all feelings of solemnity and respect out of my mind. I contrived to get ahead of my party, and stripping off my own finery, as I sat on the howdah, made my way to the Governor-General's tent to beg his lordship to come and see the Chief Secretary and Colonel Broadfoot as they arrived in camp and before dismounting from their elephants, as these two estimable gentlemen looked as if they had gone suddenly mad, and decked themselves out in a manner worthy of 'Madge Wildfire.' The Governor-General (Lord Ellenborough) begged me to explain what we had been doing, and on my informing him his lordship's indignation and surprise was extreme; and then, for the first time, I myself became alive to the impropriety of an act which, in reality, made Queen Victoria, in Eastern estimation at least, hold her Indian possessions as a mere feudatory and vassal of the Imperial house of Delhi.

(Edwardes' 'Reminiscences of a Bengal Civilian.')

XV.

SIR HENRY BARNARD'S LAST LETTER TO THE GOVERNOR-GENERAL.

The following letter was written to Lord Canning by Sir Henry Barnard three days before his death. It gives a correct idea of the difficulties of the position before Delhi:—

Camp above Delhi, July 2, 1857.

MY DEAR LORD CANNING,—Ere this reaches you, the business here will have been settled; if successfully, well; if a failure, I shall like to leave behind me a brief record of the service of the little force.

The work of reduction or re-occupation of Delhi was evidently greatly under-estimated. Delhi, when once its gates were shut, and its immense arsenal and magazines in the hands of insurgent troops, became a formidable operation to reduce. When, added to this, the passions of the people were roused, and the cry raised of a new 'Mogul dynasty,' it became as important as formidable.

With means totally inadequate, this force was sent against it, reinforced by detachments from Meerut, who were to have provided sappers, gunners, and field implements; when all had formed a junction the force barely arrived at 3,800. Meerut sent no gunners and only a small number of sappers, and these unprovided. On June 8 we started from Alipore, met the enemy at Budlie-ka-Seraï, and from thence drove them from the height above Delhi. Here the commanding artilleryman and chief engineer proposed to commence the attack; batteries were planned and erected, but the distance was too great. After eight days, I found the side of the town, which must be silenced before we got approaches, quite as alive as ever. The artilleryman admitted the distance too great, and the engineer his inability to make batteries, having positively not a single sandbag. I was promised reinforcements, and for their arrival I determined to wait. They have arrived, and now comes the decisive moment, and I confess to you I never was so puzzled. The force I have amounts to about 5,000, and comprises almost all the Europeans in the upper provinces; quite enough, if free, to re-establish the country, but quite insufficient to storm Delhi, guard the camp, and keep open my communications with the rear for supplies. If I succeed in the gambler's throw, well and good, but if I fail, the game is up, and all I can expect to be able to do would be to effect an honourable retreat, carrying off sick, wounded, and guns. To add to my distress, dissatisfaction is proved to exist in the native troops just arrived, and some have been detected in trying to tamp with the men of Coke's corps. These fellows are to be hang to-night, but the 9th Irregular Cavalry and some of the Sikh corps are known to be tainted, and would like an opportunity of doing us any mischief they could. Thus it is, with enemies without, traitors within, and a task before me I cannot in reason feel my force competent to undertake, I am called upon to decide. Much is said about the native character and aptitude at turning tail, but where the treasure is I fear the heart will be found also; for all these miscreants are laden with plunder they will not abandon, and they know full well that every man's hand is against them. They dare not fly.

My men are very tired; we have had since the action of Budlie-ka-Seraï no less than ten affairs, seven of which employed my whole force, cavalry and infantry; in each we experienced heavy losses, but inflicted greater. The traitors are, or rather were, tired; they openly said it was no use fighting, and that unless assisted they would fly in four days. Yesterday brought them the Bareilly people, so we shall have our eleventh to-morrow. After that, I think the game is over. The Gwaliors are not coming on, and we shall have defeated them all in turn. But to be useful, I must enter the city, and this will, I am fearful, be a sanguinary affair, for it is clear the sepoy knows well how to fight behind stone walls.

I hope to hear of the head of the European columns coming up from Calcutta, and then matters will begin to look up again.

Pray excuse this scrawl: it is written in a gale of wind. The rain has fallen for two days, but it is fine again.

Very truly yours,

H. Barnard.

(Sir J. Kaye's 'History of the Sepoy War.')

XVI.

Visit of Nana Sahib to Lucknow.

I must here mention a visit which was made to Lucknow in April by the Nana of Bithoor, whose subsequent treachery and atrocities have given him a pre-eminence in infamy. He came over on pretence of seeing the sights at Lucknow, accompanied by his young brother and a numerous retinue, bringing letters of introduction from a former judge of Cawnpore to Captain Hayes and to myself. He visited me, and his manner was arrogant and presuming. To make a show of dignity and importance he brought six or seven followers with him into the room, for whom chairs were demanded. One of these men was his notorious agent Azimoola.

is younger brother was more pleasing in appearance and demeanour. The Nana was introduced by me to Sir Henry Lawrence, who received him kindly, and ordered the authorities of the city to show him every attention. I subsequently met him parading through Lucknow with a retinue more than usually large. He had promised before leaving Lucknow to make his final call on the Wednesday. On the Monday we received a message from him that urgent business required his attendance at Cawnpore, and he left Lucknow accordingly. At the time his conduct attracted little attention, but it was otherwise when affairs had assumed the aspect which they did at Cawnpore by May 20. His demeanour at Lucknow and sudden departure to Cawnpore appeared exceedingly suspicious, and I brought it to the notice of Sir Henry Lawrence. The Chief Commissioner concurred in my suspicions, and by his authority I addressed Sir Hugh Wheeler, cautioning him against the Nana, and stating Sir Henry's belief that he was not to be depended on. The warning was unhappily disregarded, and on May 22 a message was received stating that 'two guns and three hundred men, cavalry and infantry, furnished by the Maharajah of Bithoor, came in this morning.'

(Gubbins, 'The Mutinies in Oude.')

XVII.

Letter from Sir Henry Lawrence to Lord Canning, on account of the state of mind in the Native Troops.

May 9, 1857.

I had a conversation with a jemadar of the Oude Artillery for more than an hour, and was startled by the dogged persistence of the man—a Brahmin of about forty years of age, of excellent character—in the belief that for ten years past Government has been engaged in measures for the forcible, or rather fraudulent, conversion of all the natives. His argument was, that as such was the case, and that as we made our way through India, won Bhurtpore, Lahore, &c., by fraud, so might it be possible that we mixed bone-dust with the grain sold to the Hindoos. When I told him of our power in Europe, how the Russian war had quadrupled our army in a year, and in another it could, if necessary, have been interminably increased, and that in the same way, in six months, any required number of Europeans could be brought to India, and that therefore we are not at the mercy of the sepoys, he replied that he knew that we had plenty of men and money, but that Europeans are expensive, and that therefore we wished to take Hindoos to sea to conquer the world for us. On my remarking that the sepoy, though a good soldier shore, is a bad one at sea, by reason of his poor food, 'That is just it,' was the rejoinder, 'You want us all to eat what you like, that we may be stronger and go everywhere.' He often repeated, 'I tell you what everybody says.' But when I replied, 'Fools and traitors may say so, but honest and sensible men cannot think so,' he would not say that he himself did or did not believe, but said, 'I tell you they are like sheep; the leading one tumbles down, and all the rest rolls over him.' Such a man is very dangerous; he has his full faculties, is a Brahmin, has served us twenty years, knows our strength and our weakness, and hates us thoroughly. It may be that he is only more honest than his neighbours, but he is not the less dangerous. On one only point did he give us credit. I told him that in the year 1846, I had rescued 150 native children, left by our army in Cabul, and that instead of making them Christians, I had restored them to their relations and friends. 'Yes,' he replied, 'I remember well. I was at Lahore.' On the other hand, he told me of our making Christians of children purchased during famines. I have spoken to many others, of all ranks, during the last fortnight; most give us credit for good intentions; but here is a soldier of our own, selected for promotion over the heads of others, holding opinions that must make him at heart a traitor.

Lord Canning to Lord Elphinstone, Governor of Bombay.

Calcutta, May 8, 1857.

The mutinous spirit is not quelled here, and I feel no confidence of being able to eradicate it very speedily, although the outbreak may be repressed easily. The spirit of disaffection, or rather of mistrust, for it is more that, has spread further than I thought six weeks ago, but widely rather than deeply, and it requires very wary walking. A hasty measure of retribution, betraying animosity, or an unjust act of severity, would confirm, instead of allaying the temper which is abroad. It is not possible to say with confidence what the causes are, but with the common herd there is a sincere fear for their caste, and a conviction that this has been in danger from the cartridges and other causes. This feeling is played upon by others from outside, and to some extent with political objects. But upon the whole, political animosity does not go for much in the present movement, and certainly does not actuate the sepoys in the mass.

('MS. Correspondence.')

XVIII.

The May Proclamation.

Fort William, Home Department, May 16, 1857.

Proclamation.

The Governor-General of India in Council has warned the army of Bengal that the tales by which the men of certain regiments have been led to suspect that offence to their religion or injury to their caste is meditated by the Government of India are malicious falsehoods.

The Governor-General in Council has learned that this suspicion continues to be propagated by designing and evil-minded men, not only in the army, but amongst other classes of the people.

He knows that endeavours are made to persuade Hindoos and Mussulmans, soldiers and civil subjects, that their religion is threatened secretly, as well as openly, by the acts of the Government, and that the Government is seeking in various ways to entrap them into a loss of caste for purposes of its own.

Some have been deceived and led astray by these tales.

Once more, then, the Governor-General in Council warns all classes against the deceptions that are practised on them.

The Government of India has invariably treated the religious feelings of all its subjects with careful respect. The Governor-General in Council has declared that it will never cease to do so. He now repeats that declaration, and he emphatically proclaims that the Government of India entertains no design to interfere with their religion or caste, and that nothing has been, or will be, done by the Government to affect the free exercise of the observances of religion or caste by every class of the people.

The Government of India has never deceived its subjects, therefore the Governor General in Council now calls upon them to refuse their belief to seditious lies.

This notice is addressed to those who hitherto, by habitual loyalty and orderly conduct, have shown their attachment to the Government, and a well-founded faith in its protection and justice.

The Governor-General in Council enjoins all such persons to pause before they listen to false guides and traitors, who would lead them into danger and disgrace.

By order of the Governor-General of India in Council,

Cecil Beadon,
Secretary to the Government of India.

XIX.

Private Letter from Lord Canning to Lord Elgin.

Calcutta, May 19, 1857.

My dear Elgin,—I wish I could give you a more cheerful and acceptable greeting than you will find in the letter by which this is accompanied. As it is, you will not bless me for it, but the case which I have before me here is clear and strong. Our hold of Bengal and the upper provinces depends upon the turn of a word—a look. An indiscreet act or irritating phrase from a foolish commanding officer at the head of a mutinous or disaffected company may, whilst the present condition of things at Delhi lasts, lead to a general rising of the native troops in the lower provinces, where we have no European strength, and where an army in rebellion would have everything its own way for weeks and months to come. We have seen within the last few days what that way would be. I cannot shut my eyes to the danger, or to the urgent necessity under which I lie, to collect every European that can carry arms and aid to the Government of India in the event of such a crisis. I do not want aid to put down the Meerut and Delhi rebels; that will be done easily, as soon as the European troops can converge upon Delhi, but not sooner. Meanwhile, every hour of delay—unavoidable delay—is an encouragement to the disaffected troops in other parts; and if any one of the unwatched regiments on this side of Agra should take heart and give the word, there is not a fort, or cantonment, or station in the plains of the Ganges that would not be in their hands in a fortnight. It would be exactly the same in Oude. No help that you could give me would make us safe against this, because it cannot arrive in time. The critical moments are now and for the next ten or twelve days to come. If we pass through them without a spread of the outbreak, I believe all will go well. If we do not, the consequences will be so frightful, that any neglect to obtain any possible accession of strength whereby to shorten the duration of the reign of terror which will ensue, would be a crime. If you send me troops they shall not be kept one hour longer than is absolutely needed. If you come with them yourself, you shall be most heartily welcome.

XX.

Proclamation of the Nana Sahib, dated July 6.

'A traveller just arrived at Cawnpore from Calcutta had heard that previous to the distribution of the cartridges, a council had been held for the purpose of depriving the Hindustanis of their faith and religion. The members of the council came to the decision, since it was a matter affecting religion, it would be right to have seven or eight thousand European soldiers that fifty thousand Hindustanis might be destroyed, and all (the rest) become Christians. This resolution was sent to Queen Victoria and received her approval. Again, another council was held, at which the English merchants assisted. It was here determined that the European force should be made equal to the Hindustani army (in numbers), so that when the contest took place, there should be no fear of failure. When this representation (from the council) was read in England, 35,000 soldiers were embarked in all haste and despatched to India, and the news of their departure has reached Calcutta. The sahib of Calcutta ordered the distribution of the cartridges with the especial object of making Christians of the native army, so that when the army became Christians, there would be no delay in making Christians of the ryots. These cartridges were rubbed over with the fat of pigs and cows. This fact has been asserted by Bengalese who were employed in the manufacture of the cartridges, and of those who related this, one has been executed, and all the rest put into confinement. They (the sahibs) made their arrangements here. This is the news from thence (Europe). The Turkish ambassador wrote from London to the Sultan to inform him that 35,000 men have been despatched to Hindustan for the purpose of making Christians of the Hindustanis. The Sultan of Room (may God perpetuate His sovereignty!) despatched a firman to the Pasha of Egypt to this effect:—"You are an ally of Queen Victoria. But this is not the season for amity, inasmuch as my ambassador writes that 35,000 soldiers have been despatched to Hindustan for the purpose of making Christians of the native ryots and troops. Therefore, in this case, whilst a remedy is in my power, if I should be negligent, how shall I show my face to God? And this day (*i.e.* conjuncture) may some time or other be my own (meaning this may some day be his own case), since, if the English make the Hindustanis Christians, they will make an attempt on my dominions."'

When the Pasha of Egypt received this firman, he, previous to the arrival of the (English) force, assembled and organised his troo at Alexandria, which is on the road to Hindustan. The moment soldiers (English) appeared, the Pasha's troops opened an artillery fire upon them from all sides, and destroyed and sank their ships, so that not a single soldier escaped.

When the English at Calcutta had issued their order for the distribution of the cartridges, and the disturbances had arisen, they anxiously looked out for the troops from London to aid them. But the Almighty, in His perfect omnipotence, had already disposed of these. When the news of the slaughter of the army from London came known, the Governor-General was greatly affected and distressed and THUMPED HIS HEAD!

Persian Quatrain.

In the beginning of the night, he possessed the power over life and property. In the morning his body was without a head, and his head without a crown. In one revolution of the cærulean sphere, neither Nadir (Shah) remained nor any sign of him.

Issued from Painted Garden of the Peischwah.

('Parliamentary Documents.')

XXI.

Sir J. Outram to the Governor-General.

Dinapore, August 19, 1857.

I purpose taking on two guns of the battery here (leaving the mountain train for service in Behar if necessary hereafter, for which I intended it), and also Major Eyre's battery to Benares, where I propose, if practicable, to organise a column to advance to Lucknow through Jaunpore, between the Sye and Goomti rivers, the only course now left by which we can hope to relieve our garrison in Lucknow; General Havelock having again retired from the attempt, and recrossed the Ganges at Cawnpore, being unable, I suppose, to cross the Sye in face of the enemy, the Bunnee bridge having been destroyed. In addition to the artillery above mentioned, I can only have the 5th Fusiliers and 90th Regiment, so weakened by detachments as to amount together to less than 1,000 men, some of the Goorkhas perhaps, and the Madras regiment now on its way up the river. But I hope to arrange with General Havelock—after effecting a junction with such troops as he can forward from Cawnpore—to cross the Ganges about Futtehpore, and pass the Sye near Roy Bareilly. I would there prepare rafts (on inflated skins) by which these reinforcements would cross the Sye. We should then be in sufficient strength, I trust, to force our way to Lucknow.

All my arrangements here will be completed by to-morrow, and no time shall be lost in pushing up to Benares, whence I hope to send back most of the steamers and flats now here and above. Aware as I am how urgently these vessels are required at Calcutta, I am very much vexed that such great and unnecessary delays should have interposed, by detentions here, at Dinapore, and other places; and your lordship may rely on my preventing any further delay that can possibly be avoided.

(Sir James Outram's 'Campaigns in India, 1857–1858.')

The Commander-in-Chief to Sir J. Outram.

Calcutta, August 24, 1857.

I have been favoured by the Governor-General with a perusal of yours to his lordship of the 19th instant, in which you propose to collect a force of about 1,000 infantry and eight guns at Benares, with a view to march to the relief of our garrison in Lucknow, by the most direct route from thence, and that the force under General Havelock at Cawnpore should co-operate with you in this movement, by crossing the Ganges at Futtehpore, and the Sye subsequently (with your assistance) at Roy Bareilly, and forming a junction with you beyond that place.

General Havelock states, in his telegraph of the 20th instant, that his force is reduced to 700 men in the field, exclusive of the detachments required to guard his entrenchments, and keep open his communication with Allahabad, and so inadequate does he consider his force to be for the defence of his post, that he states in his telegraph dated August 21, 12.30 P.M., that, if not assured of reinforcements by return of telegraph, he will retire to Allahabad. Hope of co-operation from General Havelock (by a force equal to accomplish the movement you propose, by crossing the Ganges at Futtehpore) is not to be entertained. The march from Benares, by the most direct route, to Lucknow is a long one—some 150 miles—and the population through which you would have to pass hostile. Its great recommendation, I presume to be, that you (by that route) turn, or rather, come in rear of, the many nullahs which, I am told, interpose between Cawnpore and Lucknow, and this would be an important advantage. But if the force you propose to collect at Benares were to be moved by the river to Cawnpore, and united with Havelock's reduced numbers, do you think it would be equal to force its way over the numerous nullahs, necessarily full of water at this season, which are to be found on the road from the latter place of Lucknow? By this route all incumbrances, such as sick, &c., would be left at the different stations, or pass along the road, and the troops being conveyed by steam, would suffer less than if obliged to march, and Havelock's anxiety about his post would be removed.

In offering these remarks or suggestions to you, who are acquainted with the country people and difficulties attending the movement you propose, it is not with any view to fetter your judgment and perfect freedom of mind, but I mention these as they occur to me in writing to you, and I think I may venture to say that the measures you may deem most advisable to pursue will receive the approval of the Governor-General. I hope to have the pleasure of hearing from you.

(Idem.)

The Governor-General of India to Sir J. Outram.

Telegraphic. August 25, 1857.

Upon well considering the plan proposed in your letter of the 19th, it seems open to these objections:—

The road to Lucknow by Jaunpore is bad: it lies through a country in insurrection; there would be great difficulty in keeping communications open in your rear; there would be no safe places at which to leave the sick and wounded; supplies must be uncertain; the march will be 150 miles, and will not be eased or expedited by carriage or water conveyance.

The road by Allahabad and Cawnpore is much longer, but none of these objections apply to it. It will bring you into junction with General Havelock's force, which, considering the small strength of each force, seems very necessary; and if the Gwalior regiments advance, you will have them in front. But the road by Jaunpore may have advantages of which I am not aware, and I am confident that your deliberate judgment will decide for the best.

It is not probable that the relief of the Lucknow garrison will be facilitated by the abandonment of Cawnpore; but if this should be the case, do not hesitate to abandon it. The political importance of it, and the cost of recovering it, are not to be weighed against the relief of Lucknow.

Accounts from Lucknow to the 16th were received last night. There are 350 Europeans and 300 natives, but they have 120 sick and 4 per cent. women and children, and no carriage; they cannot, therefore, cut their way out. They are hard pressed, but a reduction to half rations will enable them to hold out till the 10th of next month.

Endeavour to communicate with Colonel Inglis, and tell him

satt he is not to care for the treasure, if it should be an incumbrance, but that he may use it in any way for the release of the garrison.

(Idem.)

Sir J. Outram to Mr. Mangles, Chairman of the Court of Directors.

Allahabad, September 3, 1857.

I arrived here on the evening of the 1st instant, and had hoped to be overtaken yesterday by the troops which were to follow in two hours after I sailed from Benares on the morning of the 3rd, but they have not yet (8 A.M.) made their appearance. I hope they will arrive in the course of the day, and in the meantime everything is prepared for their onward march. I trust I shall join Havelock at Cawnpore by the 10th or 11th, and that then no time will be lost in forcing our way to Lucknow and relieving the garrison, as I confidently rely on doing.

We have no direct accounts thence, but I am pretty sure that they are not in such stress as represented—even to the length, it is said, of negotiating for terms!—reports set about by the rebels no doubt. Indeed, an officer likely to be well informed writes from Cawnpore on the 31st ultimo: 'Lucknow is all right and in good spirits.' The amount of reinforcements I am taking on to General Havelock, and his confidence that they will suffice, you will gather from the enclosed copies of telegraphic messages which have lately passed between us. In coming up the river, I have made every disposition the means at my command permitted for the security of the principal stations bordering thereon, and I trust they will suffice so far; but of course I could not provide military means for ridding the districts of the gaol birds and budmashes let loose on the country by the blundering of the authorities at Dinapore. I, however, suggested to the civil authorities to augment their police, and to impress on the zemindars, &c., that they would be held responsible for keeping the peace within their own limits. By such means Behar and Tirhoot ought to be kept tolerably quiet, until troops can be released from their more pressing duties in advance. The abandonment of Goruckpore by the Goorkhas was a sad mistake, and has encouraged an invasion in that quarter from Oude, which would never otherwise have been attempted. I trust, however, that the evil will not spread further in that direction, and that the Goorkhas may yet be induced to resume their position at Goruckpore for the present, in addition to Azimghur and Jaunpore, which they are now holding with great advantage, securing those districts from incursions from Oude. I trust my next will be from Lucknow; and my object in writing this hasty note, which I am told will be in time for the mail, is to relieve you from the anxiety which the critical position of those at Lucknow must naturally inspire. I rely their holding out till we can advance, and in that case that we shall succeed.

XXII.

Order of the Day of Sir J. Outram and Brigadier Havelock.

Cawnpore, September 15, 1857.

The important duty of relieving the garrison of Lucknow had been first entrusted to Brigdadier-General Havelock, C.B., and Major-General Outram feels that it is due to that distinguished officer and to the strenuous and noble exertions he had already made to effect that object, that to him should accrue the honours of the achievement.

Major-General Outram is confident that this great end, for which Brigadier-General Havelock and his brave troops have so long and so gloriously fought will now, under the blessing of Providence, be accomplished.

The Major-General, therefore, in gratitude for and admiration of the brilliant deeds of arms achieved by Brigadier-General Havelock and his gallant troops, will cheerfully waive his rank in favour of that officer on this occasion, and will accompany the force to Lucknow in his civil capacity, as Chief Commissioner of Oude, tendering his military services to Brigadier-General Havelock as a volunteer.

On the relief of Lucknow, the Major-General will resume his position at the head of the forces.

Cawnpore, September 16, 1857.

Brigadier-General Havelock, in making known to the column the kind and generous determination of Major-General Sir J. Outram, G.C.B., to leave to him the task of relieving Lucknow, and rescuing its gallant and enduring garrison, has only to express his hope that the troops will strive, by their exemplary and gallant conduct in the field, to justify the confidence thus reposed in them.

(Sir J. Outram, 'Campaigns in India, 1857–58.')